W9-ANG-893

FOR FAITH AND FORTUNE

Statue of Liberty–Ellis Island Centennial Series

Board of Editors
Roger Daniels, Chair (University of Cincinnati)
Jay P. Dolan (University of Notre Dame)
Victor Greene (University of Wisconsin–Milwaukee)

A list of books in the series appears at the back of this book.

FOR FAITH AND FORTUNE

The Education of Catholic Immigrants in Detroit, 1805–1925

JoEllen McNergney Vinyard

UNIVERSITY OF ILLINOIS PRESS

URBANA AND CHICAGO

Publication of this book was supported by a grant from the
Ellis Island–Statue of Liberty Foundation.

This book is printed on acid-free paper.

Library of Congress Cataloging-in-Publication Data
Vinyard, JoEllen McNergney.
For faith and fortune : the education of Catholic immigrants in Detroit, 1805–1925 /
JoEllen McNergney Vinyard.
p.   cm. — (Statue of Liberty–Ellis Island Centennial series)
Includes bibliographical references and index.
ISBN 0-252-02405-2 (cloth : acid-free paper).
ISBN 0-252-06707-X (pbk. : acid-free paper).
1. Catholic Church—Education—Michigan—Detroit—History—19th century.
2. Catholic Church—Education—Michigan—Detroit—History—20th century.
3. Children of immigrants—Education—Michigan—Detroit—History—19th century.
4. Children of immigrants—Education—Michigan—Detroit—History—20th century.
I. Title.
II. Series.
LC503.D48V56   1998
371.829—dc21   97-45321
CIP

FOR THELMA KEEGAN MCNERGNEY,
WITH LOVE

When the Irish Catholic—we speak only what we know—with a heart, half broken, bade farewell to his native fields, to feudal landlords, a hireling magistracy and Protestant opression, he did so with the firm faith of finding a promised land in America. Daily as the sun went westward over his ship, nightly as the beautiful evening star arose, he said in his own heart, "In America I shall be free! and my children will grow up free to practice their faith, and prosecute their fortune!"

—*Detroit Catholic Vindicator,* April 30, 1853

Contents

Acknowledgments

I am the third generation of female teachers in my family. We span a century. The women who went before me walked to their rural schools, often through miles of mud or snow; they "dressed up" for their students, worked to prepare lessons, and worried over the students' troubles. They went home at the end of the day to hang out laundry, to cook, clean, and raise children, sometimes alone. Their wages paid not only for day-to-day necessities but also for farms, homes, and the education of their children. The way they lived their lives helped make my career one they could not have imagined to dream for. I have thought of them often while writing this book. I admire them beyond measure and will not forget.

Memories of students, friends, and teachers have also peopled my head as I mulled over ideas about education. Especially the teachers. Faith and fortune aside, education in a democracy should communicate and promote a sense of personal worth. For embracing that end, I thank Merle Bauer, Gordon P. McKay, Harold Hutcheson, Gordon Kenyon, Arthur Mendel, and Sam Bass Warner, Jr. This book has reminded me that I have been fortunate as a student.

More people than I can list have provided advice, assistance, and support with this project. I could not have undertaken it without the faculty research fellowship and the sabbatical leave granted by Eastern Michigan University. The Earhart Foundation generously funded a semester's leave for the final stages of research.

Several archivists and librarians have gone out of their way to share knowledge and time. Sister Celeste Rabaut, IHM, is responsible for the origin of this project, having permitted a group of my seminar students to use the Archives of the Sisters, Servants of the Immaculate Heart of Mary in Monroe, Michigan, as an experience in primary research. Once having discovered the wealth of material available at this gem of an archive, I kept coming back. The current archivist, Sister Rose Matthew Mangini, IHM, helped search for the last necessary records and photographs and shared her considerable experience of Detroit Catholic schools. Sister Mary Carmeline Biewlawski, OSF, director of the Archives of the Felician Sisters, Presentation of the B.V.M. Province in Livonia, Michigan, spent hours pouring over folders and photographs with me and shared priceless stories of her days as student, novice, and professed sister. Sister M. Camille, SSJ-TOSF, not only identified important materials in the Sisters of St. Joseph Archives in Stevens Point, Wisconsin, but also and without qualm mailed them off for me to use, as did the Sisters of Christian Charity archivist Sister Mary Thecla Malawey, SCC. Elizabeth Yakel and her successor, Roman Godzak, were invaluable in helping locate information at the archives of the Archdiocese of Detroit, as were Alice Dalligan and her successor, Noel Gordon, at the Burton Historical Collection of the Detroit Public Library. Sister Anna Mary Waickman, IHM, who has preserved a fine collection on Catholic history at Marygrove College, made the library home to me. And, as with every project I have brought through their doors, Francis Blouin, Jr., Nancy Bartlett, and Karen Jania of the Bentley Library at the University of Michigan once again joined enthusiastically to offer aid, advice, and bring out cart after cart of file boxes.

People in the Archdiocesan Office of Education were unfailingly helpful in providing records of schools that had been closed, a marked contrast to my efforts to find public school information. Catholic parishes and schools all around Detroit welcomed me to residency in storeroom, basement, hallway, or whatever space they had, making their meticulous historical records available without hesitation or bureaucracy. I especially thank Father Malcom Carron, SSJ, for providing access to the University of Detroit High School files; Brother George Synan, FSC, at De La Salle High School for access to the files of the St. Joseph Commercial College; and the staff members at St. Vincent, Most Holy Trinity, St. Casimir, and Sweetest Heart of Mary parishes.

Olivier Zunz, Leslie Tentler, Jeffrey Mirel, and John Rury shared their insights and information and extended support in a variety of ways; their own fine research on Detroit saved me countless hours and pointed me in important directions.

Merle Henrickson, even in the midst of illness and moving from Detroit, helped me to understand public school building policies and map the buildings. My departmental colleagues, Della Flusche, Lou Gimelli, and Roger King, read sections of the manuscript and offered encouragement at critical junctures. Nancy Snyder, time and again, picked up anything and everything I let drop through the cracks.

Sister Marie Liguori Ewald, IHM, has extended her unshakeable faith to me and mine for more than thirty years; she is the finest combination of teacher, scholar, religious woman, and family friend we will ever know.

Robert McNergney, professor of education at the University of Virginia and the right kind of zealot, has shared countless hours talking about the power schooling has to change lives for the better or to wound, cheat, and defeat. He is equally impassioned about family loyalty; I am grateful for all that he is, an extraordinary brother. Maggie McNergney and Sandy Price have devoted years to translating all our high-minded talk into elementary classroom reality. Special women of good hearts, they have kept me sane by example; each deserves far more than a place in heaven, a decent wage and retirement plan, or a mention in some history book. Maureen Des Roches, friend nonpareil, has been indispensable for more, much more, than all the time she devoted to every chapter of this manuscript.

Matt and Andy Vinyard have grown up not only tolerating my obsession with teaching and writing but also taking it in stride and even with pride. I thank them both for their unspoken conviction that any right-thinking mother would spend hours of her days and nights typing in the study. But I thank them especially for the other hours—like those I spent on some set of bleachers cheering a good save or hit or catch or throw. Teaching and writing are fun, as I often said, but they have mattered most all along.

Finally, I owe more than words can say to two people. Dale Vinyard loved and supported me without fail until the day he died. Sid Gendin picked up the pieces of my life and put them back together with his; I have no doubt that he will love and support me without fail until the day one of us shall die. That an Irish Catholic woman who grew up in a small Nebraska town could chance upon two such remarkable men—one a Methodist political scientist who grew up in Wauwatosa, Wisconsin, the other a Jewish philosopher who grew up in Brooklyn, New York—explains in no small way my passionate belief that education offers paths we could not otherwise have followed.

INTRODUCTION

WHEN they left any record of their lives, ordinary immigrants, by word and deed, registered their efforts on behalf of their children. For foreign-born and native-born alike, the present centered on their children's future. If there was not a common vision among those who peopled America, there came to be a shared recognition that education could make a difference to children when it came to practicing faith and prosecuting fortune. How much formal schooling, what type, for what reasons, and under whose auspices were the questions with which people grappled. We live, still, with the consequences of the answers they crafted.

This book discusses the complex roles Catholic schools played within the fabric of Detroit—the schools that, for more than a century, educated a substantial share of the city's extensive immigrant and second-generation population. Detroit is especially valuable as a case study of urban education. It represents, as a nineteenth-century city, the midsized commercial town of the midwestern urban frontier. Then, across the first two decades of the twentieth century, Detroit metamorphosed into the nation's fourth-largest city, the most powerful example of America's manufacturing might. Throughout a history stretching from its French foundations in 1701 the city was home to a continuing flow of foreign-born Catholics. The parochial schools they introduced played an integral part in the city's ability to accommodate its bursting, polyglot population. Separate parish schools became the fixed habit during a seventy-year era bracketed by the "school question" controversy of the 1850s, when Catholics sought tax money for their schools, and the "anti-parochial school amendment" controversy of the 1920s, when others tried to mandate that all children must attend public schools. Both initiatives were prompted by a complex web of local circumstances played out against the backdrop of national enthusiasms.

Detroit's nineteenth-century mobile population was a microcosm of certain national patterns, as Yankee migrants from the East and immigrants from Northwestern Europe settled in together, newcomers in search of opportunity. But whereas the great eastern cities such as Boston, New York, and Philadelphia were established by Protestants, Detroit was founded by French Catholics. History and circumstance led French, German, and Irish Catholics to mingle with Yankee Protestants and German Lutherans in neighborhoods, workplaces, and political parties. At first, for more than forty years, they cast about in common to educate their children however best they could manage. Nonetheless, education became a lightning rod for the religious differences among them once schooling appeared critical to ensuring a child's faith and chance for fortune. Time and again, Detroit would reflect the dilemma that baffled and divided Americans: In a democratic society, what is the appropriate role of schools? Ethnic parish schools emerged out of that debate as one answer.

In the 1850s, during what local newspapers called the "school question," Catholics sought tax funding to go their separate way because Protestants and their version of the Bible dominated the fledgling public schools. Alone and divided internally over the wisdom of this campaign, Catholics were unsuccessful in a three-year effort to get a share of public money targeted for education. Nonetheless, they preferred the hardships of paying for their own schools rather than accepting the risks they perceived in Protestant-run public schools. Protestants preferred to let them go their own way rather than find some agreeable accommodation. Nearly 40 percent of all children who attended school in Detroit during the last half of the nineteenth century went to parochial schools.

The separate ethnic parish schools often had only religion in common. Despite outsiders' perceptions of them, what went on in one Catholic school or another depended less on any dictates from the papacy or church councils than on the heritage and purposes of parents, pastors, and teaching sisters—especially the sisters. Each school's parish-based distinctiveness was a significant part of its appeal to Catholic families. The many schools sifted Irish children from German children from Polish children and then, later, the more assimilated second- and third-generation middle class from the poorer working-class Catholics. Some parishes were able to initiate high schools of enviable quality, whereas others struggled to provide even six elementary grades from which children emerged unequipped to reach farther yet secure in the faith, culture, and language of an older homeland. The role parochial education played within Detroit's economic and social equilibrium evolved, until by the mid-1920s more than sixty Catholic schools together enrolled nearly fifty thousand students.

In the first two decades of the twentieth century Detroit was radically reshaped by the auto industry. It transformed nearly everything, including the schools and the residents' notions about education. Unlike in the diversified economy that characterized nineteenth-century Detroit, the avenue of upward mobility had narrowed. Most jobs were in factories, where certain employment and a good daily wage presented powerful enticements to youngsters and their parents. Yet new white-collar management spots and the professions were within reach of both the immigrant and native-born white child who went to a good school and worked hard. How much and what kind of education could make all the difference. In addition to recognizing that reality, Catholic parents and prelates worried, as before, What of faith as well as fortune? Others worried, as before, What of democracy given so many who were new to it?

Detroit's parochial schools had continually managed to attract a more impressive share of children than Catholic schools in most any city in America. Some long-time natives, both in Detroit and in Michigan itself, fretted anew over the dogmatic training they assumed Catholic school children likely received. The fearful rallied to promote the anti-parochial school amendment in 1920 and again in 1924. Had they won their campaign at the ballot box, the amendment would have required all Michigan children to attend public school until the age of sixteen. By now, however, Catholic schools had come to serve a variety of interests beyond those of the separate Catholic immigrant communities. They were a tax-saving and a fiscal boon to overcrowded public schools; they also represented a considerable real estate investment, anchored neighborhoods, and offered the means to keep new immigrants segregated and out of public schools. Prominent outsiders praised parochial schools as models of efficiency, thrift, order, and, selectively, of proven high quality. Many residents agreed that Catholic schools symbolized the right to free choice in a democracy. Voters twice supported their right to exist in Michigan even before the U.S. Supreme Court reinforced that same position. Out of their experiences, thousands of Catholic and non-Catholic Detroiters concluded that separate schools were to public and private advantage and outweighed any costs. Between the 1850s and the 1920s Detroit's Catholic schools carved out their places.

There is a sense today that the successes of American education explain much that is admirable in our history and that the weaknesses may help explain our national shortcomings. In 1966 James S. Coleman's *Equality of Educational Opportunity* proclaimed the nation to be "at risk," thereby launching one more era of analysis and debate among "experts" about what went wrong with schools and how to do better. For all the advantages of hindsight, those who value history's lessons are not always in agreement about which of them to pronounce admirable, nor do they concur on which particular remedy will best address national shortcomings. Detroit is a paradigm of the complexities that make the lessons of history so difficult to unravel.

Education's promise, with all its various interpretations among Americans of diverse persuasions, has long called forth a hodgepodge of responses. Often these responses have come to bear with special force upon the nation's heterogeneous urban centers. Despite a persistent faith in formalized schooling as the means to a more just and civil society, Americans need to grasp more carefully the extent to which education has long depended on chance, on people somehow confident enough to be of generous and tolerant spirit.

PART 1

THE EARLY YEARS

1 On Common Ground

Education is common ground. All parties can here meet;
all sects here unite.
　—John D. Pierce, October 5, 1852

For the first forty years of the nineteenth century, Detroit was a small town, growing from fewer than a thousand to just over nine thousand people. Newcomers, mostly New England and New York Protestants with a few Irish, Germans, and British scattered in, layered on the established French community. Detroiters had their differences, often acrimonious and usually when strong personalities clashed over property, politics, or matters of romance. The same strong personalities, along with the gentler and timid, more usually pulled one another through—through a fire that destroyed the town in 1805, occupation by the British in the War of 1812, cholera epidemics, and economic hard times. They spoke often of dreams for a better future. For the first forty years, they cast about in common to educate as many of their children who needed schooling as best they could provide it. They paid little mind to one Bible version in preference to another. Ability to read a Bible was what mattered.

In 1837 Michigan became a state with a new constitution noteworthy for its provisions on education. Detroit was the capital, the second-largest city in the Old Northwest, and the place where residents' resolve to educate their children had an important chance to be realized. Whether they harkened back to Puritan forebears or had themselves sailed from Europe, one immigrant expressed the hope that nourished them all: "In America I shall be free! and my children will grow up free to practice their faith, and prosecute their fortune!"[1] Because of their shared recent past, there was reason to believe that Detroiters were in accord. They viewed the promise of "democracy" much as Alexis de Tocqueville publicized it, an opportunity for deeds and ambition to count for more than wealth or family. Schooling would be democracy's advantage, democracy's salvation.

But from 1837 onward, despite the new constitutional provision that others acclaimed as a model, Detroiters could no longer find the common ground they needed to transcend their religious and ethnic differences so they might take advantage of tax-provided education. Times and people changed. Detroit had new political stature, expanding economic opportunities, and greater diversity among its growing population. Incoming residents had no intention that their children should miss all that America promised. Part of that promise came to be interpreted as the right to read one's own Bible in school. Once they became embroiled in debate over the separate Catholic and Protestant versions of the Bible and approaches to reading it, Detroiters could not recapture a sense of shared commitment; when it came to the next generation, they feared to put faith at fortune's risk.

THE TERRITORIAL ERA

Michigan became a separate territory in 1805, relinquished by the British just nine years earlier when they finally agreed to the Jay Treaty and withdrew from the area. Decisions about organizing the Old Northwest had already been made in the 1780s by the Congress under the Articles of Confederation and at the Constitutional Convention. Detroit, with its cabins, small shops, and barter economy, was part of the little-known western frontier when American settlers began to trickle in. It was one of the young country's oldest communities, however, and it had its own traditions. French Roman Catholics had settled Detroit in 1701, and their Ste. Anne's Catholic Church was the town's first permanent building. Shifting from one structure to another, Ste. Anne's remained the only religious congregation in the community for 115 years, until the First Protestant Society organized. The town had developed on a foundation as unmistakably Catholic as New England towns were Protestant.

The strongest base for local education was almost always Ste. Anne's, dating from the first organized effort in 1760 when the Ste. Anne's priest and the trustees recruited a schoolmaster born and educated in France. With a few lapses, one form of school or another operated under the patronage of Ste. Anne's members despite the French and Indian War, the American Revolution, and the accompanying shuffles both in population and in governments.[2] Meanwhile, the elite often chose more select forms of private education. Starting with the settlement's founder, Cadillac, some French families had sent their children to study in Montreal or Quebec. When the

British won the region in 1760, officers and government administrators left their children in school back East or in England. When the Americans took possession in 1796 the few families in the vanguard also left their children behind in schools.

Other families grouped to organize subscription schools. Much as with the arrangement at Ste. Anne's, these were supported by parents who got together, hired a teacher, and shared the cost of candles and wood to light and heat the school place—usually the teacher's home. Often, several of these schools operated around town at the same time under the direction of schoolmasters and schoolmistresses of varying talent, ability, and integrity. In some only boys attended, in others only girls. In at least one subscription school in the early 1790s, a few pupils were children of French parents and a few were children of Indian or black slaves.[3]

Reverend David Bacon took pride in 1801 that the children "of nearly all the principal men" attended his school. But Bacon, a Congregational minister who preached in the courthouse on Sundays, apparently alienated parents by the heavy dose of Puritan theology he brought to the classroom so that they began to withdraw their children after a few months. Whether properly or not, Bacon's brother-in-law and assistant blamed the Roman Catholic priests, whom, he said, "had great influence over those who were not Roman Catholics."[4]

When more Protestant Yankee migrants began to trickle in after the War of 1812, they necessarily acknowledged the long-established Catholic interests. They understood Detroit was not Boston, Albany, or New Haven, where their own families, friends, and traditions were the well established. Nor was it New York City, which was more than 95 percent Protestant in 1800; there, upper-class philanthropists attracted city and state funds to their Free School Society and monopolized education during the first four decades of the century.[5] Education in Detroit came not from some single elite cadre trying to control the lower class, but it came piecemeal from a variety of groups who gave their notions a try. A habit emerged: Multiple schools dependent for their form upon any few who took the trouble, schools initiated with the faith that money would somehow be found to keep the effort going and reliant on the appearance of willing teachers.

Although Detroit had little but fish and cider to export when the first steamboat made its appearance in 1818, and with some easterners warning settlers away from a region that they deemed wanting in healthful climate, fertile soil, and "civilizing influences," a grandiose scheme to systematize education was already taking form as "Catholepistemiad." It was one of the earliest of episodic local dreams that would spin out temporary banks, aborted canals, single-issue newspapers, and railroads to nowhere. In 1817 the Territorial Legislature approved the Catholepistemiad, or University of Michigania, a design for education from the lowest primary grade through college. At the time, there was little disagreement about this vision. It was the chimera of a handful of respected territorial leaders—Gabriel Richard, who was the priest at Ste. Anne's from 1798 to 1832; John Monteith, pastor of the First Protestant Society from 1816 to 1820; Augustus B. Woodward, territorial judge from 1805 to 1824; Lewis Cass, who was territorial governor from 1812 to 1831; and William Woodbridge, who held various key political posts for long years after he arrived in 1815. The collaborators were ethnically, politically, and religiously a diverse group; all were well educated, even by standards of the day. For Richard, Monteith, and Woodward, the intellectual architects behind Catholepistemiad, learning was a passion more than a mission.

Each man did have his private purposes, although biographers and historians could rightly praise the "pioneers" for cooperating toward a "common end." Richard, who reputedly read seven languages and had the largest library in the region, did not want French Catholic Detroiters to go without education and thereby lose future "situations" to the Yankees, whose children would be better able to qualify for civil and military positions because they would more likely be able to read and write.[6] Princeton-educated Monteith, based in Michigan as part of the Protestant missionary thrust to the frontier, aimed to extend the civilizing influences of East Coast Protestant institutions. William Woodbridge, an advocate of views that eventually led him to the Whig Party, insisted newcomers must learn "our complicated system of government" and form habits "upon our model" in the interest of a culturally homogeneous community.[7] The Democratic Cass had received a solid education at Phillips-Exeter; ever-practical, the tireless promoter of Michigan also owned considerable land in the territory and recognized the value of schools as an attraction for a larger share of westward migrants. Woodward, educated at Columbia College and a friend of Thomas Jefferson, gave the educational system its high-minded title and much of its form. He was an eccentric visionary—mocked by a contemporary as one trying to make cucumbers from moonbeams—but he was also a hard-headed land speculator who stood to profit if settlement increased.

The private purposes of these early school supporters were not in conflict. They all wanted schools that offered Michigan children the chance to grow up economically competitive, and they wanted pupils to emerge steeped in an appreciation for the democratic institutions that were, they believed, the safeguards of competition. Catholepistemiad was to offer an opportunity.

It was not intended as an obligation for all children nor as the exclusive means for schooling. Just two years earlier, in 1815, Gabriel Richard had set about planning for a Catholic school system in the Michigan Territory that envisioned separate schools for boys and girls in every parish.[8]

The public school system as envisioned in 1817 did not threaten any purse, power structure, or prayer book. For financing the plan intended to depend heavily upon tuition, lotteries, and public subscription rather than relying on tax support. Costs were controlled by the enabling legislation. The professors of the university, to be appointed by the governor, would establish the lower-level schools, hire the teachers, determine the curriculum, and choose the books. The emphasis in the curriculum was upon basic skills for the younger children and a classical course of study for the older students. Nothing in the plan envisioned the podium as a sectarian pulpit. The original act made no mention at all of religion, but a subsequent act in 1821 declared that no person, from president to professor to pupil, was to be refused "for his conscientious persuasion in matters of religion."[9]

Upon recommendation of Judge Woodward and with concurrence of Governor Cass, Secretary of the Territory Woodbridge named Reverend Monteith to be the first president and hold seven professorships, and Father Richard became vice president and held the remaining six professorships. They were chosen, apparently, out of regard for their dedication to the cause rather than for any concern to balance religious representation. The respect Monteith and Richard commanded was essential, given the broad powers the act conferred on the president, vice president, and professors. Neither man was deluded about the lack of popular enthusiasm for "extensive literary establishments." They decided to focus on the "primary parts of education."[10]

The governor and judges provided an appropriation for a two-story building, quickly erected in the center of Detroit; the lower floor was to be a primary school and the upper a classical academy. In the winter of 1818 the Classical Academy became the first school to open. Its purpose was to provide advanced study for older children who already had a primary education. Monteith recruited the teacher from his old college in Pennsylvania, but the following winter the man died of typhus and the venture then lurched from one teacher to another through the 1820s. Instead of functioning like a public institution, the school operated more in the nature of a subscription school. Various residents, French and American, searched out teachers from Princeton, Yale, and other colleges in the East. One group appealed to the president of Princeton in 1820 for help finding a "gentleman of exceptional moral character, well qualified to . . . teach the Greek,

Latin and English Languages" together with other subjects.[11] Four years later the search was on again, and although Monteith had left the Michigan Territory in 1821 he found Detroiters a teacher—this time from among the students at Hamilton College, where he held the chair of languages.

Richard struggled to keep the venture alive, but he became distracted by other matters after he went to Washington for a term as territorial delegate in 1824. Spread thin, he still dreamed of educational ventures. "God knows," he wrote to a friend in 1825, "how many other projects, great and small, go through my head, of schools and missions for the Indians, for the deaf and dumb, for poor children, etc."[12] At about the same time, Judge Woodward lost his final local political struggle and left Michigan. Affairs of the university devolved on trustees lacking the interest or ability to carry out the founders' ambitions.

With the University of Michigan itself still unrealized, the rudimentary high school course offered through the Classical Academy was the only form of higher education in the territory. Nonetheless, by 1827 the board of trustees of the University of Michigania withdrew responsibility for it. Trustees had been authorizing a salary of $500 for successive teachers, but now they claimed that funds were insufficient for continued support. They were likely influenced also by public criticism that the classical curriculum was not a practical training for the needs of everyday life.[13]

The trustees had no better success carrying out their charge to provide primary schooling. Hoping to educate a substantial group of children economically so as to reassure the public, Monteith and Richard had decided at the outset to follow the Lancasterian model, which organized older children to monitor and drill younger children under supervision of one teacher. Originated by Joseph Lancaster, who was English, from its introduction into the United States in 1805 the system gained praise because it seemed a viable means to offer education to the poor. Monteith was familiar with a Lancasterian school in Albany and used his Presbyterian contacts to recruit a teacher from there. The school opened in August 1818, a few months after the Classical Academy began. As of the following April, the primary program enrolled 183 children.[14]

The Lancasterian system aimed to educate poor children through an essentially religious program, yet Lancaster, a Quaker, contended that education ought not be "subservient to the propagation of the peculiar tenets of any sect."[15] He wanted Protestants to join in a common effort to teach ethical and moral values. Catholic and Protestant pupils in the Detroit Lancasterian school learned to read with the Bible as their text. No record describes whether they read the Catholic Douay or the King James Bible, although, because the teacher was Protestant, they likely used the version familiar to him. Perhaps children brought whatever their parents sent along from home. Still, it was money, not religious problems, which soon caused the primary school initiative to unravel. University of Michigania trustees lacked funds to pay the teacher's promised salary, and those students who were expected to pay tuition were often in arrears. The first teacher left in 1821. After two more men tried and gave up, this plan for quasi-public primary education ended in January 1824. Neither a common school nor an infant school that followed gained permanence.

Clearly, although a public system of education had the intellectual support of a coalition of respected leaders—Catholics and Protestants, Democrats and Whigs—these well-placed men could not imaginatively or politically marshal the funds to establish it on a firm footing. In every year from 1827 to 1833 the Territorial Legislature passed or amended acts on behalf of common schools. Generally, the legislation said, each township must provide for education, and because the territory had not yet begun to receive sufficient income from the reserved school lands the legislature made funding the responsibility of elected township officials. The legislators' directives about establishing, conducting, and reporting on township school districts doomed the process. In Detroit, one of the few communities sufficiently large and compact for a district plan, critics complained that the Territorial Council had no right to tell citizens how to provide schooling for their own children with their own money.[16] Detroit's Common Council ignored the common school laws with impunity.

The problem of developing a public pool of money for schools was exacerbated by episodic crises such as the Panic of 1819 and by residents' determination, in good times, to spend according to their personal purposes. Even the comparatively wealthy First Protestant Society failed to pay Monteith the salary owed him, an important factor in his decision to leave Michigan. Public schooling, especially the Lancasterian system, was less costly than private schooling, at least by the first teacher's accounting. He reported that total expenses in 1818 and 1819 were $1,800 less than it would have taken to educate the same number of children privately. But, in fact, many parents were paying nearly as much as they might have for a private school because the "public" school had heavy dependence on sliding-scale tuition. Parents of 158 of the 183 children were expected to pay between $7.50 and $10.50 for the nine months of schooling that first year. Only twenty-three students were admitted at the "indigent" rate of $1 for each of the three quarters.[17] Likely, tuition-paying parents perceived little financial advantage to such "public" education compared with the cost of private schools, where they might exercise more parental prerogatives and negotiate the rate in the bargain.

Given all the circumstances, there is little wonder that it was dozens of independent teachers who educated Detroit children into the 1830s. According to one estimate, two-thirds of Detroit's children between the ages of five and sixteen were in school in 1834.[18] They were scattered among twelve private schools, including the Free School, which, with the help of donations, educated poor children.

Parents shifted children from one school to another. One resident explained to his sons' current teacher that he was withdrawing his boys not out of dislike or dissatisfaction but to enroll them in a new school that had just opened because the youngsters would "benefit from the change."[19] Much in the manner of present-day private schools, teachers were advertising for pupils by 1818 and 1819—at the same time the Classical Academy and primary school were getting underway. The advertisements were intentionally distinctive. One was aimed at parents who might want particular attention paid to "politeness and moral conduct of the pupils," while another offered evening school "for the instruction of Gentlemen in the French language." In one "School for young ladies" there would be "no additional charge" for geography, maps, English, grammar, elocution or needlework; still another advertised for both sexes. Nearly all teachers claimed to be "well qualified in every respect."[20]

One group of friends from locally prominent French Catholic families made education their lifelong concern: Elizabeth Williams, Elizabeth Lyons, Angelique Campau, and Monique Labadie. Three were still in their teens when Father Richard recruited them soon after the turn of the century to help start an academy for girls. Richard instructed them in teaching and, in his 1806 will, arranged that in the event of his death his personal goods and any money owed him would go to two of the women to fund the Detroit school they founded. When the priest drew up the series of resolutions aiming toward a Catholic school system in the Michigan Territory, it was in conjunction with the women who hoped to organize as a religious order and staff the schools. None of them, seemingly, regarded the idea of Catholic parish schools as incompatible with the public University of Michigania system that Richard began to promote a year later. The religious order did not materialize, but three of the four women never married. Moving about from Detroit to rural Michigan settlements or to Indian schools, the women continued to be educators throughout their lives. The last of them survived until 1851. Monique Labadie married the prominent and wealthy Antoine Beaubien. Remaining childless, she used her husband's resources to fund free schools and, near the end of her life, bequeathed a sizeable fortune to endow the elite Academy of the Ladies of the Sacred Heart.[21]

All along, the idea driving public common school planners was the need to provide education for poor children. The rich could be expected to look to their own education, but families without assets or initiative must be helped along in the right direction. Governor Cass never tired of making his party's point that the promise of America included the chance to serve in government, which in turn called for a moral and enlightened citizenry. Even leaders politically opposed to mass participation agreed that those in better circumstances should take on the obligation to educate the poor; it would redound to their benefit. According to their experiences, men such as Cass and Richard expected that those who could afford it would educate their children privately.

Michigan was growing faster than any other state or territory in the Union during the 1830s—from 31,639 in 1830 to 212,167 by 1840. It was during this decade of dizzying change and adjustment that denominational schools began to have new appeal. Promoters saw religious schools as the best means to advance cherished values, and parents viewed them as their children's most likely opportunity for learning. Initiatives began to come not only from newcomers in the community but also from long-time residents who were discouraged by the failed initiatives to organize public schools. The search for workable alternatives promoted schools separated along lines of religion and nationality.

At this same time, political influence began to play a more significant role in access to resources. In 1829 the governor and judges set aside a lot in the center of town for educational purposes; they swiftly granted it to a group of Protestant stockholders who, in anticipation, had formed an association to open a female seminary. The association was a league of the city's Presbyterian, Methodist, Baptist, and Protestant Episcopal denominations, with Governor Cass himself as president. Even though the Detroit Female Seminary's prominent backers had the free lot to spur them on, it still took six years before the three-story, eighteen-room brick building opened its doors "to promote the great cause of Female education." Girls who enrolled understood the Bible was a cornerstone of instruction from teachers who relied on "appeals to it, to conscience, and a sense of duty" for "moral improvement." To minimize fractiousness among the Protestant denominations, controversial topics on religion, politics, or morals were "strictly excluded."[22]

About two years before Protestants opened their Female Seminary, daughters from Catholic families could study "all the attainments which are necessary in society" at the "Female Academy of St. Clare's Seminary."[23] Started in 1833 by eight Poor Clare sisters, the academy attracted French, German, and Irish Catholic pupils, but its reputation for excellence—and perhaps the mere fact of its existence—encouraged territorial governor Stevens T. Mason to bring his two young sisters from Emma Willard's Seminary in Troy, New York, so they could study with the Poor Clares. William Woodbridge, whose daughter and niece attended in 1834, was probably representative of Protestants who put their young females in the sisters' charge until they had their own substitute. He had "insuperable objections" to a Catholic seminary but knew it was the established rule of the Poor Clares never to interfere with the religious education of the day scholars.

Tuition in the seminary was about $6 per quarter, depending on the curriculum. One family paid in milk, a common enough practice. Concerned for children whose families had nothing even to barter, bishops often required religious orders to provide free schools as a condition for allowing them to operate tuition schools in the diocese. The Poor Clares were also teaching as many as a hundred poor pupils in an English and German Free School by the late 1830s.[24] Because the diocese provided little or no funding for such charitable undertakings, the money (and milk, vegetables, firewood, and meat) from tuition-paying students in the sisters' private seminary subsidized those who taught in the free school.

The Detroit Ladies Free School Society, whose steering committee was primarily composed of Presbyterians, opened schools for poor children "of every denomination" in 1832, with the "object" to "take these children and bring them under the culture and moral restraint of a school."[25] They tapped husbands, friends, and relatives for donations and patronized the money-making bazaars and social gatherings they arranged. In 1837 their three schools enrolled two hundred pupils.

Boys from families of some means studied with private tutors, and residents generally made fewer attempts to institutionalize education on their behalf than they did for upper-class girls or the poor. One school for boys, St. Philip-Neri College, started in 1836, inspired by Bishop Frederic Rese's hope that it would serve as the foundation for a Catholic seminary. The bishop was willing for "pupils of all religious denominations" to attend "under certain restrictions." Advertisements did not specify what those restrictions were, but interested local residents knew that the teachers were two Oratorian fathers from Belgium and a young Irish diocesan priest and the tuition was $3 per quarter. The student body numbered about thirty boys in 1839, when the school closed after both Belgian priests died.[26]

Meanwhile, Catholic schools structured according to nationality developed in the form of distinct classrooms operating separately under Ste. Anne's roof (fig. 1). The Irish organized Most Holy Trinity parish in 1833, and by 1838 they started Trinity Church Academy in the basement of Ste. Anne's. Ninety children attended that first year, sixteen of whom were orphans housed and educated by members of the parish. By 1841 two hundred English-speaking children—probably most of them Irish—plus three hundred French children and forty Germans were attending the day and Sunday schools in the basement of Ste. Anne's.[27]

The Poor Clares closed their schools and left Detroit in 1839 after a dispute with Bishop Rese over finances, but Monique Labadie Beaubien and Elizabeth Williams moved into the vacuum and established the French Female Charity School for poor girls. Beaubien financed it, providing free tuition, books, and supplies. Williams taught the school's forty pupils until

Figure 1. Ste. Anne's Church, with its twin spires, dominated the town's center through the 1840s, but the Irish and German immigration, booming apace with the migration of New York and New England Protestants, would soon transform institutional development as well as the landscape. (Vertical File Photograph Collection, Michigan Historical Collections, Bentley Historical Library, University of Michigan)

she died in 1843, replaced then by a younger woman she had helped train.[28] On behalf of the type of girls who had attended the Poor Clares' select academy, Beaubien also began her correspondence—and the persuasive talks with her husband about a bequest—that brought the prestigious Madames of the Sacred Heart to Detroit in 1851.

The variety of private attempts to establish schools in the 1830s, both the successful and the failed, proved more consequential than the efforts of earlier decades because public school plans were underway once again. Locally, education received heightened attention in the 1830s as just part of the bundle of national enthusiasms energizing that expansive decade.

THE OPPORTUNITIES OF STATEHOOD

Michigan's possibilities began to seem quite impressive to refreshed old-timers and to the vigorous newcomers who came in such numbers that they helped boost the territory to statehood. Almost every cause afloat in the North seemed worthwhile to some group. But there was also an increasing sense of urgency to "make things right" while the time was ripe. The American Home Missionary Society sent a representative to Michigan in 1831, the Michigan Anti-Slavery Society organized in 1832, and the American Temperance Society spawned a Michigan branch of the society by 1833. The cause of publicly supported schools, dormant since the mid-1820s, revived as part of this Yankee thrust to better self and others.

The design, organization, and funding scheme for public education took shape in the hands of two men, John Pierce and Isaac Crary. More purposefully than Monteith, Richard, and Woodward before them, both regarded the cause of public education as a mission. There was no organized society in Michigan promoting education, and it was, in principle, a cause that captured a wider spectrum of public approval than any other. But there was ultimately less money than the planners had counted on and more difficulty over religion than they anticipated.

Pierce was born in New Hampshire, educated at Brown University, and licensed to preach as a Congregational minister in 1824. The Home Missionary Society sent him to Michigan, where he organized the First Congregational Church in Marshall in 1831. From his earliest days he used the pulpit to preach the importance of education, which, he believed, would develop moral powers to will, to choose, to refuse, and to distinguish right from wrong.[29]

Isaac Crary, a young lawyer "of good Puritan stock" from Connecticut, arrived in Marshall about a year after the Pierces and lodged in their home.

Out of long conversations about their shared pride in New Englanders' past accomplishments and with joint optimism for the future in the more fertile Michigan, they concluded that education must provide the link between the solid New England and the malleable frontier. In 1835 Pierce and Crary read about the strides toward universal education in Prussia, where the government established schools, allocated funding, trained teachers, and required attendance in a centralized system headed by a minister of state given strong executive authority. Convinced that in the right hands centralized education could promote democratic values, the two were well positioned to promote their plans when Michigan leaders decided to make the push for statehood that year.

Andrew Jackson was president, and political friends and foes shared a growing recognition that legislative acts at the state level might accomplish goals of every sort. Yankee migrants were especially anxious to transplant familiar laws and institutions. Certain Michigan had more than the sixty thousand residents it needed to apply for statehood, the governor and Territorial Council ordered a special census in 1834. Upon learning the count was more than ninety-two thousand, the Territorial Council immediately called for an election to choose delegates for a constitutional convention. On May 11, 1835, ninety-one delegates from across Michigan convened in Detroit to prepare a constitution and request statehood. Issues concerning public education attracted considerable attention as the delegates deliberated—down the street from the Female Seminary that had just opened and within a few blocks of the Poor Clares' seminary and Ste. Anne's schools.

Isaac Crary was a delegate. He moved to establish a committee on education, chaired it, and wrote the article on education that the delegates adopted. The innovative article provided for a system stretching from primary grades through the university, but it was grounded in a plan for funding unlike the previous Woodward-Richard-Monteith scheme. Unlike Ohio, Indiana, and Illinois—the other three states already admitted from the Old Northwest—Michigan's constitution provided for state control of education and stipulated that the state, not separate townships, would appropriate profits from sale of public lands designated by the Northwest Land Act to fund education. The legislature was to pool the proceeds from those land sales, creating a perpetual school fund to finance a share of the cost of public education. Interest from the fund was to be parceled out to school districts, and every district was to operate common schools at least three months each year. The constitution also mandated a state superintendent of public instruction appointed by the governor, who would administer education as a system. Pierce thought that this provision was critical for keeping education "perpetually before the public mind" and protect it from falling prey to the whims of legislators.[30]

The constitutional framers in 1835 proved uncommonly attentive to issues concerning separation of church and state. Delegates had, after considerable discussion, voted against inviting clergy to open their sessions, and they also rejected any recognition of a Supreme Being in the constitution. In several sections of the constitution, careful wording incorporated measures to guarantee religious freedom and prevent any denominational group from gaining hegemony. The prevailing mood similarly was on the side of public education free from sectarian control of any sort.[31]

Of the original cadre who promoted the 1817 legislation for a system of schools under the University of Michigania, only Cass and Woodbridge remained. Both were supporting the Protestant's new Female Academy, but they eagerly endorsed the constitutional provision for public schools. So did the pastor of Most Holy Trinity, whose parish children, studying with the Poor Clares, were soon to stake out their own Irish school in Ste. Anne's basement. Without dwelling much on the matter, most Detroiters seemed to expect private school initiatives to continue alongside tax-funded common schools, anticipating some democratic compromise to accommodate religious differences. They were willing to try anything and everything, just as they had all along.

After some delay caused by angry boundary disputes with Ohio residents, Michigan was admitted to statehood on January 1, 1837. With statehood came 1,067,397 acres of land for public schools.[32] Crary, elected to Congress, recommended that the governor appoint John Pierce superintendent of public instruction. Horace Mann (who graduated from Brown University three years before Pierce) was the new secretary of the Massachusetts State Board of Education and just beginning the career that would establish his reputation and bring reform to Massachusetts. Free public education had just begun in Pennsylvania in 1834. Michiganders congratulated themselves that they were embarking on plans as grand as anything easterners contemplated.

Between 1835 and 1837 Pierce had traveled throughout the East to meet with politicians and educators and to attend two conventions on education. He prepared a detailed report of proposals, which he submitted to the new legislature. Almost at once, however, the Panic of 1837 derailed everything but the need for education. The value of land dropped, including sections targeted for the state's education fund, which had been selling for an average of $12 an acre. Besieged by requests from terrified speculators and discouraged farmers, a sympathetic and compliant legislature reduced the minimum price from $8 an acre to $5 and required only one-fourth of that amount be paid.[33] Even with such generous reductions, previous buyers defaulted. Constitutional provisions that were supposed to ensure public education had quickly proven of little consequence when it came to financing schools in hard times. Economic and political self-interest mattered more.

By the time Pierce left the post of superintendent in 1841, the common school fund had shriveled. Meanwhile, the legislature had made several modifications to the school law that reduced the amount a district could levy as a tax and also required parents to pay for the school's fuel.[34] Public schools were paid for by state allotments and a district tax plus rate bills paid by the parents of students. If the state allotment went down, rate bills went up, and that, in turn, disposed parents to withdraw their children.[35] In 1840 Detroit received $854 to apportion among the seven district schools, which had an aggregate enrollment of 895 students. Holy Trinity parish, struggling to absorb its own children, petitioned the state legislature that year for a subsidy equal to the school tax parishioners paid, perhaps inspired by the similar effort underway in New York. At the time, the request was reported favorably out of committee to the legislature, but there is no record that any money went to Father Martin Kundig or his parishioners.[36] Even if the votes had been there, money to allocate was dwindling. In 1841 the city received about half the subsidy from the common school fund it had received in 1840, and all the district schools had ceased operating by the end of the year.[37] There were twenty-seven private schools, but public schools were losing ground again.

Although he had not succeeded with the school building program for which his plan called, Pierce had hammered home the idea that the state must be committed to the future of public education. In the *Journal of Education,* which he founded and kept alive from 1838 to 1840, and in his frequent reports to the legislature the first superintendent emphasized the theme that democracy depended on education even more than on constitutions and forms of government. "Without education, no people can secure themselves against the encroachments of power," he warned.[38] The missionary had spread his vision of education and fired the zeal of others.

Dr. Zina Pitcher, a Detroit physician and regent of the University of Michigan since 1837, was well acquainted with Pierce's convictions. Serving as mayor of Detroit in 1841, when the public schools closed, Pitcher headed a Common Council committee to improve education in the city. In a house-to-house canvass the committee found 2,093 children between the ages of five and seventeen of school age but only 714 were in school, all necessarily attending the city's twenty-seven private schools.[39] To certain people Detroit seemed proof of the dire warning Pierce had given in his first report to the legislature: Wherever there are flourishing private institutions, "They have uniformly had a pernicious influence upon the common schools." In towns with well-supported private schools, free schools "will be found, without exception, to be in a miserable condition."[40]

Although the distinction would soon be lost by common school promoters, Pierce had not targeted Catholic schools as a "pernicious influence." Rather, his experience as an easterner led him to view private schools as elitist enclaves, their existence working against broad-based education of the poor to the detriment of democracy. Public schools were to be prized precisely because "all classes are blended together; the rich mingle with the poor, and are educated in company . . . and mutual attachments are formed."[41] In fact, however, at Ste. Anne's, which was the only site with "substantial enrollment" in 1841, many pupils came from marginal or poor families.[42]

Both Catholic and Protestant leaders were making an argument becoming common in urban areas: Children who were not in school were learning vices on the streets that would injure not only the children themselves but also harm the public.[43] Neither personal safety nor property ownership were to be found "among an ignorant and vicious people . . . the child uneducated in knowledge is thoroughly educated in the school of depravity." Such individuals were a danger to the community.[44] Once again, as in the early era when Richard and Monteith joined forces and as in 1835 when the state constitution was up for debate, prominent Catholics threw support behind another public school initiative.

Holy Trinity's Martin Kundig, the city's most influential Catholic pastor, joined Pitcher in convening a public meeting on the heels of the school census canvas. Pitcher was a Whig but had won the mayoralty with support of Irish voters; they were disgruntled with Democratic Party leadership just then and found it easy to support Pitcher, who had headed a local drive on behalf of the Irish Repeal Association. The assembled citizens agreed with the city council's request to petition the legislature to levy a property tax that would support free schools and for a board of education with two persons from each ward.[45] Education was, in itself, a value they believed was well worth their attention; at the time, Michigan residents ranked sixth in the nation in the proportion who could read and write—ahead of all the other states in the Old Northwest.[46] The legislature authorized Detroit to be one school district in an act that said all schools organized under the board of education should be public and free to children between the ages of five and seventeen.

In March 1842 Pitcher and others backed Douglass Houghton for mayor because, among his other qualifications, he actively supported their "free school" aims. Houghton won despite vigorous opposition from some of the large property holders.[47] Voters also created the first board of education, selecting two members from each of the six wards. Within two months, a free primary school opened in each ward. According to plan, the primary schools met from May until November, and then middle schools took over the buildings for the following six months. Black children were provided for, but in a separate school that also opened in 1842. Pitcher became president of the board of education the next year.

In one of its first decisions, in 1842, the board of education excluded the Bible as a school book. Judging the Protestant and Catholic population "nearly equal in numbers," the board members feared these divergent groups could not otherwise be brought "to unite in the same system, and place their children under the same regulations." Their report assured the legislature that the board did indeed regard the Bible as the "textbook of all moral obligations" but realized it was "the source of all the bitterness of sectarian animosity." Rather than "sacrifice their fixed purpose of establishing a system of free schools," the members "deemed it advisable to exclude the Sacred Scriptures altogether."[48] This decision echoed the sentiment at the constitutional convention six years earlier, but the chance for maintaining such a position was already almost past. The board's easy accommodation in 1842 belonged more to earlier times than to emergent realities.

THE SOURCE OF SECTARIAN ANIMOSITY

Within three years the Detroit school board backed away from its original religiously neutral stance. From its inception, the board was almost all Protestant, but the number of militant Presbyterians and Baptists edged up. Protestants pouring in during the 1840s were often evangelicals who vied to win converts from other Protestant denominations or from among the unchurched. Various sects made ardent demands for the Bible in schools, each one seeking recognition as the defender of religion. The *Michigan Christian Herald,* which spoke for Baptists, began publication in 1842, determinedly certain that Catholics, slavery, drink, and trains running on Sunday were all dangers to the institutions of God and man.[49] The paper was especially active in mounting the campaign for Bible-reading in school.

The *Christian Herald* promoted the position which other Protestants seized upon as a "compromise:" It pronounced the King James Bible the only English translation not "sectarian" and therefore deemed it should be uniformly acceptable. According to the Baptists' way of thinking, since Catholics wanted to exclude the Bible unless it was accompanied with their own explanations, theirs was the self-serving position. Reading the King James Bible was accordingly represented as the "non-sectarian" act; failure to use it would be giving in to sectarianism promoted by Catholics.[50]

In 1844 a newly elected board member introduced a resolution that held that although students must not be coerced to study the Bible when their parents objected, teachers should choose either the Catholic or the Protestant version and read it without comment. The resolution was defeated, but the debate continued, and on February 3, 1845, the board shifted to support the position that nothing in its bylaws prevented teachers from reading from a Bible of their choice as long as they did not proselytize.[51] Leaving the choice of Bible to teachers was no compromise. It reminded Catholics that nearly every teacher hired was a Protestant. In a show of satisfied self-righteousness, and with an eye to voters, the board had its resolutions printed in the daily press.

Catholics paid less attention to board elections than their Protestant neighbors, perhaps because many of their children were studying in parish classrooms or in Catholic-taught free schools. Too, Irish and German immigrants did not yet constitute bloc votes, nor did they control any ward or make common cause with others who happened also to be Catholic. Often only one Catholic served at any time on the board. Daniel Campau, from a respected old French family, represented the Second Ward and served as the board's first treasurer. James O'Callaghan, who was Irish, was on the board in the mid-1840s, but there was no concerted Catholic drive to elect their own partisans.[52]

Archetypical of those who came to exert considerable influence on the board was the lawyer D. Bethune Duffield. His father was George Duffield, minister of the Presbyterian Church from 1836 to 1868. His brother, a minister, gained permanent recognition as the author of the militant hymn "Stand Up, Stand Up for Jesus." His Bethune grandparents were educational pioneers in New York. D. Bethune Duffield was a Whig and then a Republican and an "uncompromising abolitionist"; he brought considerable righteous zeal to the cause of education. Duffield was on the board for more than a decade, retiring in 1860. Seconded by the efforts of his father, he helped mold the public schools in a thoroughly Protestant cast.

With public schools underway, and promoted by many of the same families involved in opening the Detroit Female Seminary, that private joint-Protestant venture closed in 1843 for lack of financial stability. Potential pupils could comfortably attend the public schools, with the best and most convenient likely to be in the sections of town where wealthier Protestants lived. By contrast, Catholics found increasing reason and encouragement to continue their separate schools. Some Catholics were making expansive plans side by side with Protestant public schools throughout the 1840s.

The faltering efforts of the 1830s, far from discouraging them, had given energetic immigrants the start of their own ethnic parishes and schools. In Ste. Anne's basement in 1841 there was the "substantial school" described in Pitcher's report which, if in an overstatement, educated "nearly all of the children of Catholic families then resident in the city."[53] Ste. Anne's housed about 440 students divided among Trinity's Academy, the group of children from Ste. Anne's own parish, and the class of German children. Elizabeth Williams and her successor were tending to poor Catholic girls in their French Female Academy. The new generation of young Catholic women wanted to teach at least until they married or, like Williams, in preference to marriage. And from December 1841 there was a new Catholic bishop, Peter Paul Lefevere, whose personality, conception of duty, and concern for authority made him less cooperative in local affairs than his predecessors.

A Belgian, Lefevere had come to the United States to do missionary work and for ten years had traveled the wilderness of Missouri and Illinois. The Detroit diocese appointment, a significant promotion for him, gave Lefevere charge over a far-flung area that his predecessor, Frederic Rese, had left in severe financial straits by overspending on land. He also inherited an undisciplined clergy, who, coupled with the antagonism of other bishops, had helped drive Rese out.[54] One of his parishioners, preferring Rese, would ultimately assess Lefevere kindly—a "rough diamond" whose polish had been rubbed off by his missionary years and whose "gruff ways were not pleasing to the elite of Detroit," who were difficult to please at best.[55] A complicated man whose actions made a variety of interpretations possible, Lefevere seemed concerned only with his responsibilities as he defined them. In the area of education, he felt an especially heavy obligation to safeguard tenets of Catholicism.

Lefevere arrived just a few months before the free primary schools opened. One of the bishops who came for his consecration in the fall of 1842 was John Hughes, then locked in the highly publicized struggle over control and financing of education in New York. Lefevere embraced Hughes's notions about the dangers public schools presented. Lack of Catholic instruction loomed "more disastrous" than the scarcity of priests in his diocese; he saw "with dread" the "rapid progress of indifferentism in religion" portending "the total loss of faith if we can not properly remedy the situation."[56] He proceeded vigorously to encourage the developments in Catholic education that were underway.

Neither Lefevere nor his successors would be the only deciding factors for local Catholics when it came to educating their children. Still, the strong-willed and determined Lefevere remained as bishop for twenty-eight critical years during the formative era of school development in Detroit, and he exerted significant influence—by promoting separate parish schools, by bringing in teachers necessary to make Catholic schools attractive as well as viable, and, ultimately, by alienating those Protestants who might otherwise have helped amenable Catholics identify some shared ground in a single system.

It was the trustees of Ste. Anne's who forcefully prompted Lefevere's initial search for teaching sisters. Although Ste. Anne's was his cathedral church, the lay corporation held the title and leased it to bishops contingent upon certain conditions. One was the requirement to establish a free school and orphan asylum. Once the Poor Clares were gone, Bishop Rese did not meet that condition, so the firm-handed trustees had been publishing legal notices to cancel the lease.[57] Under threat of losing the cathedral, Bishop Lefevere set about finding sisters to make a free school possible. After some negotiation with their Emmitsburg, Maryland, motherhouse, the bishop brought the Daughters of Charity to Detroit. In 1844, two years after the public schools opened, the newly arrived sisters started St. Vincent's Select School for Girls and two free schools, one for girls and one for boys. Children "flocked to us from all quarters," one of the sisters recorded when the free schools opened their doors.[58] St. Vincent's Select School moved into a new brick building in 1852 with 150 paying students and continued to offer free school education as well.[59]

The bishop arranged an additional free school for poor girls as a consequence of Monique Beaubien's bequest, which brought the Religious of the Sacred Heart to Detroit. They opened their academy for daughters of wealthy Catholics in 1851, as she intended, but the bishop asked the sisters to extend their work beyond their traditional mission to the upper classes and open a free school because Detroit Catholics were principally "the laboring class of people."[60]

Always aiming for free parish schools above all, the bishop welcomed a small group of women who wanted to start a new religious congregation. Settling them at Monroe in 1845, he anticipated that these sisters, Servants of the Immaculate Heart of Mary, would come to provide the pool of inexpensive teachers his diocesan parishes needed.

The encouraging development of a diocesan community based in Monroe coincided with successful overtures the bishop and individual parishes made to other religious communities of men and women. By the fall of 1849, after some years of effort, Lefevere succeeded in bringing a contingent of Christian Brothers, who took over the school at the Germans' St. Mary's parish. Then, from Milwaukee, the German-speaking School Sisters of Notre Dame arrived to teach younger children and older girls at St. Mary's in 1852. Meanwhile, the Irish, who had initiated the ethnic church and school in the 1830s, were about to move their boys out of basement schools and into a new brick building adjacent to Holy Trinity Church.

Hugh O'Bierne, a local judge, claimed 1,300 Catholic children were being educated "in religion, in morals, and in science, without one cent of charge to the public" by the school year of 1852–53.[61] Although the *Detroit Daily Advertiser* may have exaggerated the figures because the editor was anxious to stress the importance of public schools, public school enrollment totaled about 2,900.[62]

Enthusiasm for parochial schools developed within the Catholic community at the same time public schools were becoming more overtly Protestant. Still, other Protestant groups, many of them German Lutheran immigrants, were also embarking on separate school efforts. St. John's German Evangelical School opened its doors in 1843, St. Matthew's started a school class in 1846, and Trinity Evangelical Lutheran School organized in 1850.

By focusing nearly all their attention on Catholic-Protestant quarrels over the Bible, outspoken school champions, whether Catholic or Protestant, minimized the importance immigrant parents placed in transmitting their own heritage—and, for Germans, their language. More ominous, when public school officials did address the special needs of immigrant children, from the outset it was with the purpose of bringing them into "our culture." Bishop Lefevere had no patience with Catholics who insisted on priests of their own nationality, but he did appreciate their need for a priest who spoke their language. He encouraged seminarians to study French, German, and English, and he allowed ethnic parishes to multiply.[63]

Developing in tandem, church schools and public schools were siphoning money from those residents who contributed for the former and paid taxes for the latter. The cost of "free" public schools edged up. As early as 1843 it became apparent to the legislature that the primary school fund on which Pierce and Crary planned would not be adequate to the task. Taxes would have to provide more of the financing. New enabling legislation allowed Detroiters' school assessments to rise continually across the 1840s. Moreover, the board issued bonds for construction, increasing the number of primary schools to thirteen by 1848. Projections for public education became ever more expansive. When the state government moved to Lansing in 1847, the board took over the old capitol in the center of town, where it organized the first union school, a combined primary and middle school under one roof.

By the 1852–53 school year, every ward but the Third had a public school, albeit in makeshift quarters. In the First Ward nearly a hundred children studied in a "large room" on the corner of Wayne and Congress, and another brick building on Abbot was the site of a primary and a middle school for 225 students. The Second Ward had three schools with one hundred students each. In the Fourth Ward a house "usually" served 160 to 170 students and another "colored school" met in the African Episcopal Church. The capitol school in the Fifth Ward initiated the union school, and primary and middle school attendance there had reached 700; another 125 children from that ward studied in a house on West Park. A house with two school rooms and three more rented rooms gathered in four hundred Sixth Ward students; a brick union school on Larned in the Seventh Ward also enrolled four hundred; and, in the Eighth Ward, a new "beautiful and costly" building had five hundred students.[64] Suspicious Catholics did not doubt the motives for putting this particular temptation in a ward where 1,864 of 4,188 people indicated they were Irish Catholics.[65] It was almost across the street from the new brick school that Holy Trinity parish had opened the same year at a cost of $1,500 to parishioners. As an indication of the import the Eighth Ward school meant to have, its principal was the brother of the Detroit school superintendent.[66]

To those Catholics carefully assessing the situation, it began to be unmistakable that influence in political councils mattered and that decisionmakers from top to bottom were arrayed against them when it came to education. Regents at the fledgling University of Michigan mollified critics who charged the university was "ungodly" by designating professors to represent the Presbyterian, Methodist, Baptist, and Episcopal churches. There was no gesture to Catholics. One after another, state superintendents had a powerful voice in the halls of the legislature, impressed newspaper editors, and influenced the Protestant-dominated colleges; they sided with people and expressed ideas Catholics came to perceive as the opposition. Pierce's successors were men like him, educated in eastern Protestant colleges and consumed by the concern to transmit those values and institutions. Franklin Sawyer, the second superintendent, was an editor of the vigorously anti-Catholic *Detroit Daily Advertiser.*[67] Oliver Cromwell Comstock, the state superintendent in 1845, was an ordained Baptist minister who recommended that the Bible be read each day in school. Denying the King James Bible was sectarian, he said that Bible-reading was time well spent because its lessons would exert "a healthful influence" on students' "discipline, tuition and improvement."[68]

A new state constitution adopted in 1850 had, as a key purpose, more provisions that would limit executive power because voters had become wary of excessive government. The state superintendent of public instruction was now to be elected rather than appointed by the governor. That could have been little comfort to alert Catholics, however. Few of the legislators were Catholic—three of the 104 in 1852, according to one tally.[69] Moreover, Catholics' voting power was concentrated in Detroit, and the recent decision to shift the capitol to Lansing signaled the growing political influence of towns and farms where Protestants dominated. Indeed, from 1850 to 1881 every superintendent was a Protestant, born either in New England or New York.[70]

Ira Mayhew was particularly visible as state superintendent, appointed by the governor between 1845 and 1849 and back in office when voters elected him from 1855 to 1859. In a series of lectures in 1849 to the legislature, he clearly understood that he was among friends when he pointed out, "It is one of our cardinal principles, as Protestants, that the more they read the Scriptures the better."[71] Protestants should note how effective the "Romanists" were with their school children: "It is astonishing to see with what tenacity children thus educated cling to the superstitions and absurdities of their fathers; and it is because their religion is wrought into the very texture of their minds, in the schools as well as the churches." He viewed Bible-reading in public schools as necessary and proper. After all, Papists, Jews, and Mohammedans taught their religion to their children, so "why should not Protestants do the same?"[72]

Mayhew openly represented public schools as the province of Protestants. His sentiments duplicated those of the Detroit school board and the university's regents. The Michigan House of Representatives so heartily approved the superintendent's lectures that the members unanimously passed a resolution requesting Mayhew to publish them "in book form" to be "diffused throughout the state and nation."[73]

Such blatant proselytizing offered the opportunity to rally lagging Catholics around Bishop Peter Paul Lefevere's resolve for Catholic schools. His alarm had been intensifying. Proliferation of public schools threatened to bring higher property taxes on the one hand, yet at the same time it offered a free alternative to budding Catholic schools. The parish school was proving to be an important attraction in the German and Irish communities. Still, parents had to make a careful decision whether to pay tuition especially because the city's low-cost real estate put the possibility of property ownership within reach of even the laboring classes (chapter 3). There were danger signs in the Irish Eighth Ward. Because Trinity's school enrolled only boys, parents who had daughters were looking favorably upon the new neighborhood public school, where, by an agreeable accommodation, a Catholic schoolmaster taught Catholic children upstairs and a Protestant schoolmaster taught Protestant children downstairs.

The vigilant decided it was time to act once Mayhew's *Popular Education* appeared in 1852.[74] Catholics responded with a petition to the legislature, requesting a portion of school taxes for their schools. The idea was first popularized more than a decade earlier by Catholics in New York and had been broached but dropped by Holy Trinity parishioners. Now the idea was resurrected—this time to become a major issue in Detroit politics.

By now there were enough separate issues to attract a pool of petitioners. Probably the ordinary Catholic storekeeper, farmer, or drayman neither comprehended the debates over sectarianism nor cared about the import of university regents and state superintendents. But they understood the warning signs of state control because many had come across the ocean to avoid it. They paid taxes for schools that chose not to teach their language, appreciate their culture, acknowledge their religion, or hire their daughters. Willingly, "rather than run any risk of their young minds being tampered with, by a non-Catholic teacher," parents made personal and financial sacrifices to open Catholic schools.[75] These schools were already costly, even the small ones. With genuine confidence in democracy, many Catholics anticipated petitioning could work. With an almost naive conviction, the faithful expected a just share of the school fund might be theirs.

Conditions that contributed elsewhere to nativists' virulence and Catholics' fears did not have the same chronic grip in Detroit. There were people on every side for whom the rallying issues of taxation, religious values, and democracy would prove merely devices to serve their own ends. But still this was not New York or Boston or Philadelphia or Cincinnati. There was a long French heritage and the recent Protestant generosity on behalf of Irish potato famine victims. Protestant and Catholic Detroiters lived and worked among one another. "Irish need not apply" signs were uncommon. There would be alarmist warnings but no riots in the streets, no houses stoned.

Detroiters would shy away from calling their fight the "school war." They would become preoccupied, rather, with the school question. John D. Pierce would ultimately be proven wrong in his dire assessment: "If we can not meet on this ground, and join our efforts as citizens of one commonwealth to promote a common good, we can meet and cooperate nowhere this side of the grave."[76] During the next seventy years and beyond, public schools and parochial schools developed independent of one another, with little mutual support or understanding, but they managed to educate thousands of children. Still, residents might have managed to accommodate their differences better than most communities had they been more thoughtful and courageous. Nowhere better is there an example of the hold exerted by the national experience.

2 The School Question of the 1850s

He was a man in moderate circumstances, but he preferred to pay for
the tuition of his children by a Catholic, rather than run any risk of
their young minds being tampered with, by a non-Catholic teacher.
—Richard R. Elliott

SUPERINTENDENT Mayhew's report, the legislature's response, and
Catholic reaction underscored the nearly impossible expectations Americans
had come to place on education. When the school question became imperative in mid-nineteenth-century Detroit, it revealed the self-protective fears
of a people, native-born and immigrant alike, driven by the optimism that
their children might have it all—"faith and fortune" and American democracy. The conflict came because men and women of all persuasions were convinced that schools must teach moral values and also that "all morals, all
virtue, are founded on religion."[1] Like other Americans, Detroiters grappled with the problem of how, in a democracy, to make disparate religious
teachings translate into common values—a task, ironically, not difficult. Despite lacking tolerance for each other's ritualistic baggage, neither Protestants
nor Catholics doubted which values were central to a child's education: the
Golden Rule and the Ten Commandments.

The ballot box would settle the immediate question about school funding. The majority would win, the minority acquiesce. Protestants would
maintain their control of public schools but not force Catholics into them;
Catholics would not pursue tax dollars for their schools but would run the
schools according to their own dictates. It was the type of compromise customary to nineteenth-century America, approved by all but the dogmatic
extremists. That Protestants and Catholics did share common values and
faith in democracy went almost unobserved in this complicated time.

THE BACKGROUND OF THE SCHOOL QUESTION

Like the very issues of school funding and school purpose, some complexities that helped unsettle Detroiters belonged to the contradictory national mood that prized legislated moral reform on one hand but personal freedom from governmental interference on the other. From about the time Michigan became a full partner in the Union, entrepreneurs large and small were scrambling for the abundant natural resources that the state's land, pine forests, iron ore, copper deposits, and waterways promised. They sought state subsidies for railroads, salt mines, and family farm purchases in order to make huge fortunes possible for a few and put decent family incomes within reach for many. With every severe downturn in the economy, sharp in 1837 and recurring throughout the 1840s, competitors vied for favorable protective tariffs, banking acts, and currency arrangements. Consistently, Detroiters opposed taxes and what they considered "irresponsible spending." A chief purpose of the new constitution in 1850 was to restrain state spending, and in 1852 Detroit voters defeated a proposal to keep street lights burning all night.

Like other Americans who sought state-enforced reform of targeted evildoers—slaveholders, drinkers, unchurched sabbath-breakers—Michigan reformers wanted to be in control of the state lest their own particular cause come under attack. Many residents judged each reform by its potential impact on them. For example, all the while pockets of Michigan abolitionists passed runaway slaves across to Canada, the *Free Press* worried about the economic effect an end to slavery might have on the North. There was a persistent urge to seek some moderate middle ground on most every issue. When it came to slavery in the territories, the state's old hero Lewis Cass was the national champion of popular sovereignty. But in the state as in the nation, those on either side of him drained his influence by the mid-1850s. The very notion of compromise could seem a betrayal of principle.

For all the national turmoil, the school question, as it came and went in Detroit, belonged very much to the interplay of local circumstances and personal relationships. Patterns added up differently in Detroit than in cities that experienced bloody riots and school wars, cities where Catholic schools would gain neither the enrollment nor the acceptance Detroit Catholic schools managed to achieve. At the time the school question emerged, class differences did not sharply divide Detroit's native-born from immigrants, but the number of poor immigrants had recently increased; ethnicity did not predictably define the city's neighborhoods, but Irish and German sections were newly obvious. Catholics and Protestants had an established habit of various partnerships, and neither clergy nor politicians could command assured allegiance; complicated local political alliances cut across class, place of origin, and occupation. Religion was becoming more significant in party allegiances, however; as the Whigs pulled in nativists the foreign-born and Catholics were pushed more dependably toward the coalition-building Democrats. Still, the political parties were so divided by the early 1850s that neither could calculate a clear direction. Every faction in town grasped the volatile potential of tax-supported public education.

In-migration, especially rapid from the mid-1840s, had helped create a community on edge, and various groups were defensively poised. The population had been multiplying since 1830—from 2,222 that year to 9,102 by 1840 and then to 21,019 by 1850.[2] At midcentury, nine out of ten Detroiters had been in the city less than a decade. Detroit had become home to so many Irish and German immigrants that 47 percent of its population was now foreign-born. According to the 1853 city directory, which surveyed residents as to their religion as well as their nationality, 11,380 of the 29,073 Detroiters were Catholic. Among Catholics, 45 percent identified themselves as Irish, 34 percent as Germans, 18 percent as French (including a group of French-Canadians), and only 2 percent as "American Catholics." Citywide, the number of Protestant Irish was comparatively slight, but there were almost as many German Protestants as German Catholics.[3]

Statewide, only 14 percent of Michigan residents were immigrants, and the proportion of Catholics in small towns and rural areas was negligible apart from localized areas where they settled together as groups of families. This urban concentration seemed especially worrisome to those who lived elsewhere in the state, who were more often sympathetic to issues such as abolition and tariffs that did not interest immigrants or to causes like temperance and school Bible-reading, which aroused many foreigners to outright opposition. Michigan's constitution of 1850 made voting laws even more lenient than before, giving the franchise to every white male with three months' residency in the state. A voter who had lived in a ward for ten days could appear at the polls, and any immigrant could hold local office so long as he had declared his intention to become a citizen by taking out "first papers." Two years after that step, the government would issue "second papers," and the immigrant could then hold state, legislative, or even national offices. The specter of machine-controlled blocs of Detroit voters danced in the heads of those hoping to mobilize voting power for whatever purpose.

Unlike their countrymen who had settled in earlier, many of the Irish who came after 1846 were "famine Irish" who had fled when the potato crop failed year after year from 1845 through 1848. Poorer than the previous emigrants, they were less skilled, less well educated, and more often had to take low-paying jobs. In Detroit at midcentury, household heads who had left Ireland during the famine were twice as likely to be common laborers as those longer in the country.[4] Newcomers gravitated toward the Irish parish, Most Holy Trinity. Once parishioners jacked up the church building in 1849, rolled it fifteen blocks westward from downtown, and set it in place at Sixth and Porter, Trinity's draw to the Eighth Ward worked like a magnet. There, for the first time, Detroit began to have a distinctive Irish neighborhood.

Even more than the Irish, Detroit's German families settled near each other. Germans of all classes bought property in a newly foreign enclave that spilled from the near east side to the edge of the city. Their physical adjustment to the city was not without conflict. German shopkeepers whose businesses lined Gratiot Street got together in 1849 to tear up part of the railroad track along the street in protest over the noise, filth, and smoke from trains running past their doors. They were outraged that the Common Council would not take their side against railroad companies, and other indignities piled up to fuel their ire. As the German neighborhood expanded eastward, families began to move into the section of the city where brothels had concentrated undisturbed during the 1840s. By the early 1850s German residents wanted city hall to rid the area of houses of ill-repute and angrily contended that because they were immigrants the mayor and council were unconcerned with them.[5]

Temperance proved one more wedge. Native-born Protestant temperance advocates increasingly singled out immigrants, especially Catholics, as excessive drinkers. Papists' lack of self-control, went the argument, meant that laws must take over where character failed. Many Catholics leaders worried over every manner of excess and were themselves vigilant opponents of alcohol. Bishop Lefevere was a staunch temperance advocate. One of his first acts in the diocese was to administer a total abstinence pledge at Ste. Anne's, and in 1842 the temperance society of Holy Trinity numbered 1,002, having enrolled men, women, and children. Still, those who obediently stood to take the annual pledge at Sunday mass no doubt made a distinction between voluntary temperance and outright abstinence mandated by law. Few Catholics doubted that any drinker should be moderate about it. But the right to drink after a hard day's work or on a Sunday in a German beer garden did seem to them part and parcel of America's freedom. Prohibition smacked of a government control that even the British government had not imposed. More important, banning liquor would seriously interfere with established businesses and jobs. Many breweries were German-owned and employed German workers, and dozens of Irish and German families made a living as neighborhood saloon-keepers.

Temperance advocates gained ground by petitioning the legislature and exhorting the public just as Catholics turned to the legislature for a share of the school fund. Michigan's version of the anti-liquor "Maine Law" won support in the legislature in February 1853 and then in a popular referendum in June—with a landslide vote outside Detroit.[6] It ushered in stringent controls on liquor wherever enforcement proved possible. Detroit's newspapers were filled with debate over the issue for months.

CITY CHARTER PROPOSALS PROPEL THE SCHOOL QUESTION

The role of the state in education began to command steady attention by December 1852, and letters to the editor staked out the opposing positions in near-hysterical hyperbole. "A Constitutional Catholic" charged that Superintendent Mayhew, to the "applause" of the legislature, recommended the adoption of compulsory state free schools on the Prussian model and would have parents punished by fine or imprisonment if their children did not attend them.[7] A counter "notice" signed by "FREE EDUCATION" warned that "petitions are in circulation" asking that public money be given to sectarian schools, with the "view of utterly destroying our noble system of public schools."[8]

It is possible that the controversy over schools might have hit and then lingered with more bitterness had not Catholics' request for school funding been entwined from the outset with council proposals for new tax-funded projects. Bishop Lefevere decided to make the move for a share of the school fund in December 1852, the same time the Detroit Common Council sought charter amendments to levy taxes and borrow money so it might proceed with civic improvements. Several proposals impinged upon church assets. Even some Catholics, jaundiced by their experiences with him, could wonder if the bishop fought more out of financial self-interest than principle. Later, residents could mute their differences by charging imprudent leaders with blame.

Establishing a public hospital, discussed for several years, was one part of the council's plan. From the time the Sisters of Charity opened St. Vincent's Hospital in 1845 and then replaced it with the larger St. Mary's in 1850, the council had contributed to the care of some patients from the poor fund.[9]

Money in the poor fund came from licenses paid by liquor dealers, but in 1852 the Michigan supreme court had ordered Detroit to enforce the legislative ruling against selling liquor licenses.[10] Short of funds, the council now cut back on the sum it allocated for each charity case and began to plan a tax-supported hospital and almshouse under city control.[11] The council also wanted the power to pave or repair "streets, lanes, alleys, sidewalks, highways or bridges" by assessing all owners who had bordering property. Furthermore, the council asked approval to expand the city's water system by selling municipal bonds. Less controversial were amendments that would give the council power to assign watchmen or policemen and made literacy in English an eligibility requirement for any city office except chimney sweeper or scavenger.[12]

The charter amendments had significant financial implications for taxpayers. Heated citizens' meetings began within a week of the Common Council's charter amendment report. Every foot of paving already in place had been subject to debate. Considerable sentiment favored the paving assessment in preference to any additional general tax. At the meetings Bishop Lefevere was prominent among the opposition, along with Father Michael Edgar Shawe, pastor of the cathedral church. The bishop made himself spokesman on behalf of the poor, arguing that individual assessments on property owners would present an unfair burden. He favored a general assessment if supported by a popular vote, opposed the almshouse, and was against the hospital because there was a "splendid" charity hospital already in the city.[13]

The bishop did not respond to charges that conversion was pressed upon Protestants at St. Mary's. Saving souls was, in fact, a goal the sisters did nourish along with their patients' health. One nursing sister recorded in her chronicle that in the winter of 1853 and spring of 1854, "A number of German Lutherans became Catholics; nearly all of them were respectable, intelligent young men."[14] But the bishop apparently failed also to muster those statistics that might have helped counter demands that he "should support his poor himself."[15] He could have demonstrated that not only Catholic immigrants but also American-born and Protestant immigrants figured prominently among the patients. In 1851, 122 of the 437 patients admitted to the hospital were born in the United States, and in 1854 the hospital served 598 Protestants and 365 Catholics[16] The sisters had accepted a responsibility that the council, so far, had tended to only with penurious subsidies for the hospitalized indigent.

In preference to substantive debate, both sides opted for public posturing and rhetoric. "A True Democrat," one frequent contributor to the various newspapers, hammered out the key accusation against the bishop: He was merely protecting his own interests. As one of the largest property holders, his paving assessments would be significant. Furthermore, the charge went, the sisters at St. Mary's hospital would no longer be able to rely on payments from the city for care of the poor. Other critics insisted that the prelate should not have the right to interject himself into public affairs, and they objected that Catholic "mobs" packed the meetings.

Father Shawe, a former professor of English literature at the University of Notre Dame, articulated the defense. Because the bishop was "as large a tax payer as almost any man in the community," certainly, "unless the fact of his being a Catholic Prelate deprives him of his rights as a citizen," he should not be denied the right to participate in the citizen meetings.[17] It was the classic dilemma dividing Americans well before and long after the 1850s: How was democracy to be ensured? For whom and from whom should it be protected?

The problem of paying for necessary public services readily focused on Catholics' request for a share of taxes to support their schools. Improved streets and a cost-efficient municipal water system garnered general popular support. The return of cholera in 1849 and 1852 underscored the need for additional attention to health care. Education, however, would be an ongoing tax expense, with its long-term benefits realized only in the future. When the bishop and his Catholic following asked that school money be spread even further, anti-Catholics could make common cause with religiously tolerant but tax-hesitant residents.

Detroiters had seen school expenditures edge upward from $1.60 per student in the 1840s to $1.90 by 1850.[18] Rapid growth in the number of schools and the obvious cost widespread education would bring meant Detroiters were anxious to get their money's worth. Once the biases of State Superintendent Mayhew, the legislature, and the school board became apparent, more Catholics began to fear that their school taxes would not only be misspent but also harmfully so if their children attended public schools. Once the bishop began encouraging Catholics to political action, more Protestants began to heed nativists who warned that an authoritarian Roman church was endangering democracy on every front.

PAROCHIAL SCHOOL FUNDING AND THE POLITICAL ARENA

On January 10, 1853, Bishop Lefevere led like-minded Catholics to Lansing with their petitions. They asked to change the Michigan school law so that tax money, equivalent to that used in free public primary schools, could be given to qualified teachers in any Catholic primary school taught in English. Representative Jeremiah O'Callaghan, who sat strategically on the House Committee on Education, wrote a bill to accomplish the division of school funds. O'Callaghan was an erudite Irish Catholic immigrant grocer who belonged to Holy Trinity parish in Detroit. The school question shook free of other issues and dominated public attention from January through the spring elections in March.

Catholic and Protestant leadership came from Detroit, but supporters elsewhere in the state, rallied by their own clergy, put their signatures and contributions to the cause. Each side snatched up familiar arguments, waved constitutional democracy as a flag, and demanded that the political process should safeguard guarantees. Samuel McCoskry, bishop of the Protestant Episcopal Church in Michigan, was quick to present the legislature with a petition whose signers opposed any change in the common school law that would "allow parents to choose teachers for their children" based on religious preferences. Bishop McCoskry warned about the consequences of placating Catholics. If such a change were indeed made by the legislature, he intended to "respectfully ask for his proportion . . . so that the people entrusted to his spiritual oversight" could employ teachers of "their religious preferences," too.[19]

Claims and counter-claims about motives poured in to state legislators. Reverend George Duffield of Detroit's First Presbyterian Church became the most visible standard-bearer in the effort to oppose the Catholics' request. Elders and deacons of Reverend Duffield's church sent a "Remonstrance," warning legislators that the "Romish priesthood" was acting "in obedience to the commands and suggestions of a foreign despotic sovereign," with the object of "subversion of the free system of schools." They maintained that "Jesuitical enterprise" and "Romish Clergy" throughout the United States were threatened by the "consequent independence of mind" that education in the Republic promoted.[20] The Presbyterian denomination and Duffield became chief targets of Catholics, who sneered that there "is no sect whose teachings have led so directly to the denial of the Divinity of Christ" and attacked Duffield as a man who "preeminently worships his own reason and judgment."[21]

In one forum or another, Protestants constantly emphasized Article IV, section 39 of the Michigan constitution of 1850: The Legislature shall pass no law to compel any person to "pay tithes, taxes or other rates for the support of any minister . . . or teacher of religion."[22] Catholics pointed to Article IV, section 31: "The Legislature shall not diminish or enlarge the civil or political rights, privileges and capacities of any person, on account of his opinion or belief concerning matters of religion."[23]

Catholic supporters of "splitting" the school tax were best represented in the local press by A Constitutional Catholic, possibly State Representative O'Callaghan or Father Shawe. In frequent letters the writer instructed Catholics with familiar points made in other states' campaigns: Public schools were influenced by Protestant thought; nonsectarian schools were undesirable because they did not teach morality; Catholics had a constitutional right to religious freedom of choice in education; and the only protection for this freedom was a fair share of the school fund.[24] According to the interpretation of A Constitutional Catholic, the Michigan constitution "unequivocally declares that no citizen shall be deprived of any of his rights because of his religious opinions."[25]

Catholics reminded legislators of their voting power and deluged the state house with copies of a pamphlet entitled *The Common School System and Public Education,* a statement of Catholic views. In contrast to Catholic complaints elsewhere, anti-Catholic textbooks received little mention throughout the course of local arguments. Perhaps because so few children had been attending public schools, parents were not particularly attuned to biases routinely written into standard texts. Somehow, Catholic defenders also generally ignored the critical doctrinal point, strongly emphasized by Bishop Hughes and New Yorkers, that school Bible-reading without "note or comment" would be unacceptable precisely because Catholics must not interpret the Bible on their own.[26] Michigan Catholics had a special concern, however, second only to receiving a share of the school fund. They firmly insisted upon an end to discrimination against hiring Catholics as public school teachers. Quite likely, this demand represented immigrant preferences for teachers who shared their same heritage and, in the case of Germans, teachers able to speak their language. It surely also reflected ambitions of the considerable number of educated, would-be teachers within the Detroit Catholic community.

Protestants dominated the legislature. By one estimate, only three of the 104 members were Catholic in 1853. Growth in the southern and middle tiers of Michigan had also resulted in the swing of power toward rural counties, enough by 1847 to weight the vote for Lansing rather than Detroit as the permanent capital. People who lived outside Detroit feared that the city might harbor dangerous classes, a concern probably exacerbated by the heavy involvement of Detroit Catholics in the request to the legislature; of the 4,104 who signed the petition, 2,753 lived in Wayne County.

Representative O'Callaghan received little support for his bill that would split school tax money to pay teachers in parochial schools. A majority of the House Committee on Education voted against it, issuing a report expressing their opinion that any change "ought not to be demanded by the friends of education of any sect or denomination." Such a change "would interrupt the prosperity and progress of primary schools . . . and would introduce confusion and discord in place of harmony and peace, and materially affect the interests of the rising generation."[27] The legislature agreed and ordered five hundred copies be printed as well as five hundred copies of O'Callaghan's minority report.[28] Only two weeks had elapsed since the petitions were delivered. The legislature considered the matter settled and turned back to its preoccupation with railroads and a canal at Sault Ste. Marie to link Lake Superior with Lake Huron.

Lawmakers did not expect that their failure to change school financing would interrupt the "progress and prosperity of primary schools," introduce "confusion and discord," and materially affect successive generations in addition to the generation then "rising." Even if they had been able to foresee the political turmoil soon to follow or the impact upon public and private education, it is likely that they would have voted the same way again out of their conviction about the purpose of "public" schools, in the interest of conserving tax funds, and in response to political pressure from Protestants, a strong presence in most legislators' constituencies.

Driven by conviction and financial need, the bishop and his steadfast adherents persevered in their determination to get a "fair share" of the tax money Catholics paid on behalf of education. Now they directed their strategy to Detroit, intending to win supportive office-holders in the spring elections nearly six weeks away. Although that venture, then and later, was usually attributed to Lefevere's machinations, he lacked the political acumen of several other American bishops and probably relied on the advice of willing allies. The campaign surely involved a number of laymen active in local Democratic politics.

For years Democrats had enjoyed electoral success by a careful, bargained unity among Catholics, Protestants, immigrants, and native-born. The Whigs often scoffed that the city's Democratic ticket had "well over half" of its slots filled by either "foreigners or Catholics." So far as can be judged, between 1850 and 1852 the party had nominated ten Americans, nine Irishmen, five Germans, and two French residents for seats on the council. Half or more of the residents in six of the city's eight wards in 1853 were foreign-born. In three wards the number of Catholics approached or exceeded half, and in two more wards about one-third of the residents were Catholic.[29] Banking heavily on their ability to influence ward caucuses, Catholics launched an effort to make their weight felt through the Democratic Party. That strategy was in contrast to Bishop Hughes's 1841 directive in New York, where he had urged Catholics to leave the two major tickets and support an Independent ticket friendly to Catholics.[30]

The political aims of Bishop Lefevere and his supporters, not set forth in any published form, can only be pieced together from newspaper accounts and evidence of their activities. It appears that in something of a blunderbuss volley these Catholics aimed to elect councilmen in the March 1853 election who would share the bishop's opposition to the planned property tax for paving, the proposed hospital and almshouse, and the water system expansion. They sought school board candidates who would be at least sympathetic to parochial schools or who, some activists imagined, might be counted on to deliver—even divert—tax dollars from Lansing to Catholic schools in Detroit.[31] Whatever Catholics hoped, however, their strategy was unrealistic. Worse, their tactics were inopportune given the extreme nativist minority waiting for a chance to make headway with public opinion.

Catholics packed ward Democratic caucus meetings in February 1853, succeeded in nominating a number of their candidates, and by these means laid themselves open to the charge of corrupting the democratic process at the bishop's instigation. Old political balances in Detroit ruptured. Other Democrats, disgusted and angry, split from the Regular ticket and put together an Independent slate with separate candidates for the offices of alderman and school inspector. Whigs, nearly moribund a year earlier, announced righteously that they would "make no nominations in view of the seriousness of the problem."[32] Instead, in a smart political strategy, they nominated their candidates under the Independent label in those wards where they had strength.

Anti-Catholicism propelled the Independent ticket in 1853, but within a year a new national political party would take form in Michigan. Electoral politics in Detroit represented the emergent realignment of Whigs and the Free-Soilers—who had distrusted each other—and also disenchanted Democrats and bigoted, extremist Know-Nothings.[33] One local Democrat described the opposition's heterogeneity as aptly as most political scientists and historians later would manage with their sophisticated tools of analysis. The Independents, he assessed, included "one-half who have always voted whig" and many others who were abolitionists and Free-Soilers, men who had supported the Constitutional provision "for the negro to vote . . . on a par with the white man; there were disappointed Democratic office seekers blocked in their own party." Among this lot were men who, to win, would try "three or four gestures, such as the free schools, Catholicism, and what not."[34] To be sure, various highly publicized national matters such as the Maine Law and the Kansas-Nebraska bill helped pull factions together under the new fusionist ticket that was advantaged by anti-Catholicism and candidates in search of slots. But all those factors combined were not enough to secure victory in Detroit for Democratic Party rivals. In 1853, and again in the spring election of 1854, it was the school question that doomed Detroit Democrats, and they would regain customary control in the city only when they could put the issue aside.

"Regular" Democrats won only in the Irish-dominated Eighth Ward. Catholics themselves were not solidly united. On the petitions Catholics from Wayne County took to the state legislature in January, the 2,753 signatures fell short of the number of Catholic adults in the city of Detroit by perhaps as many as 4,000.[35] The best analysis of the 1853 election suggests that German and Irish voters, especially those in the working classes, supported the Regulars while French Catholics supported the Independent ticket.

The *Detroit Daily Tribune* singled out the Irish laborers as a bloc vote for "their priests" when it chided "no class of our citizens" should have been so deeply in favor of street paving, because "employment thus afforded is the bread and butter of a very large number of these men."[36] Still, religion was a more important factor in the immigrant vote than class.[37] Letters in the newspapers from middle- and upper-class Irish Catholics especially revealed their fear about state-enforced education because of experiences in British-dominated schools in Ireland. Subsequent events in 1854 and 1855 lend credence to press accounts that assessed, however, that in addition to the French, the Irish and German Catholics who had been in the city for several years did not support the "Catholic" position.[38]

Reasons for Catholic defection were complicated. The established French elite of Ste. Anne's parish was not always in accord with the bishop's plans. They were among the wealthiest people in the city and able to support their own Catholic school children along with any poor French or French-Canadians worthy of help. Ste. Anne's trustees had so vehemently insisted on their right of ownership that Bishop Lefevere abandoned that church as the cathedral and between 1844 and 1848 built SS. Peter and Paul, which he named after his own patron saints and controlled securely. Further, many of the "fine" French families were loathe to be identified with the Catholic immigrants regarded as rabble in local circles. Other Catholics, too, were opposed to the high-handedness of their bishop and had already proven themselves an independent laity. The Germans delayed opening St. Mary's Church for more than three years because the congregation could not agree on whether to give the bishop title to the land, causing him to complain of "infidel Germans" as a lot and excommunicate the most offensive.[39] The Irish had risen to battle when the bishop thought to close their Holy Trinity parish and thereby create a larger congregation for his new SS. Peter and Paul cathedral.

In addition to a periodic disregard of their bishop, many Catholic voters were tied economically to Protestant employers. Others, genuinely devoted to parish schools, feared outside control would be the likely price those schools would pay for tax funding. Further, certain Catholic politicians were aware of the flaws in the Regular Democrats' plan to gain school funds in defiance of state law. James Collins, an Irishman in the First Ward, ran on the Independent ticket for alderman, whether out of dictates of conscience or political prudence.

Regardless of how they voted, all Catholics felt the effect of the failed effort; there were ominous consequences beyond lack of tax dollars for their schools. The local press began to pay considerable attention to their religion. The *Detroit Daily Advertiser* and the *Daily Tribune,* for example, although representing different shades of the opposition, railed against Catholics with extreme, bigoted characterizations: "We would as soon place the stake of our safety upon the career of a maddened horse—upon the tender mercies of the devouring flame, or the raging and remorseless ocean, as to place it within the control of the Catholic clergy."[40] Immigrants, especially the Irish, were portrayed as ignorant; who else would ask for the "riggilar Dimmercratic ticket" at the polls?[41]

Free Press editor William Storey backed the Regular Democratic ticket as a party loyalist. Storey, new to the city, scrambled to find some middle ground in the interest of restoring the Democratic Party to power in Detroit. Having just come from Cincinnati, where religious-based controversies raged in the streets, press, and political conclaves, he was aware of the school issue's fearsome potential. The position the *Free Press* staked out did not please independent Democrats or accommodate tax-hopeful Catholics, however. Storey consistently opposed any effort that might come about to divert funds from their "legitimate course" and insisted the present system of public schools "must be preserved."[42]

To serve as the "means wherein calumny might be refuted," the *Detroit Catholic Vindicator* began as a weekly newspaper within a month after the 1853 election. It was initiated by Father Shawe, probably with the financial support of Bishop Lefevere. When Father Shawe died as the result of a buggy accident ten days after the first issue appeared, Richard Elliott and several other Irish Catholics took over the paper. With the second issue, they made their chief aim clear: the "necessity of vindicating Catholic rights in regard to Public Schools." For the four years of its existence the *Vindicator* spoke for Catholics, especially to the Irish, reminding them weekly on the masthead, "Be of good courage and let us behave ourselves manfully for our people."[43] It was the only dependably sympathetic organ Catholics had. Frequently the *Vindicator* helped heighten antagonism, however, by its emotional overreactions, deliberate insults, and jeering taunts. Catholics, the paper chortled, were increasing every day and would "come to have not just a relative majority, but an absolute majority."[44]

Catholics and Protestants each took delight in passing along rumors about the other's duplicity and crazed behavior. The *Daily Advertiser* charged the *Tribune* editor, evidently too soft on Catholics, had in fact converted to Catholicism. With that, the *Tribune* responded this was a "sheer, unmitigated, malicious falsehood."[45] According to the *Tribune,* the *Advertiser*'s editor was no Whig, but a Democrat.[46] A letter from A True Democrat contained inside information from a "well-informed correspondent" that Bishop Lefevere was so wiley a manipulator that he was secretly a Whig bent on controlling the Democratic Party.[47] Before the spring 1853 election, the *Daily Advertiser* floated a warning that "Roman Catholics have fortified their Churches by planting them with cannon and muskets!" The *Free Press* reported a "rumor was around" that Protestants had collected a quantity of firearms, with the intention of firing on Catholics.[48] But once the votes were counted, even the anti-Catholic *Advertiser* was sufficiently pleased to be charitable: "Hardly an angry word passed—sobriety was the order of the day, and drunkenness, if any there was, was the infrequent exception."[49]

One year later, despite some efforts to patch the Democratic Party back together, the split was "not yet cured." As it had in 1853, the Eighth Ward caucus met at an unusual time, from noon to two, to choose delegates to the city nominating convention, perhaps so Irish activists could appear at the other ward caucuses, all customarily held on the same night at seven.[50] The *Free Press* lamented that nominees for office were not "what they should be" because Democratic ward meetings "were not well attended by the business men and commercial men and professional men of the party."[51] With paving taxes now approved by charter amendment, schools were the sole focus of Catholic critics. The *Daily Advertiser* reminded voters that the "greatest and vital question in the coming contest is, *in whose hands will the system of free schools be best cared for?*"[52] Once again, the nativist coalition gained council and school board seats.

Momentum behind the issue of tax money for parochial schools peaked in 1854. Rome proclaimed the dogma of the Immaculate Conception in January that year, setting off more trouble for Catholics. In Cincinnati a visit by papal nuncio Monsignor Gaetano led to a riot when German Free Liberals and American nativists marched on the cathedral to protest papal interference in the United States. Two people died as police battled to suppress the marchers, and there were immediate charges of Catholic influence upon Cincinnati police.[53] The Know-Nothings emerged nationally as a defined political party, and, in June 1854, Know-Nothings in Michigan formally organized. Among the party's other efforts to "Americanize America," according to local Know-Nothing pamphleteer L. W. Granger, Michigan would have a "pure *American* Common School System."[54]

On July 6, 1854, nearly 1,500 people from across Michigan brought their assorted causes to a meeting in Jackson, where they organized a fusion platform and nominated a full state ticket. Within a year that coalition of interests would take national form as the Republican Party. As the November election of 1854 loomed to offer Michigan voters the new ticket, Democratic editors warned readers that the fusionists' umbrella sheltered Know-Nothings.[55]

When fusionist and former Democrat Kinsley S. Bingham won the governor's office and the new ticket swept all offices plus a majority of seats in the state legislature, it signaled that the anti-Democratic vote had been successfully gathered together. Except for the city of Detroit, Michigan would thereafter remain almost consistently Republican until 1932. Democrats who previously defected in Detroit's spring elections of 1853 and 1854 recognized the danger of continued division in their party. The old French Catholics, long a "bulwark of the Democracy," together with the more astute Irish and German Catholics, were ever more chagrined by the bishop's lack of political sophistication and blamed him for the ill-advised campaign that had cost them political offices.[56]

The politically shrewd were not the only Catholics who came to understand the need for Protestant allies. For two years the city's Catholics had reckoned with a Common Council and school board that evidenced hostility toward them but favoritism toward others. In accordance with approved charter changes, the council taxed the Catholic hospital, orphan asylum, and church lots along paving routes. The *Vindicator* furiously complained that the Masonic Hall and "other similar favored institutions" were exempted from taxes.[57] Seeming abuses of power piled one upon another. A favored institution, Reverend Duffield's First Presbyterian Church, received an eight-thousand-pound bell, which the council announced was to serve as a fire alarm. School board president Levi Bishop visited the Eighth Ward school, where he learned of Catholic children studying upstairs with a Catholic teacher and Protestants studying downstairs with a Protestant teacher. He demanded that twenty-five Catholic students be sent down and a number of Protestant students up; it was necessary to equalize class size, he explained. Parents of both groups protested vigorously, but Bishop persisted, finally forcing the Catholic teacher to resign.[58]

Just before Christmas of 1854, when the council proceeded with plans to sell St. Vincent's Orphanage for nonpayment of taxes, residents put aside religious differences to conduct a fund-raising fair for four days. The *Free Press* and the *Daily Tribune* urged the public to attend, the Fireman's Hall gave space, and the gas works did not charge for heating the hall during the fair. The fair raised $1,500, the orphanage survived, and the *Vindicator* publicly thanked Protestants for their help.[59] By February 1855 the *Vindicator* saw "Symptoms of Returning Sanity," optimistic that American citizens were "awakening to the danger of Know-Nothings" and were showing more healthy attitudes.[60]

In time for the elections that spring, the city's Democratic Party began its comeback with a single slate balanced between foreign-born and native-born, Catholics and Protestants. Democrats nominated Henry Ledyard for mayor. Wisely chosen, the New York-born mayor was a Presbyterian of French descent and had many Catholic friends. He was also the son-in-law of the popular Lewis Cass, who had recently taken special aim against the Know-Nothings. Still scrambling to put its party's most divisive problem to rest, the *Free Press* prompted readers that it "would not work" for the *Advertiser* and *Tribune* to again disinter the "fossil remains of the school question" and try to shake the "grim skeleton" before the public. A majority, the editor insisted, was sick of "this annual bugbear" and the effort to "array religious creeds" against each other.[61]

Ledyard was successful in the election and managed to attract a number of voters back to the Democratic fold in wards that had recently gone for Governor Bingham; he won large majorities in wards that had numerous foreign voters. The Independent ticket—this time dominated by Know-Nothings—elected four aldermen, but the Democrats regained ground in the council. Still, alert observers correctly assessed the trouble this new Republican Party posed. For the remainder of the decade Democratic fortunes see-sawed in Detroit elections, depending upon that party's ability to overcome internal schisms. Ledyard's inaugural address signaled the futility of any continued Catholic effort for school funding: "Let us unite, then, with one heart and one mind. . . . Let us practice economy in the expenditure of the taxes . . . and promote the diffusion of knowledge by providing means of education for all, by our inestimable system of Free Schools."[62]

To Cass and other vigilant Democrats, the future of the Democratic Party increasingly hinged on the issue of slavery in the territories. The school question that had dominated local attention must not get in the way of party unity. All the arguments and counter-arguments that could be made had been exhaustingly repeated: about the constitutionality of tax dollars for Catholic schools, about the place of religious teaching in schools, and about democratic freedom and rights. No acceptable political middle ground had surfaced, but, in contrast to Cincinnati, where two men were killed and four wounded on election day in April 1855, there was no blood to mop up in Detroit. There was no enthusiasm for any war over schools. War over slavery was not anticipated either, but finding some political middle ground on that most pressing national issue seemed imperative to both political parties. If the Democratic Party was going to survive severe fractures at the national level, local fissures must be patched up.

To Catholics, even to the stubborn Bishop Lefevere, it was apparent they had given aid and comfort to powerful enemies by promoting a cause that could not presently be won. Many legislators did indeed believe that the Catholic clergy's effort to get "political power" over Detroit schools presaged an "ultimate aim of extending it over all the state."[63] The fusion or "Republican"-dominated state legislature elected in November 1854 had quickly reflected its evangelical and Know-Nothing influences. By February 1855 it passed a new Maine Law, bringing strict prohibition and a church property bill that gave state law precedence over canon law in governing disputes between trustees and the clergy—particularly aimed at undermining the Catholic hierarchy. The legislature also began to consider a bill to regulate Roman Catholic "nunneries and schools," which state authorities would visit on a regular basis.[64]

Bishop Lefevere veered to a new course and by 1856 was insisting the church must remain above politics. When the *Catholic Vindicator* joined the other seventeen Catholic weeklies to endorse presidential Democratic candidate James Buchanan, an outraged Lefevere placed the paper under interdict and declared all Catholics who owed money for subscriptions or advertising were forbidden to pay the paper.[65] He might have been secretly in sympathy with the Catholic abolitionists such as Thomas D'Arcy McGee, but more likely he had decided on a new tactic. Regardless, his political influence had withered, even among the faithful. The Irish chose to ignore his opposition to an additional Irish church and joined a favorite priest, Father Hennessy, to open St. Patrick's by 1860 "without a dollar from the diocese."[66]

Astute Catholics such as Richard Elliott recognized the damage the bishop had done by "his lack of knowledge of people, customs, laws, and institutions of this country" and that his "unpopular course" had hurt the laity.[67] The *Vindicator* preferred to believe it was the hated English, not Detroit

Catholics' "just" and "high-minded" Protestant neighbors, who were really behind organized nativist efforts to "introduce civil strife in America." It was all out of English hatred and jealousy over the "growing prosperity and power" of a country that was once its mere colony.[68] The prominent Elliott was just one of many ordinary Catholics who would begin the push for Catholic schools, intending to make them so respectable that decent Protestants would be gratified and detractors would find no ground for denunciation. In this ambition, aims of the laity mirrored the intentions of Lefevere and his successors.

With new determination, once he withdrew from public politics Bishop Lefevere redirected his energies to exert authority over the Immaculate Heart of Mary sisters lest they drift off to teach in other dioceses. He had paid scant attention to the congregation after welcoming them to the diocese ten years earlier. Now, however, thanks to their vows of voluntary poverty, sister-teachers became more critical than ever for affording the Catholic school plans he would not abandon.

For the present, Catholics recognized that they would have to provide their own answers to the question of how to pay for their schools. Recent experience made it apparent that public schools, vulnerable to the whims of politics, could not be counted on to uphold compromises even if they were reached. Nationwide, talk was growing about compulsory education, and in neighboring Ohio a law was proposed in 1853 to compel parents to send children to a common school for three months in every year.[69] In New York, Bishop Hughes had demonstrated that Democrats needed Catholics to win, and control had been wrested from the Protestants who had dominated through the Public School Society. Still, there were regular reports from New York Catholics that Protestant influences over education prevailed. Locally, school board intransigents such as Duffield now belonged to the new Republican Party, which had power more fearsome than the old Whigs. Detroit Catholics were in little doubt that they must claim their children for their own schools, with or without tax support.

During the school question controversy, their opponents threatened Catholics that separate schools would cause "the young Irish and the young Germans, to be set apart." So educated, such children could expect to be considered "an outside and alien element, disturbing and disturbed, a pest in politics, and a thing of Bigotry."[70] But the molders of public schools had forfeited a chance to educate all children in common by intractable Protestantism. At the same time, the school question helped advance immigrants' pride of nationality, contradicting Bishop Lefevere's intention to rally and thereby unite immigrants as Catholics. Detroit immigrants did not choose to educate their children in one Catholic system, and, dating from the 1850s, they would accelerate an enduring pattern of separate parish schools.

German parents wanted schools where their culture and language would be transmitted rather than public schools that had the outspoken intention that immigrant children "ought to assimilate themselves to our people as soon as possible."[71] But German Catholics, complaining about Irish domination in the local Democratic Party, agreed with Irish stereotypes popularized by nativists and saw no reason to educate German and Irish children jointly because religion was their only commonality. Irish Catholics, who felt "especially hurt" by the attacks of the nativist opposition, surely now would not risk sending children to public schools where "Orangemen" lurked; they wanted Irish children to learn the lessons of their special heritage unknown to teachers hired for public classrooms. Stung by cruel jibes about their ignorance and their brogue, Irish parents were not willing to have their children take on new liabilities by merging with children, albeit Catholic, whose German-speaking priests, nuns, and parents were themselves open to press insults that they were "foreigners" unable even to understand English.

Over and again the Irish editors of the *Catholic Vindicator* demonstrated immigrants' determination to equip their children with knowledge common among Americans and yet anchor them in the wisdom of the homeland:

Written for an Irish Little Girl
I could tell you of the wishing-cap, and all about the ball,
Where Cinderella's slipper, from her little foot did fall.
But you and I are Irish and methinks I hear you say,
Tell me of ancient Erin, of our old home far away.[72]

Catholics emerged from their struggles over the school question with a better awareness of their course. They would have to continue providing their own parish schools, where they could teach religion, preserve their separate immigrant cultures, and prepare their children for the same economic opportunities as Protestant children had. In the process, they would need to demonstrate their commitment to democracy and American values.

Education, parochial or public, was left to get along without broad-based financial generosity, without leadership required to be tolerant, and without students who necessarily accommodated themselves to strangers. When Detroiters resolved the question about how to fashion and fund their schools in the mid-1850s, they hobbled the best promise education might have offered generations well beyond their time. They had not been incorrect, however, in recognizing that religion and education in the long run could most appropriately intertwine only in parochial schools. As Sidney Hook has said, "When it is recalled that the community places no restriction on the voluntary study of religion and theology under denominational auspices, the demand for required instruction in them rightly becomes suspicious."[73]

PART 2

Establishing a Pattern, 1860s-90s

3 Charting the Course: The Irish, the Germans, and Their Teachers

If a school is lacking the church is only a passing thing.
—Detroit German newspaper editor, speaking in Frankfurt, 1882

THEIR encounters with public school advocates over the school question alerted Catholics to the emphasis standard-bearing "Americans" were coming to place upon education. Leaders among the immigrants, themselves educated, knew the power it provided and did not want their people left behind. Neither did they want to resort to public schooling. Pride was at stake. They did not care to appear outmaneuvered by Protestant adversaries who would jeer if Catholics now tossed away the principles they had touted to save the expense of autonomous schools. Too, concern for the spiritual and educational well-being of Catholic children was more pressing than ever because champions of the common school often sounded indistinguishable from nativists. One ethnic parish after another opened its own school, a collective commitment shouldered by parents, pastor, and sister-teachers on behalf of children whom they regarded much as a mutual responsibility.

The first generation of serious parochial schools emerged between the 1860s and the early 1890s, initially through the collision between accident and ambition more than through any careful plan. A diocesan congregation of religious women, the Sisters, Servants of the Immaculate Heart of Mary (the IHMs), established their motherhouse forty miles from Detroit in 1845; after a troubled first dozen years, they acquired a monopoly over parochial education in Detroit. The women crafted a curriculum that became the favored local model for educating children of Irish and German Catholic immigrants and successive generations as well, the children and grandchildren of immigrants. Meanwhile, nearly half of the city's German Catholic children grew up under the tutelage of another congregation, the School Sisters of Notre Dame. The German "mother church," St. Mary's, first introduced these women to Detroiters in the early 1850s, when the German-speaking sisters came from Milwaukee to teach young children alongside the Christian Brothers, who were in charge of the older boys. These "German sisters" established a reputation that endured, still, in the 1920s when most of their pupils were no longer German. Well before the new immigrant rush from Southern and Eastern Europe layered on top of the old immigrants, the course was set for Catholics who preferred to pay for the tuition of their children by a Catholic rather than run any risks.

In the thirty years following the failed campaign for tax support, the number of parish schools in Detroit increased from three to fifteen, and enrollment jumped from about six hundred to more than six thousand. More than a third of all Detroit children in school were attending Catholic schools by the mid-1880s, a ratio closely approximating the percentage of Catholics in the population.[1] Few cities even approached such growth or attendance rates. Although it was the school wars that propelled Catholics along the course already begun, this remarkable embrace of parochial education came about because Detroit Catholics, most of them Irish and German immigrants, found themselves managing to afford schools where their children could learn precepts of the faith. Moreover, they became convinced that parochial schools were also providing a superior education by secular standards.

Irish and German Immigrants: Their Jobs and Neighborhoods

Later generations of new immigrants, eager in turn to educate their children, would not comprehend all the circumstances that helped make the first era of parish schools viable. It was a time when immigrants could move in, move up the occupational ladder, and move around the city. A steady flow of Irish immigrants and the large influx of Germans meant that more than half the city's residents were foreign-born or second-generation (table 1). More than eight of ten Irish and about a third of the Germans were Catholic.[2] By their numbers, energy, and persistence, Irish and German Catholics overwhelmed the influence of old French families within the diocese. Yet they did not come in such a rush or in such uniform poverty as to undermine their own chances in the local economy.

Steady rather than sudden population increases helped promote a diversified economy able to absorb workers who came with a range of abilities, and upward mobility was within reach of the hardworking or savvy immi-

Table 1. Immigrant Groups in Detroit, 1850 and 1880

	1850		1880	
Birthplace	Number	Percentage of Detroit Population	Number	Percentage of Detroit Population
German Empire	2,855	14	17,292	14.9
Ireland	3,289	16	6,775	5.8
England and Wales	1,245	6	4,200	3.6
Scotland	474	2	1,783	1.5
France	282	1	721	0.6
Other[a]/Canada	1,782	8	10,564	9.1
Poland	—	—	1,771	1.5
Switzerland	—	—	421	0.4
Holland	—	—	275	0.2
Belgium	—	—	240	0.2
Austria	—	—	128	0.1
Italy	—	—	127	0.1
Miscellaneous	—	—	230	0.2
	9,927	47	54,645	39.0
Detroit population	21,019		116,340	

Source: Compiled from *Compendium of the Seventh Census of the United States: 1850* (Washington: A. O. P. Nicholson, Public Printer, 1854), pp. 117–18, and U.S. Bureau of the Census, *Tenth Census of the United States, 1880,* vol. 1: *Population* (Washington: Government Printing Office, 1880), 536–41. a. Most in this category, a designation used only in the 1850 Census, were of Canadian birth.

grant. Catholics, more significant than ever as consumers as well as producers, were not often handicapped by religion or nationality when it came to finding jobs. Only about one-third of the city's Irish and German immigrants worked as laborers.[3] For the Irish, that contrasted sharply with the situation of their countrymen in Boston, nearly two-thirds of whom were in the lowest manual work.[4] Younger immigrants, especially, found skilled jobs as carpenters, painters, plasterers, or plumbers. They worked in iron and steel foundries, railroad car factories, the stove industry, shipbuilding, or in carriage and wagon firms. Immigrants were less well represented in the professions than the American-born, but there were professionals and businessmen within the immigrant communities. Nearly one-fifth of the second-generation German and Irish family heads owned businesses. Often they were small, family-operated shops serving their own neighborhoods; still, some proprietors were recognized as "solidly respectable," and a few belonged even among the city's prominent.[5]

Wages for day laborers and skilled workers were above the New England and Middle Atlantic states, better also than in any surrounding state except for Illinois.[6] Many foreign-born were earning enough to provide more than just basic essentials. In contrast to sea coast cities where single immigrants congregated, Detroit's Irish and German immigrants arrived as families. Often the couples had been married for some years.

In a highly mobile nation, immigrants who "stayed put" gained certain advantages, and a substantial core did stay on in Detroit. Almost half the Irish and a quarter of the Germans who lived in Detroit in 1850 were still in the city a decade later; more than two-thirds of the Irish and half of the Germans in Detroit in 1870 remained in 1880.[7] They fell heir to vacancies in a wide variety of occupations, they learned about housing options, and by putting down roots they improved their chances for institutional development. As a solid base, they were able to help ease in arriving countrymen. The choices immigrants made with their money gave them a reputation, even among detractors, as responsible homeowners willing to sacrifice for their children and their faith.

More than one-fourth of the total area of Wayne County remained unimproved at midcentury; even near the center of town, lots were affordable. The chance to buy land was part of the lure pulling immigrants to Detroit, and they helped make the city's rate of homeownership one of the highest in the nation, an accomplishment maintained throughout the nineteenth century and beyond. By the early 1880s, about half the working-class Germans and Irish owned their own homes. Among immigrant businessmen and professionals the proportion was even higher.

Families chose to locate in one part of the city rather than another for a variety of reasons. Immigrants were less likely than native-born Americans to have grandparents or relatives with them and because neighbors took on those roles for each other, being near countrymen had added importance. Once early Irish arrivals settled on the west side of Woodward and moved Most Holy Trinity there, many more Irish families gravitated to "Corktown" or farther westward, where they built new neighborhoods with new Irish parishes. Germans first concentrated on the east side of Woodward near their St. Mary's with its German priests. Other German families edged eastward until so many were so far from St. Mary's that additional German parishes were warranted, one after another.

Individual decisions added up in such ways that nineteenth-century Detroit did not develop tight, separate ethnic sections despite these dominant patterns of Irish on the west side and Germans on the east side. Public transportation was poor and streetcar fare bit into wages; consequently, immigrants sometimes opted for houses close to work as long as they were not the only "foreigners" of their nationality in the area. Real estate developers fostered mixed neighborhoods by buying tracts of vacant land, platting it into lots, or offering lot-plus-cottage in various price ranges.[8]

Many Irish families lived along streets on the east side and many Germans were amid west-side Irish. Mixed in, too, were heirs of the old French families, Americans, Canadians, pockets of British, Scots, Belgians, and, from the late 1870s, a growing number of Polish families. A single block or two might also represent a range of occupations, from professional to peddler. These nineteenth-century neighborhoods were more complex by many measures than those that would evolve in the early twentieth century when work and income came to divide Detroiters by geography. This complexity shaped institutional development.

Irish and German families might live on the same block yet have little cause for serious interaction, because their private lives centered around the separate parishes they built. The right to ethnic rather than territorial parishes was an accepted reality in the American Catholic Church. And because ethnic parish boundaries overlapped, within every few blocks there might be two or three Catholic churches, each with its own school.

Within each immigrant parish, the common bonds of nationality helped transcend differences in wealth or status. The mix of classes was an important source of strength because the parish trustees and priest could tap pockets of the wealthier and commandeer the talents of members who had more skill than money. Parishioners knew what one another had to offer and did not hesitate to ask for it on behalf of a common cause. Schools were always at the top of the list, "the life and soul of our parish."[9] Sometimes when the bishop gave his approval for a new parish the organizing committee decided that school construction should start even before the church went up.

Immigrants' eagerness to become homeowners and church builders won approval from the local press and watchful Protestants who were aware that many foreigners were proving as anxious as native-born Americans to educate their children. Some Protestants remained angrily unreconciled to a curriculum they believed centered around "Popery" and notions "dangerous" to democracy, yet there were others who began quietly to recognize the savings all these separate parish schools meant for taxpayers. With most Detroiters preoccupied with the Civil War and then postwar development, there was no serious effort to force Catholic children into public schools or even to extend public queries into parochial classrooms until the nativists reemerged in the late 1880s. Educators scrambled, meanwhile, to do their best with the children they had.

Public Education

When Catholics and Protestants first struggled for control of school funds, neither side had much of an educational plan in place. Even though Michigan had, in John Pierce, one of the "great pre–Civil War architects of universal schooling," the practicalities of public education confounded local schoolmen into the 1880s and beyond.[10] Law required townships to levy a "mill tax" for school support, and the amount seesawed from 1 to 2 mills until 1879, when it stabilized at 1 mill.[11] There was never enough money to provide free books or seats for the number of potential students. There were never enough qualified teachers, either. The Michigan Normal School, which opened in 1853 in Ypsilanti, graduated only about thirty students a year during its first twenty-five years. Most were trained through brief institutes and special classes. Efforts to certify teachers by examination were "a complete failure" so far as the state superintendent judged in 1866, and the system of supervision intended to improve schools was "equally a failure."[12] Upon strong recommendation from the state superintendent, graded schools began to rationalize the progression of students through a curriculum that was taking form by 1876.[13] Not until the 1890s were significant improvements made in course offerings and physical facilities, however.

Toward the end of the century, the *Detroit Evening News* assessed, "The schools have been going to the dogs . . . for nearly a generation."[14] Certainly, the city's public schools did not prove able to attract students. Although they enrolled nearly four times more children in 1884 than in 1850, public school enrollment kept sliding in comparison to the school census. At midcentury, six of ten children between the ages of five and seventeen were in public school, but by 1884 only about four in ten were.[15] Many children still did not go to school at all, except between the ages of eight and thirteen. Compulsory education laws went unenforced, and job possibilities became more available for youngsters as the city industrialized. Newer German and Polish immigrants were more likely than other parents to send their sons and daughters to work, but even among native-born white Americans a sizeable portion over the age of twelve were working.[16]

Catholic leaders never relaxed in their worry over the lure public schools might have, but the faithful did not waver in their preference for parochial education. The growing number of parish schools steadily attracted almost a quarter of Detroit's school-age children and educated more than a third of those who did attend school.[17] Local Catholics were able to act on their preference because congregations of religious women were willing and anxious to teach as their mission. In the first generation of parochial school development, the sisters made parochial schools desirable not only because of their religious emphasis but also because the women appreciated the immigrant origins of pastor and parents, taught immigrant children the skills they needed as Americans, and labored for bare subsistence wages—sums they often helped parishioners come up with by one means or another. The sisters and the "sisters' schools" were an integral part of the Catholic immigrant enterprise.

ESTABLISHING A DIOCESAN SISTERHOOD: THE SISTERS, SERVANTS OF THE IMMACULATE HEART OF MARY

Like those who tried to give shape to public schools, bishops, priests, and the Catholic press made intermittent forays into matters of method, content, and policy. Few offered any coherent guidance other than a certainty that Catholic schools must be guardians of "faith and morals." In this era, the hierarchy's major contribution was to develop and foster a diocesan community of teaching sisters: the Sisters, Servants of the Immaculate Heart of Mary.

Starting in the 1860s and until the large Polish schools with their Polish sisters emerged in the 1880s, the Immaculate Heart of Mary sisters taught nearly eight in ten Detroit parochial school pupils. To the extent that there was any "system" of Catholic education, the IHMs provided it as the common denominator among several immigrant parishes. The content, philosophy, and instructional style that came to characterize local Catholic education in the formative Irish and German era related significantly to the development of this congregation of women. Parents' support for parochial schools reflected their conviction that the IHM sisters taught not only precepts of the faith and respect for children's heritage in a classroom atmosphere marked by "so many favors and especial kindnesses" but also provided a better education than public schools.[18]

Nearly all IHMs were immigrants or the daughters of immigrants. Much as the immigrant community itself took form, this community of religious women developed out of the combination of personal choice, networks of acquaintances, and chance circumstances. The sisterhood originated in the fall of 1845, when Bishop Lefevere agreed to welcome Sister Theresa Maxis Duchemin and Sister Ann Constance Schaaf, who left the Oblate Sisters of Providence, a faltering Baltimore community "of color." They came to help Father Louis Gillet start a school at Monroe, forty miles south of Detroit. The women had first met Gillet and Lefevere when the clerics visited the sisters' Baltimore convent in 1843. It was in the course of their own encounter in Baltimore that Lefevere persuaded Gillet, a fellow Belgian and Redemptorist, to move to southeast Michigan. Gillet, meanwhile, had captured Sister Theresa's imagination with his dreams of a women's religious community and a school in Michigan.[19] Soon after Sister Theresa and Sister Ann Constance joined Gillet in Monroe, they attracted twenty-three-year-old Therese

Renauld, who came from her father's Grosse Pointe farm as the little congregation's first novice, newly named Sister M. Celestine; together, the women and Gillet opened a day school and a boarding academy for girls.

Sister Theresa Maxis took on the role as superior general of the new community. She was a thirty-five-year-old mulatto whose mother had originally come to the United States from San Domingo at the age of ten. Educated and experienced as a teacher in a school for black children, Sister Theresa spoke French and English. The thirty-four-year-old Sister Ann Constance [Charlotte] Schaaf was also a Maryland-born mulatto with experience teaching the French-speaking black children in the Oblates' schools. The independence that brought the pair to Michigan helped them persevere even though Gillet fell into disfavor and left the diocese shortly after their arrival. The small band of women soon took the official name of Sisters, Servants of the Immaculate Heart of Mary and changed their traditional black habits to the royal blue that distinguished them thereafter from other sisters who came and went in the diocese wearing brown or black garb.

Since Theresa Maxis and Ann Constance were light-skinned, their origins were not apparent, but the new community was ethnically diverse from the start. Several of the first women to join came from Michigan's French Catholic families, but others were French Canadians or Northwestern Europeans. Word about the new IHM congregation spread through personal connections. Diocesan priests told women in their parishes, Monroe Catholics wrote to relatives, and Belgian missionaries passed information across the country and on to Europe. Three Irish women made their way to Monroe from New York City upon the recommendation of a Redemptorist they encountered there. Many of these first women to join the IHMs were in their twenties, some even older. Several were from wealthy or middle-class families, and they brought a variety of abilities—talent in music, needlework, and drawing. Several were bilingual in French and English or German and English. A few had experience as teachers. All were attracted by the congregation's teaching mission.

The women spent considerable energy in the early years clarifying their role within the local Catholic power structure. The only two types of female religious communities possible in the nineteenth-century church were papal (approved by the pope as a branch of a male order) or diocesan (responsible to the local bishop). Papal orders were centuries old, but the idea of diocesan congregations developed after the French Revolution, and lines of responsibility for them were ambiguous until canon law finally clarified issues of jurisdiction in 1900.[20]

The IHMs were classified as a "congregation" and were diocesan. But the women who joined assumed their voluntary association, and the simple rather than solemn vows they took gave them a measure of autonomy. Bishop Lefevere had his own definite intentions for the sisters, however. He expected these women, dedicated to serving an educational mission and accepting a life of voluntary poverty, would fit with his aim of providing affordable Catholic schools in his diocese. Preoccupied in the early 1850s with the effort to gain tax support for Catholic schools, he devoted little attention to the sisters for several years. Then he learned in 1857 that Mother Theresa was corresponding with the bishop of Philadelphia about staffing schools in that diocese.

The IHMs were exploring possibilities in Pennsylvania because they were anxious to extend their teaching mission. They were also distressed because the Redemptorists had left Monroe as a result of a quarrel with Bishop Lefevere and the bishop made no effort to send any other priest for eight months. Sister Theresa Maxis worried about their future.[21] After a decade in Michigan, the congregation numbered nearly twenty, and yet their work remained confined to a total of a hundred or fewer students attending their boarding academy and day school, Monroe's small German parish school, and a rural parish about ten miles away. Lefevere viewed their overtures to the Philadelphia diocese as unacceptable, an initiative that would drain off the sisters' services at a time when he wanted to open more schools and make them tuition-free to compete with public schools. Understanding that the effort to get tax money was a lost cause, at least temporarily, he was well aware that these women were financially important for the future of education in his diocese. He moved to assert authority in a power struggle that demonstrated not only the subordinate place of women in church work but also the discordance among immigrants about how the American Catholic Church should conduct business.

Suddenly and without notifying Mother Theresa, Bishop Lefevere sent Father Edward Joos to Monroe, bearing a letter that announced to the startled sisters that this "man of God" would now be their "Spiritual Father and Director." Joos was Lefevere's close friend and a fellow Belgian. Both men were comfortable with this form of organization that was common in Belgium, where female religious communities had priest-superiors.[22] With few U.S. precedents to claim, the women nonetheless regarded the bishop's action as preemptive, dictatorial, and undemocratic. Joos, after just one year in America, seemed a foreign intrusion. But Lefevere was unconcerned over any discontent, insistent on discipline, and intolerant of any and all Catholics who objected to priests he assigned to them.[23]

For the next two years, as the "former" superior of the IHMs, Sister Theresa Maxis chafed under Joos's reduction of her authority, and she continued to seek schools in Pennsylvania. Clerics in the diocese of Philadelphia began claiming the right to negotiate with sisters from the Detroit diocese. Finally, in the spring of 1859, Joos alerted Lefevere, "I think it is almost necessary that you should come Yourself as soon as possible."[24] Lefevere arrived at Monroe the day after he received the letter, reproached Mother Theresa for being headstrong, discharged her, dispatched her to Philadelphia, and named a new superior. Soon after, the bishop dismissed other IHMs who were teaching in the diocese of Philadelphia. By midsummer half the sisters at Monroe had gone to a separate congregation they established in Pennsylvania. Lefevere, convinced of their duplicity, considered discrediting Theresa Maxis by exposing her mixed-race background. He also wrote scathingly about her display of the "softness, slyness & low cunning of the mulatto" and accused her of sexual misconduct with Redemptorist priests.[25]

The twelve women who remained behind in Monroe were now well aware of their boundaries. The lesson—that for years after was mentioned by all participants only obliquely as a time of "trials"—was given permanence within a year when the IHM congregation and the bishop came to a revised agreement about the regulations under which the women would operate. This "Rule" detailed duties, outlined obligations, and specified the bishop's power over their internal affairs. The congregation also gained legal status under Michigan law by incorporating in 1860. One article in the document of incorporation declared that their purpose was to care for orphans, perhaps inserted by Father Joos, who wanted the sisters to develop this role. It may also have been part artifice to avoid any trouble with legislators who continued to oppose separate Catholic education. The IHMs did operate an orphanage for the next fifty years, but it averaged two dozen or fewer children a year, and the women never wavered from their chief mission of teaching.

On behalf of fulfilling this purpose, the sisters realistically set about parlaying demonstrations of obedience and the well-placed connections of Joos into favoritism for their community. Pragmatically and, in time with evident affection, they accepted "Father," as they familiarly called Joos. They listened to his sermons, agreed with his religious values, were grateful for his active help training teachers, and appreciated his intervention if any parish pastor proved troublesome. Nonetheless, they proceeded to exercise their right to elect the mother superior, and their own leaders made the key decisions about teaching assignments and schools the IHMs would accept.

Joos, who retained the title of director until he died in 1901, proved particularly useful to the sisters because of his influence within the diocese. Proud of his position and "his" sisters' accomplishments, Joos promoted the IHMs at every opportunity and gave them important visibility within the male-controlled church. During his long life he was the confidant not only of Lefevere but also of Lefevere's successors, bishops Caspar Borgess (1870–87) and John Samuel Foley (1888–1918). Joos was the first priest in the Detroit diocese to be named a monsignor, briefly administered the diocese between Borgess and Foley, and was named administrator of the diocesan board of education once it was established in 1887. The various bishops went regularly to visit their good friend Joos in Monroe. Nationally important Catholics such as Bishop John Ireland knew him and traveled to Monroe at his invitation. Visits centered around the IHMs' motherhouse, where bishops presided over religious feast days, attended ceremonies large and small, and ate Sunday dinners.

Trust in the sisters developed along with this familiarity, and even Bishop Lefevere was soon reassured. One after another, the succession of Detroit bishops signaled their respect. The sisters managed to establish a privileged place and gain an educational monopoly that other communities came to describe as the "long blue line," a reference to the color of their habits. Well into the twentieth century, their religious "competitors" would charge that the IHMs shut out other sisters at will and took whatever Detroit schools they wanted.[26]

The monopoly began to develop in the early 1860s once the "troubles" were conclusively resolved. Initially, as the only diocesan congregation of sisters, the bishop or parish priests requested the IHMs because they were available locally and were well known among the Belgians who amounted to thirty-nine of the eighty-eight priests in the diocese as of 1870. Moreover, they had sisters who could communicate with various immigrant groups.

They took charge of their first Detroit school in September 1861 at St. Joseph's, the new east-side German parish, so German immigrants should not "labor under . . . disadvantages" of a poor education.[27] St. Joseph's priest, a Belgian recently arrived from the American College of Louvain, asked "Father Joos's sisters" to teach the girls in his parish. When school opened there were eighty pupils. By January, one sister began teaching smaller boys along with girls, and by the time warm weather came there were so many more students that the sister often taught them in the yard.[28] The congregation's leaders were careful to designate a "German teacher" for every class who would tend to those children unable to communicate in English.[29] Pleased parishioners contributed money for a new school house. Opened in 1867, it had four rooms for boys and four for girls, one of which was an academy for "young ladies."[30]

Requests for the sisters' services multiplied. With their ranks growing to nearly eighty in the 1860s, they were willing to accept invitations from new schools. IHM sisters began teaching Irish- and American-born boys at SS. Peter and Paul Cathedral School in 1864, French children at Ste. Anne's in 1865, and black children at St. Augustine School for Colored Children in 1867.

St. Augustine was their most short-lived endeavor. The sisters took it on at the request of the Ste. Anne's priest and provided a room in their cathedral convent for the thirty-five boys and girls until the bishop built a wood-frame school behind SS. Peter and Paul. Unlike their other pupils, these children were not Catholic; their conversion was perhaps the primary goal of the priest and sisters and Bishop Lefevere. When Lefevere died and Bishop Borgess arrived, he showed less interest in the school. After what the IHM chronicler at the cathedral convent then regarded as "long years of experience," the sisters "found it impossible to bring the children to religious principles." Because none showed any desire for baptism, it was "thought proper" to close the school in 1870—just three years after it opened.[31] By then, the sisters were increasingly preoccupied with Catholic immigrant pupils.

Their nineteenth-century monopoly of Irish education began with Most Holy Trinity boys in 1867 and the girls soon after. From that base, they staffed each parish the Irish opened. When young Irish families began settling to the west of Trinity, they built St. Vincent's. By 1874, with enough children for a school, they invited the IHMs and set about developing a rival to their old home parish school at Trinity. Meanwhile, on the east side of town, Jeremiah Dwyer, an Irish stove manufacturer, opened a factory and "surrounded himself with a flock of Irish" who founded Our Lady of Help parish. In 1875 the IHMs opened a new school there with two hundred English-speaking Irish children. French children from the neighborhood went instead to the school taught by secular teachers in the new parish of Sacred Heart. Then, back on the west side, in 1878, Irish tobacco manufacturer Daniel Scotten moved his tobacco business to the edge of the city on Fort Street near Clark Park. Expanded, it gave new jobs to many, including the Ratigan family and "a whole brood of Madigans"[32] from Holy Trinity. They built Most Holy Redeemer and asked the familiar sisters in blue to start their school in 1882.

In these same years German Catholics opened three more parishes in addition to St. Mary's and St. Joseph's. As they moved, parishioners preferred teaching sisters they knew. Catholics who migrated from St. Mary's to its new "daughter parish" requested the School Sisters of Notre Dame, who sent teachers from their Milwaukee motherhouse. Young families who left St. Joseph's and its IHM school for the west side invited the IHMs to come along; their new parish of St. Boniface opened its school in 1872. Meanwhile, between 1864 and 1871 sisters went to staff eight schools in small towns and rural immigrant parishes in the diocese, some German and some Irish. In one mixed parish, they pragmatically set up a "dual school," where German and Irish children studied separately.

Their ethnic diversity was a significant reason the IHMs were sought after in the post–Civil War era. One of the few religious congregations native to the United States at the time, they attracted women who had immigrated or who were the daughters of immigrants, reflecting patterns that had been defining Michigan's population since the 1830s. Of those who entered the congregation during the 1860s, forty-two were American-born; some were from eastern cities like Buffalo, Rochester, and Baltimore, but twenty-nine were born in Michigan. Typical of the local Catholic population, many of the American-born were daughters of Irish immigrants. At least nineteen sisters had both parents born in Ireland. The Irish dominated also among immigrant sisters. Of the thirty-eight who were foreign-born, twenty-four were Irish, four were from Germany, four from Canada, two came from Switzerland, two from France, one from Scotland, and one from Belgium.[33]

As the number of sisters increased, so did their kinship ties throughout the diocese, another source of strength for the community. Several sisters had brothers, uncles, or nephews ordained as priests in the diocese, some serving in high places. Many IHMs were daughters, sisters, or nieces of parish trustees, Detroit businessmen, lawyers, and politicians. One sister regularly corresponded with her brother, who was for many years the editor of the *Michigan Catholic* newspaper. She "never failed to remonstrate with him and to present a milder and more dispassionate view of the subject" when she thought he was too radical.[34] On some points, the sisters were more radical than he. When he began disapproving the University of Michigan after the turn of the century, for example, they ignored him and continued sending sisters there for degrees.[35]

THE IHM EDUCATIONAL PHILOSOPHY

Their position as a diocesan community, their ethnic diversity, and their ties to well-placed families helped put the IHM sisters in one school after another in Detroit. But they built their reputation by developing a distinctive philosophy and a thoroughgoing system of education carefully followed. Their characterization of one sister upon her death spoke to their shared commitment in life: "She had the right philosophy of education and she lived up to its principles. A pupil to her meant a child of God gifted by nature and grace. . . . She realized that the teacher's part was to help the child make the best of the gifts God had given him. . . . This she did by inspiring confidence in her pupils, confidence in their own powers and confidence in the teacher."[36]

According to the IHM convictions, the "right philosophy of education" was represented by their St. Andre System. Starting in the early 1860s and for almost a century thereafter, the community grounded their parish school curriculum, their teacher-training program, and their philosophy of education on a model brought from the St. Andre Normal School in Belgium. In practice, however, their form of the St. Andre System became a unique blend of European and Catholic humanist theory, along with ideas echoing the psychologist G. Stanley Hall, mainstream American Protestant values, and nineteenth-century feminism. Generations of Catholics who passed through their schools called it the "IHM way." Sisters, too, would remark among themselves, "There's the easy way to do things and then, there's the 'IHM way.'"[37] By the 1870s the sisters' all-encompassing plan had become central to their popular image.

A chain of personal relationships brought the core St. Andre System of pedagogy from Belgium to the Detroit diocese just when the IHMs were regrouping after the bishop split their congregation, their time of "trials." In 1861 Sister Theresa Persyn, a Belgian nun, was referred to Bishop Lefevere and then to Father Joos for help with her desire to go to America and teach Indians. Joos was willing to welcome her to the IHM community and sent word through his cousin, rector of the American College of Louvain, that Sister Theresa should first be encouraged to study at the St. Andre Normal School. Recently started in Bruges, it was noted among Belgian Catholics for its teacher-training program. The woman agreed, and after a period of study she set off for America in 1861 in possession of "very valuable manuscripts for an academy," as the rector of Louvain who sent them alerted his cousin, Father Joos.[38]

These manuscripts represented the thought of Felix Antoine Dupanloup, the French bishop-educator who was one of the liberal group resisting the new conservatism of mid-nineteenth-century European Catholicism.[39] Dupanloup's theories had just been introduced into the teacher-training program for sisters at the St. Andre Normal School of Bruges. Now, the manuscripts from Belgium became an important link between European liberal Catholic humanists and educators in the Detroit diocese.

Dupanloup was highly regarded at the American College at Louvain, an institution Lefevere had helped establish. Lefevere and Joos readily gave their authorization to translate the imported program so it could be used to train the IHMs. Sister Theresa Persyn, forty-six when she emigrated, helped with the translation and then turned over the task of preparing teachers to others while she took the position of mistress of novices. She would die in 1901, one day after Father Joos, without ever encountering the Indians who were her original reason for coming to Monroe.

In a pattern of teacher-training they would continually repeat, the mother superior and her closest advisors deliberately selected those women considered their most outstanding teachers, had them learn the program thoroughly, and then had them form and monitor the other sister-teachers according to Dupanloup's precise directives. A few sisters set to work making copies of the translated manuscripts so each convent "mission," as they called their schools, would always have the guidelines at hand for reinforcement.

IHM sisters were practioners of the Dupanloup philosophy even before American liberal bishops like John Ireland became its champion (chapter 4). To the advantage of their program, the IHM community admitted only women who had completed high school. Newcomers to the convent were often in their twenties, with some advanced schooling or with experience as teachers. That made it possible to focus on the philosophy and methods of teaching rather than on basic subject matter or mastery of information.

Because they were opening schools so rapidly, they began implementing the St. Andre System as soon as it was translated, if sometimes "only on the broadest lines." For more than seventy years, until the diocese imposed a uniform curricular plan, the sisters carefully followed the philosophy and methodology in all of their schools. Approximately every twenty years they would establish a committee to spend long hours reevaluating their approach. Always they concluded by reaffirming it with only slight modification to suit the times and new educational research. This comprehensive plan shaped IHM schools in different ways than either the public schools or those parochial schools staffed by other religious communities.

Reinforced by strong support of parents, priests, and bishops, the St. Andre system of education became a paradigm in the Catholic community. In part, it was the ideal model because the nuns impressed the bishops by their work with students. Too, Joos, who studied it carefully, wrote lengthy articles in the *Western Home Journal* and in the *Michigan Catholic,* extolling its virtues and urging its principles upon parish priests at every opportunity. But the education IHM schools provided gained acceptance also because it served so many separate interests successfully.

The plan was an amalgam. Dupanloup provided the theory. The St. Andre teacher-training system provided principles of education, pedagogy, methodology, and school administration. The place of Catholics and women in America provided immediacy to a group of idealistic teachers grounded in the realities of immigrant life.

The Dupanloup message clearly reflected the influence of Rousseau (1712–78) and Pestalozzi (1746–1827). Like Rousseau, the St. Andre System insisted that education must prepare men and women for the different roles they would be called upon to perform by virtue of their different natures. Also like Rousseau, Dupanloup's philosophy called for the child's freedom to participate in learning, but toward an end the teacher had already predetermined. Like Pestalozzi, Dupanloup emphasized character formation—the development of values, principles, and habits.[40] These ideas resembled the child-centered psychology which, by the 1880s, had gained importance among American educators such as G. Stanley Hall and William James.[41] The Dupanloup philosophy emphasized the divine, however. This French Catholic bishop put the child at the heart of the educational program as "the depository of all the gifts of God, of the hopes of humanity."[42]

Repeatedly, in philosophy, purpose, and pedagogical style, Dupanloup emphasized the dignity of the child; the respect teachers must give to the child; the liberty of the child's nature, intelligence, and will; and his right to follow his vocation in life. There was value in teaching the poor because "the soul of the poor is before God like to that of the rich . . . the poor need the consolation of our holy religion . . . religious principles are indispensable to a poor girl for the preservation of her virtues."[43] The charge fit well with the sisters' immigrant constituency.

Dupanloup's plan aimed especially toward character development in order to form "the man of reason, the man of the heart, the man of character, the man of his century and of his country."[44] That lofty charge fit well with the goals of nineteenth-century American society. The sisters found no problem applying the same energy to female pupils as to the future "man of his country." The character formation of women necessarily included training appropriate to roles they must play in society. As Dupanloup stressed, it would be the female's duty as mother to give the child "the first moral and religious principles." She would be the one "who regulates the details of all domestic affairs and so ruins or supports her house."[45]

Unlike the education Rousseau planned for Sophie in *Emile* or Dupanloup envisioned for females, the nuns knew there was an alternative to life as wife and mother—theirs—and that in America, a woman, especially if she was a poor Catholic immigrant, might have to do more than tend to her home and family. Toward the end of educating females as they saw them, the IHM sisters soon were going off on their own, beyond Dupanloup's charge. In practice, the curriculum they designed had much in common with nineteenth-century feminist thought.

Because so many women came to the IHM convent already mature and educated, it is possible that they were familiar with contemporary writers. Certainly the congregation was more open to outsiders than many sisterhoods; they brought in lay teachers and speakers, allowed a breadth of reading material, and, for a time, even housed the Irish immigrant activist Mary Harris Jones. Later well known as "Mother Jones," her radical efforts to organize miners would earn her brickbats and widespread condemnation from laborers' opponents. Most likely, the women arrived at the notions that came to characterize their schools through a combination of others' influence, instinct based upon experience, and their own assessment of what was needed.

Whatever the sources, their ideas on the education of girls did closely resemble the recommendations and philosophy of Catharine Beecher in her *Treatise on Domestic Economy.* Whether or not they borrowed from her, the sisters were often in line with this solidly Protestant woman. Widely considered a national authority on how the American home should be organized and how women should be educated for their roles, Beecher was more radical than some of her champions realized.

Beecher's book, published in 1841, introduced theories, open to various interpretations, on the education of females. The strongest reading emphasized that in certain respects women were not just equal but superior to men. Although Beecher could accept a hierarchical society as consonant with Christianity and necessary in human relations, she maintained that the hierarchy did not presume inequality and the order of subordination was not always the same. Women were superior in "manners pertaining to the education of their children," she wrote.[46] It was a position that mirrored the IHMs' notion about their relationship to priests in whose parishes they taught. The sisters also shared Beecher's thesis that men and women in America had tasks and functions that were different yet equally deserving of respect. And more like Beecher than Dupanloup, they considered women's tasks so important as to be deserving of a superior education.

The IHM program of education focused on girls, in part because their private academy and boarding school at Monroe admitted only girls, as did the parish high schools once they began to introduce them in the early 1880s. A few of their courses, described as "ornamental," were designed with the sole purpose of providing skills and information women would need. One such class was domestic economy.

Whether it was the sisters' own imaginative course or borrowed, their domestic economy had the same name as one that Beecher outlined and regarded as the key to women's education. Beecher insisted that girls must have not just "simple skill training" but the solid theoretical knowledge upon which principles guiding domestic practice should be based. Necessarily, for example, they must study physiology and the digestive system in order to understand which foods would be "healthful." With not only this class but also with their emphasis on a full range of science courses and laboratories, IHM schools echoed her insistence on rigorous "theoretical knowledge." Sometimes highminded goals could serve a few immediate and practical purposes, too. "I have just come from domestic economy," a student in the motherhouse academy wrote her friend. "I washed dishes this morning and wiped dishes last week."[47] Domestic economy class that semester did offer some variety because, according to another girl, "Mame works in the kitchen, Ella in the refectory, Fanny and Frances in the recreation hall and [Aggie] in the music hall."[48] Beecher herself would have approved this work as an important means for the girls to exercise.[49]

Also on behalf of their "girls," the sisters wrote their own manual, *Good Form*. The question-answer format read like a catechism and was intended to indoctrinate a litany of social skills, poise, and good manners associated with middle- and upper-class longtime Americans at their best. "Name two things of which a true lady never speaks unnecessarily," one typical question demanded. The appropriate answer, "Of her health and of her servants," was to be memorized by the girls, some of whose mothers were servants. The answer to "How is the foolish woman known?" left no room for doubt: "By her frivolous manner and the desire to attract attention." From *Good Form* drills, the daughters of immigrants learned how to register at a hotel, walk down a street, set a luncheon table, eat asparagus, radishes, and pickles, and avoid "looking like a monkey" when eating a banana.[50] In contrast to Beecher, who wanted to encourage the expression of "gentler emotions" but left their development to chance, the sisters' girls rehearsed proper attitudes. The very first lesson in *Good Form* was firm: "The well-spring of all true courtesy is Christian charity, a habitual feeling of respect and courtesy for others."[51] The teachers confidently expected memorized lessons would become automatic habits.

The IHMs' emphasis on the total development of their students particularly pleased observers. Some local laymen, widely read, followed developments in other cities and had their own ideas about appropriate education. The Catholic press regularly offered such convictions as, "Our girls especially need" an education that teaches "that money can not buy happiness, that men and women are superior to accidents of station and wealth; that truth and virtue, moral beauty and intellectual strength are more desirable, more admirable and lovable, than fine dresses, costly furniture and a bank account."[52]

Boys studying with the sisters inherited, especially in the upper grades, a curriculum designed by women for girls. Detroit's Irish and German Catholic parents sent their sons to grade school as commonly as their daughters, and classrooms usually had about an equal number of each. Church authorities did not want sisters to teach boys over twelve, but in practice the age crept up because many twelve-year-old boys had not yet made their first communion. A lack of teaching brothers and the cost of hiring laymen meant the age rule finally proved too difficult to enforce, despite Bishop Borgess's best intentions.

Parish schools were widely regarded as important for "sheltering" girls. They held boys, in part, by competing successfully with offerings in public school. In the 1860s and 1870s the IHMs insisted that both boys and girls must learn English grammar and composition, spelling, reading, mental and written arithmetic, geography, and history. At the upper levels there was more composition and history, along with algebra, rhetoric, chemistry, natural philosophy [physics], astronomy, botany, zoology, and geography. In addition, there were ever-present classes in sight-singing, drawing, and penmanship. For many parents, however, the significant difference that set the parish school curriculum above that in public schools were the classes in Christian doctrine [catechism] and sacred history that held "first place" in every grade.

While most basic subjects were the same as in public elementary schools, the books were not. The IHMs selected a list of textbooks different even from those nationally popular among Catholic schools.[53] Carefully chosen, the books were used year after year so parents could save money by passing them down from one child to the next. Acknowledging the expectations of parents, German schools added books and courses in German language and culture, but instruction in all regular classes was in English.

As they developed their educational philosophy and extended their own preparation, the course offerings in IHM schools became more deliberate. Outlined in a half-dozen pages in 1872, the curricular plan was nineteen pages in 1890 and more than a hundred pages by 1910. Music, modern languages, and domestic economy, along with art and a commercial course, took on more than their previously ornamental status. Earlier than many, the sisters insisted on the laboratory sciences, along with Latin, Greek, philosophy, and literature; such courses fostered "desirable qualities" of both mind and character.[54] They shared convictions common among educators that the purpose of a liberal education should be "the formation of habits of investigation, of correct reasoning . . . of accurate analysis, and of vigorous mental acts."[55] And, like other religious school educators, Protestant or Catholic, the IHMs shared the grand vision that their work might "bring countless, souls, even in this life, to 'refreshment, light, and peace.'"[56]

If rising to the challenge seemed difficult to their children, parents supported the sisters. "You are not old enough to understand all these things," one mother wrote to her daughters, warning "dont, dont my children stoop to sympathize" should there be "chronic grumblers" who "are always finding fault with things."[57]

The IHMs drew upon existing ideas to formulate their curriculum, but, finally, they were responsible for its design. Their philosophical approach and methodology came almost directly from the St. Andre System and the theories of Dupanluop, which the imported Belgian plan incorporated. This system left no detail to chance. It outlined even the "order of the day" and prescribed the type of examinations. Because discipline must promote rather than weaken a child's positive characteristics, certain forms of punishment were not used: corporal punishment, tactics that would humiliate, and chastisements disproportionate to the offense. The St. Andre System specified intellectual levels and skills teachers must master along with the necessary personal qualities. Dupanloup was precise: Teachers must show evidence of "goodness, evenness of mind and temper," plus good judgment, memory, and studiousness. Not enough to be even-tempered and well prepared, the teacher had to be joyful about her work, because "devotedness" and "evident happiness in associating with her pupils" would be key to her authority.[58] It was an educational program so ambitious as to be impossible to achieve, but it was also sufficiently concrete to provide a constant set of guideposts toward the infinite perfection of teacher, pupil, and school.

In an effort at systematic training, the sisters began a normal school at the motherhouse in 1876. Their St. Mary's Academy in Monroe became a laboratory school where young sisters were drilled according to Dupanloup's directives. To prepare for class, teachers must first recall what they had taught the day before, outline the present day's lesson, and gather examples and comparisons. Once before her class, a teacher must hold attention by "animation," by communicating on the same level of her "young audience," by frequent questioning, by showing the usefulness of the information, by removing distractions, and by variety. A teacher must not teach superficially, must make exercises practical, and must avoid telling amusing stories that would lose time.[59] And, of course, she was to speak in a "sweet" voice and look happy all the while.

The instructors monitored students and reinforced one another tirelessly. Classroom teachers wrote notes to students each week, commenting on their work and behavior. Teachers also met each week to discuss their own successes and failures. In the summers, all sisters returned to Monroe to study, hear speakers, attend classes, and prepare for the next year's students. By their total absorption in the work of teaching, they formed their character as a collective corps of professionals. At one point in the 1870s, the sisters sought and received permission from the bishop to have their second meditation in the evening "expunged" in order to extend study hours for all teaching sisters.

They carefully bound themselves, through their constitution, to adhere to the course of study as they arranged it at the motherhouse. Use of the planned curriculum, the sisters knew certainly, was not up to "personal feeling" when they were out in their parish missions.[60] Because their pupils made up such a significant share of Catholic school students, this uniformity in content, purpose, and style meant that thousands of children received an education in common, regardless of their economic class or nationality.

THE FACTOR OF ETHNICITY

When the first Diocesan School Board took a systematic count in 1887, Detroit's parish schools enrolled 6,351. Of that number, more than 1,300 German children studied with IHMs and the other 1,451 were divided among the Franciscan Brothers, Sisters of Christian Charity, and School Sisters of Notre Dame. The five distinctively Irish parishes, enrolling 2,239 children, were all taught by IHMs. More usual was the situation in Chicago, where several separate Irish congregations taught in the various Irish parishes while German School Sisters of Notre Dame and German branches of the Franciscans, Benedictines, and Holy Cross orders divided their immigrant children among them.[61]

Attractive because of their ethnic diversity, the IHMs made shrewd or perhaps instinctive use of this advantage. When a woman joined any Catholic religious congregation, she took a new religious name. Her former name, status, and previous background were set aside, no longer to be of importance or mention. Still, an IHM sister's nationality was never lost upon the other sisters, however charitable their stereotypes might be about the "solid German presence" of one or the "cheerful Irish humor" of another.[62] And when it came time to assign nuns to various parishes, the superior and her assistants often matched teachers to the ethnic background of pupils (table 2). Based on the records for five Detroit schools through the 1920s, ethnicity was taken into account also when assigning each sister-superior to serve as principal. The Irish parishes had Irish superiors, and the Germans had German superiors. It was a practice they would continue long after Irish and German immigration waned.

72   *For Faith and Fortune*

Table 2. Assignment of Sisters and Ethnic Identification

	Irish		German	
	Number	Percent	Number	Percent
American-born to Americans	28	25.5	10	13.8
Irish-born or Irish parentage	49	44.5	16	22.2
German-born or German parentage	13	11.8	33	45.8
Other nationality	11	10.0	8	11.1
Parentage unknown	9	8.2	5	6.9
	110	100.0	72	99.8

Source: IHM Sister Personal Files, Monroe Motherhouse Archives, Monroe, Mich.

Note: Irish schools are Most Holy Trinity, 1867–1903 staff records, and St. Vincent, 1913–29 staff records; German school is St. Joseph, 1862–1929. This is based on a 66 percent Irish sample and a total German sample.

The German language was taught in German Catholic schools until World War I, so there was indeed a need to assign some sisters who could handle those classes. Yet that need does not account for the overall pattern. IHM leaders obviously recognized the educational advantages when teachers shared a common background with students and parents. The arrangement also made it easier for the sisters to work with pastors, who nearly always belonged to the same ethnic group as parishioners.

Occasionally, a sister was assigned back to the priest and parish of her childhood. When Sister Rosalie arrived at Most Holy Trinity School in the 1870s, the parish neighborhood remembered her well as one of the Flaherty children who attended the school not long before. There Sister Rosalie stayed for the next fifty-two years of her teaching career. When she died, it was written that "she loved everybody and everything" about the parish, "even the Trinity cats."[63]

Quirks individual to each parish were accommodated, in part, by maintaining a stable core of faculty. As in the case of Sister Rosalie, some sisters spent many years in one parish even though it was common community practice to rotate sisters. Sometimes priests made specific requests on behalf of parishioners "very anxious to have [a sister] come back who has gained the affection of everyone."[64] On the Sunday before school started each fall, many a child hurried to church to see if her "beloved sister" was back or if some "dreaded unknown" sat in the front pew instead.[65] Records of Most Holy Trinity, St. Joseph's, and St. Vincent's show that there were always familiar faces. Of a group of 182, two in ten were in the same school for seven or more years. Many others shifted back and forth and were well known in the parish.[66]

Character formation of teachers, such a fixed part of their teacher-training program, helped keep individual tendencies in check. Sisters who might have had an inclination to humiliate some child or favor another were reprimanded by a principal-superior citing Dupanloup's directives. They knew one another well, however, and when they could IHM leaders tried to ensure success or at least avoid trouble by matching a sister's personality with her classroom charge. By the time a sister died, the IHM congregation routinely congratulated its good judgment when it memorialized her. "Naturally retiring and timid," one sister had spent her years of teaching in the primary grades, where "her gentleness bore a charm that invited the confidence of the young."[67] The sisters held the firm idea that boys and girls responded to different types of teachers. Some were tapped specifically to teach boys when it was apparent, as in the case of one, "She possessed those traits which preeminently fitted her to be a boys' teacher."[68] Another's "wonderful insight into the psychology of boy nature" was credited with her successful training of many "priests and professional men of Detroit."[69] The unremarkable were appreciated for what they could offer. Sister Cecelia, her compatriots knew, "was neither a brilliant scholar nor teacher; hers was the plodder's way." But as a follower she gave "guidance" that leadership could not have provided.[70] The community of teachers found a place, too, for the few unable to handle a classroom. A sister who was especially "timid and had a great dread of meeting strangers" spent a helpful life in charge of the household in one of the larger parish convents.[71]

Although their St. Mary's Academy in Monroe was the laboratory for the IHM curriculum, Most Holy Trinity became the model for all that was involved in operating a parish school. Even their move into Trinity school, edging out another community, demonstrated the dynamics of diocesan politics. The oldest Irish parish, by the late 1850s Trinity had a school for girls taught by the Daughters of Christian Charity from Emmitsburg, Maryland, and one for boys taught by the Christian Brothers. The Christian Brothers withdrew to concentrate their efforts where they could make enough money to better support their own community, however, and the IHMs took on the school for boys in the fall of 1867, opening it to those under the age of fourteen. The numbers grew from twenty or thirty on the first day to 228 at the school year's end in July.[72]

At about the same time, a new priest arrived in the parish, a Belgian trained at the American College of Louvain. He began pressing the Daughters of Charity. He made the school tuition-free and then was unable to pay them regularly, but the final straw came in the summer of 1874 when he sent what their superiors deemed a "very unreasonable letter," insisting that outsiders must examine the children's progress. Frustrated and annoyed, the Daughters of Charity decided to give up the mission. Quickly, as their annoyed mother superior viewed it, "The Sisters of the Immaculate Heart took possession of what *had been the labor of fifteen years.*"[73]

The Trinity parishioners had just constructed an impressive four-story brick school building, and now, with boys and girls united under the IHMs, almost eight hundred attended the grade school (fig. 2). By 1881 an academy provided an abbreviated high school course for girls patterned after St. Mary's Academy (chapter 7). The community assigned Sister Veronica Mulligan to be superior and principal for the first few years; she was Irish and regarded as one of their best teachers. Once Trinity was off to a solid start, she went to head the IHMs' new normal training school in Monroe, taking practical lessons from the parish with her.

The Daughters of Charity probably took some satisfaction when they observed that their successors "have had a difficult time of it."[74] Any difficulty related not to disagreement with the priest or parishioners, however, but centered around the problem of school expenses. Sometime in the late 1860s or early 1870s, the salary settled upon for teachers was $20 a month, or $200 for the year. The amount remained the same, despite increased living costs and expenses involved in certifying teachers, until 1919, when Bishop Michael Gallagher finally decided that teachers would receive $250 a year, a figure that matched salaries of nuns in other cities. In Boston, as late as 1910, sisters received housing without board and $200 a year.[75] Sisters were not certain to receive even the fixed stipend, however. Because there was no centralized system, each parish was responsible for its own obligations, and sometimes the pastor could not pay at all. The problem was particularly acute at Trinity because, given its large enrollment, the faculty often included as many as thirteen or fourteen teachers. Concerned to keep class size manageable in their schools, the IHMs always assigned more teachers than was common in schools taught by other religious congregations. At Trinity, the sizeable faculty posed a considerable expense to parishioners who were also paying for their new school building and trying to keep tuition fees at a minimum.

Financing Trinity became a joint effort among parents, pastor, and sisters, a creative juggling of contributions each was able to make and a pattern common in most other parishes throughout the city. It was at Trinity, apparently, that the IHMs first devised a plan to use a musically talented sister to help the parish priest afford the others' salaries. Irish-born Sister Scholastica Coakley, who had a strong musical education when she entered the convent, went to Trinity in 1877 under the agreement that she would receive a regular teacher's salary but would also give private lessons. All she earned in excess of her $200 salary would be turned over to the pastor to

Figure 2. Most Holy Trinity School (1867), only a few blocks west from the city center, drew Irish families to the Eighth Ward neighborhood and served as the model for many other parochial schools. (Archives of the Sisters, Servants of the Immaculate Heart of Mary)

help him pay the other teachers. Sister Scholastica stayed almost to the time of her death in 1908, all the while helping hundreds of children appreciate music and transferring their fees to support the school. Tuition was nonetheless unavoidable, but it remained low; music lesson money often amounted to as much or more than the total tuition collected. Typically, in 1894 Trinity collected $1,090.50 from music lessons and $945.85 from tuition, and in 1900 music revenue amounted to $1,388.13 and tuition totaled $1,083.35.[76] It was a creative means to draw money from families able to afford private lessons to subsidize families who could barely afford tuition and to assure, meanwhile, that the sisters were paid. Other parish schools seized upon the same plan.

The Trinity account book remained often in arrears. It listed $882.37 as a "Floating Debt" owed to the "Sisters of the I.H.M." in the late 1880s. This was by far the largest of the debts on the ledger, possibly accumulated over several years.[77] Trinity pastors did their part, supplementing church revenues with money they received for saying funeral masses and the special Christmas collections they might otherwise have pocketed. In 1886 that added $315 from funerals and the "entire Christmas collection" of $354. At one desperate point, Trinity's loved and loyal Father James Savage lent the church $2,295.42.[78] Fund-raisers were constant. Trinity's August Festival in 1886 raised $2,108.50, and the December supper and concert in the school hall brought another $250. Annual matinees and musicales, book sales, and food sales all brought in small but helpful amounts. Indeed, a careful piecing together of resources meant that Trinity parents had to pay tuition averaging 8 cents per year in 1880 and still less than $1.70 a year for each student in 1894.[79]

Wherever they taught, the sisters shared the same straitened circumstances as most of their parishioners and, like the neighborhood families living nearby, the sisters practiced constant economies. They had their own convent gardens, made their own clothes, and even mended their own shoestrings. The IHM motherhouse was the headquarters of a substantial farm that the congregation owned and operated. In the summer when sisters were through teaching, and between attending classes, they did much of the farm labor alongside their hired help. They grew, picked, and packed food to take back to parish convents when they went in the fall; they also tended sheep, cattle, chickens, and then canned the meat. Thinking of the upcoming year, in summers sisters traded still usable items among themselves and searched out leaves, bugs, and anything free on the farm that might help teach some lesson. Leaders reminded them, "don't slash and dash as if we were made of money" when it came to necessary purchases made during the school year. "We are not the Madames," an IHM superior chided one sister who wanted extra materials for her classroom, a reference to the Madames of the Sacred Heart, who focused on teaching children of the wealthy in private academies.[80]

Parents appreciated the sisters' contributions and sensitivity to the financial problems working-class families faced. It was one more reason to support parochial schools, where the faculty understood, "Better to do without an education altogether than to teach the daughter of the mechanic to be ashamed of her father's position."[81] A series of lengthy articles in the diocesan newspaper in the 1870s praised the St. Andre System as ideal for Catholic education, and the local press and parish newsletters frequently gave coverage to the sisters or their pupils' accomplishments. Even classroom arithmetic contests between boys and girls merited press attention.

Nagging fears about the lure of public schools kept local Catholic leaders vigilant. One of the purposes of developing Trinity's school was the awareness in the late 1870s that three hundred parish children attended public schools.[82] Of all the neighborhoods, Trinity's Eighth Ward was the one most dominated by Irish Catholics, and so the local public school was perhaps the most acceptable to parents because in it their children had a comforting strength of numbers. The pastor made no attempt at explaining such significant public school enrollment to the bishop, unlike priests who, with even a few parish children in public schools, made certain to record that "mixed marriage" or "indifferent parents" were at fault. Trinity began to hold its own from the mid-1870s, once the IHMs took over and the Irish Father Savage settled in to become a local legend during his thirty-year stay. Sisters, pastor, and parents joined forces to make the public school unattractive compared with the social activities, religious ceremonies, and friendships that centered around the parish grade school.

In German parishes staffed by IHMs, the same sense of community endured, centered around the parish school (fig. 3a–b). Pastor and parents attended the annual "public examinations" to admire what the children had learned during the school year. And, year around, they turned out for the exhibitions of one sort or another intended to raise money for their school. At the end of the century, parish children were still conscientiously pleasing their elders by delivering their lines in German in such familiar old plays as *The Princess and Peasant*.[83]

Despite these demonstrations, some members of Detroit's German Catholic community feared that children in the IHM parish schools were at risk

Figure 3a. St. Joseph's parish, still predominantly German, had the largest enrollment of any Detroit parochial school in 1894, the approximate time these children assembled in their best clothes for the annual class photo (see also figure 3b). The boys, among the five hundred listed in attendance, were taught by six Christian Brothers. The girls, among the 475 who regularly attended in 1894, were taught by fourteen IHM sisters. (Archives of the Sisters, Servants of the Immaculate Heart of Mary)

Figure 3b.

of becoming too Americanized, too "worldly." In preference to either the IHMs or the public schools, they persistently opted for sisters more to their liking: the School Sisters of Notre Dame from Milwaukee.

THE GERMAN SISTERS: THE SCHOOL SISTERS OF NOTRE DAME

For more than a decade before the new St. Joseph's opened its school with IHM teachers, parishioners at St. Mary's were sending their children to study with the School Sisters of Notre Dame. Their allegiance held, prompted not only by early familiarity but also because some pastors and parents appreciated the School Sisters' uncritical acceptance of the German language as a teaching tool. Moreover, the School Sisters traced their origin to the homeland.

The impetus to establish schools in the United States for German Catholics with teachers of their own kind had gained a timely boost in the mid-1840s from King Louis I of Bavaria. Concerned for the souls of emigrants who left for America, he began prodding the Bavarian province of the School Sisters of Notre Dame to send teachers to join the Redemptorist missionaries working among the German Catholics. The king promised to use a part of the mission money at his disposal to pay the women's traveling expense and build a convent in the United States. A group of four professed sisters and one novice set sail in June 1847, accompanied by the mother superior who went along to help them get settled. They were encouraged by King Louis' assurance: "I shall not forget you in America. I shall not forsake you."[84] Within a year, however, the Revolution of 1848 forced him to abdicate. By then, word about the School Sisters of Notre Dame was spreading through the Redemptorist network, German parishes were requesting their services, and the sisters—all of whom had volunteered for the American assignment—were committed to their intentions.

Milwaukee, with its large German population of "refined, cultured people who were clamoring for just such religious teachers," was the site the women chose for their American motherhouse. In 1850 they established their center in a solid, two-story brick home the local bishop purchased for them, using the money King Louis had provided for that purpose.[85] They would retain a novitiate in Baltimore where they had first settled and in the 1890s open another novitiate in New Orleans. Ten more sisters who arrived in 1849 were the last group who came from the Bavarian motherhouse. Schools were spreading so rapidly in Europe that more women could not be spared for America. Nonetheless, the School Sisters were soon a presence in one city after another because women joined the community in what the founders viewed as "astonishing numbers," thanks to "the zeal of the Redemptorist Fathers, the Fathers of the Society of Jesus, and many of the diocesan clergy."[86]

Detroit Germans and their Redemptorist priests at St. Mary's hosted the sisters when the women traveled through in 1848 to explore possibilities in the West. German Redemptorists had recently come to the Detroit diocese to work among the immigrants and had taken on the responsibility for the new St. Mary's parish.[87] The parishioners had erected a school and hired a German schoolmaster. Now, with the possibility of sisters who might teach their children, Redemptorists and parents requested the visiting sisters to assign some of their members to Detroit. Carefully observant and in much demand, the women pronounced St. Mary's "still too weak to undertake a school."[88] Instead, they accepted schools in Baltimore, Philadelphia, Pittsburgh, Buffalo, and Milwaukee.

It was not long before the Detroiters prevailed. When the Christian Brothers arrived to open classes at St. Mary's in 1852, the School Sisters of Notre Dame came to take charge of the girls, the smaller boys, and the parish orphanage for girls. It was the beginning of their long-term association with German Catholics in Detroit. A new and impressive four-story brick building opened in 1855 to be a combination school, orphanage, and sisters' residence. By then, the parish numbered nearly four thousand, and the school boasted five hundred pupils. Because there were never many orphans, the Redemptorists soon found homes for them among parish families so their quarters could be used for classrooms. Heavy German immigration and greater interest in schooling pushed enrollment up after the Civil War; again, there was a new building. When Sacred Heart formed as St. Mary's "daughter church" to accommodate the crush of German Catholics on the near east side, the pastor asked for the familiar School Sisters. In time for the 1875 school year, the mother superior sent additional teachers to Detroit.

As with so many other religious communities of women, one leader was especially responsible for the School Sisters' direction and educational philosophy, in their case, Mother Caroline Friess. Mother Caroline was among the first little group who came to the United States, and she was granted full charge of the American branch after sailing back to the motherhouse in 1850 to persuade her European religious superiors that the American School Sisters must be released from strict rules of the cloister if they were to work successfully among immigrants. Sisters teaching in America needed to speak to one another so they could discuss their pupils, she explained. Moreover, she was convinced that the teachers needed to talk with parents face to face, not from behind a shielding grate, and to attend the parish church rather than separate themselves in a convent chapel. The European superiors decided modifications were worth making if this would help the School Sisters carry out their mission in "a distant part of the world."[89]

By the time she died in 1892, Mother Caroline had given the habit to more than three thousand young women and opened 265 schools in the United States and Canada.[90] The few biographical sketches in the community's 1928 historical account describe women who were well educated. Sister Theophilia came in 1848 with the second group of arrivals from the German motherhouse. She had been educated in Munich by the Sisters of Loretto from England. Sister Seraphica, born in 1837 in Maryland to a plantation owner, had gone to a private school presided over by an "English gentleman," then to the Academy of Visitation Nuns in Washington, and she studied also with the prestigious Ladies of the Sacred Heart. Sister M. Gregory, born in Canton, Ohio in 1838, went to public school there and then to the Normal school. She taught for several years before joining the School Sisters of Notre Dame, where Mother Caroline reportedly "welcomed her with joy" because the "need of qualified English teachers was still great" at the time she entered in 1856.[91]

Mother Caroline, herself half French, made the decision soon after settling in Milwaukee to accept women of any nationality who preferred the School Sisters over other congregations. Yet most School Sisters of Notre Dame in the nineteenth century came from German families, immigrants or the second generation, and among Detroit Catholics they were customarily viewed as the "German nuns." Standards for admission contributed to the School Sisters' uniformity. Applicants were young, not to be under thirteen or above twenty-seven, and they had to arrive in good health as well as being free of "conspicuous corporal defects." Each candidate had to affirm she was making the choice to enter religious life without being coerced, had to prove she was of an "irreproachable reputation," and had to document her "legitimate birth" to "respectable parents." Each potential sister also had to come from a financially solid family so she would not have any lawful obligation to support poor parents, grandparents, or repay any debts. It was not enough to meet these certifying qualifications; the School Sisters would not allow any candidate to proceed through the novitiate unless she had an aptitude for the teaching profession as well as for religious life.[92]

In search of financial stability, certain congregations of women diversified their work, usually dividing their ranks into teachers and nurses. The School Sisters persisted in their original teaching mission, however, a focus that helped advance their professionalism. Usually the candidates completed their schooling after entering the convent. Within the Milwaukee motherhouse, priests or sisters who were proficient in English drilled the novices while Mother Caroline took on the task of training them as teachers aided by other members of the congregation whom she regarded as especially accomplished.

According to Mother Caroline's dictates, "the first requisite of a Catholic teacher" was the ability "to teach her pupils to know and to love God." Then the battle would be "half won."[93] Although the School Sisters probably did not have a thoroughgoing curricular plan throughout most of the nineteenth century, the women absorbed a certain basic philosophy at the motherhouse: religion, character formation, and mastery of skills "in the secular branches" entwined as the organizing principles in their classrooms.[94]

Every sister left for her fall assignment understanding she was to be a missionary who must make catechism and Bible history as "attractive as possible" to the children; "harsh measures" were never to be used when teaching these particular subjects. Sisters had to write weekly plans for their own guidance—and undoubtedly for the watchful eye of the sister-principal—specifying what they would include in the secular fields, which prayers they would teach, what instructions they would provide for youngsters preparing to receive the sacraments, and which virtues they would stress in each part of the day. Sisters who taught older pupils tried also to equip them to give "intelligent answers" to people who ridiculed the Catholic Church.[95]

Like the sameness in the weekly lesson plans and the sisters' long black habits, the classrooms mirrored one another. Pupils' double or triple desks lined up facing the teacher, whose desk was centered in front of the middle aisle; sometimes two blackboards flanked her desk, resting on easels so they could be lowered or raised according to a child's height. A crucifix and holy pictures decorated the walls, along with maps and charts usually made by the sisters. Depictions of St. Joseph, the German patron saint, were typically conspicuous. Pupils celebrated his day, March 19, with as much enthusiasm as Irish parish school children lavished on St. Patrick on March 17.

Mindful that the School Sisters' mission was to the poor and immigrant Catholics, Mother Caroline usually declined the idea of opening academies for older girls. Some other communities of women operated day and boarding schools for the daughters of the wealthy as in Europe and, from the 1880s, the more established parishes began adding upper grades to their elementary programs to serve daughters of the aspiring working class. Even in the face of criticism, Mother Caroline insisted it was necessary to help "preserve the faith among the masses first," because otherwise there would be little need in the long run for many higher institutions.[96]

From the writing on the blackboards to the decorations on the walls, their elementary schools were unmistakably German. In contrast to some Polish congregations, however, the School Sisters did not make Old World language and culture a centerpiece of the curriculum. They regarded instruction in German more as a practical necessity in order to teach catechism and Bible history—their first priorities—to children who so often understood nothing but German when they arrived in school. The School Sisters remained steadfast in their original priority: They had come to America with the intent of keeping German immigrants faithful to the Church. They hoped to win back lapsed or lukewarm parents through their children; it was important to reach out to those children in the language they could understand and to maintain the language tie between the generations as well.

Because Catholic parents and pastors commonly left the choice of parochial school books and materials to the teachers, the School Sisters selected books that met their purposes. They purchased books in common for all of their schools, often through Edward Hussey's Catholic bookstore in Milwaukee, which opened soon after they first arrived there to cater to local German Catholic families and schools. Occasionally, they sent away to suppliers in New York City, Philadelphia, and Baltimore. Bible histories, catechisms, readers, and a variety of other books were in German.

Once the first diocesan school board organized and began to visit each Detroit parochial school in 1887, a majority of its members were displeased when children proved less proficient in English than in German or Polish. Like most in the Detroit Catholic hierarchy, the pastors on the board agreed with those in the American church who favored acculturation (chapter 4). Persuaded by that perspective, they championed the IHM curriculum and regarded the School Sisters as too tolerant of the German language. Although several IHM schools taught German as a language, boys and girls who studied with the School Sisters spent a portion of their day studying in German.

Visitors from the Diocesan School Board tersely noted that examinations were "fair considering that both German and English are taught," but overall they gave pupils at St. Mary's a lower than average rating.[97] The school might have been assessed differently by visitors from the sisters' home diocese, however, because Milwaukee bishops and priests were among the most staunch defenders of ethnic pluralism (chapter 4).

There were long-standing differences of opinion among Detroit's German Catholics about which of their parishes had the best school and which religious community had the best teachers. The board's assessment did not visibly sway the School Sisters' loyal constituency. Had parents been dissatisfied with the School Sisters, they would probably have taken action. When a new pastor at St. Mary's removed the Christian Brothers in 1875 and replaced them with Franciscans, parents caused so much trouble in the parish that the bishop removed the priest.[98] Far from being disenchanted with the School Sisters, parishioners and pastor agreed that the entire school should be turned over to the women in the early 1890s when the Franciscans announced they were leaving. By then, with more than 1,100 pupils between St. Mary's and Sacred Heart, the School Sisters of Notre Dame were instructing nearly 18 percent of the city's parochial school children.[99]

The School Sisters continued to be important to the next generation. St. Anthony's, another German parish they staffed from 1895, became one of the city's largest parochial grade schools. In 1912 they agreed to teach in Detroit's only Italian parish school, and they also remained at St. Mary's and Sacred Heart long after Polish, Hungarian, Italian, black, and Mexican families had replaced the original German parishioners. Even then, in the 1920s, "Old St. Mary's" would often be described as one of the "German" schools and its teachers as the "German sisters."

Satisfied Parents

Detroit Catholics were reinforced in their choice of Catholic schools by the continuing alliance of public education and Protestant influences. The vindictive nativism of the 1850s was no longer in evidence, but neither side relinquished old convictions. Public school educators in Michigan agreed that readings from the King James Bible were at the "very root of our national being." Without dissent, Michigan teachers at the state association meeting in 1869 adopted a resolution that "the Bible should not be excluded from our public schools, and that such exclusion would not, in our opinion, render the schools more acceptable to any class of our citizens."[100] Local Protestants shared President U. S. Grant's widely publicized position that federal and state governments should "leave the matter of religion to the family altar, the church, and the private school, supported entirely by private contributions."[101] When midwestern bishops met in the Fourth Provincial Council of Cincinnati in 1882 Bishop Borgess strongly supported their mutual agreement to "continue support of our Catholics Schools . . . while waiting a change in the public school system, in which our rights as citizens will be recognized and conceded."[102]

Although not alone in facing a hostile public system, Detroit Catholics had turned to the parochial school alternative more enthusiastically than their co-religionists elsewhere. In Chicago, Catholics faced serious discrimination and had a profound suspicion of the public schools, yet half of all Catholic children attended public schools throughout the first one hundred years of parochial school development in that city.[103] Similarly, in Boston more Catholics were choosing public rather than parochial schools. Moreover, the lower attendance and slower rate of parochial school building was not due to the poverty of Boston Catholics, because children of the poor were more likely than the wealthy to attend parochial schools.[104] The real surge to establish schools did not come in Boston until after the Third Plenary Council of 1884 mandated it, and the rise of ethnic parishes led to an effort to bring French-Canadian, German, Polish, and Italian sisters who could speak the pupils' languages.[105] In New York, too, enrollment in parochial schools lagged well behind the increase in Catholic population. As a proportion of the city's total school population, the percentage in New York City's parochial schools was 1 percent less in 1870 than in 1840.[106]

Among Detroit immigrant Catholics, satisfaction with their parish schools may have become more important than their mistrust of public education. They were pleased with their accomplishments and intent on maintaining those "of as good a quality as schools established by the public."[107] If critics would "slander" Catholic education as "too religious," the local Catholic press reminded readers to respond by pointing to Mozart, Petrarch, Dante, and Cervantes, all products of Catholic education.[108] Comfortable with the sisters who taught their parish schools, parents did not really fear the type of Dickensian teacher whose widely reported cruelty to her local public school students gave the *Michigan Catholic* editor a golden opportunity. One could expect, he pointed out, to encounter such a "cold, cruel and repellent puritan spirit" in a public system that emphasized cramming facts, many "absolutely false," rather than the "kindly sentiments of the human soul."[109]

Too, although local Catholic rhetoric railed about parents' sacrifices to afford schools unsupported by tax dollars, direct tuition fees remained low. The amount varied considerably from parish to parish, as, in the typical year of 1880, from the average per pupil charge of 4 cents at St. Vincent's and 8 cents at Trinity to $2.20 at Our Lady of Help and the unusually high $5.10 parents paid at St. Boniface.[110] There were always discounts for families with several children in school, or understanding priests marked accounts "paid" if parents could not manage what they owed.

By the early 1880s a generation of Detroit Catholics had pieced together the reasons, form, and funds for educating their children separately. When the Third Plenary Council met in Baltimore in 1884 and decreed that Catholics must attend Catholic schools, Detroiters were already set on the course. Of the sixteen city parishes on the eve of that council, fourteen conducted schools, compared with a rate of merely 40 percent for all Catholic churches nationwide.[111] One report states that the Catholic population of Detroit was 37,950 in 1884, with 5,827 pupils in parochial schools.[112] All the various statistical reports taken together point in the same direction; 25 percent to 30 percent of all Detroit children enrolled in school in the 1880s were in Catholic schools. That approximates the proportion of Catholics in the total Detroit population.

Most parochial school students belonged to Northwestern European immigrant families who were anxious to share in the promise of America as they understood it. Even if they had never heard of the nationally prominent Catholics writers, Orestes Brownson and Issac Hecker, intentions of most local Catholics matched those of Brownson and Hecker, who hoped to harmonize church doctrine and American democracy.[113] Few Detroit immigrants could recognize that they had come to share and promote the American habit of privatization. Better, parents understood they had accomplished a measure of security and control when it came to educating their children.

Having initially taken refuge in parochial schools to protect their children from Protestant religious teachings, Detroit's Irish and German Catholics were coming to value the additional advantages parish schools offered. They were proud when their teachers and classrooms received high marks from church authorities once they began evaluating parochial schools. They congratulated themselves that an educated second generation was making rapid progress into skilled, professional, and business occupations. And they were also relieved to set their children apart from the Polish Catholics who were rapidly increasing in number and visibility.

By the mid-1880s Irish and German Catholics were poised for expansion into more new neighborhoods with more new parish schools, and they had begun to provide high schools for their grade school graduates. When the pope, the American church hierarchy, and prominent laymen joined forces to urge them on, it was encouraging but not necessary.

4 Promoting the Cause: Prelates, Polish Immigrants, and the Public Schools

> . . . the school is an important factor in the forming of childhood and youth—so important that its influence often outweighs that of home and Church.
> —from decrees of the Third Plenary Council (1884)

THE Catholic hierarchy made parochial education a major issue across the last quarter of the nineteenth century. It was a period of high-power church politics and extraordinary growth in the number of Catholic immigrants. From the Vatican to the small neighborhood parish, the clergy claimed responsibility for the children who attended Catholic schools, and they assigned blame for the children who did not. Detroit's bishops and priests lined up to promote the school cause. They took pride in local successes; Catholics continued adding new parish schools until there were twenty-three within the Detroit city limits by 1900. Papal admonitions, church council decrees, and prodding from priests contributed importantly, yet they were only a part of the impetus.

Public schools continued to help parochial schools thrive, dominated as they were by Protestant interests in their physical location, curriculum, administration, and zeal. There was also the impact of the new Polish immigrants who, determined to preserve their culture and language, fought among themselves in the process. Bitter turmoil within the Polish community prompted Irish and German Catholics to distance themselves. Detroit Catholics had no interest in a unified school system; each ethnic community was too independently successful to risk making common cause. In the last decades of the nineteenth century, leaders and laity tried to harmonize the separate education of their children with the democracy prized by Americans of every persuasion. Some of these Catholics were hopeful optimists, and others were worried pessimists. Most all were persuaded that theirs was a worthy endeavor.

Men in the church hierarchy and in the Catholic press were convinced that religious freedom was the great advantage America offered. In the United States, Catholic children could lay claim to an education incorporating their religious values. Church spokesmen carried on as if their pronouncements should and would preserve this right, which must not be compromised in a free land. American bishops solidified their position across three plenary councils held between 1852 and 1884 that assembled them all under leadership of the senior metropolitan bishop, the archbishop of Baltimore. Each council dealt with issues particular to the church on this side of the Atlantic. Bishops drafted legislation which, with the approval of the pope, intended to achieve unity and uniformity for the Catholic Church throughout the nation. Education was always a topic prominently linked to their primary purpose of perpetuating the faith.

The First Plenary Council of Baltimore said bishops should establish schools in connection with all churches in their dioceses and church revenues should provide for competent teachers. There was little coordinated follow-up, however. The Second Plenary Council busied itself, in 1866, with statements on theological topics, the role of bishops within the church, and concern over the large number of Catholics living in slums.[1] In 1884 the Third Plenary Council made Catholic schools and parochial education a cornerstone of the discussion, and it was the subject of one-fourth of the bishops' decrees.

In the years between the Second and Third Plenary Councils, the number of Catholics had grown significantly, and more Catholic children were ready to be educated at a time when public schools were increasing in number. Free public high schools signaled that secondary education was becoming an asset. Detroit's diocesan newspaper editorialized about the need to catch up, fretting, "In Detroit, the great body of Catholic youth (by which we mean boys from twelve years and upwards) *of necessity* receive their education in public schools."[2] With new intellectual currents emerging, public educators seemed vulnerable to books such as Darwin's *Origin of the Species,* published in 1859, and Herbert Spencer's *Education,* published two years later. Catholics saw signs of danger in the growing emphasis on natural science, economics, and modern social problems to the detriment of the classical education they long valued. Adding to the mix, Protestant evangelism was losing its former influence, and the religious aim of education within public schools was in disrepute among reformers. Far from being pleased with this development, clerics worried that such a shift might make public schools more attractive to some Catholics.

THE CONSERVATIVES

A few vocal Catholic leaders, clergy and lay, pressed educational issues and in the process spoke for the contingent who came to be labeled "conservatives." They provided arguments and debating positions for Catholics. Chief among these self-appointed watchdogs over immigrant education were Bernard McQuaid and James McMaster.

McQuaid, Bishop of Rochester, began lecturing throughout the country by 1871, three years after he was named bishop. He strongly opposed the move toward secularization in public schools. He wanted religion to be an important foundation of the curriculum in all schools and wanted the state to provide both the financial support and moral justification for it.[3] McQuaid's position that Catholics had a right to their fair share of public funds for education was not new, of course, and it would not succeed. But his insistence that parents should have priority over the state in matters of education reinforced both Catholics and those Protestants who agreed with him that religion must be the foundation of education and that it was "unmitigated despotism" for the government to be "meddling with the duties and work of families." The *Michigan Catholic* gave him page-one status, approving his conviction, "If there is any one principle, over and above all others, underlying our Democratic-Republican form of government—it is this that the political State should not undertake to do for the people what the people can do for themselves."[4]

James McMaster was even more vehement in defense of Catholic education than his ally McQuaid. McMaster edited the *New York Freeman's Journal and Catholic Register.* It was one of the leading Catholic publications in the country, and McMaster was the most influential layman in the nineteenth-century American church.[5] He presented the zeal and paraded the credentials of one who had come to his religion by reasoned choice, not birth. Son of a Presbyterian minister, McMaster had converted to Catholicism when Union Theological Seminary refused to ordain him because of his Anglo-Catholicism.

McMaster, publisher and Catholic activist, became particularly outspoken in matters of education when the "Poughkeepsie Plan" first came to his attention. The plan was a creative attempt designed by a Poughkeepsie, New York, priest to fund Catholic education with tax money. In 1873 the priest rented the Poughkeepsie parochial school building to the municipal school board for a nominal fee during school hours. Only Catholic children attended. The priest nominated Catholic teachers, and the board passed on the nominations and paid the teachers. During regular school hours the children studied secular subjects. Before and after hours, when the school was no longer rented to the board, teachers provided religious instruction. Priest, parents, and the Poughkeepsie school board were content. James McMaster was not. It was "a bargain with the devil," and such schools, he inveighed, "cannot in conscience be attended."[6]

McMaster feared state-funded Catholic schools because of European examples. He followed developments in France closely and was upset by the state's action against religion in 1871 after the Franco-Prussian War. Bismarck's Kulturkampf in Germany and czarist reaction against Polish Catholics in the Russian empire added more reasons to avoid all church-state entanglements. In 1874 McMaster made a formal appeal to Rome, broadening his attack on public schools. He asked the Sacred Congregation for the Propagation of the Faith to intervene, convinced that American bishops were not taking sufficient action against parents who sent children to public schools. Rome, he urged, must order clergy to refuse absolution to those parents. McMaster offered the Vatican several reasons for objecting to public schools for Catholic children. Schools would determine the victory for faith or infidelity in the United States, he maintained. Public schools would undermine the Catholic faith because the books children used there were full of false representations, incorrect facts, and "calumnies" against the church. In public classrooms pupils would read from the Protestant Bible or say Protestant prayers. If that was not enough to convince Rome, he also warned about the danger of sexual perversion because children of both sexes up to the ages of sixteen, eighteen, or even twenty sat opposite each other or mixed together.[7]

The New York layman had disproportionate influence in Rome because of his conservative convictions and well-placed connections within the Vatican. McMaster's concerns became their opinions. Within seven weeks of his appeal a questionnaire went off to American bishops on the condition, influence, and role of American public schools. Some members of the hierarchy were not satisfied with the reply, which the bishops sent jointly. In November 1875 the Vatican issued a formal instruction to American bishops. Catholics in a particular area could go to public school if their bishop approved it, said the directive, but it was not good to do so, and bishops should ensure safeguards such as classes in catechism.[8]

The American bishops met the instruction with silence, but Detroit's Bishop Borgess shared these same concerns and soon began implementing procedures to deny parents the sacraments if they sent children to public school when a parochial school was within walking distance of three miles. When no parochial school was available, parishes in the Detroit diocese provided weekly catechetical instruction.[9]

The instruction provided the first detailed statement on American education. With it the papacy declared, "For the Catholic children of the United States of America evils of the greatest kind are likely to result from the so-called public schools."[10] It was nine years after the instruction when the archbishops and bishops convened the Third Plenary Council in Baltimore upon Pope Leo III's request, and that position formed the basis of the council decrees on education.

ROLE OF THE THIRD PLENARY COUNCIL

As Baltimore Catholics prepared to host the council, Archbishop James Gibbons explained its purpose. The pope wanted the assembly to consider "the best means for promoting the salvation of souls" in America.[11] Throughout the sessions, from November 9 to December 7, 1884, the fourteen archbishops and sixty bishops demonstrated a conviction that education was significant not only for the salvation of souls but also for the salvation of civilization. Education must foster religion because the school was so important in forming youth "that its influence often outweighs that of home and Church."[12] Schools teaching religion provided a bulwark because a "civilization without religion would be a civilization of the 'struggle for existence, and the survival of the fittest,' in which cunning and strength would become the substitutes for principle, virtue, conscience and duty."[13] Religion must not be shut out of the school and kept just for home and church, or a generation would be trained to consider religion good for home and the church "but not for the practical business of real life."[14] The assembled men felt a sense of obligation and urgency.

The bishops met in the long shadow of the Kulturkampf and attacks on the church in Europe. They warned that "avowed enemies of Christianity" were banishing religion from the schools and proclaimed it was in the best interest of the American nation for schools to include religion. They wanted friends and foes to understand that the church was making an "honest endeavor" to give the state better citizens by making them better Christians.[15]

To Catholic bishops and lay activists like McMaster, the position seemed clear enough but it confused and angered public school advocates. To that constituency it seemed as if Catholics wanted public schools to teach religion and objected to secularization yet opposed public schools because of the religion they taught, insisted Catholic children must attend parochial schools, and wanted tax support for these parochial schools. It appeared that Catholics wanted religion out of public schools but would then object on the grounds that such schools were un-Christian. Critics had identified the

Catholic position but failed to comprehend it because they dismissed Catholic charges of Protestant bias in public schools.

Pronouncements from the Third Plenary were clear evidence, in any case, that Catholics as well as Protestants had come to identify religion as essential to their interpretation of democracy. Newer to the land and its institutions, often feeling under siege, the church hierarchy used the Third Plenary as a forum to signal that Catholics, as loyal Americans, would defend their democratic right to religious freedom. The bishops wanted to be sure that Catholic schools were not only a presence but also measured up to American standards of education. Accordingly, the Third Plenary's education measures had two primary objectives: to multiply Catholic schools and to perfect them. Hard-liners won language that commanded, not just encouraged, school construction. Each parish was to open a primary school within two years. That was clearly a goal rather than a realistic demand, but a priest could be removed if he neglected his obligation to establish a school. Negligent parish communities were to be "reprehended" by the bishop.[16]

Caspar Henry Borgess, Bishop of Detroit, was among the hard-liners on the school-establishment issue. From his arrival in 1870 until his resignation in April 1887, Borgess involved himself in organizing, building, and staffing schools. During his years as bishop he convened five synods, and education held a high priority at each meeting.[17] By the time of the Third Plenary, Borgess offered his experience as reason for denying sacraments to parents who sent children to public schools. Having relied on exhortations for twenty years, he had accomplished little, he told the assemblage. Priests in the diocese had failed to enforce his 1877 mandate requiring them to deny sacraments to parents who sent children to public schools without sufficient reason. Ultimately, parents complied, as he saw it, only when he made it a reserved sin—meaning that the erring parent could not receive the sacraments until applying to the bishop.[18]

Borgess openly disagreed with Archbishop Patrick Feehan of Chicago, Plenary Council chair of the committee on parochial schools. He disputed Feehan's claim that good Catholic schools taught by trained teachers would persuade parents to send children willingly. In making his case, Borgess apparently discounted a series of appeals he received just the year before from parishioners who begged for good teachers, complaining their teacher "may have a very flowery education, but our school is not properly managed, and our children learn very little, especially the boys." They had assured him they would "humbly submit" to his last order, which obliged them to send their children to a Catholic school, "if we can have a school where our children can get an education."[19] He also disregarded the substantial school enrollment in the Detroit parishes, focusing instead on troublesome rural and small-town churches. Bishop Borgess sought council support for a strong hand.

Rather than issue a uniform mandate, however, the Plenary Council compromised. A deliberately worded statement empowered bishops to make their own decisions; parents were bound to send children to parochial schools unless permitted to make other arrangements by their bishops. The assembled prelates did bind themselves to admonish any parishioners who failed to support the expenses for parochial education. They agreed to send pastoral letters, deliver sermons, and even hold private conversations to let Catholics know clearly about the "serious neglect" of their duty.[20] And in their formal pastoral letter to the "Clergy and Laity" at the conclusion of the council, the archbishops and bishops were moved to "implore" that parents not take children out of school early but rather give them "all the time and all the advantages that they have the capacity to profit by."[21]

On the matter of quality, the Third Plenary Council pronounced it was not enough for Catholics to act on the principle that "it is better to have an imperfect Catholic school than to have none." They must "not relax their efforts till their schools be elevated to the highest educational excellence."[22] Bishop Borgess was again at the forefront of those pushing for concrete means to improve academic standards. Priests in his diocese had been studying the idea of a school board since the fifth synod met in 1881, and they had discussed the need to examine Catholic school teachers. The council now gave such efforts official status.

The bishops decided each diocese was to establish a school board of priests to administer teacher examinations. Board members could choose also to inspect schools and approve textbooks. Each religious congregation was to establish a normal school to train their sisters for teaching. The bishops rounded off their recommendations by encouraging parochial high schools and urging wealthy Catholics to help establish and fund Catholic colleges. As the capstone of their aims, the bishops provided for Catholic University. When it opened in Washington, D.C., in 1889, it included a sisters' college on the campus to educate nuns for their duties as teachers.[23]

On the whole, the Third Plenary decrees focused on numbers, on improving the count: a school in every parish, more children in attendance at those schools, a school board in each diocese, teachers taking examinations to determine mastery of content, and a normal school in each sisterhood. It was the stuff of which annual reports to chanceries were made. The substance of parochial education was another matter entirely.

It was beyond the council's ability to decree how Catholic schools might accommodate cultural pluralism, Catholic doctrine, American "respectability," and occupational opportunity, all the while funded by people mostly in the working class. Such, however, were the real concerns that preoccupied parishioners, exasperated priests, and confounded bishops. Historians of the Catholic Church in America point out that the Third Plenary Council ended the era of ecclesiastical organization and ushered in a period of conflict.[24] Within a short time after the council adjourned, church leaders were disagreeing with one another in the pulpit, press, and in appeals to Rome. There was never a solid front at the Baltimore meeting, and for fifteen years a bitter dispute raged over the interpretation and adaptation of rules laid down at the council.

AMERICANISTS VERSUS PLURALISTS

On one side stood the Americanists. Often described as the "liberals," most clergy in this group were Irish and, as the designation implied, wanted the Catholic Church to be firmly planted within the American culture. Four bishops were the major spokesmen. Archbishop John Ireland of St. Paul took the lead on issues dealing with education. Ireland supported the need for Catholics to cooperate with public schools and offered defense of the public schools. He briefly attempted cooperative efforts similar to the Poughkeepsie Plan in the communities of Faribault and Stillwater in his Minnesota diocese. Archbishop Gibbons of Baltimore took up the task of explaining Catholic dogma to Protestants and became the spokesman who pointed out how Catholicism fit with American values.[25] John Keane, Bishop of Richmond, became rector of the new Catholic University when it opened and eloquently defended the Knights of Labor and the rights of workers. The fourth key Americanist, Bishop John Lester Spalding, gained his position among the leaders primarily because he defended their rights. Spalding, Bishop of Peoria, did not agree with Ireland and the others about accommodating to assimilation. He believed immigrants had the right to maintain their own languages and ethnic schools. But, finally, when men such as Keane and Ireland came under attack from Rome, it was Spalding who came forward as an important and vocal champion of their right to act without interference from abroad.

Like the Progressive Era reformers, Catholic Americanists belonged variously to the Democratic and Republican parties. Their defining characteristic was a shared enthusiasm for America, for democracy, and their faith in the opportunity of Catholics to become full partners in what they optimistically saw as a land of unbounded possibilities. Upon being told by the pope that he was too loud in his admiration for America, Keane allegedly responded, "Please God, I will never be less loud."[26] Clergy and laity on the Americanist side agreed with the question as Gibbons formulated it: Catholics must decide "whether the church is to be honored as a bulwark of liberty and order, or is to be despised and suspected as an enemy of [American] institutions."[27] Americanists promoted the use of English in churches and schools and hoped to eliminate the foreign image of the Catholic Church in America to free it from attacks of bigotry and anti-Catholicism.[28] Bishop Borgess, who numbered among hard-liners on matters of establishing parish schools, stood with the Americanists in the desire to avoid any stigma as a "foreign" church. Just then on the brink of trouble with his Polish parishioners, Borgess understood this danger better than most.

Most German bishops were on the other side in alliance with a number of Irish bishops. Historians sometimes refer to these churchmen as pluralists because they favored ethnic parishes; too, they are labeled protectionists and conservatives. Pessimistic about human nature, they generally thought children had "awful possibilities for evil" unless held in check.[29] The group continued to fear that too much contact with Protestant-dominated American institutions would undermine Catholicism among intellectuals and unsophisticated alike. In common, pluralists advocated ethnic schools and churches where children's language and culture could be appreciated. They opposed public control over parochial teacher certification, curriculum, or school standards.[30] They believed the Third Plenary Council had endorsed their position. In the years after the council, each side continued to seek involvement from Rome in defense of its position.

In their arguments, churchmen focused most on broad outlines: the acceptable extent of compromise with public schools, the place of religion in school, and the value of assimilation or the justification for pluralism. Significant differences in educational philosophy surfaced. Key among them was a sharp division over how much and what type of education women should have. Liberals such as Ireland and Spalding wanted women to be able to realize their full potential and applauded their demands for higher education. In contrast, their opponents insisted that women, emulating Mary, could find a complete life in the home and church work.[31] The Americanists became enthusiastic about the same educational theories the IHM sisters had been implementing in Michigan since the 1860s. The French humanist Dupanloup, who provided the foundation for the IHM curriculum and methodology, was Bishop Ireland's hero. Ireland, Gibbons, and others held to the notion that teachers should respect a child's individuality, should take students "as God made them," and should bring out their special talents. They admired the ideas of Frederick Froebel, despite his religious radicalism, and believed that schools should encourage a child's curiosity rather than stuff young heads full of memorized lessons. Conservatives like McQuaid strongly objected, arguing that it was the role of schools to impart information rather than encourage curiosity among the naive.

The quarrel ranged widely. In addition to the nature of Catholic schools, there were conflicts over Catholic University, Catholic participation in labor organizations, and the demands raised by the German layman Peter Paul Cahensly, who insisted that the church recognize German immigrants' right to ethnic parishes and greater representation within the hierarchy. With each side calling upon supporters in Rome, onlookers, including President William Henry Harrison, some U.S. senators, and the *Chicago Tribune,* decried the power of "an Italian priest living in Rome" who claimed any say over any issues in America, especially those dealing with education.[32]

All these controversies were given due attention in Michigan. Neither Bishop Borgess nor his successor, Bishop John Foley, commanded national notice inside or outside the church. But in the Detroit diocese each attempted to make his mark. Borgess, opposed to ethnic self-interest and insistent on parish schools and concerned to improve their quality, is sometimes considered among the reformers. In his dark view of human nature and his constant efforts to legislate against all occasions that might encourage sin, he was temperamentally aligned with conservatives. When Foley came to head the diocese in 1888, he shared the Americanist views of his mentor, Archbishop Gibbons of Baltimore. Foley also agreed with Ireland's ideas on education and refused to sign a protest when the papal delegate to the United States supported Ireland's views; he was the only bishop in the Province of Cincinnati who withheld his signature.[33] Both Borgess and Foley attempted autocratic mandates when they could; nonetheless, both promoted ethnic parish schools because their Catholic constituents and parish pastors, finally, gave them little choice.

DIOCESAN EFFORTS TO EXPAND SCHOOLS AND ESTABLISH COMMON STANDARDS

While the debate between Americanists and pluralists preoccupied some, Bishop Borgess focused on managing matters of local concern. Convinced as he was that Catholics must not attend public schools, the bishop was equally determined to make parochial schools meet exacting standards. The Third Plenary reinforced his resolve. He convened a Seventh Diocesan Synod in 1886, where, at his insistence, the assembled priests approved a wide-ranging set of regulations that served as broad guidelines for the next thirty years.

The synod approved the goal of a school beside each church and reaffirmed the 1878 synod proposal to encourage financial support from the general parish revenues so children could attend without charge. They agreed that no child should be turned away from a parochial school because of a family's poverty. Throughout the proceedings, clerics were careful to assert their right to control parish schools; serious conflicts in the Polish community at the time made them especially wary of undue interference from bishop or parishioners. As before, priests would continue to hire or discharge teachers, subject to the bishop's approval. They were also the authority on religion in the parish school. Christian doctrine classes, taught twice a week in half-hour classes for all children, would be their province.[34]

The assembled priests agreed to establish a diocesan school board, even though they were not all enthusiastic about doing so. It was an idea they had debated at meetings for five years. Bishop Borgess was an insistent proponent, seeing this as essential in his effort to bring uniformity and improve quality. The synod proceeded to elect the first board members, in line with proposals from the bishop, and gave them impressive responsibilities: to certify teachers through examinations, to develop a uniform curriculum, to select textbooks, and to visit and report on every school. With great zeal, board members took up their tasks at once.[35]

In the first year of operation, the board began examining all instructors in the diocese who had been teaching for fewer than five years. Public school teachers had been subject to examination or various means of certification since the 1850s, depending on vigilance in each local district, and teacher preparation was gaining attention in many states.[36] By administering tests, Borgess and the board expected to push religious congregations to educate their teachers more carefully. Moreover, they intended to signal outsiders that Catholic school teachers had to meet standards, too.

Each priest on the board traveled from school to school within his assigned district during the 1887–88 school year. They orally quizzed pupils, observed discipline, looked over physical conditions, and scanned pupil attendance records. Then they wrote assessments in the first thorough report of diocesan parochial schools. In the preface, board secretary Father Peter Baart reminded all readers that the board's role was not to write up schools "in eulogistic strain" but rather to give statements of fact.[37] The forty-five-page report proceeded to praise some schools and teachers, but it criticized others, usually for poor pupil examinations, poor discipline, or problems both teachers and students had with the English language.

Those who mistrusted the board from its early planning stages continued to be displeased. The board was, as they charged, an effort to oversee areas that previously had been left to the parish priest and the sisters in each school. Parishes with problems resented having their weaknesses on display and, further, sometimes regarded board decisions as biased. The decision to exempt teachers from certifying examinations if they had taught for five years favored the longer-established IHMs over new congregations such as the Polish Felicians who were just building their numbers. Priests who had IHMs teaching in parish schools dominated the board and wanted their practices to be the norm, especially when examiners found IHM pupils generally ranked higher in "scholastic standing" and demonstrated better discipline than students who had other teachers. Father Joos, who administered the diocese at the time of the first report, openly preferred the IHM model. Some parishes felt the board failed to take their special circumstances into account when urging a common standard. Polish priests especially saw problems with uniform texts and curricular plans. In other instances, sisters and priests whose schools had an established reputation for excellence saw no need to be visited or judged. Certainly, the IHMs were never enthusiastic about a strong school board, even though they won its praise. They realized centrally made decisions would interfere with their independence.

Bishop Borgess resigned in April 1887, just as the first board members began their tasks, and so in its earliest stage of operation the board lost its powerful advocate. Almost at once, political pressure brought revisions in the board's composition and purview. The original five-member board was expanded to include a sixth priest, Father Paul Gutowski. Prominent as a power broker in the Detroit Polish Catholic community, he had offered support for Borgess when Polish critics attacked the bishop. More significant than the expansion of board membership, however, was the erosion of the board's activities. Soon, if quietly, board members surrendered any plan to bring about a uniform curriculum and common textbooks. By 1889, with the new bishop, John Foley, school inspection became the business of district boards composed of pastors in each of the five districts or "deaneries." The central school board was left with the examination and certification of teachers as its primary role. There would be no thoroughgoing effort to meld a parochial school system until the 1930s. Parochial schools remained as separate as the ethnic parishes.

Any advantages of unifying all parish schools seemed insignificant when many Catholic priests and laity compared them with the advantages they expected to gain by retaining parish school independence. That became particularly apparent as Bishop Borgess was pressing a centrally controlled system. Serious internal disagreements developed within the Polish community and sparked conflict with the church hierarchy, and Polish parishioners emerged from the fray convinced they must retain local control. Meanwhile, the highly publicized disputes confirmed other Catholics in their desire to avoid the Poles. Not so unlike the civil disturbances Detroit would experience in the late 1960s, trouble in the Polish community surprised contemporaries.

THE DEVELOPING POLISH COMMUNITY

The Polish community that began forming from the 1840s had grown without much notice. Most who arrived across the late 1850s and 1860s were Prussian Poles in search of economic improvement. They spoke and understood German, settled in the German east-side neighborhood of Detroit, worshiped in the two German Catholic churches, St. Mary's and St. Joseph's, and sent their children to those parish schools.[38] When Borgess arrived from Cincinnati to become bishop in 1870, there were nearly three hundred Polish families. Leaders within the immigrant community, many of them small businessmen or professionals, were beginning to make plans for their own church. They were especially anxious for a school where their children would learn Polish history, culture, and language.

Borgess was not among the American bishops, Irish and German, who pursued a plan to mix Poles with the older ethnic communities. There were those in the Detroit church who believed Polish immigration would not be a long or significant movement.[39] But Borgess was willing to entertain the request for a Polish church once the Resurrectionist Fathers, an order of Polish missionaries anxious to place their members in America, assured him he could find priests.[40] He then gave leaders in the Polish community approval; they could collect money to build a church.

A committee of four purchased a lot at Fremont (later Canfield) and St. Aubin, then at the northeastern edge of the Polish settlement. On July 14, 1872, St. Albertus was dedicated as the first Polish church in Detroit.[41] In a show of support and religious solidarity usual at church dedications, members from Detroit's other parishes came to celebrate the accomplishment. Even before they erected the wooden frame of St. Albertus, parishioners had organized a school in a house rented by the newly appointed pastor, who took charge of the pupils himself. Within a year the school was so crowded that the parish needed a new building.[42]

Within ten years the parish that started with three hundred families had quadrupled to 1,200 families and seven thousand people. The Polish community spread northeast from the German neighborhood to surround St. Albertus. Most immigrants continued to arrive from Prussian Poland, but now more came from peasant families. Being Polish was becoming synonymous with belonging to Detroit's working class. The Poles pushed forward the industries and construction projects that relied on cheap labor. Men and boys found jobs at breweries or blacksmith shops. The strong paved streets, dug sewers, laid rails for street railways, or put in water pipes for new housing. The fortunate found skilled work as brass finishers, molders, and polishers or in the stove works. Women and girls worked as domestics, in bean factories, or on farms. Some younger women ventured off in pairs or groups to work downtown in hotels and restaurants. A few found tailoring positions, but many more hired on in the factories making cigars, cigarettes, chewing tobacco, or matches until they could marry.[43]

After long days on the job or while temporarily unemployed, Polish immigrants built their homes. Family members did as much of the construction as they could, traded with friends for tasks they could not handle alone, or hired some acquaintance who had specialized skills. Small lots and small houses helped keep costs of home ownership down, sometimes as low as $400 to $600 in the Polish neighborhood of the 1880s. Often immigrants managed to build without going into debt or taking out a mortgage. To maintain their families, couples commonly rented out a room, a basement, or a backyard shed. Living arrangements were cramped. As many as ten or more people of assorted ages and relationships often lived under one roof. But the neighborhood that developed around St. Albertus and the smaller Polish community emerging to the far west were both brand new. Detroit Poles did not suffer the secondhand housing or crowded tenements so many immigrants inherited in urban America.[44] It took an enormous effort, and Poles were proud of their accomplishments.

The tightknit Polish community was absorbed in its own concerns. These interests centered importantly on the church and school that reinforced this world of their own within America. Willing to help friends and relatives build homes, Polish immigrants were willing also to go so far as to mortgage even their own hard-earned homes for their parish church or parochial school. Given the sacrifices they made, they expected attention to their concerns from those who should understand them—especially their neighbors and their priests. Their German bishop, Caspar Borgess, should at least appreciate them as faithful Catholics.

In the late 1870s and early 1880s Polish Catholics in Detroit had reason to be as optimistic about their place within the local church as within the city's growing economy. In the single year of 1882, after a decade of unsatisfactory pastors or shared pastors, the Polish community welcomed three Polish priests and also became the permanent center for a congregation of Polish nuns.

Father Dominic Kolasinski, an Austrian Pole, emigrated to assume leadership at St. Albertus in 1882. With its seven thousand communicants, it was the city's largest parish. The new priest and parishioners began at once to talk about plans for a brick building to replace the wooden church, now ten years old. Meanwhile, after six years of requests, Poles on the city's west side gained the bishop's approval to build a church so they could end their trek across town to St. Albertus.

Father Paul Gutowski, a Prussian Polish refugee from Bismarck's Kulturkampf, came a few months after Kolasinski to establish that new parish, named in honor of St. Casimir. Gutowski apparently had the support of Kolasinski, who had been helping the hundred west-side families organize their church until a new priest arrived.[45] St. Casimir's opened in April 1883, at Twenty-third and Myrtle, gathering in Polish immigrants who settled along both sides of Michigan Avenue from about Twentieth Street on beyond the city boundaries at Twenty-fifth. Almost at once, Gutowski and his parishioners were making plans to replace the wooden building with a magnificent structure modeled after St. Peter's in Rome. Between 1887 and 1890 they built it at a cost of $126,000.[46]

The third new Polish priest in town was Joseph Dabrowski, chaplain and director of the Felician Sisters, who relocated their American center from Wisconsin to a new motherhouse across the street from St. Albertus. Gaining these sisters was a major source of pride for Detroit Poles. Known properly as the Congregation of St. Felix of Cantalicio, Third Order of St. Francis, the Warsaw-based Felicians were the first European congregation of Polish sisters to establish a province or division in the United States. For many years they would be the largest group of Polish nuns in the country, responsible for the education of thousands of Polish children in several states (chapter 5).

On top of these impressive accomplishments, plans soon started for a seminary in Detroit that would train Polish-American priests who could minister to immigrants. It was the first such undertaking in America, a long-cherished goal of Father Dabrowski. The idea of such a seminary coincided with the need Bishop Borgess had for priests. His problem was becoming more severe in the mid-1880s, when there was only one priest for every thousand Catholics. Borgess, no advocate of ethnic rights or separatism, was nonetheless realistic. Citing the difficulty in obtaining from Poland "a sufficient number of good and zealous pastors," he approved Dabrowski's request to build a seminary in the diocese in March 1884.[47] The next month, the priest bought two acres just two blocks north of St. Albertus and the new Felician motherhouse. The Seminary of SS. Cyril and Methodius opened in December 1886, with Father Dabrowski as rector.[48]

Meanwhile, events had so sharply disrupted relationships that the seminary opened more in an atmosphere of grim resolution than the confident optimism that characterized the Polish community when the project was launched two years before. The city's Polish Catholics had been absorbing burdensome costs to build and operate their institutions. All three Polish priests—Kolasinski, Gutowski, and Dabrowski—were bent on ambitious projects at the same time, and each persevered despite the stock exchange collapse in the spring of 1884 and the financial panic that followed. The Felicians also were expanding their original building, already cramped for space.

The Polish people were tugged from one project to the next for their time, labor, and money. Many were immigrant couples relatively new to the city or to marriage and in the midst of supporting growing families and building or adding to their own homes. Careful about money, they expected their priests to be accountable and careful, too. They struggled to balance pride in their Polish churches and institutions with the demands on their strained incomes. A small group of established families with better incomes and professions battled to maintain some control when clerics asserted authority.[49] Bishop Borgess was bent on implementing policies just set forth at the Third Plenary Council, which, he believed, underscored his position and required his authority. It was not an easy time.

CONFLICT WITHIN DETROIT'S POLISH CATHOLIC COMMUNITY

Tensions ignited at St. Albertus. Father Kolasinski signed contracts with builders for a large red-brick neo-Gothic structure in February 1884. The new St. Albertus church would be 208 feet long, and the top of the cross on the spire would reach 200 feet into the sky. It would have steam heating and incandescent lights. Seating 2,500, the magnificent new building would be the largest church in Michigan. The charismatic priest persuaded parishioners to go along with the elaborate and costly scheme. There were trustees, however, who disagreed with such indebtedness. While plans were still talk, twenty-four parishioners lodged a complaint with the bishop against Kolasinski's ideas. As one objection, they charged the pastor was draining the school of funds needed for expansion, and because there was no room for them parish children were being forced into public school.[50]

Even though two complainants had mortgaged their property to buy the original site for St. Albertus in the 1870s, the bishop held title to both the land and church according to established church practice and state law. The issue of parish property ownership caused battles in numerous other Polish

American communities; dedication of St. Stanislaus Church in Chicago had been delayed for two years because of an ownership dispute between bishop and parishioners.[51] Polish nationalists in the United States were particularly vocal about the "injustice" of Irish bishops and Roman popes benefiting from Polish contributions. As the Detroit Polish community became more factious, some reports mistakenly identified Westphalia-born Borgess as Irish. The Detroit bishop was determined to stand firm in his diocese against what he saw as the danger of laymen asserting control or claiming authority. He supported Kolasinski, and the building proceeded. Soon after, when the bishops assembled at the Third Plenary they ruled that a parish and its wealth belonged to the bishop and that priests were accountable to their bishops only, not to trustees or parishioners.

Bishop Borgess was equally determined to keep his priests in line. Kolasinski's parish enemies kept up their litany of complaints, asserting—unjustly—that he was guilty of sexual immorality as well as financial misdeeds. Affidavits piled upon statements embellished by rumors. Still, building proceeded, and on July 4, 1885, the bishop dedicated the new St. Albertus. The flamboyant, high-living Kolasinski disclaimed continuing charges of mismanagement and refused to turn over the books when the bishop demanded an audit.

Incensed by this defiance of his authority, Borgess dismissed Kolasinski in November and told parishioners that Father Dabrowski would take over their pulpit temporarily. Dabrowski had not been a parish priest in the Detroit diocese. Devoting his time to educational efforts at the Felician motherhouse and Polish seminary, he had proven cooperative in his dealings with the bishop. He had served as the bishop's main interpreter of events going on inside Kolasinski's troubled parish. Still, Kolasinski had many supporters within the parish, perhaps a majority. They were outraged that the bishop had dismissed him without a hearing and had handpicked a successor.[52]

Identifying the Felician sisters with Dabrowski, a group of women stormed into St. Albertus school, chasing startled students and nuns from the building. The incident was followed by street brawls between Kolasinski's accusers and defenders. On December 4, 1885, the bishop closed St. Albertus just five months after the celebrations that marked its opening; the church would remain locked until June 24, 1887.

For a while, churchmen did not realize that this stern action would fail to bring the immigrant community to obedient order. Kolasinski had refused to vacate the parish house and proceeded to feed his supporters' anger, describing Borgess as one more example of Prussian oppression of Poles.

He also gave an interview to the *Detroit Free Press* in which he claimed Dabrowski wanted to gain control of St. Albertus to pay off the Felicians' building debts and "throw the entire support of the cloister upon this parish."[53] Poles divided into the Kolasinskiites and the Dabrowskiites.

In the period from December 1885 through the spring of 1887, east-side immigrants carried on in what the local press termed the "Polish Wars." Some historians of the events would later chronicle seven "recorded" Polish "riots."[54] Two men died during the course of the street fights, and the Detroit police were constantly needed in the neighborhood. The "Polak quarter" was regularly in the news. Here was no academic debate around bishops' mahogany council tables over the issues of Americanization or ethnic representation. The Polish Wars alerted all other Catholics as well as Protestants to the rapidly growing, independent, and volatile Polish population settled so heavily in the northeast section of Detroit.

Kolasinski did not vacate the rectory until spring in 1886, when he finally went to the Dakota territory for a brief ministry. It was a sojourn one prominent Polish priest-historian at the time described as the priest's Elba.[55] Bishop Borgess resigned in April 1887. Exhausted and discouraged, he surrendered his ambitions for education to the school board, turned the administration of the diocese over to Father Joos, and left it to his successor to resolve the problems in the Polish community.

For two years after St. Albertus was closed, Father Dabrowski ministered to hundreds of parishioners who attended mass at the Felician motherhouse chapel. St. Albertus was finally reopened after Borgess left, Dabrowski went back to guide the Polish seminary and direct the Felicians, and a new priest came to the church. Meanwhile, Kolasinski's loyalists defied the church hierarchy and bought land on Canfield, a few short blocks west of St. Albertus. First they began a school and then a church in this new schismatic parish, soon named Sweetest Heart of Mary. By December 1888 Father Kolasinski was back from Dakota to preach to them.

The new bishop, John Samuel Foley, had arrived in November 1888, and he took up the task of getting the "Polish troubles" under control. Initially, he tried to draw off Kolasinski's supporters by establishing another Polish parish, St. Josaphat's, in the neighborhood. Despite numerous irregularities in Kolasinski's new parish accompanied by highly publicized disputes involving the priest and some of his original allies, the parishioners and pastor completed Sweetest Heart of Mary Church in 1893. Sweetest Heart was deliberately more massive and more magnificent than St. Albertus or St. Josaphat's. Kolasinskiites, ten-thousand strong, were unrepentant in their support for their priest even though Bishop Foley had excommunicated them. Gradually, Foley developed better relations with many Catholic Polish leaders. Of necessity, pressed by Rome, he came to an uneasy peace with Kolasinski and his maverick congregation, and when Kolasinski met certain conditions for reconciliation Bishop Foley agreed to dedicate Sweetest Heart in 1894. On the surface, the dispute was resolved, at least in terms of meeting requirements of the church.

The *Michigan Catholic* had joined secular newspapers to deride and chastise the "poor simple-minded people" who supported Kolasinski.[56] Despite praise for the "better class" who supported the bishop, the reputation of the entire Polish community suffered. Few, if any, understood how complex the issues were. Polish supporters of Kolasinski, like those who called for his removal, had come to an "American" interpretation of their rights within the church. In Poland, wealthy individuals or families held the right to name their parish priest because they contributed so heavily to church support. In the United States, churches like St. Albertus were built by the work and contributions of most members. To them, they believed, belonged rights inherent in a democracy. To build, to pay, but to surrender title to a bishop or suffer the financial mismanagement of a priest seemed a particular injustice in such a democratic land.[57] Even at Sweetest Heart parishioners remained unwilling to turn over financial control to Kolasinski although many had earlier risked everything, including the rite of burial in consecrated ground, out of determination to support him. For years several trustees fought until, with the majority on their side, they took management of church funds from Kolasinski; all the while, parishioners still offered near-adoration to him as their spiritual leader.[58]

When all the events are aligned, it is apparent that disagreements in the Detroit Polish community had begun turning angry just a year after the Third Plenary Council. The Seventh Diocesan Synod met during the period when St. Albertus was still closed. The school board began examining teachers and visiting classrooms just when this large Polish parish was reestablishing its school. Many national Catholic spokesmen who were on the side of the Americanists saw the turmoil in Detroit as all the more reason to hasten assimilation. It seemed that here was reason for a common parochial school curriculum that would emphasize habits of democracy and citizenship as a prime goal. Advocates of pluralism saw, instead, the importance of maintaining ethnic schools and local parish control rather than risk more such publicized standoffs within the church; they argued the case for gradual assimilation.

Certainly, the worst fears of men such as Ireland and Gibbons were confirmed, for disruptions in the Polish community contributed to anti-

Catholic activists. But other factors piled on to fuel the backlash. Catholic opponents were reinvigorated by the specter of Irish and Germans, who were beginning to emerge from Catholic schools to join a rising middle class. The panic in 1884 and 1885 followed by the Depression of 1893 helped heighten prejudices against working-class immigrants. In 1893 the Polish community once more drew particular attention when a crowd of Polish laborers tried to force a road crew on Grand Avenue to lay down their shovels and give others a chance to work. Another scuffle between Polish workers and the Wayne County sheriff's deputies over piecework wages left three dead and several injured.[59]

ANTI-CATHOLICISM REINVIGORATED

Inopportunely, Rome's growing involvement in the debates between liberals and conservatives in the American church came at the same time Protestants were becoming more watchful of Catholic immigrants. To provide a presence and an interpreter on whom he could rely, in 1893 the pope sent Archbishop Francesco Satolli from Italy to live at Catholic University as a permanent delegate from the Vatican to the American church. Neither conservative nor liberal Catholics were pleased by the pope's effort to supervise American affairs more closely. Anti-Catholics were particularly displeased with what they saw as a dangerous attempt to retain influence over Catholics in a democracy where they might do damage as a voting bloc. By an overwhelming majority, Michigan voters passed a constitutional amendment in 1894 that disenfranchised aliens.[60]

Fertile ground for nativists, Michigan was a center of the American Protective Association almost from the time it was founded in Clinton, Iowa, in 1887. Members of the APA pledged never to vote for a Catholic or employ one when a Protestant was available; those who were in the working class agreed never to join with Catholics in a strike. The APA newspaper, the *Patriotic American,* was published in Detroit. Editor William Traynor was president of the state council and moved into the leadership post of the national APA based on his strong record in Michigan. The national secretary also lived in Detroit.[61]

Well-established enemies of the "Catholic influence" joined: men from the fraternal groups such as the Orange lodges, Patriotic Order of the Sons of America, and the Junior Order of American Mechanics.[62] Many APA members were Republican voters, often men who were influential in the Michigan Republican Party. Others who did not go so far as to join shared the same anti-Catholicism and helped forge a powerful minority bloc. Education, always a favorite focus among nativists, predictably turned out voters. The time was ripe to stress school issues within the political arena.

In Detroit the public school board was a waiting vehicle. Accusations of corruption had continued despite the board's restructuring through the introduction of at-large elections in 1881. And although both the *Free Press* and *Detroit Evening News* held firm for the advantages of the twelve-member, at-large board, the Republican state legislature reversed that arrangement in 1889. Now there was to be one school inspector from each ward. That did not help immigrants gain much influence because they were dispersed among so many of the city's wards and had disparate ethnic and religious interests. Immigrant causes could be overwhelmed by the more focused Protestant American vote. By 1891 Detroit voters elected a majority to the school board who were sympathetic to the American Protective Association.

Within a year, the majority ruled that teachers who had not received the whole of their education in public schools could not be hired. The board's action reflected the impact education was having within the Irish and German communities. Until the late 1880s most public school teachers were Protestant; meetings of the Michigan State Teachers Association provided an annual forum for speakers who attacked Catholics as enemies of the American school system.[63] But Catholic girls eager to be teachers were beginning to come forth from the new Catholic high schools or the public training programs. Because parochial schools depended almost entirely on nuns, the public system offered their only chance, a slim one. One letter to the *Detroit Journal* reflected an attitude shared by those who would block them: "I say there should not be a Catholic teacher allowed in our school under any consideration. Do you find one Protestant teacher in their schools?"[64] The board did back off from its extreme position to require, instead, that non-public school graduates must take a series of examinations in order to be considered for jobs.[65]

Protestantism was pervasive without any help from nativist zealots. Along with the teachers, those who held responsible administrative positions were Protestant by word, deed, and background. All three Detroit superintendents between 1863 and the turn of the century were rural or small-town, native-born Protestants. One, William E. Robinson (1886–97), was highly visible in the Masons and in several other Protestant fraternal lodges regarded as hostile by many Catholics.[66] All three superintendents remained above the acrimonious exchanges board members sometimes carried on with Catholics. Nonetheless, the superintendents helped identify the public schools as Protestant-led, and they accurately reflected public school constituents. Apart from a small group of intellectuals who advocated the genuine separation of school and state from religion, most public school parents were committed to the need for Bible-reading and moral education. If Detroit Protestants described the nineteenth-century public school as "our school," Detroit Catholics surely agreed with that assessment.

In return, Catholics opposed spending money on public schools. A committee of prominent Protestant Detroiters had taken on a two-year study of the free public high school in 1881. Predictably reporting in favor of it, they cited the service it provided to the working-class children as the "poor man's college."[67] Quite probably they were trying to counter Catholic critics. The *Michigan Catholic* editor, who stayed abreast of the committee's work, pointed out that children in working-class families had to leave school for jobs and wondered if perhaps publicly funded high school education benefited the children of the wealthy at the expense of everyone else. The same charge was made by the president of the Detroit school board in the mid-1890s when he complained it was a "class school" with "too many Fauntleroys."[68]

The *Michigan Catholic* also strongly opposed the move to provide public students with free books when that was proposed in 1890. The paper said Catholics were already providing a free education for others and should not have to buy books, too. Nonetheless, the board agreed to free books in 1892. In their demands for cost-cutting, Catholics were sometimes bedfellows with APA members and board conservatives who denounced "fads" and what they saw to be frivolous waste on class materials such as newspapers rather than sticking to the three R's.[69]

Charges that instruction costs were excessive were inaccurate. Low salaries and high class loads made the per-capita student cost in Detroit lower than for any city but Louisville.[70] The large number of Catholic students not educated at public expense contributed significantly to this low cost, of itself not a good sign about public schools. In fact, the sum of Protestant and Catholic educational decisions added up in the last decades of the century to an underfunded public system, schools which, according to the local press, had been "going to the dogs" for a generation. Intending variously to put an end to parochial schools or force more money from those who insisted on them, thirty-two of thirty-five members of the Michigan House of Representatives voted to tax churches and their institutions in 1892. It was a bill aimed principally against Catholic schools and might have succeeded had it not roused leaders in other religious denominations because of its effect on them.[71]

Established Catholics worried over the broad implications of all the animosity that was resurfacing. A few tried to win respectability, at least for themselves. John Atkinson, a prominent Catholic attorney, became an advocate of public schools, and the *Detroit Evening News* obligingly covered his opinions. In one front-page interview, Atkinson said that parochial schools made Catholics subject to prejudice and put them at social and economic disadvantage. Their separate education, he stated, made them unfamiliar to others in the community with whom they must do business, win elective office, or gain posts.[72] The *Michigan Catholic* was quick to point out that Atkinson had his political future most in mind. When he died, the paper noted that he had sent his children to parochial schools. Atkinson's arguments had not managed to persuade other prosperous middle-class Catholic leaders to support public schools, either. Holding their ground, Catholics began to see equilibrium return.

Various combinations within the electorate deflected bills that might have given anti-Catholicism more legislative force. In 1896, for example, when the Detroit school board went back to a long-dormant issue and ordered compulsory readings based on the Bible, influential German freethinkers, a prominent local rabbi, and several Protestant leaders helped defeat the issue by mustering those who were opposed to sectarianism in public schools. By the time the Michigan supreme court decided by a four-to-one majority in favor of the board, its book, *Readings from the Bible, Selected for Schools*, had already been recalled from classrooms and the texts were not used again.[73]

The Catholic middle class was sufficient in size and respectability that mainstream newspaper editors and politicians were reluctant, finally, to attack its members; moreover, once the depression waned, the general mood of hostility toward foreigners diminished. The APA failed to maintain momentum and went into a decline.[74] Locally, reformers within the Republican Party had begun to look for votes among Polish Catholics whom Democrats ignored or took for granted. Polish and German working-class voters helped Republicans elect the progressive Hazen Pingree mayor of Detroit in four successive elections between 1889 and 1895 and then governor of Michigan in 1896 and 1898. Republican reformers avoided the APA voters in their party, and immigrant Catholics were willing to ignore them, too, so long as Pingree supported lower street car fares, lower utility prices, and help for those hurt by the depression. Throughout this period, middle-class Irish and German Catholics continued to be committed Democrats with many representatives in leadership positions.[75] Nationally, Catholic leaders made the same type of deliberate choices and were often on opposite political sides. Bishop Ireland was a long-time Republican advocate, influential in the 1896 Republican platform and a supporter of McKinley. His friend and fellow Americanist Keane remained a staunch Democrat and advocate of labor organization.

Catholics did not fit into fixed or predictable categories within church politics either, despite all efforts to apply labels of "liberal" or "conservative," Americanist or pluralist. Some, then and later, interpreted Bishop Foley's acceptance of Kolasinski and Sweetest Heart parishioners as a defeat for Americanists. The Americanists were, and often still are, described as the church liberals, in part because they supported assimilation. Yet Kolasinski had ridiculed Dabrowski's Polish seminary as provincial. And Dabrowski, the ally of "reform" Bishop Borgess and Foley, an Americanist, was a leading champion of Polish language, culture, and parishes. The Felicians, with his tutelage, presented one of the most unwavering courses of Polish education offered in any of the nation's Catholic schools. The emphasis on ethnic rights and pluralism, seen as conservative in the late nineteenth century would, of course, be viewed very differently a century later. Similarly, the Polish Wars, which were portrayed as an example of foreign behavior, can instead be seen to be a sign of Polish immigrants' success as Americans. Sufficiently established as home and church builders, they had enough self-confidence to exert their demands and independence.

The Sum of It: Catholic Children in Parish Schools

There were incongruities in the debates behind all the closed doors, in the street brawls, and in nativists, reformers, and immigrants sharing the same political party. The anomalies spoke most of all to the conflicting self-interests, self-protective impulses, and misperceptions that defined the 1880s and 1890s. Children variously reaped gains or bore the brunt.

Americanists were defeated within the church in the years between 1895 and 1899. The pope's apostolic delegate to the United States shifted his support to the conservatives, their spokesmen were forced out of positions, and the American church turned to "bricks and mortar." Locally, it made little difference; Detroit Catholics had already made their decisions. Events of this era coincided to shape education with a finality that would hold sway for the next two generations.

Catholics of every nationality and class were confirmed in their determination to build schools alongside their churches. Because they had chosen also to continue a pattern of ethnic parishes, ethnic schools proliferated. By 1900 Detroit had six Polish parishes and six Polish schools. Catholics who were not Polish found this agreeable. Polish schools would help safeguard the principle of parochial education and yet make it unnecessary to share their own facilities or teaching sisters. With Polish children in separate schools, Irish and German children would not meet them to fight or marry.

Preoccupied with their own schools, Catholics were also distracted from Detroit school board politics. Accordingly, the Protestant-controlled board could proceed to ignore any needs of the new settlements at the outer wards of the city. Protestant voters, meanwhile, came to look more favorably upon parochial schools as a means to segregate immigrants and thereby protect their own children who attended public schools. With effects of the 1893 depression lingering, public school budget cuts reduced the 1896–97 school year to thirty-eight weeks, cut twenty-five teachers, and put a thousand children on half-day sessions.[76] It was clear that, at least in the short run, the self-supporting parochial schools kept the public system from a desperate financial quandary. By 1900 attacks on Catholic schools lessened and demands that immigrant children belonged within the "American" public schools quieted.

Although both bishops Borgess and Foley were convinced that Catholic children belonged in Catholic schools, they were able to give only intermittent attention to them. The diocese was growing so rapidly in numbers and complexity that they were preoccupied by administrative problems— staffing concerns, difficulties in some parishes between priests and parishioners, the "Polish problem," court battles over titles to church land, and challenges to their authority from the state legislature.[77] The bishops stood firm in their insistence on parochial schools, but it was up to the pastors to manage them and the parents to support them.

Parish priests, anxious to retain prerogatives, opposed a strong central diocesan school board and demanded the right to select teachers. Parents concurred with the need for Catholic education and proved willing to pay the price for parish schools. Both priests and parishioners usually shared a preference for a certain type of parochial school education and, toward that end, made deliberate choices among congregations of sisters when staffing their schools. Occasionally, they would decide to dismiss one group of nuns and invite another, but once the basic decision about teachers was made, most pastors and parents respected the sisters' authority except in such unusual episodes as the strife in the Polish community. More commonly, priests were preoccupied by the obligation to provide necessary sacraments for congregations that sometimes numbered several thousand souls; parents were harried by demands of families, homes, and earning money.

And so it worked out. During these decades of intense concern about Catholic education in the late nineteenth century, most Catholic children in Detroit went to ethnic parish schools when they went to school. In those schools, the education children received depended most of all upon their teachers.

5 Polish Parish Schools: The First Generation

> We are going to build a Poland here thus: a Pole who was born on
> American soil will never be like a European Pole, but we want him to
> be a Catholic believer, to speak Polish, to know Polish traditions and
> history, and for the rest let him be a Yankee.
> —Jan Barzynski, editor of *Pielgrzym* [The Pilgrim], to the vicar
> general of the Resurrectionist Order in Rome, 1872

WHEN fall came in 1887, the year the diocesan school board began examining teachers and visiting classrooms, groups of nuns prepared
for the returning rush of pupils. The three dozen IHM sisters in long blue
religious habits and black veils were a familiar sight when they arrived at
the train station and headed off for their six different parish assignments.
At about the same time, east-side children who lived around St. Mary's and
Sacred Heart passed the word that their sisters—the black-garbed School
Sisters of Notre Dame—were back from Milwaukee. Children in Polish
neighborhoods helped the brown-robed Felicians carry supplies from the
motherhouse to their three schools.

Among them, the IHM, Notre Dame, and Felician sisters would instruct
almost 5,500 of the 6,300 pupils who enrolled in the city's Catholic schools
that year. In common, the sisters would teach the seven sacraments, the basic
doctrines of the Catholic faith, and not to rest back against the pews when
kneeling at mass. In almost every other respect their classrooms were as distinctive as their blue, black, and brown habits.

As the number of parish schools in Detroit increased, Catholic education came to be less uniform. City historian Silas Farmer described the
physical appearance of parochial school buildings and tallied the number
of their scholars in his meticulous 1880s chronicle, but he did not dwell on
how different the school day was for children in one building compared to
another. Without reflection, he recorded that girls at St. Mary's "German
Schools" were "in charge of the Sisters of Notre Dame from Milwaukee,"
that at St. Vincent School "the female department was placed in charge of

the Sisters of the Immaculate Heart of Mary," and that St. Albert's school was "conducted by five Polish Franciscan Sisters."[1] Parents, pastors, and children—especially when they grew to adulthood—recognized the contrasts, however. And, customarily, they endorsed their experiences. Across the last decades of the nineteenth century, when Catholic schools alongside ethnic parishes became a significant and differentiating factor in Detroit, a Catholic education turned out to be, above all, what its teachers could plan, teach, and subsidize. Some children were more fortunate than others.

A generation of Polish children, many the first in their families to receive much education at all, began crowding into their parish schools by the late 1880s. Their numbers alone dramatically changed the scope of Catholic education in Detroit. By the turn of the century, the six Polish Catholic schools had a total enrollment of nearly five thousand. That meant that even before the auto industry brought a quick rush of new immigrants, almost 40 percent of the children in Catholic schools were Polish.[2] So, too, were most of their teachers.

The Felician sisters attained an early lead as the major educator of Detroit's Polish Catholics from the time they arrived at St. Albertus in January 1880. Closely associated with Father Dabrowski, they shared almost automatically in his reputation. His friends, like his enemies, were theirs. Ultimately, he had more friends than enemies in the Polish community; he also had the support of Bishop Borgess and, later, of Bishop Foley. By 1900, when the Felicians were staffing St. Albertus, St. Casimir, St. Josaphat, and St. Stanislaus, they were responsible for two-thirds of all Polish children attending Catholic school. Most other Polish children attended Sweetest Heart of Mary or St. Francis of Assisi under the tutelage of the School Sisters of St. Francis based in Milwaukee. Once again, as with the IHMs, a complicated skein of personal relationships among adults affected the education of thousands of Polish children, and the opinions and abilities of a few critically placed individuals had enormous impact.

FROM EUROPE TO AMERICA: THE FELICIANS' BACKGROUND

Dabrowski and the Felicians agreed from the beginning of their association that Polish culture and the Catholic religion that gave it meaning must survive among the immigrants. That premise brought priest and sisters together initially and provided the core of their educational program. Dabrowski had come to the United States and on to Wisconsin in 1870 to work among Polish immigrants. Missionary work was one of his few options, because he could not return to his home diocese of Warsaw after participating in the 1863 uprising against czarist Russia. When the failure of that insurrection ended his studies at the University of Warsaw, he moved on to the new Pontifical Polish College in Rome. He completed his education at the Pontifical Gregorian University and in 1869 was ordained for missionary work in America. Within a short time after emigrating, he wrote to the Felician superior in Cracow, the sisters who had arranged for him to bid farewell to his mother and brother at their convent. He asked them to help him again by sending teachers to educate Polish children in America.

The Felician community was not yet twenty years old at the time. Organized in Warsaw in 1855 by a few daughters of Polish professionals and wealthy landed gentry, their basic mission was to raise the level of education and morality among peasants.[3] Forced by czarist suppression to leave Warsaw, they reassembled in Cracow in 1865 and continued their work, aiding victims of the plague, the aged, sick, and orphans, as well as Polish revolutionaries. But they persisted in their initial purpose to improve the condition of the poor. Father Dabrowski's invitation to America expanded the opportunity. Mother Magdalen Browska, the superior general, sent off five sisters in 1874 to establish an American province in Dabrowski's rural Polonia, Wisconsin, parish.

Perhaps Dabrowski had observed that other immigrant groups found nuns to be a source of cheap labor in their schools. His strong convictions were undeniable, however. Throughout his life he would continue to believe, as he expressed to Mother Magdalen in 1874, that only a religious community of Polish origin could meet the needs of immigrants because "a foreign religious order . . . does not understand the spirit and traditions of the nation."[4] Most often in America the "foreign religious order" teaching Polish children was German in origin. As Dabrowski saw it, Polish immigrants faced something of the same struggle they had experienced in Europe, where their heritage, the "spirit and traditions of the nation," were at risk from outsiders' control. The Felicians shared his concerns. As Sister Monica Sybilska, named superior of the American province, reportedly reminded a less purposeful young nun years later, "Sister, remember it was for the Polish language that I crossed the ocean."[5]

Just as Dabrowski and the Felicians emigrated, Polish spokespersons in the Prussian sector were urging a fight against Germanizing campaigns to belittle Poles. They should remain proud, they were reminded, and demonstrate their superior abilities. One Polish-language newspaper in Kashubia challenged, "If you are a shoemaker make better shoes, if you are a blacksmith do a better job on the cart . . . if you are a Polish housewife make better and cleaner butter, have better vegetables, linen, fruit, and poultry than the Germans have. In this way you will save yourself and Poland."[6]

The same message served a purpose in Polish Catholic schools in America. Dabrowski and the Felicians would craft a curriculum grounded in their early dismay about German influence that threatened to overwhelm Poles not only at home but also within the American church. That unvarying, protective impulse would transfer almost automatically to a concern that Americanization threatened the Polish language and culture.

The five sisters who first emigrated to Wisconsin were the only European-trained and European-professed Felicians in the American congregation, but their ranks expanded by drawing from among American-born Polish women or by gaining women who emigrated specifically to join the Felicians in America. Between their arrival in 1874 and 1894, the year in which Mother Monica stepped down, the American province grew to 262. During those crucial formative years, the original core of sisters provided the link to the mother superior in Poland and to the goals of the European-based congregation. Felicans in America, even those who had never seen Poland, felt a heavy obligation to carry out daily duties in just the same manner as the sisters back home. Their missions, after all, were parallel.

The American-based sisters were continually reminded of their obligations and responsibilities in directives that arrived from Father Honorat Kozminski, their "spiritual director" in far-away Poland. A Capuchin assigned to the congregation when it originated in 1855, Honorat Kozminski dominated the women until his death in 1906. American Felicians, buffered by the ocean and supported by Father Dabrowski, who better understood the demands they faced, occasionally ignored his orders. But they had emigrated to reinforce the Polish religious culture in America, and the religious rule they followed belonged to that culture. For the most part, they agreed with Father Honorat's dictates and adhered to them. Honorat, charitably described as "authoritarian, narrow, suspicious, pessimistic and anti-intellectual," insisted that American Felicians follow a way of religious life so strict that it interfered with their effectiveness as educators.[7]

Mother Monica shared Honorat's rigid, self-abnegating approach to Catholicism. Her outlook was important because she was a key influence on the American province as a founder and superior from the outset to 1894. It was upon Father Honorat's suggestion that she had entered the congregation at the age of thirty-two when she found herself widowed. By the time she arrived in America, having accepted and fulfilled many difficult assignments, she was fifty and an experienced administrator who had firm convictions concerning the governance of a religious order. Her good qualities would be memorialized: She had "ceaseless energy," she was an independent thinker, and she feared no challenge. But she was also severe in judgment of others, unyielding, and irascible. Mother Monica viewed difficulty as punishment for sins; other sisters noted she thrived on "mortification," taking on extra fasts and bodily penance. As superior, she insisted on childlike obedience from the sisters and demanded that they expect the same from those under their charge. According to her view, all mortals should recognize themselves as sinners. Presumably, joy could wait until heaven, but, of course, redemption was never sure. Mother Monica's lessons were hard for the sisters she led and hard, in turn, when passed on to their students.

This style and philosophy were tempered by Mother Monica's assistant, Sister Cajetan Janiewicz (fig. 4), who was eventually to emerge from Mother Monica's shadow to become the most important figure, with Father Dabrowski, in the development of Felician education. Although equally rigor-

Figure 4. Sr. Cajetan Janiewicz was the most important woman in the development of the Felician sisters' schools. For more than thirty years she helped write texts, train teachers, and organize new schools in one Polish parish after another. (Archives of the Felician Sisters, Presentation of the B.V.M. Province, Livonia, Michigan)

ous about following the vow of poverty, Sister Cajetan was kind, gentle, and appreciative of others' good qualities. She would long be remembered as joyous about her work and faith yet haunted by feelings of inadequacy. Her lifelong lack of self-confidence and her belief that Mother Monica's harsh dislike of her was justified did not paralyze her effectiveness, however.

From the sisters' arrival in Wisconsin, Sister Cajetan took on the responsibility for school planning. Over the next thirty years she designed curricula and, alongside Father Dabrowski, wrote dozens of texts used in Polish schools throughout the United States. Raised in an affluent and cultured Warsaw family, she had already completed normal school training when she entered the convent at the age of twenty-nine in 1868. It was Sister Cajetan who traveled to each new Felician school to help it get underway, negotiating between parents, pastor, and sisters and then moving on once she had identified a sister to take over as principal. Long before she was named superior of the Detroit province in 1900, Sister Cajetan had become the woman most responsible for the form and content of Felician schools. Against formidable odds, she struggled to guarantee that teachers would be well prepared and would understand classroom management. Above all, she insisted they must remember that love was the most fundamental principle of education and the key to a child's heart.[8]

The other three of the original five Felician sisters had supporting roles. Sister M. Wenceslaus Zubrzycka, a cousin of Father Dabrowski, would work in America as a teacher, administrator, and superior at several parish schools and at a home for the aged until her death in 1923. Sister Vincentine Kalwa was the youngest of the group. Only twenty-three when she came to America, she took on various tasks such as housekeeping, almsraising, and some teaching. But she had hoped for a chance to do hospital service and, after fourteen years when the Felicians still could not offer that possibility, Sister Vincentine transferred to the Sisters of the Holy Family of Nazareth. The fifth member, Sister Raphael Swozenlowska, received her religious habit one day before leaving for America. Her religious name was bestowed deliberately in honor of Raphael, the patron saint of travelers. Sister Raphael took care of household duties in Wisconsin and then at the motherhouse in Detroit when the sisters transferred there. Both Sister Vincentine and Sister Raphael were members of the "second choir." In America as in Europe, Felicians were organized into two choirs, or classes. One choir consisted of those who governed, directed, and taught; in the other choir were the sisters who devoted themselves to domestic duties and manual labor. Together the five original immigrant sisters represented the variety of talents, attitudes, and roles that encouraged other young women to join them.

THE FELICIANS IN DETROIT

When the Felicians opened their school in Polonia, it was the first in America to be staffed entirely by Polish nuns. Polish priests across the nation began to request their help, but even the most enthusiastic parishioners could hardly equal the welcome that Michigan Polish Catholics gave the sisters. The day the train pulled into the Bay City station in 1878 to bring a little group of Felicians to their first school in the state, the parish band was waiting and entertaining an assembled crowd. Men, women, and children led the astonished sisters through the streets with "all the fanfare of a parade," and many people even fell to their knees in gratitude.[9] Within two years the Felicians agreed to send teachers to Detroit, which had an even more established Polish community centered around St. Albertus parish. From that time onward, the Felician congregation was integral to the education of the city's Polish Catholic children, and, in turn, Detroit's Polish community fostered the development of the Felicians.

St. Albertus parishioners had started their school in a house in 1872, the same year they established the parish. In January 1880, when Sister Cajetan and the three other sisters arrived, the school had an enrollment of 350. From the outset when seventy families founded St. Albertus as an alternative to continued attendance at the Germans' St. Joseph's parish, parents harbored the concern that also motivated the Felicians. They feared their children would soon become more German than Polish in a school where they associated with a German majority and had classes in the same language that was forced upon Poles in Europe. Delighted at the chance to have the Polish sisters at St. Albertus, parishioners had willingly agreed to provide a house, furniture, fuel, light, and a combined yearly salary of $720 for the women.

The earnest and substantial Polish community impressed a sympathetic Mother Monica. In the process of visiting Detroit to make arrangements for the Felician sisters to teach at St. Albertus, she came to believe, "If the Congregation will continue to exist in America, Detroit holds great promise for its future."[10] Soon she wrote to Cracow, asking permission to transfer the motherhouse from Polonia to Michigan's largest city. She offered convincing arguments: Detroit had a large and growing Polish population, a German bishop who was supportive of the Felicians, a climate less severe than Wisconsin that would be better for the ailing Father Dabrowski, and more priests who could help Dabrowski tend to the sisters' spiritual needs. The leaders in Cracow agreed to make Detroit their new American center.

With news that the motherhouse would be in Detroit, Polish families dug deeper into their precious wages and spare time. Other Detroiters,

Catholics and some who were not, came forth with money and building material. Dabrowski purchased land across the street from St. Albertus and contributed several hundred dollars from his own pocket for bricks to begin construction. An adjacent parcel of land was donated by the owner, a German, who wanted the sisters to be protected from any undesirable building that might have disturbed their convent life. The sisters did much of the fund-raising. Although the School Sisters of Notre Dame and the IHMs had their own rules against seeking alms, the Felicians did not hesitate to accept this practice as part of their religious obligation. Now, they traveled in pairs to Polish settlements during summer vacation to offer $1 certificates ("bricks"), which they had printed up. In return for each donation the sisters promised their prayers.

Ground-breaking took place, and the bishop blessed the convent with much ceremony on an October Sunday in 1880. A procession wound its way from Campus Martius at the center of the city eastward past the German churches, picking up their men's societies and church groups as it moved along to the Polish east-side neighborhood.[11] Within two years, fifty-seven postulants, novices, professed sisters, and the orphans for whom they cared had moved from Wisconsin into the completed three-story building that had a chapel, convent, novitiate, and orphanage. The Felician motherhouse was the first substantial Polish Catholic structure completed in the city. Almost upon completion it was overcrowded and additional wings were necessary. By 1897 the building had become twice its original size.

Father Dabrowski also took up permanent residence in Detroit, and upon settling in he proceeded with plans for his SS. Cyril and Methodius Seminary to train Polish priests. The seminary was two blocks down the street from both the motherhouse and the new St. Albertus church Father Kolasinski was just then beginning. Polish Catholics sent wood to heat the seminary, money to support it, and their sons to join it. By 1890 the Polish seminary enrolled sixty-five students, most of whom were middle-class Polish Detroiters.[12] The Felician motherhouse and the seminary gave Detroit a nationwide reputation as the center for Polish education, recognition that helped temper the concurrent bad publicity about the city's turbulent Polish community.

These institutions offered a permanence that encouraged incoming immigrants to settle in the neighborhood. In turn, the growing Polish population provided a ready supply of applicants for the seminary and convent while insulating the institutions from outsiders. For years, many women who became Felician sisters came from local families. Ninety of the 317 new candidates admitted to take vows between 1875 and 1900 were from Michigan.

Forty-seven were from Detroit, and most others came from Polish settlements in neighboring states. Only fifteen candidates arrived directly from Poland.[13]

The education of Polish children took form alongside the persistent dilemma that dogged Felician leaders. Given the nature of recruits who entered the convent, it was necessary to provide would-be teaching nuns with a basic elementary education even before they could be trained as teachers. At the same time, there was a desperate need for teachers in the Polish parish classrooms where enrollees multiplied so rapidly. Only if the Felicians refused to meet parish requests for teachers could incoming young postulants and novices remain at the motherhouse long enough to be educated sufficiently. Torn by internal conflict over this quandary, Felician leaders pressed on to do it all the best they could manage.

To increase the number of sisters so they could meet the need for them in elementary schools, Mother Monica began accepting girls into the convent even before they reached their teens, although that was counter to prevailing policy in Cracow. Most of those who joined the American Felician community after 1882 were fourteen or fifteen; a few were as young as nine.[14] They came usually from immigrant families recently out of German Poland. Their parents were of a lower class than the Felician leaders in either America or Cracow who had been educated by tutors and private academies in Europe. Sister Cajetan despaired over the shortcomings of girls she must shape into teachers. She wrote to the congregation's superiors in Poland and complained that the American candidates being admitted to the convent were daughters of immigrant peasants, unfamiliar "with the high culture of the upper class." They were "simple humble souls who couldn't even say their prayers."[15] In a rare criticism, Sister Cajetan also lamented that Father Dabrowski, "whose self-abnegation leaves him totally unsophisticated," was not much help in correcting the lack of refinement in prospective nuns.[16]

Many girls hoping to become teaching sisters arrived with only a rudimentary reading and speaking ability in the Polish language and none at all in English. Once within the motherhouse walls, nearly all the "aspirants" to the sisterhood needed to master elementary school lessons before proceeding to a secondary program or to the capstone normal school course. The quality of instruction in Felician-taught parish schools depended significantly—well into the 1920s—on the basic education provided for these young women in the motherhouse academy where they studied.

All the while disapproving of the admission of girls so unprepared, Sister Cajetan helped Dabrowski put together the curriculum for the academy. Studies in this motherhouse school evolved over the 1880s and began to take definite form during the mid-1890s. By that point, the twenty or twenty-five girls who came to join the congregation each year went either to a preparatory program designed for those who had not completed elementary school or to the secondary division. The secondary division had one level for beginners and another, which corresponded to the first two years of high school, for advanced students. From there the plan called for girls to proceed to the normal training program. By 1904 the Felician leaders were finally able to add a third year of high school, and in 1914 a fourth year (chapter 7).

The academy was available only to those girls planning to become Felician sisters. Apart from SS. Cyril and Methodius, where boys studied for the priesthood, it was the only secondary school in Michigan with instruction in Polish. For many years it was the most advanced secondary education program for Polish sisters available in the United States. Not until the turn of the century were other Polish religious congregations of women sufficiently organized to attempt such an institution as the Felician Academy.

Father Dabrowski insisted on hiring secular teachers for English classes at the academy so students might learn from "native Americans." The earliest records, dating from the end of the century, list two laywomen as English teachers and another who taught music. Two sisters and Dabrowski completed the faculty roster. One of those sisters must have received all but her very earliest education from Dabrowski himself, because she had joined the Felicians as a young girl while they were still in Polonia.[17]

Until his death in 1904, while also responsible for priests studying at the Polish seminary, Father Dabrowski was central to the Felician Academy's program of instruction. The young women sampled from the range of knowledge he had learned at the University of Warsaw, the Pontifical Polish College, and the Gregorian University in Rome. Academy lessons focused variously on church history, mathematics, physics, chemistry, natural history, botany, zoology, physiology, astronomy, hygiene, Latin, sacred scripture, liturgy, Polish literature, European and American history, and penmanship. Painting and drawing, vocal and instrumental music, drama, plain and fancy needlework, and good manners rounded out the program when there was time. The energetic priest introduced the young women to photography, book binding, and whatever other hobby occupied him at the moment.[18]

It seems likely that Dabrowski taught almost entirely in Polish. Students entered from Polish-speaking families, and English was a second language at best; too, there was little time to translate his own university lessons into English. His urgency to educate these "aspirants," whom he jestingly called "half-sisters," must have mandated lessons in their common language. Apart from their English classes, academy students probably had little occasion for using English within the convent walls. And even in the last years of the nineteenth century, when more girls came to the convent with English-speaking ability, a mother superior who spoke only Polish allowed only Polish in the convent. Apart from any English texts, she limited sisters to Polish in their leisure reading, which had to be from spiritual books.

Dabrowski offered instruction in Latin, and even if the sister-pupils could not understand the language of their church well they could absorb the basic dictate he repeated often: "Roma locuta, causa finita" (Rome has spoken, the case is closed).[19] It was a message to pass on to little children along with catechism lessons. There were no debatable issues in the church so far as they were concerned. Sisters and pupils should leave the serious matters to Rome and attend to their own tasks.

Most girls who entered the convent's academy were eager students, often regarded at home as the family bookworm. It was not unusual for children of Polish immigrants to make life decisions at an early age. Their earnings were essential to the family, their beds were needed by younger children, and their opportunities for prolonged reflection were rare. Girls understood that they would need to work before they could hope to set up housekeeping. Polish girls in Detroit went to work in higher proportions than any but Russian Jewish immigrant girls. By 1900, 56 percent of all Polish daughters aged twelve to twenty were at work. Once they married, they could anticipate a life of childbearing. Detroit's Polish women between the ages of twenty and forty-nine had a high fertility rate: 1,264 per 1,000 married Polish women aged twenty to forty-nine.[20]

The Felician Academy on St. Aubin Street represented a marked contrast to the lives their mothers, aunts, and married sisters led. Even the convent-prescribed clothing was appealing. Young women studying to become Felicians wore dark dresses, usually blue, with long sleeves and high collars covered by starched, crisp pinafores. Days in the academy were as predictable as the clothing. Studies, playtime, food, and work proceeded according to regular schedule. Nevertheless, there were moments of leisure that offered a chance to read, study, and pray. There were companions who shared their interests as well as the chores of ironing, scrubbing, cooking, and polishing. Still, convent life could be harsh and lonely. Girls were not permitted to go home once they arrived to join the sisters, but they could have visitors once a month. Of the 167 admitted to the academy between 1883 and 1890, 57 abandoned the program. The rest successfully completed their studies.[21]

Upon taking up life as a nun, girls became part of an educated professional elite. By the early twentieth century teaching sisters made up an estimated two-thirds of the professional workers in the Detroit Polish community.[22] Indeed, if a young Polish woman hoped for a career, the convent was one of her few avenues. Once married, she was expected and needed at home. Poles had the lowest percentage of married women in the work force.[23] Life as a permanently single working woman was an unfamiliar option, especially within the Polish immigrant family. A daughter called to a vocation in the church, however, was the answer to many a parent's prayers. Once young women advanced through the convent's stages, few left. Like sisters in many other religious congregations, most would spend their entire lives as teachers.

Girls who entered the Felician community might find themselves teaching very soon. The ideal program as outlined by Dabrowski and Sister Cajetan aimed to move girls from the academy to normal school training. After completing normal school they would spend another year studying for their religious vocation and practicing for their career by working under master teachers. But Dabrowski's eagerness to open schools for Polish immigrants undermined this plan almost from the beginning.

When he first asked sisters to join him, he alerted the superior in Cracow that Catholic schools in America must "be on par with the public schools" because, he warned, "the Protestants strive for a thorough education."[24] Before long, however, he was urging the superior in Poland and Mother Monica in Detroit to staff additional schools without delay. "I believe the Felicians are obliged to take these schools, if at all possible," he wrote in 1884, "since the well being of our people, the good of religion and the welfare of the community are at stake."[25] He grasped quite clearly that success in America was heavily influenced by education. "If the sisters must refuse schools, the young people move on to jobs, where in no time, these poor wretches are struggling for survival among the godless."[26]

At the time, his gloomy prediction about children moving into jobs was probably well founded for Polish children in Detroit. There was, after all, the shortage of classroom space in Detroit public schools, especially those in Polish neighborhoods. Furthermore, public schools were neither equipped nor willing to tend to special needs of Polish-speaking children. Even in Polish parochial schools, students usually studied for only a few years. Schooling was an expensive luxury when a child's wage could help meet pressing family expenses. At any rate, the general superior in Poland and the mother superior in Detroit agreed that the choice was Catholic school or no school for Polish children.

Intent on the need to "exert a good influence" as Polish and religious women, the decision makers in the Felician congregation chose to ignore dissent from some sisters who argued that incoming sister-candidates were not adequately prepared or sufficient in number to send off. Mother Monica refused to turn away any parish wanting help. Unlike a diocesan congregation such as the IHMs, Felicians were not limited to one geographical area. By the early 1890s they were staffing thirty-eight schools from Massachusetts to Wisconsin. Between 1894 and 1900 they added fourteen more institutions including orphanages and a temporary shelter for immigrants in New York City.

That meant that the most able girls must be rushed into classrooms. Confronted by their own problems, pastors sometimes betrayed less concern for a sister's educational qualifications than for her presence. As one bluntly wrote, "Mother, you have no idea how effective the habit is in managing school children and in correcting their bad behavior." He wanted the superior to send a sister, "Even if she's yesterday's candidate dressed in religious garb."[27] In the worst situation, the superior would call forth the tallest girl from the academy, equip her with the habit and "bonnet" (a postulant's white-veiled headdress), and send her off to handle a classroom of seventy or eighty children only a few years younger than the sudden teacher.[28] It was an emergency, the superior would assure the disapproving Sister Cajetan. Her response to "emergencies," along with her continual acceptance of new schools, created constant tension in the motherhouse over teacher preparation.

Necessarily, Dabrowski and Sister Cajetan set aside their ideal program and revised the course of study to fit into vacation weeks and Saturdays to accommodate those whose educations were interrupted by teaching assignments. There was little time for educational philosophy, detailed training in methodology, or practice under a master teacher. Most Felicians were teaching before they had completed even the abbreviated two-year high school course.

Meanwhile, bishops insisted on Catholic schools and pressed teacher training on nuns. Yet because the Third Plenary Council decreed that each religious community should establish its own normal school to upgrade teacher quality, the church hierarchy unwittingly compromised the effectiveness of teacher-training programs that emerged. Following the bishops' dictate, each group of nuns developed a separate program isolated from other congregations. There was duplication of resources and effort; worse, there was neither sharing of ideas nor healthy external criticism. The bishops expected new diocesan school boards to make sure that standards were set and met, but Detroit's board—one of the few actually established—quickly fell short of its own ambitions.

The most lasting thrust of the Detroit diocesan board was the examination and certification of teachers. When the board initiated examinations for all teachers in the diocese who had less than five years' experience before August 19, 1886, the stipulation had special significance for the Felicians. Few of them had been teaching for five years before 1886, so few were protected from examination. As a papal community, the Felicians were not responsible to local bishops, nor were they clearly bound by diocesan regulations on matters such as teacher certification. Nonetheless, community leaders in Poland agreed with those in Detroit that every effort must be made to meet local requirements.

Worried sisters hurried back from parish convents to spend Saturdays and vacations studying in the motherhouse alongside the young academy girls. Dabrowski brought professors from the Polish seminary down the street and hired the superintendent of adult education in Detroit to provide lectures. In the first round of testing in 1888, fifty-four Felician sisters received certificates. Most qualified for the lower primary level. With nearly two hundred assigned to classrooms, many had yet to meet even the minimal standards. Because Detroit was one of the few dioceses that did put examinations into effect, it surely must have occurred to harried and pragmatic superiors to assign the less qualified teachers to Felician schools in other states.

A Divided Polish Catholic Community and Education

While they grappled with the need to educate their sisters, the Felicians had to deal also with the turmoil in Detroit's Polish community. They found themselves target of verbal abuse and physical threats once the bishop removed Father Dominic Kolasinski as pastor of St. Albertus and replaced him with Father Dabrowski. But like Dabrowski, the sisters did not waver from their intended mission. After all, Felician sisters—including Mother Monica—had been driven from Warsaw by state politics. They had persevered in Polonia, Wisconsin, even though Dabrowski's church had been set on fire and local Polish tavern-keepers had tried to kill him with gunpowder put in hollowed logs amid his woodpile because he changed the site of the parish church to a location distant from their businesses.[29] In a separate event, their Polonia convent caught fire accidentally, and so they built another. Not easily intimidated or discouraged, they now held their ground in Detroit.

In the period from December 1885 through 1887 during the Polish Wars, children whose parents were in the "loyalist" Dabrowski faction attended classes wherever the Felician sisters could reassemble them.[30] At first, with St. Albertus church and school closed, the children studied at the motherhouse. When the Polish seminary opened in December 1886, some children collected there in a part of the third floor set aside for them.

Identified as they were with Dabrowski, the sisters became targets of the opposing parish faction who were incensed all the more by Kolasinski's charge that Dabrowski wanted control of St. Albertus parish funds to defray motherhouse building debts.[31] Although money was always a concern for the sisters, the official Felician history would later maintain they were not in debt at that time. Most likely, Kolasinski was using this charge as one more means to rally allies, but the sisters remained suspect in the eyes of some Polish families for years.

By one account, as many as five thousand men, women, and children stayed loyal to Kolasinski. Kolasinski himself placed the number of families at just under three thousand.[32] Kolasinskiites were distinguished principally by their strident demands for parish autonomy; Kolasinski also had more supporters among the poor and working-class immigrants than did Dabrowski. Certain of his advocates pointed to these distinctions, convinced that a "class of men . . . got the ear of the bishop."[33] But the controversy brought bad blood in many families, with "husband and wife, father and son, brother and sister" divided against each other.[34] On each side, men and women were willing to fight bishops or priests, neighbors or nuns; they were determined to do whatever it took to retain a say in the parish institutions for which they paid.[35] In one episode during the summer of 1886, Kolasinskiites turned on the motherhouse. Dabrowski was in Europe and the bishop lived many blocks away, so with those primary foes out of reach the Felicians were a convenient symbol. Individuals in the angry street crowd hurled threats at the sisters and stones through the windows of their orphanage.[36] Children learned that nuns did not command automatic respect when certain issues were at stake.

Children whose parents were in the Kolasinski faction went to a school their elders set up in a large frame house at Riopelle and Canfield about two blocks down the street from St. Albertus. No records remain from the earliest days, but the school began perhaps in March 1886, within four months after the bishop closed St. Albertus school. By August 1886, when the academic year started again, there may have been nearly two hundred children at the counter-school, and by 1888 the number had grown to four hundred.[37]

The teacher at this new school was Anton Dhugi. He was a man deep into intrigue during the controversy, castigated by the *Michigan Catholic* as "cunning and wicked" and described in the Detroit secular press as "ringleader of the Kolasinskiites."[38] Dhugi was of uncertain education and background. He may have been a blacksmith in Poland; perhaps he was a lay Jesuit who had been rejected by that order. In the United States only a few years, he was almost illiterate even in his native language, yet he was the principal and often the only teacher in the alternative school. On Sundays in the schoolhouse Dhugi led the Kolasinski faithful in hymns, prayers, and the rosary as a substitute for Sunday mass. Critics charged that he made a handsome sum as a schoolmaster and from Sunday donations.

Dhugi was initially a confidant and champion of Kolasinski. Once the priest returned in December 1888 to reclaim his flock, however, the two headstrong men came into conflict. Amid more public quarrels and notoriety, Kolasinski, Dhugi, and various other parties sued each other in court. In May 1889 Dhugi finally left town, forfeiting bail on the remaining charge that he had seduced and impregnated one of his students upstairs in the schoolhouse.[39] With Dhugi gone, once again school children necessarily shifted to other arrangements.

Some may have enrolled in the Campbell Public School, the neighborhood school on St. Aubin just two blocks south from St. Albertus. It opened in 1874, six years before the Felicians arrived at St. Albertus. Campbell, despite its cupola and two large wooden front doors, was not nearly so impressive as most public schools built or rebuilt in other city neighborhoods during the 1870s and 1880s.[40] The curriculum followed the standard Detroit public school pattern, providing reading, language, arithmetic, geography, spelling, history, government, drawing, music, and writing.[41] The faculty was standard, too; none of the teachers at Campbell spoke Polish. Enrollment did not keep pace with the parochial schools. However troubled the Polish community might be, most parents elected to have their children educated in Catholics schools or not at all.

During these difficult years the Felicians scrambled to do the best they could with children placed under their charge. They shifted loyal St. Albertus pupils to the motherhouse or on to the Polish seminary. Meanwhile, they staffed St. Casimir's school on the west side from its opening in 1883. Between 1885 and 1886 they taught at the small Bohemian parish of St. Wenceslaus and then added St. Josaphat's school to their responsibilities in 1890. Children at each of these parishes had the same course of study that Sister Cajetan and Father Dabrowski had outlined for their first school in Wisconsin in the mid-1870s. Sister-principals either followed or tinkered with the plan, depending on who was available to teach. The challenges were extraordinary.

DEVELOPING POLISH PARISH SCHOOLS

St. Albertus had just reopened in the summer of 1887 when the new school board visited as part of its first examination of diocesan schools. "Under the circumstances," the board acknowledged, student performances "were not unsatisfactory." But the wooden school building was "not very good," and the school had no maps or charts. Compared to other parishes at the time, St. Albertus parochial enrollment statistics were sharply imbalanced. St. Albertus school had 342 pupils, but 550 Catholic children from the parish were in "non-Catholic" schools. Quite possibly a number were in the renegade school that Dhugi was teaching, which the board did not recognize or visit. The report, dated December 31, 1887, charitably anticipated that, "Within a year, however, a very decided change for the better may be expected throughout the School."[42] Two years later when the examiners returned they again had to make allowances for the sisters and their pupils: "Considering the circumstances and difficulties with which the Congregation had to contend, we can say, that the Knowledge is satisfactory, and after having overcome the obstacles, this school shall reach to a high standpoint of learning." The priest-examiners did not hesitate, nonetheless, to label St. Albertus pupils' knowledge only "satisfactory" rather than awarding the "good," "very good," or "very satisfactory" ratings customary for most schools.[43]

There were problems also with educational progress at St. Casimir's. The pastor, Paul Gutowski, was a recently added member of the school board, and his west-side parish was geographically removed from the factional troubles burdening St. Albertus. Smaller than the St. Albertus congregation, St. Casimir's managed to enroll 450 pupils. Father Gutowski reported that only three children in the parish attended non-Catholic schools in 1887.[44]

But the school had weaknesses that the examiners could not overlook. The visitors were willing to admit there might "be occasion of excuse" for "the irregularity of attendance" because children had to come from a distance and the school suffered from a "want of sufficient room of accommodation." Even allowing for that excuse, students "did not meet the expectation." It was also the one Detroit parochial school in which discipline was rated just "satisfactory" rather than "good" or excellent." The Felician sisters at St. Casimir's were charged with blame, because "a deficiency of proper knowledge of Pedagogic showed its bad effect."[45] It was the only negative comment about teachers in the entire report on diocesan schools.

Board members made little note of the wide range in class size from one parish school to another, nor did they comment on the effect class size might have had on learning. In the late 1880s St. Casimir's school was in a building that also served as a church. Eight to ten children jammed into desk seats meant to accommodate four. At one point, eighty children were without seats until a parishioner's complaint prompted Father Gutowski to purchase more desks. Still, the building was crowded beyond expansion, and for two years during the 1890s groups of students went to school in the partitioned parlor of an adjacent small house. The house was being built by Father Gutowski's sister, and at his request she agreed to make rooms temporarily available for the children.[46] Whether they lived in the large east-side Polish community or on the western edges of Detroit, Polish school children spent their days trying to learn in an environment of uncommon physical hardship.

As new parishes and schools were added, they only duplicated these conditions for the ever-increasing population of immigrants rather than alleviating persistent problems. Mother Monica committed the Felicians to St. Josaphat's parish when the bishop insisted on organizing it, and she sent four sisters to start the school year in 1890–91.[47] In 1898 the Felicians also agreed to take on St. Stanislaus once the school was opened. Soon after the turn of the century, nearly 2,800 children studied at the four Felician schools in Detroit. The faculty for those schools totaled only forty.[48]

The strain took its toll on the women, and, beleaguered, they sometimes turned on each other. In addition to the external problems in the Detroit Polish community, Felicians battled among themselves over educational philosophy, enforcement of their congregational rules, issues of authority, and their relationship to leaders back in Cracow. Personality and power struggles were especially bitter. Always at odds with Mother Monica, Sister Cajetan went back to Poland in 1890 when Mother Monica began her last four-year term as superior. Then in 1894, reinvigorated by her observations in Europe and supported by a new Detroit superior, Sister Cajetan returned to resume her work. She and Dabrowski revised the plan developed twenty years earlier in Wisconsin. All Felician schools would henceforth use this new curriculum until the next revision came in 1913.[49]

As it had earlier, both the school curriculum and the Felician normal school program remained an amalgam of conservative Catholic European influences and American educational expectations. Polish children in Detroit's parochial schools faced a wide array of classes in two languages. The 1894 plan prescribed that children in their first year of school were to use English for reading, spelling, arithmetic, verses, and composition. As they advanced to the later grades, they were also to use English in geography, nature study, American history, and government. Through grade seven, Polish was the language for catechism, Bible history, poetry, church history, literature, Polish history, art, and music. Students were expected to write compositions in Polish at every grade through the sixth. Only by grade eight would all instruction be in English.[50] But the fact was that Polish parish schools did not extend beyond grade six. St. Albertus did not graduate an eighth-grade class until 1908.

Given the range and number of courses in the Polish language, it was continually a problem to find appropriate texts. Set on their course, Dabrowski and Sister Cajetan tapped a few other sisters to help write, compile, and print their own books. Between 1877 and 1904 the community published forty-five texts for use in their own schools and for sale to other customers. Most were entirely in Polish. The solution to one problem exacerbated another. More than thirty years after she started preparing the first generation of Felician teachers, Sister Cajetan found it necessary to remain vigilant about the sisters' lapses into Polish. At noon intermission, she remonstrated, and "always during the school children's English class," sisters must remember that "the English language is to be used."[51] The scoldings did little to modify the basic problem. As late as World War I, most children arrived in school rooms able to speak only Polish, and many sisters remained more fluent in Polish than in English.

When the Felicians and Dabrowski initiated the practice of writing their own texts, Bishop Borgess authorized the endeavor. Bishop Foley apparently continued the habit of approval even though he sided with Minnesota's Bishop John Ireland and the other Americanists in favor of acculturation.[52] Both Borgess and Foley were concerned about alienating Polish Catholics for fear of lending support to the local dissidents. Because Dabrowski was their firm and best clerical ally on that front, perhaps the bishops pragmatically although grudgingly accepted the ethnic-language texts. For Polish school children, the course of study inevitably set them farther apart from parochial and public school children who were learning from English texts, but it preserved for them the language and culture their elders valued.

POLISH SCHOOLS AND THE SCHOOL SISTERS OF ST. FRANCIS

At the same time Felician schools were implementing their revised curriculum, another congregation of nuns was gaining a foothold in the education of Detroit's Polish children. When St. Francis of Assisi parish school opened in 1892, the School Sisters of St. Francis came from their Milwaukee motherhouse to staff it. Priest and parishioners, on Kolasinski's side during the diocesan conflict, preferred this congregation of women over the Felicians even though the School Sisters were predominantly German.

Kolasinski's Sweetest Heart of Mary parish made the same choice. When its new two-story brick building opened in August 1894, five School Sisters of St. Francis took charge of the pupils. From the Sweetest Heart tower, a new bell chimed over the neighborhood, summoning parish children from along the same blocks as St. Albertus school four blocks east of Sweetest

Heart and St. Josaphat, three blocks west. Sweetest Heart's congregation had doubled since the late 1880s to reach nearly ten thousand by the mid-1890s. In the first fall, five hundred children enrolled in the parish school; the following year Sweetest Heart's school had eight hundred.[53] Although many in the congregation were new to the city, old animosities prevailed. Parishioners appreciated the uneasy reconciliation, just effected, between Kolasinski and Bishop Foley because it brought them back within the rites of the church and diocese, but neither priest nor parishioners wanted Dabrowski's Felicians at their school. Between them, by the turn of the century, St. Francis of Assisi and Sweetest Heart enrolled nearly two thousand Polish children, all studying with the School Sisters.[54]

The School Sisters of St. Francis were a German order founded in Wisconsin in 1874, the same year the Felicians arrived in Polonia. The community had originated with three women who emigrated when Bismarck's Kulturkampf closed convents. They stayed for a while in Milwaukee with the German School Sisters of Notre Dame and then organized their own separate congregation when a German priest invited them to staff his parish school forty miles north of Milwaukee. Like the Notre Dame Sisters, they were committed to preserving the German language and culture along with the Catholic religion. They agreed to staff the one- and two-room schools that were opening alongside new rural Wisconsin German parishes. Girls from small towns began joining the convent, and others came from Germany with that intent. Demand for the sisters' services quickly outpaced their numbers. Confronted by the same kind of dilemma the Felicians faced, the School Sisters' superior, Mother Alexia, made the same decision as the Felicians and rushed her newcoming sister-candidates to the classrooms.

The School Sisters of St. Francis located their motherhouse in Minnesota, but once there they came under Bishop Ireland's purview. He attempted to bring them into line with his notions, insisting they must stop accepting postulants from Germany, must teach English in their schools rather than German, and must train their teachers adequately. Determined that the community should make its own decisions, Mother Alexia withdrew from Minnesota and moved her headquarters to Milwaukee, where the bishop agreed with her commitment to the German culture and the population of Germans was large enough to occupy the School Sisters of St. Francis as well as the School Sisters of Notre Dame. Meanwhile, the Polish population in and around Milwaukee was growing rapidly, and School Sisters of St. Francis began teaching in several large Polish parishes. Polish girls from their classrooms joined the congregation. By the turn of the century there were nearly seven hundred School Sisters of St. Francis, and likely eighty or ninety of them were Polish.

Most of these girls were born in Poland and had recently come to the United States with their parents. As in the case of the Felicians, girls joined the School Sisters' congregation when they were quite young. Often the aspirants had only a weak grasp of Polish and wrote little or no English. They were probably little different in this regard from young German girls entering the convent. Rejecting admonishments of men such as Bishop Ireland, leaders rushed postulants and novices out to meet the need for more teachers. By 1900 the School Sisters of St. Francis were staffing ten Polish schools, and nearly seventy of their sisters who were Polish were in classrooms.

The superior tapped those she identified as the best in the congregation to take on administrative responsibilities. Both St. Francis of Assisi and Sweetest Heart acquired Polish principals as well as Polish teachers.[55] Well aware of the volatile situation in Detroit's Polish community and the aggressive personalities sisters might encounter there, the mother superior carefully considered strength of character as well as a sister's Polish heritage when she made teacher placements. It is not surprising, therefore, that three sisters at Sweetest Heart became leaders once Polish nuns asserted independence from the School Sisters of St. Francis to form the Sisters of St. Joseph congregation in 1901.

One of the women first assigned to Sweetest Heart, Sister Mary Boleslaus, played a significant role in shaping and enforcing educational practices among the School Sisters of St. Francis. She would also be influential upon the Sisters of St. Joseph. Children studying with either the School Sisters of St. Francis or the Sisters of St. Joseph were shaped according to three basic aims. The "end in view" of education, as Sister Boleslaus enunciated it, was first to plant the "seed of solid virtue and religion," which would "guide the children on the way of salvation." Second, children should learn "the science that will be most useful to them." Finally, education should train children "so that they will not only be good Christians and law-abiding citizens themselves, but be able to inspire others with a love for all that is true, noble and good."[56] For years, there seems to have been no detailed plan that might have elaborated on how to accomplish those aims. Equipped, presumably, with no more and no less than personal determination, knowledge, and understanding of the faith, sisters set about doing what they knew they must.

Like the Felicians, sisters at Sweetest Heart and St. Francis of Assisi found it a considerable strain to keep up with their religious obligations while attending to teaching responsibilities. School Sisters of St. Francis spent Sundays learning basic practices of religious life. They passed entire evenings all week long in a common study hall or community room under the ever-present principal, who was also their convent superior. While she watched mistrustfully, insisting on proper attention to their studies, the sisters poured over academic subjects together. One year the major focus was on Polish grammar, because few of the sisters were literate in the language they had learned at home from parents who had themselves emigrated with little education. In another year the emphasis was on arithmetic. Yet another time they took up nature study with books borrowed from a helpful professor at the Polish seminary. After class each night came one more hour spent planning the next day's lesson for pupils. If there was time for it, sisters could read approved religious books, but newspapers and periodicals, like other contacts with the world, were forbidden.[57] This meant that any practical application of issues of the day could not be brought into their classrooms. It is likely that the sisters did not know that teaching "current events" was a hotly debated point of pedagogy among public school teachers, administrators, and parents, with advocates of the three R's insisting that the issues of the day and newspaper reading certainly did not belong in the classroom.

Young teachers learned by example from older sisters, who had usually acquired what pedagogy they knew on their own through experience. If a school could spare the principal from a class assignment, she rotated through the building, helping novices with lesson plans and taking over classes so the young teachers could observe. Students and teachers alike learned select lessons, depending upon the superior's particular concerns. In some years penmanship in the Palmer Method was stressed; at other times the emphasis might be on mental mathematics. Given the obstacles created by crowding, large class sizes, and the transient immigrant children, discipline was always a major priority. Students were expected to obey rules without question; order was demanded when they walked to and from church and also inside classrooms. The principal did not hesitate to step in when she decided a teacher was too lax or incompetent.

Sweetest Heart and St. Francis of Assisi parents approved of discipline. It was one facet of the "good Catholic education" that would provide their children with "an antitoxin" to the dangers they faced "amidst people belonging to diverse denominations."[58] They approved also when the sisters in their parishes took a determined stand on behalf of their Polish heritage.

A New Polish Sisterhood: The School Sisters of St. Joseph

Almost every year one or two girls from Detroit decided to join their teachers permanently by entering the School Sisters of St. Francis. As the number of girls entering from Polish parishes grew, friction in the congregation increased. Polish sisters complained among themselves that they were treated like second-class citizens by the German-speaking sisters who began, ran, and constituted the majority of the School Sisters' congregation. The aggrieved minority charged that German sisters belittled the Polish culture, making them feel inferior and undesirable. They felt singled out to take on domestic work, especially once the School Sisters opened a sanatorium in Milwaukee. Polish girls reported to their priests and parents back home that they were forbidden to speak in their native language and that German sisters reminded them that many had come to the convent without the customary dowry. They were told the sanatorium would be disgraced if patients knew the School Sisters of St. Francis included Polish women. The girls' parents and Polish priests were sympathetic to their tribulations, agreeing that vows of obedience surely did not mean anyone must take such treatment.

Ethnic friction came to a head when six young women from the Polish parish in Stevens Point, Wisconsin, objected to household assignments in the sanatorium. Thereupon the mother superior, Sister M. Alfons, sent them home. Stevens Point priest Luke Pescinski inquired into the affair, and an irate father sent two angry letters. Sister Alfons responded that the girls were not intelligent enough for teaching but would not accept appropriate duties so there was no place for them in the School Sisters of St. Francis.

The Polish sisters' perceptions of prejudice against them were likely well founded. Yet if the congregation's statistics for that era are accurate, at least seventy of the eighty or ninety St. Francis sisters of Polish descent were teaching and only a small group had other duties.[59] Between 1892 and 1907 it was common for the congregation to send unprepared girls, both German and Polish, to teach. The situation involving the six girls from Stevens Point happened, however, against a backdrop of the School Sisters' refusal to staff parishes on demand, a refusal that harried Polish priests had already come to view as discriminatory.

Animosity was compounded when, after dismissing the girls who wanted to be teachers, Sister Alfons notified Father Pescinski that she did not have enough teachers for his Stevens Point school. "Although it grieves me," she wrote, "I am compelled to inform you that on account of a lack of Polish sisters we are unable to staff your school next year."[60] Withdrawing School Sisters was a tactic she used frequently when parishes failed to meet her conditions or caused her aggravation. Between 1874 and 1903 the School Sisters of St. Francis withdrew from nearly half the schools they accepted.[61] Annoyed with the Stevens Point priest and parishioners who questioned her judgment, the mother superior was again asserting her prerogative to decide where her sisters would teach.

It was one more affront to Polish parishes and not to be ignored, a group of pastors decided. After all, the six Stevens Point girls were eager for the chance to teach, and other Polish sisters still within the congregation were also dissatisfied over their treatment. The course of action seemed evident to Father Pescinski, and, after consulting other Polish priests, he concluded that a new community of Polish sisters was necessary.

Stevens Point belonged to the Green Bay rather than the Milwaukee diocese, and Green Bay's Swiss German bishop supported Pescinski even though it put him at odds with a long-time conservative ally, the bishop of Milwaukee, who did not approve of plans for a new religious community. Each bishop was anxious to secure a pool of teachers, and the Milwaukee diocese stood to suffer if Polish women seceded from the School Sisters of St. Francis congregation based there. Complicated and often bitter negotiations went on among bishops, priests, representatives of Rome, and members of the School Sisters of St. Francis. Even before agreement was reached, forty-six Polish sisters and novices separated from the School Sisters in the summer of 1901 to form the new Sisters of St. Joseph.[62] Their motherhouse was in Stevens Point, and Father Pescinski became their spiritual director.

Priests and a few sisters from Detroit's Sweetest Heart and St. Francis of Assisi parishes formed the inner circle involved in starting the new congregation. Bishop Foley apparently left the decision to the sisters who were faced with the need to make individual decisions about community allegiance. Kolasinski had died three years earlier. The new Sweetest Heart priest, also Polish, appealed to the sisters' "Polish hearts," stressing the new congregation was important for the souls of Polish children. Eleven of the twelve sisters at Sweetest Heart joined the group of forty-six who launched the Sisters of St. Joseph. After some hesitation, the twelfth sister canceled her signature and chose to remain with the School Sisters. She was the homemaker-sister at Sweetest Heart, and it did not matter to her, she explained, whether she washed Polish or German pots and pans. She wanted only to be at peace and so returned to Milwaukee.[63]

Angry because the priest at St. Francis of Assisi had demonstrated support for the new congregation, the School Sisters' superior wielded her customary weapon and announced she was withdrawing her nuns from his parish. Hastily, three of the new Sisters of St. Joseph traveled across town from Sweetest Heart to sit prominently in a front pew at mass, where previously the School Sisters had been a familiar fixture. Their presence reassured parents who had preferred even German School Sisters of St. Francis to the Felicians. By the time the school year began, reinforcements had arrived. In the fall of 1901 St. Francis of Assisi had a superior, seven teaching sisters, and one candidate. Sweetest Heart had a faculty of the same size. Parents and pastors were delighted with their "exclusively Polish religious congregation."[64]

With 850 children enrolled at Sweetest Heart, it was the city's largest Polish parish, but the new congregation of women was determined not to shortchange either of their Detroit schools. Despite being shifted from one congregation's teachers to the other, the children found sisters who, to their eyes, looked exactly as they had the school year before. Their school day, like the course of study, remained much the same also. To mark their difference from the black-robed School Sisters of St. Francis, the St. Joseph sisters simply added two knots to the five in the white Franciscan cords worn around their waists. Those seven knots honored the seven joys and sorrows of their patron, St. Joseph.[65]

Despite their stable facade the teachers felt under severe strain. In October of their first year as a new congregation, Bishop Sebastian G. Messmer from their home diocese of Green Bay and Father Pescinski from Stevens Point traveled to Detroit when a "distressed sister" wrote they were suffering criticism for separating. Old hostilities were still determining attitudes within the immigrant community. To supporters of Dabrowski and the Felicians, the defection of sisters at Sweetest Heart provided just one more instance of typical rebellion in that parish. Some accusers claimed the St. Joseph sisters had joined the Independents in the schismatic Polish National Church. St. Joseph Sisters reported receiving telegrams, letters, and messages "from all sides." To the end of her life one recalled the public reaction in Detroit, where "we were spared neither slander, criticism, nor innuendoes."[66]

Children, on whose behalf a disciplined, Catholic Polish education was intended, felt free on occasion to taunt nuns. On one outing teachers and children from Sweetest Heart were riding in open streetcars past St. Albertus when several parish children in the street grabbed up mud and leaves and hurled the filth at the group. Mockingly, they called out, "Kolachy, Kolachy! [Kolasinskiites] The Independents are riding by!" Sweetest Heart pupils screamed back, "Dombruchy! Dombruchy!" [Dabrowskiites].[67] The old conflict of seventeen years' standing had become part of the new generation in the new century.

Other familiar dilemmas dogged the just-established Polish congregation. As with the Felicians, almost immediately there were more requests for their services than there were sisters to send out. The sisters they did have often lacked even basic skills in language, science, and mathematics. In general, the Polish sisters within the School Sisters of St. Francis were young. Of the original "pioneers" who left to start the St. Joseph community, about half were under twenty-five. The community experienced rapid growth by quickly taking in eager young girls from Polish parishes; accordingly, the task of educating the would-be teachers was beyond available resources. The community that started with forty-six young women in 1901 had 183 members teaching in twenty-three parishes by 1908. The congregation more than doubled soon again. By 1917, 406 sisters staffed forty-three parishes in nine states as far-flung as Connecticut and Texas. One young woman went to Stevens Point to join the convent on a Saturday in October 1901 and by Monday was standing dressed in a borrowed habit before a class of sixty children.[68]

As had Dabrowski, Father Pescinski intended to provide well-prepared teachers for Polish schools. At the outset he ambitiously anticipated that St. Joseph candidates "will apply themselves to study for three years to be educated adequately for teaching." He planned to have them attend English classes at the normal school in Stevens Point and study the Polish language "under qualified and cultured teachers from the old country."[69] For years his ideals went unrealized. Father Pescinski had neither time nor background to take on a program of instruction like the one Father Dabrowski initiated for the Felicians. Pescinski was tireless, but he was trained to be a parish priest and his higher education was limited to the Milwaukee seminary where he studied in the 1870s. Nor was anyone in the St. Joseph congregation adequately prepared to take on the task of teaching incoming sisters. As a first step, three young women aged fourteen, fifteen, and sixteen were sent to study at the Stevens Point normal school to get ready for the task of training others. Meanwhile the sisters relied "happily" on the comfort that some women were "born teachers," a notion common within American society generally.[70]

Sacrifices and Privations

Across the last decades of the nineteenth century and well into the twentieth, Polish Catholic school children learned lessons, habits, and values from teachers who gave their lives to the profession—women who saw this as a "mission." The sisters' work in the classroom as professionals was inseparably linked to their own "formation" program in the convent, where they trained to fulfill their mission. Polish sisters, whatever their congregation, had many similar experiences. Discipline was the basic constant. The Felicians' Mother Monica was convinced that "severity and harshness prepare the foundation for virtue in these sisters."[71] Reminders of personal unworthiness were unremitting. The message Father Honorat conveyed in one letter from Poland to Detroit was usual: "All great things in the Church were accomplished by means of poor and useless instruments, beginning with the Apostles and coming down through you."[72] Humbled as they were, sisters might gain confidence—and righteousness—from being on a continuum with the sainted Apostles.

Poverty was another cornerstone of proper convent life. Sisters must always prove their "poverty is in good order," Honorat reminded the Felicians. In the huge Felician motherhouse, sister superiors interpreted poverty to mean that even floor varnish was forbidden; scrubbing and scraping wood floors made for a constant duty. Labor-saving, time-saving devices were disapproved. Class-consciousness sometimes motivated demanding convent routines. When electric lights were to be installed in the Felician motherhouse, the sister-director of education and the mistress of novices wrote separately to the mother superior in Poland to register opposition. They maintained that the girls were already putting on airs because of new laundry machines. The mother superior in Poland shared the concerns. In her judgment, "These simple girls who are required only to study and to work in the fine arts" were already living above their class and liking it. On the issue of electricity, Father Honorat did counter with the position that menial service or manual labor were not so important as time for study.[73]

Ordinary comforts were few. Memoirs of Polish sisters reveal almost continual privation and physical discomfort. One little band of sisters had their first meal in their school convent sitting on the floor, with a tipped-over washtub serving as a table.[74] Another group slept under a roof so ruined that they covered their beds with umbrellas to keep off rain. In some parishes sisters lived in crude, wooden-frame buildings that doubled as school downstairs and convent upstairs. A faculty of Felicians taught and lived in a remodeled stable, a "temporary" arrangement that lasted six years. When they came to the motherhouse each summer they brought a "fragrance" that clung to them thanks to the "former residents of their convent, the shiny black steeds."[75] Bishop Foley found to his astonishment when he first visited the Felician motherhouse that sisters sat only on benches or the floor. Chairs were deemed an unnecessary luxury. Food, too, was restricted. A spartan dietary standard long ruled against much milk, butter, or fruit in Felician kitchens. Apples were an unusual treat, saved for holy days, congregational celebrations, or for sisters with poor health.[76] Sisters described their life-style and experiences as sanctifying; they found glory in sharing poverty as they imagined St. Francis must have known it.

Similar lessons were passed on to their school children. At Sweetest Heart convent, where they lived without any labor-saving devices, sisters spent noon hours washing and hanging out laundry and encouraged students to use the two-hour lunch break for chores at home. From one schoolhouse to another, children shared in the demands of a scrupulously clean poverty.

Time was carved out of the curriculum for them to help dust, straighten, carry, scrub, wax, and sweep. Even three generations later children convenienced by wax paper would put sheets of it under their feet and scoot up and down the aisles on Friday afternoons to ready the classroom for the coming week.[77] The virtue and necessity of toil were unending.

For sisters there was a physical as well as a psychological toll exacted by relentless days starting before 5 A.M. and short nights spent in crowded sleeping quarters cold in winter and stifling in summer. Not only was the work hard and nutrition poor, but there were also no sterilization techniques. Tuberculosis and influenza raced through convents. Between 1888 and 1900, from a core of three hundred, the Felicians lost thirty-two sisters, all under the age of forty.[78] The School Sisters of St. Francis, working twelve-hour shifts in the Milwaukee tuberculosis sanatorium, were hit by the disease they helped others overcome. The St. Joseph Sisters decided in 1929 to buy a large convalescent home in Denver for their sick sisters. Ten years later they discontinued the practice of indicating dates of birth on sisters' tombstones because so many St. Joseph nuns died distressingly young.[79]

Sisters were unable to ward off serious disease, in part, because they neglected early symptoms. A sister who felt ill saw no choice but to carry on because no one was available to take over her class and she knew it would be impossible to combine her eighty or a hundred pupils with another class of the same size. Moreover, Polish mothers superior often disdained weakness of any sort. Although Polish school children did not become familiar with the phenomenon of the substitute teacher, surely they must have been accustomed to a teacher so burdened or ill or exhausted that she had no patience left for them.

From the earliest days of training Felician teachers, Sister Cajetan worried, perceptively, that the life-style of poverty and the rigors of religious piety imposed by Mother Monica threatened the community's reputation in the classroom.[80] Once she became mother superior herself at the turn of the century, Sister Cajetan made changes. She improved the diet and restricted Felician sisters from washing the floor and curtains in their convent homes so often, warning, "Frequent scrubbing is an obstacle to the sisters' performance of duty and a hindrance to their study."[81] Parish altar societies should be asked to take on more sewing and mending of church linens and vestments, she suggested, because sisters needed to spend time on their duties as teachers and to care properly for their own grooming.

In part, sisters' hardships reflected the real poverty common within the Polish community. Congregations of religious women were integral to an economic system that managed to afford both religion and education by fostering private enterprise within a framework of communal sharing. It was a habit more reminiscent of peasant Europe than industrialized America.

Sisters worked for salaries. Polish parents, like other Catholics, had no doubt that sisters should be paid. Salaries and methods of school financing varied, however, depending significantly upon individual parish circumstances. In Detroit teachers' pay was generally comparable, regardless of teaching order or ethnicity of parishioners. From the nineteenth century on into the twentieth, each sister received between $170 to $200 a year. Occasionally the need for lay teachers or the presence of male congregations who taught boys made average salaries higher at one parish compared to another.[82] Teachers in the religious women's communities earned less than half as much as inexperienced first-year teachers in public schools, and even within the Catholic community there were long-standing inequities. Priests always received more money than sisters and retained individual control of it. And at St. Albertus in 1893, while the organist and choir earned $480 for that year's services to the parish, the twelve teachers received a total of $1,067.[83]

The sisters' stipend was an amount slightly higher than wages of immigrant women in the city. In 1883 women in tobacco factories averaged 72 cents a day, and laundresses who worked by the day received 77 cents. In a survey of industrial and day workers, the average daily wage for immigrant women was 78 cents at the time.[84] Unlike other working women, sisters received a variety of money-saving benefits. Parishes provided their housing even though that often meant much the same type of accommodations as nearby families, with perhaps an outhouse and little heat. Relatives, friends, parents of pupils, and neighbors brought the sisters homegrown vegetables and supplies. One sister proudly told a *Free Press* interviewer, "The convent never bought an armful of wood since its first year in Detroit."[85] Catholic professionals offered doctoring, dentistry, pharmaceutical supplies, and legal advice at reduced rates or often free.

Well aware of the financial exigencies, sisters helped keep costs down and took on fund-raising projects for part of their own salary support or for special school needs. School Sisters of St. Francis did "fancy work" to sell, and as in many other communities sisters who taught music gave private lessons. Some congregations of women worked toward solvency by becoming entrepreneurs. The Felicians sometimes bought or were given several lots around a convent, and then as property values rose they periodically sold them.[86] They also had a flourishing in-house textbook operation. Polish schools around the country placed ever-growing orders. One 1880 mailing to Resurrection Parish in Chicago included four hundred readers at 25 cents each and four hundred geography books at 30 cents each. With no royalties to pay, with Mother Monica handling the bookkeeping, and with sisters in the motherhouse recruited to print, bind, pack, and mail, book profits were assured. Selling books was also a way for parishes to help their own treasuries. When sending the order to Chicago, Mother Monica reminded the priest that he could raise the price above his costs: "Dear Father, you can sell [the readers] at 35 cents and [the geographies] 40 cents."[87]

The School Sisters of St. Francis bought three sanatoriums in the 1890s—one in Milwaukee, one in Germany, and another in Italy. It was their deliberate plan that the facilities would attract wealthier people than the immigrant parents who supported schools; these clients would provide indirect subsidies to sustain the schools. The Milwaukee sanatorium absorbed nearly a hundred sisters as nurses, technicians, dietitian, bakers, cooks, and kitchen assistants. They worked twelve-hour days, seven days a week without such conveniences as carts or elevators. The sanatorium effort meant, especially in the years from 1892 to 1907, that the congregation's program for educating sisters as teachers regressed. It was also during this period that the Polish sisters within the congregation became so disgruntled that many left to form the Sisters of St. Joseph. The sanatorium initiative was just one more instance of a costly compromise intended to make Catholic education affordable.

When he first arrived in Detroit, Bishop Foley hoped to accomplish free parochial schooling for all the city's Catholic children. Despite concerted efforts to keep school costs down, however, few schools could operate without charging parents a modest sum. Across the last years of the nineteenth century annual tuition remained under $4 at most schools, and usually tuition combined with parish contributions was enough to balance budgets. Financing varied from parish to parish. St. Casimir and St. Josaphat schools remained dependent on tuition to cover the entire cost of operating through 1912.[88] At St. Albertus, all parishioners took on a share of the school's annual expenses. In 1893 and 1894 total tuition collected amounted to $1,002.75, and a transfer from the "ordinary revenues of the church" added another $1,349.14 to meet expenses. Parishioners also collectively paid $7,400 that year for the new school and for debt interest. That pattern persisted. In 1901 and 1902 tuition at St. Albertus brought in $3,989.90 toward expenditures totaling $7,074.81.[89]

Meanwhile, Catholics grappled with heavy indebtedness for their buildings, often paying for church, rectory, convent, and school all at the same time. The 1,500 families at St. Albertus (fig. 5) faced a parish debt of $73,000 in 1894, the largest for any parish in the city. But the proportionate share

Figure 5. Over several decades, working-class Polish families helped the Felician sisters add wing after wing to their motherhouse and orphanage. As it appeared in this 1924 photograph, orphans lived on the first floor, and students and the academy occupied the second floor, separated only by a curtain from the professed sisters. Their rooms were at the front near the chapel and are identifiable by the round stained-glass windows. The top floor was home to the novices and aspirants. (Archives of the Felician Sisters, Presentation of the B.V.M. Province, Livonia, Michigan)

was even greater at St. Casimir's, where seven hundred families dealt with a debt of $40,000. St. Josaphat, expanding rapidly from two hundred families to eight hundred between 1894 and 1900, was hard-hit by the Panic of 1894 because so many of its parishioners were new to the city. In October of that year, parish board members negotiated sisters' monthly salaries down from $16 to $14.[90]

One source calculates that, nationally, Polish workers earned an average of $300 to $360 a year at the turn of the century and spent $46 on the church.[91] Building and operating costs for Polish parishes in Detroit suggest that most local immigrant families were spending well over the national average. Sometimes the strain of providing for home, family, and church led even to riots for jobs. In the midst of the lingering depression of 1893–94, three men died and several others were injured when a scuffle broke out between Polish workers and the Wayne County sheriff's deputies over piecework wages.[92] Another bloody clash developed on Grand Avenue in Detroit when a crowd of Polish workers tried to force a road crew to lay down their shovels and give others a chance to work.[93] Notwithstanding the hard times, parishioners whittled down debt and continued to insist on building parochial schools. By 1900 St. Albertus's debt was down to $33,000 from the $73,000 of 1894. Thirteen years later it was completely debt-free.[94]

THE WORTH OF IT ALL

In the last two decades of the nineteenth century Polish immigrants—parishioners, sisters, and priests—had methodically focused time and resources where they believed this would make a difference. They had stabilized community institutions: a seminary for Polish priests, another for training nuns, an orphanage, and six churches with tall steeples and organs and stained-glass windows. They also had rectories, convents, and the six schools. Their pitched battles for a say in matters of money and control were more physical yet no more bitter than in the public school arena, where Republicans fought Democrats, free-thinkers fought evangelical Protestants, and reformers fought entrenched interests. This generation of Polish pioneers, many illiterate and getting by on laborers' day wages, had initiated and funded schooling of proportions not attempted by any one generation of previous newcomers, immigrant or native-born. Their children would have opportunities they had not known.

There is another equally plausible interpretation, however. By 1900 it was too late for the generation of Polish children who had grown up in the last two decades of the century; they had already missed important stepping stones. Too few children attended or stayed long enough in the schools their parents, priests, and nuns provided. The handful who did learned too little compared with their educated contemporaries. Furthermore, the Polish community lagged at least twenty years behind older immigrants and native-born residents in equipping their sons and daughters with a high school education. Polish children who came of school age in the 1880s and 1890s lost out while adults attended, finally, to needs of their own.

The huge churches with stained-glass windows and organs provided proud immigrant men and women of the working class with symbols and a sense of security as well as accomplishment. Yet those churches—together with the solid Felician motherhouse, the impressive Polish seminary, and the rectories for priests, convents for nuns, and expanding school buildings of brick—took a significant share of family incomes. Sons and daughters had to leave school too young and go to work for wages that could compensate for their family's donation to the church and school.

Religious leaders such as Father Honorat, Father Dabrowski, Mother Monica, and Mother Alexia were bent on paternalistic enforcement of an Old World culture that once gave them better educations than they could now transmit in turn. There were sisters, rigid in their course toward salvation, whose effectiveness in the classroom was thereby too limited. Personal aggrandizement and political self-interest meant that clergy as dissimilar as Kolasinski, Dabrowski, Borgess, and Foley were more attentive to safeguarding children's souls than safeguarding children's material opportunities. All the while, *Michigan Catholic* editors pressed respectability and applauded enrollment figures.

Meantime, adults in the broader Detroit secular community tended to their particularized concerns. Some public school officials profited from textbook sale deals. Reformers extolled theories of Pestalozzi, Herbart, and Froebel; pinchpenny opponents countered, claiming concern for the three R's. None of them debated whether it would be wise to meet the needs of Polish-speaking children by providing public school teachers who could speak their language. English-speaking Catholics joined English-speaking Protestants in disdain for new immigrants and in the desire to protect their own children from them. Grappling with budget demands, reluctant taxpayers and office-seeking politicians failed the children whose working-class parents were helping create industrialists' private fortunes.

Most everyone "meant well" by his or her own standards. Personal ambitions and private visions were played out in the forum of the American church and nineteenth-century urban democracy. Polish children of the 1880s and 1890s inherited church institutions and factory slots. It was more than their parents started with. The next generation would have to carry on from there.

PART 3

CONFIRMING THE HABIT IN A CITY
TRANSFORMED, 1900-1920S

6 Parish Grade Schools Multiply

She loved God—all humanity—and us.
—Sylvia Tackowiak, remembering Sister Mary Felicia, SSJ,
her principal

IN the first three decades of the twentieth century Detroit was transformed by the auto industry. Ransom Olds initiated mass production of automobiles just after the turn of the century, and by 1904 Detroit was already the volume leader in the nation. Mergers and stock companies and the moving assembly line were in place before World War I. Not long after the practical Model T first appeared in 1908, mass production made its sale price slide, and Henry Ford was bigger in folklore than in life even before he introduced the $5 day in 1914. Huge plants and factory wages were like magnets. Miners from the Upper Peninsula, immigrants from European villages, and Michigan farmers headed for Detroit, sometimes with their families and sometimes alone. The population soared from 285,704 in 1900 to 1,568,662 by 1930, and annexations stretched the city from its comfortable turn-of-the-century confines of twenty-three square miles to seventy-nine square miles. Another half-million people lived outside the city limits in the sudden suburbs and sprawling metropolitan area.

If the auto economy altered the city, the opportunities of its children changed just as dramatically. A little education became all a boy needed before he grew up enough to take a factory job; it was all a girl needed to work behind a counter. These waiting jobs also loomed as a threat. Study harder, stay in school longer, or otherwise face a life as factory hand or sales clerk. When it came to educating the children of immigrants, greater burdens were on grade schools than ever before. Many long-time Americans held that if a grade school education was all a foreigner's child would receive, then it must promote democracy, dispense with hyphenates, and instill respect for public authority. Meanwhile, many Catholic immigrants decided that if a grade school education was all their children would receive, then it must teach the important basics American children needed, ingrain faith, preserve Old World values, and instill respect for parental and religious authority. And then there were the second- and third-generation immigrant Catholics who wanted a grade school education that would provide a stepping stone to high school and college; ingrain faith; instill respect for civil, parental, and church authority; and, in the bargain, develop the ability to make informed judgments that educational reformers such as John Dewey were touting.

Grade school for children between the ages of seven and fifteen had become a matter of law and a fact of life. Ninety-five percent of Detroit's youngsters aged seven to thirteen conformed to the expectation by 1920. Even among the fourteen- and fifteen-year-olds who could more easily get work permits, attendance was 88 percent. Educating children not only assumed new proportions but the task also seemed more worrisome because Detroit was essentially a city of foreigners and second-generation immigrants. Twenty-nine percent of the residents had been born in a foreign country, and another 35 percent had at least one foreign-born parent. Of the 120,738 children aged seven through fifteen who attended school in 1920, 75,389 were the children of foreign parents or were themselves foreign-born.[1] Then, too, there were the third-generation immigrants who still identified with the ethnic community of parents and grandparents—typically Irish or German or Polish.

Local immigration patterns mirrored national trends (table 3). Central and Southeastern Europeans were becoming more significant, and the numbers arriving from Northwestern Europe were in decline. The 56,624 Polish immigrants constituted the largest single group in Detroit. Hungarians, Russian Jews, and Italians were newly important, beginning numerically to edge out arrivals from Northwestern Europe. The substantial and established German population continued to grow, however, and there were still more Detroiters who had arrived from England, Ireland, Scotland, and Belgium than from countries such as Rumania, Czechoslovakia, and Yugoslavia, where emigration had begun to take hold.[2]

These newcomers meant unprecedented complexity not only within the city but within the Catholic population. During Bishop Foley's era (1888–1918), the number of Catholics soared from 40,000 to 325,000.[3] When it came to educating their children, new Catholic immigrants often arrived at the same conclusions as immigrants who had settled into Detroit before them. They elaborated on established patterns, and, accordingly, the num-

Table 3. Foreign-Born and Second-Generation Population of Detroit, 1920

Birthplace	Foreign-born	Second-Generation[a]
Canada	59,702	51,114
French	3,678	5,839
Poland	56,624	104,561
Germany	30,238	45,099
Russia and Lithuania	29,931	17,497
England	17,195	12,522
Italy	16,205	8,729
Hungary	13,564	26,880
Austria	10,674	20,090
Ireland	7,004	6,028
Scotland	6,993	3,089
Belgium	6,219	1,371
Rumania	4,668	731
Greece	4,628	—
Syria	3,781	—
Yugoslavia	3,702	—
Czechoslovakia	3,351	—
	290,884	348,771
Total Detroit population (1920) = 993,678		

Source: U.S. Department of Commerce, *Fourteenth Census of the United States, 1920,* vol. 2: *Population* (Washington, D.C.: Government Printing Office, 1920), 742, 936.

a. Countries as constituted prior to World War I.

ber of parochial students doubled within every twelve- or thirteen-year time span from the late 1880s (table 4). In most years nearly a third of the city's grade-schoolers attended parochial schools. As of 1925, almost fifty thousand Catholic children filtered into the sixty-three parish schools within Detroit's boundaries.[4]

Parochial school growth was the result of new parishes formed and new schools built. City annexations generally brought in sparsely settled farm-

Table 4. Parochial School Enrollment in Detroit for Selected Years

Year	Parishes	Schools	Enrollment	Percent Increase	Teaching Orders
1887	18	15	6,351	—	7
1900	28	23	11,704	84	7
1913	42	35	22,788	95	9
1925	73	63	49,181	116	11

Source: Calculated from the annual Catholic directories; *Sadlier's Directory* was used through 1895 and *Hoffmann's Directory* for the years from 1896.

land, while heavily populated enclaves such as Highland Park and Hamtramck, already incorporated, resisted Detroit's sweep. Because of patterns of land use and development, some parishes and their schools were being built at the outer reaches of the city while others were still emerging in or near the central city core. Second- and third-generation Irish and Germans who were able to take advantage of white-collar work the auto boom generated headed off to mingle in new middle-class neighborhoods, where they started churches and schools (fig. 6). Meanwhile, recent immigrants either reshaped the ethnic character of old central city parishes or, in greater numbers, sorted themselves out around the widely scattered industrial plants to initiate separate ethnic neighborhoods, tightly settled enclaves that were patched together by the streets that led to the factory gates.

In contrast to nineteenth-century Detroit, where families of various occupations might live side by side, working-class immigrants now had little contact with people who made their livings in offices, professions, or substantial businesses. Ethnic parish schools separated children according

Figure 6. These children at orchestra practice in the Blessed Sacrament School music room (about 1910) experienced the advantages that came with belonging to an upper-class parish such as this one, the cathedral for the diocese. Other youngsters, often those whose parents were recent immigrants from Southeastern or Central Europe, meanwhile attended parochial schools that lacked sufficient seats or books. (Archives of the Sisters, Servants of the Immaculate Heart of Mary)

to nationality, sometimes holding firm into the second and third generations. Territorial parish schools began to divide children according to class, just like the public schools down the block. In the shadow of the factories and tall office buildings that were changing the urban landscape, the variety among parochial grade schools was part of the pattern.

THE HUNGARIANS

Hungarian immigrants, 4.7 percent of the city's population by 1920, were a significant slice of the new factory-working Catholics. The trickle of early arrivals had turned into a small flood once word spread to the East Coast about jobs at plants like Michigan Malleable Iron Company. Michigan Malleable welcomed Hungarian workers when it opened in 1898 and began to recruit them actively from other cities once managers realized they were experienced iron molders and core makers. The company was in Delray, a factory section sandwiched between the Rouge River on the west, railroad tracks and cedar-block paved Jefferson Avenue on the north, and the Detroit River to the south. Soon Delray was one of the most concentrated Hungarian communities in the United States.

By 1900 nearly thirty Hungarian families already owned property in Delray, and the original French and German settlers had started to move out. Delray became a Hungarian enclave, a recreated Old World village. The first establishment was a Hungarian saloon that opened in 1902 and did all kinds of business beside selling liquor. People brought money to deposit, and the saloon became a kind of bank, with the proprietor and his wife helping customers send money back to Europe. They also sold steamship tickets, real estate, and general merchandise, and at the bar men could buy overalls and women could purchase groceries. Meetings of every sort were held in the hall above the saloon.[5]

Annexation in 1905 added Delray to the city's west side despite the opposition of the Hungarians who preferred to maintain village independence. Other factories located in the area, and Delray became Detroit's first mill town. By 1920 Detroit had more than twenty-five thousand residents who were Hungarian by birth or parentage, and the majority settled in Delray, whether they worked there or not.[6] Hungarians hired at Henry Ford's Highland Park plant, several miles to the north and east, preferred to make the street car trip back and forth so they could live among their own kind. Once the huge Ford River Rouge plant opened in Dearborn during World War I, it was even more convenient to Delray. Feature stories in the Detroit press liked to say there were more Hungarians in Delray than any place in the world but Budapest. With plentiful neighborhood factory jobs, Hungarians concentrated in the ranks of semiskilled and unskilled wage labor more than any other group of immigrants.[7]

Most Hungarians who settled in Detroit were from peasant families in the old country. One study found that 80 percent were born in communes having fewer than five thousand inhabitants.[8] Unlike the Hungarian peasants who migrated to Budapest to break away from what they regarded as the oppressive control of their villages, the Detroit Hungarians had no desire to break away from the old culture. Instead, they hoped to return to their home villages with higher social status because of the wages they earned in America.[9]

Many of the initial Hungarian immigrants were young single men, and Detroit was usually their second or third place of employment in America. They came planning to make money and go home, but trouble in their homeland and opportunities in America changed their plans. They sent for brides and settled in, unconcerned that Delray's streets were "mostly mud" or that railroad cars "thundered through contemptuously like the Twentieth Century going through Podunk."[10] By 1920 nearly seven in ten Hungarian households were nuclear families: father, mother, and young children without extra relatives or boarders. Most lived in neat little wooden homes. One study found that at least 35 percent of the Hungarian families on typical blocks either owned or were buying their homes.[11]

The children all knew each other and knew, too, that "everybody's dad" worked at Solvay Chemical, Michigan Malleable, or the foundries, the rolling mills, or the shipyards.[12] Men learned enough English words to get by on the job, and children were learning English in school. For most Hungarians of every age Delray was their entire world. Women, especially, might be in the community for fifteen or twenty years without once going to the center of Detroit. They were less likely to know English because, as one explained, "Why should I learn this funny English language, when I do not have to? . . . None of my neighbors know how to talk English. If these American people want to talk to us so badly, why don't they learn our language?"[13]

Because Detroit was not a port of first entry, Hungarians migrated with friends they had met in other Hungarian colonies in America. Those associations became important bonds, uniting Delray's Hungarians regardless of what village they originally came from or what religion they professed.[14] A majority were Roman Catholics, and in 1906 their Holy Cross was the first church organized. Other Hungarians followed the Catholics' lead, and Delray soon boasted St. John the Baptist Hungarian (a Byzantine Rite

Catholic Church), the Synagogue of the Hebrew Congregation of Delray, the First Hungarian Lutheran Church, the First Hungarian Baptist Church, the First Hungarian Reformed Church, and the Hungarian Pentecostal Church.[15] A Federation of Hungarian Churches and Societies held weekly meetings that made an effort to reproduce meetings of the Hungarian parliament. Delegates of the different societies were represented according to their conservative or radical tendencies; those from the Hungarian Town and Country Club were on the president's extreme right, and those from the Communist societies on his extreme left.[16]

A Hungarian-born priest, Father Hubert F. Klenner, was Delray's Catholic pastor for nearly twenty years. When Father Klenner was ordained in 1902, the bishop assigned him to St. Elizabeth's, a German parish on the east side. From there he traveled back and forth to Delray. Sometimes it took almost a whole day or night to make a sick call all the way over to Delray's hospital. Catholic Hungarian children also presented another problem because they had a choice of two grade schools, either the public school on nearby West End Avenue or the parochial school with the Germans at St. Elizabeth's—a long trek for youngsters. At any rate, they did not speak much English nor did they understand German.

Within a short time Father Klenner and a few Hungarians began taking up a collection, and in 1904 they bought land for a church and school of their own. Two years later, the immigrants celebrated the opening of Holy Cross. The little building on South Street was within walking distance from any corner of Delray. Theirs was an accomplishment equaled by only a few Hungarian communities in the United States. Even though there were a half-million Hungarian Catholics in the United States, they had started just thirty-one parishes and ten parish schools by 1909–10.[17] Residentially more concentrated than many of their countrymen, Detroit Hungarians nonetheless struggled to afford Holy Cross. It would be 1925 before they finally opened a solid brick church as their neighborhood's proud landmark. Even then, it was not so grand as some of the large, steepled buildings in adjacent working-class Polish neighborhoods.

The few prosperous Hungarians in Detroit, members of the intelligentsia, did not contribute to institutions their working-class countrymen built. Long-standing antagonism held firm on each side. Peasants hated the highly placed Hungarian engineers and professionals in Detroit, seeing them to be an extension of the aristocracy that monopolized the land and exploited them at home. The privileged Hungarians retained disdain for the peasants and identified with the upper-class American attitude toward them. As one Hungarian auto engineer explained, "I belong to the Detroit Yacht Club and enjoy very much the associations I have made. . . . I became aware of these Hunkies of Delray a few years ago, as a result of labor trouble in one of our plants. You surely would not expect me to associate with such people as they are."[18]

The "Hungarian" Catholic church began, like so many other ethnic parishes before it, as a combined church, school, and living quarters. When the school opened in January 1907 it had two classrooms on the front of the church. One served as kindergarten, first, and second grades, and the other room held all the older children. The sister-teachers lived upstairs.[19] The first year, as parishioners accounted to the penny, they managed to collect $5,872.47 to support both church and school, of which $185.50 went for a salary for the two sisters and another $214.35 for their furniture. For the next few years they "got by." Spending less than $4,500 annually, they kept the school free for all children until 1915, when small tuition fees had to be added.[20]

Hungarians were accustomed to a system of church financing in which the government required people to pay a church tax to the denomination of their choice. Without this type of support in America, Hungarian congregations had to devise other methods, because contributions were never sufficient to meet expenses. Delray churches hit upon the idea of jointly sponsored steamboat excursions to Bob Lo Island in the Detroit River. For a single fee, a family could board the boat with all their friends and neighbors in the morning, spend the day playing and picnicking, and return at night. The boat even made a separate run in the afternoon to take men back in time for the late work shift and pick up men who had been working all day so they could have a few hours on the island.[21] The event became a chance for the entire Delray community to share in fun while raising money for their churches. Less exciting and more constant was the work of the mothers, aunts, and grandmothers who made up budget deficits by their unending round of bake sales, noodle sales, craft sales, and church suppers.

The sisters who came to open Holy Cross school were Dominicans, a community of mostly German and Irish women who had organized a motherhouse in the 1880s in Adrian, Michigan, about eighty miles southwest of Detroit. It was the first time they managed to gain an assignment within the city, relegated elsewhere as a result of Bishop Foley's "strange indifference" to their community.[22] The bishop discouraged priests from hiring them, regularly making his preference for the IHM congregation quite plain to all, including the Dominican sister superior. The Dominicans decided they must have been allowed into Holy Cross only because it was small, foreign, and on the outskirts of the city.[23] Possibly Bishop Foley had some inkling of the difficulties the school would present.

There were no Hungarian sisters among the Dominicans to communicate in the language children knew from home, and the cultural gap between the sisters and the Hungarian parents was as wide as their language differences. Children were regularly reprimanded by anyone and everyone in the neighborhood who observed them misbehaving. Still, certain actions considered errant by American standards were tolerated by the Hungarian community. Hungarian adults judged it acceptable for children to steal coal from the railroads, for example, especially if it was for their parents or church. One Delray church reduced its fuel bill by more than half because its steward bought only stolen coal. The act fit old attitudes that approved stealing firewood from a noble's estate. Hungarians did not condone stealing from a person—"only the Gypsies steal from a man." But they never saw the man who owned the railroad, so it was "just like the estates in Hungary." Why, indeed, "should not the poor people get their coal from it?"[24] The rationalization was foreign to the Dominican sisters, one more example of the "strange" Hungarian way of thinking that was beyond their indulgence.

As one student remembered it, the sisters faced a group of students who were a "most intractable and unmanageable crowd." He thought perhaps his compatriots' unruliness stemmed from the public schools "from which we were recruited" and where "we were given greater liberties," or maybe "we believed that members of a religious order would be more lenient and less inclined to corporal punishment." Each student also knew that "if things got too hot" in school "he could always elect to go to work."[25] It was common for "sister" to chase someone around the room with a ruler. Necessarily, the pastor took a hand in the school beyond the mandated catechism classes and the perfunctory classroom visits expected of priests. When a student got too rowdy, one of the girls would be sent for "outside assistance," and "father" would come to "restore order" with—in the case of Father Klenner—his dreaded "mighty left arm." For the worst offenses, students took a trip with father across the hall to the "atonement room." Little wonder that serving as an altar boy at a funeral mass was a prized treat. A parishioner's demise meant getting out of school work for most of the morning, plus a "nice long ride in a horse-drawn carriage to the cemetery."[26]

The school helped reinforce dividing lines between Hungarian Catholics and others who lived in Delray, with German Lutherans among their favorite adversaries. Protestant boys called out "Catlikkers" at Holy Cross boys, who responded with taunts of "Dutch." But sometimes they went to school together. Holy Cross could not expand fast enough once compulsory school laws and parental interests made grade school necessary. By 1923 the priest reported there were five hundred in the parish school, but another five hundred were in public school "because there is no room for them."[27] Until outside pressures began to build, however, few Hungarian children went past fifth or sixth grade. Andrew Untener became the first graduate from the eighth grade in 1910. He was followed by a girl and a boy in 1912, a boy in 1913, and four boys and a girl in 1914. Some years there were no eighth-graders at all. The list of graduates did not become long until 1922, when twenty-seven children completed the eighth grade, an unusually large class for the decade.[28]

Parents made the decisions about whether a child would stay in school or withdraw. Often as many boys as girls were in the eighth grade, even though boys could find ready work if they quit. Andrew Untener was glad to stay on, at least as he remembered it, but recalled that his friends were delighted when their parents took them out to help provide income. The crowded church-front school did not have even the physical attraction of well-equipped, bright, comfortable schools in some working-class parishes. It must have seemed that school lessons were a "most humdrum life compared to working at the Michigan Sprocket Chain or driving some grocer's delivery wagon, and getting paid for it, to boot!"[29]

Efforts to strengthen the school were often derailed or delayed by conflicts among priest, parishioners, and sisters. Control of parish finances was a major issue at Holy Cross because parishioners were determined to supervise the funds they contributed, even though their priests were most always fellow Hungarians. Despite Bishop Foley's remonstrances, they established their stand at the outset with Father Klenner. Parishioners did not see any need to take on the extra expense of enlarging the two-room school until Father Klenner's successor insisted on adding four classrooms and two clubrooms in 1921 when he arrived. His quick building spree brought on a $42,000 debt, which was "not looked upon favorably by some parishioners." Part of their dissatisfaction may have been with this pastor's origins in Minnesota rather than in Hungary. After a tenure of a few months, he "accepted an invitation" to move to Cleveland.[30] Hungarian-born Father Louis Kovacs replaced him.

Parishioners paid off the school debt within just a few years in order to gain the bishop's permission to build a new and larger church. Father Kovacs was well liked by Bishop Michael Gallagher, and he had won permission to build. He also found a Hungarian-born architect, and men from the parish helped with the building to keep costs down. Despite their common end, the people and priest had many disputes before they celebrated the opening in 1925. And, because their money had paid for the school and then paid for the new church, parishioners were unmoved when Father Kovacs complained that the parish council had no right to keep the Easter and Christmas collections, which were traditionally considered gifts to the priest. Such demanding parishioners were giving him heart trouble and high blood pressure, the aggrieved Kovacs wrote to his sympathetic bishop; he could not get needed rest.[31] Father Kovacs died before he could be transferred. Whether or not they felt remorse, the Holy Cross laity persevered in asserting their financial role with his successor, Father Desiderius Nagy. Trying to placate them on some fronts and ease his own trials, Father Nagy turned his attention to the school—and was soon in a conflict with the Dominican sisters who had operated it for the twenty-three years since it had opened.

The priest was anxious to establish a stronger Hungarian presence in the school. He felt "insulted and betrayed" by the mother superior because she had not kept her promise to send two sisters to learn the Gregorian chant method used in a Hungarian school in New York. Ethnic differences were at the root of this disagreement over music. Most Dominicans were American-born daughters of Irish or German parents, some were second- or even third-generation. Father Nagy felt "the lack of mutual respect is the best source of possible fights later in the future" and accordingly asked the mother superior to withdraw her teachers. He had "decided to make the necessary steps and to fulfill the long cherished desire of the Detroit Hungarian Catholics after Sisters of our own blood."[32]

Father Nagy believed that the interests of the parish could be served better by Hungarian sisters who "could understand the parents." That would also mean, in turn, that any priest at the parish "would be relieved of a good portion of his worries." Here Father Nagy spoke from experience. Because a high percentage of the Hungarian adult population did not understand English, the pastor had served as interpreter between parents and the sisters, who did not speak Hungarian. He thought it was also possible that "girls wishing to enter the convent will find less opposition from the part of parents, if we will have Hungarian Sisters around here."[33]

The Dominicans were quite willing to withdraw. As their superior made the case to Bishop Gallagher, "They are frightened and discouraged and in addition to these small woes they are suffering the loss of the privilege of daily Holy Communion."[34] This was a sacrament priests sometimes withheld in order to discipline or drive out nuns they preferred to be rid of. By the fall of 1930 Holy Cross was under the direction of the Daughters of Divine Charity from Arrochar on Staten Island in New York, who operated other Hungarian schools in Toledo, South Bend, and Chicago.

The Hungarian parochial school always struggled from lack of students as well as lack of money. Even though the neighborhood expanded steadily

Holy Cross school grew slowly. In 1925, according to the board of education's city census, Delray accounted for more than 45 percent of the total Hungarian population, by then approaching thirty thousand citywide. Nonetheless, Holy Cross school had only 454 pupils. That made it one of the smallest parish grade schools in Detroit except for those in the declining central city or parishes that had just started. Because Hungarians living on Detroit's east side could not send their children several miles across town to Delray, they either became a substantial minority in some central parish schools such as St. Joseph's and St. Mary's or they attended public schools.

Father Nagy was convinced that the well-being of the broader Hungarian community was at risk unless Hungarians looked after their own. Toward that end, he tried to use his influence to "advise the people of Delray" that what was good for Hungarian-operated businesses was good for Delray's Hungarian churches, schools, and organizations. Hungarians must "patronize always their own independent merchants" rather than the chain stores that were moving in, he warned. The chains did not pay for advertisements in church bulletins or make donations toward church activities. Chains were interested "only in profits" and not "in schools or other civic projects."[35]

By then there were other signs that Hungarian Delray was at risk. Old-timers had died, youngsters moved on, and Armenians, Poles, Italians, blacks, and gypsies edged into the cheaper houses. A well-publicized murder case demonstrated one highly unusual consequence of neighborhood turnover. "Aunt Rose," the Hungarian "witch" of Delray's Medina Street, was reputed to have caused the mysterious deaths of many men during the 1920s in order to collect their insurance. Yet no Hungarian would testify against her because neighbors believed her claims that she could "cast an eye" on them, making their children sick and causing their husbands to lose their jobs. The state could not gather enough evidence to convict her, and she went on collecting the insurance of dead men. When she committed a twelfth murder in 1931 police were at last able to acquire enough evidence because five black newcomers on the street willingly provided detailed accounts.[36]

The episode was almost too bizarre to hint at what population changes could bring, and the depression held many young people at home longer than they might have stayed. Other second-generation couples who did set up housekeeping beyond Delray's borders came back for Sunday mass, to shop in Hungarian markets, and to gather with friends. Their children, however, commonly went to school in their new neighborhoods. Holy Cross did not venture to add a high school, and some of its students went on to the public Southwestern High School. "Of course, the result was not always very edifying," the pastor wrote to the chancery. As a remedy, in the early 1930s the parish entered into an agreement with the nearby All Saints parish, which began to take tuition-paying Holy Cross students into its high school. Father Nagy was determined to "find some way" of raising the money to pay for tuition and books for poorer students.[37] The depression was, by then, making the Hungarian community more aware that their young people should not grow up dependent upon factories or the largess of management.

THE ITALIANS

Italian immigrants were moving into Detroit at the same time as the Hungarians and slightly outnumbered them by the 1920s. A few Italian families had made their way to Detroit as early as the 1850s. Others collected, most from Genoa, Lombardy, and Sicily, until the Italian community became sufficiently obvious to warrant local attention. Newspaper articles began complaining about Italian organ players who begged on streetcars and Italian women who peddled their wares on the street, all the while accompanied by their exhausted small children.

The first permanent Italian priest, Father Francis Beccherini, immediately took a door-to-door census when he arrived in 1897 to see if there were enough Italians to build a church. The count was 207 families, with 1,103 adults and 630 children.[38] Sufficiently encouraged, the priest had no way to anticipate either the growth or the complexities ahead. Within the next two decades word about Detroit lured Italians directly from their homeland or from East Coast cities. Meanwhile, labor trouble and cyclical depressions brought hundreds more from the Upper Peninsula's iron and copper mining counties, which had nearly 2,400 of the state's 3,000 Italians in 1890. By 1920 there were 16,525 Italian immigrants in Detroit and another 12,522 who were the second generation, most with both parents born in Italy.[39] Within another ten years the Italian population nearly doubled again.

Father Beccherini and the other Italian priests who joined his endeavors found that it took more than numbers to develop a base for thriving Italian religious institutions. In later years, "looking back" newspaper articles would recall that the Italian immigrant peasant had come for "a house and a job and a chance to educate his children."[40] Even such nostalgic accounts did not record any impelling desire to preserve religion, language, or culture—the intent that figured so prominently in the collective memory of most other nationalities.

Neither the jobs Italians found nor the homes they chose were as concentrated when compared with other new immigrants such as the Hungarians or the Poles. Almost half the Italian men avoided the huge industrial work force that absorbed thousands of immigrants and second-generation Detroiters. Instead, they either scattered, often to such low-paying slots as sewer-diggers and day laborers, or sought self-employment, even if it meant street-peddling for a marginal income.[41]

From the early twentieth century onward, Italians settled predominantly on the near east side of Woodward, initially in the boardinghouses and cheaper homes within a mile of city hall. In 1910 the Fifth and Seventh wards housed a majority of the city's Italians. As the wave of newcomers continued they began to merge with other working-class whites, whose eastward advance replaced the original German residents north of Gratiot, south to the river, and three or four miles out along Chene, Joseph Campau, and McDougall streets to East Grand Boulevard. Here and there small Italian colonies split off to the house-and-land parcels that Italian real estate agents actively marketed. Elsewhere on blocks bordering various auto factories Italians were a significant presence clustered among the Polish and German working class. One neighborhood, "Cacalupo," was sufficiently marked by Italian settlement that it earned periodic attention from newspaper reporters. Cacalupo was in the area at Harper and Gratiot where streetcars ended their east-bound runs from Detroit, made a loop, and turned around. Still, Italian businesses and institutions were not concentrated along a main street or in a single area, and many Italian "centers" moved at least once or twice to follow a shifting constituency.[42]

That early residential mobility was one of several challenges confronting the bishop and other churchmen when they began trying to fit the Italians into the established ethnic parish mold. More than in some cities, Detroit's Italians were from all parts of Italy rather than from only one or two regions of the country.[43] Arriving from separate regions, Italian immigrants did not have a strong sense of national identity. They referred to one another as Neapolitans, Genoese, Piedmontese, or Sicilian. Because they preferred to settled with family and regional friends when they could, the first two Italian Catholic parishes represented and reinforced their differences.

The earliest, San Francesco, was dedicated in 1898 soon after Father Beccherini's census established that enough interested Italians were willing to pay for and support a church. Located at the corner of Brewster and Rivard, San Francesco was more than a mile north and east of the city center. It was convenient for the sixty-two families of Lombards and fifty-four families of Genoese the census identified but well beyond the sixty families from Sicily whose ranks were expanding on the south side of the city along Fort, Congress, and Larned. The Sicilians continued to attend SS. Peter and

Paul, the Jesuit church within their neighborhood. Father Beccherini went back and forth to tend to all Italian Catholics. In 1902 the Jesuits loaned him a building, and he brought the Sisters of Charity, who opened a school with ninety-seven children. But that effort did not last long. In another effort the League of Catholic Women of Detroit began a center in 1906, with the Italian children as their specific target. Josephine Brownson and several of her friends made over an unused carriage barn to provide entertainment and religious instruction for them, but the women volunteers could not offer a systematic education.[44]

Finally, too overloaded with the growing San Francesco, Beccherini appealed to the Jesuits for help and in 1907 an Italian Jesuit arrived, Father Giovanni Maria Boschi. By then, the Sicilians had become an unwelcome presence at SS. Peter and Paul and were relegated to the Sodality Chapel behind the church because they did not behave with the same "austerity" as the other parishioners. Whether from former practice or because they could not understand the English sermons, communicants chatted, turned around, smiled at friends during the service, and opposed the idea of pew rent. Father Boschi took a door-to-door canvass and discovered that there were now 350 Sicilian families, including two thousand males and a thousand females. It was time for a new church.[45] With Bishop Foley's approval and Father Boschi's insistent prodding, Italian Catholics raised money, including more than $1,000 from a wealthy Protestant woman who had organized an Italian kindergarten a few years earlier. Holy Family parish opened in 1910 at Hastings and Fort streets. The bishop established the territorial boundaries. Holy Family was to serve all Italians south of Gratiot and Grand River; those to the north were to attend San Francesco. Holy Family was, from inception, widely regarded as the "Sicilian" church.

Holy Family's school was initiated within a year after the church when several Italian men's societies approached Bishop Foley and won approval to build a hall and school on the property beside the church, with the understanding that the societies would have free use of the hall and the right to rent it out. Nervous over the reputation the Sicilian and Italian "element" had in the city, whether as gangsters, radicals, romeos, or racketeers, Bishop Foley did not agree to their generosity without stipulations. They could proceed on the condition that those using the hall met with no objection from the "Right Reverend Bishop of the Diocese." Moreover, the societies must agree "never to use the Hall for any irreligious or immoral purposes and to be obedient to the Bishop of the Diocese."[46]

From the start, all parties focussed most of their attention on the hall. It was not an auspicious beginning for the school, and parish records are contradictory about its existence. According to the annual *Catholic Directory* listing, it appears that three Madames of Sacred Heart operated a school at Holy Family from 1912 to 1914 and that three lay teachers who succeeded the Madames conducted the parish school through 1915. The pastor's report for 1913 states, however, that Holy Family "has not yet its own school." Rather, "the Sicilian children"—sixty boys and seventy girls—were attending Sacred Heart, a nearby German parish school. A much larger group of five hundred attended public school. In the blank where each priest was to account for public school attendance of his parishioners, Holy Family's pastor said that some lived far from the parochial school, whereas "others prefer public schools."[47] The conflicting reports for 1913 may mean that a few grades were provided for a time under the auspices of Holy Family. Whatever type of school it was, according to Catholic directories the enrollment at Holy Family school peaked at 134 in 1912–13, even though the parish had a thousand school-age children on its rolls. By 1916 any separate effort had been abandoned.

Neither the succession of Italian pastors nor concerned parents surrendered their ambition to have a parish school. Still, Bishop Foley evidenced little support, and his prejudice against Italians, especially Sicilians, persisted. He disliked their independence and periodically challenged their seeming irreverence. On one occasion he refused church burial to a non-churchgoing Italian who died without last rites, and in another show of authority he would not allow the Italian flag to be admitted into Holy Family during a procession because the Italians had taken Rome from the pope in 1870.[48]

Soon after Bishop Gallagher came to head the diocese in 1918, Holy Family's pastor tried anew to call the chancery's attention to educational needs in the parish. "We have no school," he wrote, claiming that the parish numbered "over twenty thousand souls!" In 1922 the anxious priest sent another letter asking permission to start a fund-raising drive to build a school. He offered precise figures to make the case: The parish had grown to 1,300 families, and among them were 3,085 children under the age of sixteen, with 358 going to Catholic school and 1,187 to pubic school. An "O.K." penciled in red on the letter granted the bishop's approval to start collecting money.[49] The priest and some parishioners raised $80,000 within seven months and bought five lots at Joseph Campau and Catherine streets, already several blocks to the east of the church but situated so as to "bring the parish buildings about to the center of the Italian colony." By then, however, the timing was wrong.

Although Holy Family had opened just a dozen years earlier, the building was already becoming a monument to revisit for sacramental occasions rather than a neighborhood anchor. Confronted by an influx of black migrants into their central city neighborhoods during the 1910s and early 1920s, Italians joined the outward march of whites. Within the year of the school fund drive a "very serious change" became apparent, as the disappointed priest necessarily explained to his bishop. Instead of the expected move of Holy Family parishioners to new homesites near the school location, at least twenty of the pastor's "very best families" had "scattered to distant parts of the city," and others contemplated moving "no later than the spring of 1924 to distant parts of the city." Many who were leaving had pledged large sums to the school, money that would no longer be forthcoming. There was no reversing the trend, the pastor assessed. "As the Italians move away the colored people move in," so the neighborhood was "fast becoming a colored settlement." Even if the school were to be built, "It would have to be abandoned soon after."[50] The lots were sold but there was no school, although Holy Family drew Sicilians back to attend the church long after they had moved away.

San Francesco, farther to the north, was still beyond the line of black settlement, and with a more stable congregation and the continued presence of Father Beccherini it fared better. The parish opened a school in September 1912 in an old frame building Father Beccherini rented from the nearby Sacred Heart parish. He arranged for the School Sisters of Notre Dame from Milwaukee to staff it, the same congregation that already conducted three parish grade schools in Detroit, including Sacred Heart and St. Mary's where several Italian families had enrolled their children.

Seven sisters, none of them Italian, were on hand to introduce the 240 pupils to San Francesco school. The women did not record any pleasure over the building—in contrast to their enthusiasm for the "well-equipped modern building" they accepted that year for a Chicago parish.[51] Finally, in September 1923, San Francesco parishioners managed to provide a new school building with eleven classrooms, an auditorium, and a large roof garden where children could play without danger from the heavy traffic in the area. The sisters pronounced this facility "well-lighted" and "thoroughly modern." In the 1928 history of their congregation's work the School Sisters of Notre Dame proudly recorded that "the Italians of San Francesco Parish say, without fear of exaggeration, that theirs is the finest Italian school in the United States."[52] It was the only Italian parochial school in Detroit, but nonetheless the grade school grew slowly compared to the immigrant population. Enrollment climbed to 457 by 1917 and to 558 in 1925.[53]

Two more small Italian parishes opened: Santa Maria in 1919 and Church of the Madonna in 1924. Santa Maria was far to the north, near the enclave of Highland Park with its huge Ford factory where many Italians worked. Monsignor Giuseppe Ciarrocchi, who started the parish in a storefront, would remain its guiding force until he died in 1954. The parish opened a school beside its new church, where by the mid-1930s the sisters of St. Dorothy finally provided Detroit Catholic Italians with the first teaching staff who were themselves Italian.[54] The small Church of the Madonna on the city's west side did not attempt a school.

Detroit Catholics involved in various efforts to organize Italian immigrants kept a wary eye on the competition. In 1909 an activist Italian Catholic joined in partnership with a Presbyterian minister to publish the city's first Italian-language newspaper, *La Tribuna Italiana*. The diocese responded by 1910, initiating *La Voce Del Popolo*. Edited by Monsignor Ciarrocchi, the newspaper emphasized religious themes and objected to almost anything *La Tribuna* supported, even the bust of Columbus that various Italian organizations jointly contributed to the city. Ciarrocchi maintained that the money could have been better used for a hospital, school recreation rooms, a library, or a cemetery.[55]

Catholics leaders were especially sensitive about Protestants who were courting Italians. Some Italians had arrived in America as avowed Protestants; others who exhibited no particular religious enthusiasm or affiliation were deemed potential recruits. Two daughters of wealthy Protestant families began the first kindergarten for Italians in 1895. The first Italian Presbyterian mission formed in 1898, the same year San Francesco opened. A succession of Italian ministers tried to develop the congregation, formally organized as the First Italian Presbyterian Church of Detroit in 1914. Soon, Presbyterian leaders were as exasperated as the Catholic chancery as a result of coping with the independent Italians. For several years the presbytery had to devote as much attention to restraining the church's eager, activist, and vocal Reverend Giuseppe Buggelli as it did to the Italian Presbyterians. He wanted to convert all Italians, insisting that the papacy was responsible for delaying Italian unification among the many other problems it caused for Italy. Presbyterian leaders, however, insisted that the minister should concentrate on the churchless or wayward rather than Roman Catholics. Buggelli's extremism and bitter fights over financing, and a growing conviction among Presbyterian leaders that some services should be conducted in English rather than Italian, weakened church outreach. When Buggelli finally left in 1922 the First Italian Presbyterian Church had only 140 members.[56]

By the early 1920s Detroit also had an Italian Baptist Church, Italian Methodist Episcopal Church, and an Italian Christian Church. Those small congregations were affected by the same population shifts that hindered

Catholic Italian institutional development. The original building that the First Italian Presbyterian Church purchased from departing Germans in 1910 was in turn sold to a black congregation about eight years later. Italian Presbyterians would move east twice. Upon final relocation in 1943 the congregation decided to become Faith Presbyterian Church because the children "no longer consider themselves Italians, but just as Americans."[57]

When it came to encouraging religion among Italians, Catholics and Protestants shared a common problem: Many Italian men were nonchalant, cynical, or outright hostile about any organized church. Few were so outspoken as the attention-seeking anarchist who interrupted Reverend Buggelli at one open-air meeting in the Italian community, shouting, "We want dynamite and not God."[58] Far more usual were the Italian men who sought or acceded to important church sacraments such as baptism and marriage and who anticipated that their wives and children would practice all the familiar rituals regularly. Typical, perhaps, was a local Italian professional man who had marched into Rome with Garibaldi supporters in September 1870 and remained "not religious at all" throughout his life. His wife's "very religious" attitude was a bone of contention in the household, yet he sent their daughter to study with the IHMs at St. Vincent's and then on to a convent school.[59]

Still, from one city to another, Italian Catholic parents lagged behind other immigrant groups when it came to providing for their own parish schools, and they did not take advantage of schools in nearby parishes, either. Chicago had ten Italian Catholic parishes in 1910 but only one had a school.[60] About the same time in New York, more than seven times as many Italian children were in public as parochial school. In Philadelphia twice as many Italians were in public school.[61] Detroit had only San Francesco's school with its five hundred students in the mid-1920s, and a majority of Italian parents persistently opted for public school when, by law or by choice, they sent their children to school.

In a 1921 nationality survey, Italian students amounted to 4.8 percent of the Detroit public school enrollment. That represented more than their share of the school-age population, given the high proportion of single adult males who swelled figures for the Italian community at large. Italian children were much more likely to be in public intermediate schools than either Hungarians or Polish immigrants.[62] That pattern made Italians an important target when, during the summer of 1926, the St. Vincent de Paul Society canvassed the homes of Catholics whose children attended public schools to request that they be sent to parochial schools. Many more parents promised than responded, and so the next summer representatives went door to door again. This time the society offered to underwrite costs of books, paper, and even carfare for children living at a distance from a Catholic school. The incentive attracted 1,500 new children, most of them to schools on the east side. The School Sisters of Notre Dame viewed this infusion as something of an invasion because most of the children "were entirely foreign" to the Catholic school environment and brought deficiencies and problems of discipline that were "taxing the strength of the sisters almost beyond endurance."[63] The seventy-seven pupils San Francesco gained represented nearly a 20 percent enrollment increase. Teachers probably regarded it as a mixed blessing when the numbers soon declined again.

Historians frequently offer Italians' general alienation from institutional religion as a reason behind the unwillingness of Italian American Catholics to support their churches and give their children a parochial school education. Scholars emphasize complaints of early-twentieth-century bishops that Italians, especially from Southern Italy and Sicily, were "unexcelled in their ignorance of religion."[64] It seems evident, however, that several factors combined to keep Detroit's Italian children from attending parochial schools, regardless of whether parents were generally alienated, ignorant, or not—special problems that their priests and concerned laity could not easily surmount.

Because so many Italian men worked outside the industrial structure, their wages were often less than even those of unskilled Hungarian factory workers in Delray. At the same time, the Detroit housing market made inexpensive home-ownership tantalizing; a child's earnings could put that dream within reach. In addition, when jobs were not tied to factory districts, neither were homes. Italians sought housing wherever they could best afford it, and although they lived predominately on Detroit's east side they did not cluster in such tight communities as Poles and Hungarians and were more likely to move sooner and farther from an initial place of residence. They did not, unlike their countrymen in New York or Boston or Newark, recreate "something of the village atmosphere they left behind."[65] As a practical consequence, Italian ethnic parishes had to extend their boundaries and gather communicants from distant corners of the now far-flung city. That, in turn, meant a longer walk if children were to attend a parish school of their own.

When Italians tried to send children to closer parochial schools already established in other immigrant parishes, they found themselves a "foreign" minority whose language and culture were not included in the planned curriculum. By 1913, for example, the old German St. Joseph's parish had come to include a thousand Italians along with Hungarian, Syrian, Polish, and Irish immigrants, but the school's orientation was still toward the Germans even though their ranks were thinning. Similarly, St. Mary's, the German "mother church," described its school as having the "most polygot attendance of any school in the city" in 1930. But rather than absorbing those children, the more established parishioners, sisters, and clerics often liked to think that their school "came to the rescue" of a succession of newcomers.[66]

With that intention, St. Mary's took in and separated black children in the lower part of the school in 1901 and allocated some of those same rooms to Mexicans when they began arriving in large numbers by 1920. Coleman Young, a black child whose father had converted to Catholicism, was proud to be at such an "outstanding school" as St. Mary's, and he worked hard for the grades that qualified him for a scholarship to one of the city's best Catholic high schools. After he grew up and became the city's first black mayor, he often talked of his still-vivid grade school experiences. St. Mary's Boy Scout troop had disbanded rather than accept him as an assistant junior scoutmaster. When he arrived to enroll in Catholic high school, he was asked, "What are you, Japanese?" When he answered, "No, brother, I'm colored," the application was torn up in his face, regardless of his good grades at St. Mary's.[67]

Dividing lines were far less rigid for Italians than blacks, but in Detroit as in most places in America they were among the least tolerated of new immigrants. The city's police force organized a Black Hand squad by World War I to deal with perceived Italian crime.[68] Understandably, perhaps, Italian businessmen and professionals were preoccupied more with their countrymen's image than with matters of their education, religious or otherwise. When Italian businessmen developed their own Chamber of Commerce in 1921, the group busied itself with tasks intended to encourage Americanization, self-help, and the improvement of Italian respectability in general.[69] Prospering Italians whose families had been well established before the turn of the century kept a careful distance from the new immigrants. Minerva Maiullo, the second-generation Italian wife of a prominent second-generation Italian lawyer, devoted her time to her family and a myriad of civic and Catholic charities favored by Detroit's upper class. Her autobiography demonstrates her love for Italy's culture, art, music, and architecture. Yet the obviously philanthropic woman does not mention the Detroit Italian community that emerged after 1900, or its institutions, or any connections she might have had with it.[70]

Detroit's large Italian working class remained unprotected by the numbers, institutions, and established spokespersons that helped buffer Irish, Germans, or Poles from their detractors. There was no common neighborhood where they could pool their resources to establish a parochial school, they were fragmented by regional differences carried over from Italy, and there was no community of Italian sisters to tend to their children. Priests, bishops, and the Catholic press urged Italians to carry out their obligations as Catholic parents, but the tuition-charging parochial schools were, finally, not much more hospitable than the free public schools.

THE BELGIANS

Although Belgian clergy gained a dominant foothold in the developing diocese during Bishop Lefevere's time, the Belgian immigrant community expanded only gradually across the nineteenth century. But drawn by the city's economic boom and then propelled by the war in Europe, the 1920 census indicated that Detroit had accumulated 6,261 Belgian-born and another 3,089 who had one or both parents born in Belgium. In 1930 nearly nine thousand were born in Belgium. Detroiters claimed theirs was the strongest Belgian community in the United States.[71]

Most of the city's Belgians were Catholics who settled in, members of the diocese and residents of the city, with less tension or attention than many other Catholic immigrants. The early arrivals were an occupationally diverse lot. Several were skilled brick-makers who chose homes around the brickyards on the city's east side. One Belgian who arrived in the 1850s established a furniture firm on the east side and offered employment to his countrymen, a practice continued by his sons who operated the large factory at the turn of the century.[72]

Belgian families planted small gardens around their doorsteps, just as at home, and a Belgian neighborhood developed sufficient visibility to earn a name of its own: "Cucumber Lane." Because they were on the edge of the city, several families were able to buy acreage that extended their gardens into small farms. Pumpkin Hook Way became a "suburb" of Cucumber Lane, and east-side Belgians began hauling produce to sell year-around at Detroit's Eastern Market. Their hothouse rhubarb became a speciality, occasionally acclaimed as a Belgian "invention." Once the brickyards declined around 1900 from lack of clay, former brick-makers were able to turn to truck gardening.[73] Meanwhile, these early arrivals initiated clubs, organizations, and institutions that expanded to accommodate the Belgian influx during the first decades of the twentieth century.

Most Belgian Catholics worshiped at Ste. Anne's downtown because its French-speaking clergy and French Canadian parishioners offered the most comfortable option they had. Nonetheless, Belgians hoped America would provide an escape from the French language and culture that influenced their homeland. Adding to their discontent, Ste. Anne's pews were rented out by the year to longtime parishioners, and outsiders such as the Belgians had to stand in the back of the church during mass.[74] As soon as they had sufficient strength of numbers, Belgians asked the bishop to allow them the same opportunity as the Irish, Germans, and Poles—a church of their own.

In 1884 Belgian Catholics celebrated the opening of Our Lady of Sorrows located on the near east side in a church they purchased from German Lutherans and then remodeled. After a move in 1887 the church settled finally in 1910 at Meldrum and Berlin. The congregation had been declining because Belgians were scattering farther eastward, and the new location was thought to be better situated. In 1911 the pastor at Our Lady of Sorrows, Father Henry Syoen, reported that the church had about four thousand members, mostly Belgians and Hollanders.[75] Meanwhile, Father Syoen began a campaign to persuade Bishop Foley to let the parish invite Dominican Sisters to open a school alongside the new church. Dominicans probably did not have any Belgian women among their ranks; rather, they matched the general Belgian interest in an "American" education for Catholic immigrant children. Most important, the sisters were eager to come to the parish at a time when it was difficult to persuade religious communities to accept new schools. Nonetheless, the bishop told Father Syoen to seek some other congregation. Our Lady of Sorrows and the Belgians must have seemed more consequential than the more alien Hungarians in remote Delray where he tolerated the Dominican presence. Still the pastor persisted. When the bishop relented, the sisters rushed from Adrian even before a residence was ready and had to live for three months in one side of the rectory.[76] Within its first year Our Lady of Sorrows boasted four schoolrooms, all eight grades, 268 pupils, and five teachers.[77]

When the bishop agreed to the first Belgian parish there was no need to stipulate geographical boundaries. Our Lady of Sorrows was to stretch "wherever a Belgian is in need of a priest, no matter where he or she may be located."[78] Father Henry Syoen continued to feel an obligation to the entire Belgian community from the time he arrived in 1907 until he died, still at the parish, in 1941. Our Lady of Sorrows routinely served as a center for activities even though Belgian immigrants and the second generation were always scattered about the east side and then beyond into the Mt. Clemens and Utica area of Macomb County.

A second church, St. Charles Borromeo, was also intended as a Belgian parish when it opened in 1887. To the south and east of Our Lady of Sorrows, it was almost a "suburban" church at the time and quickly developed the multiethnic character that would become more common in suburban parishes. Along with Belgians, St. Charles attracted Irish, Dutch, and Polish families who had no national parish of their own close by. Within a decade the congregation also included Italians, Germans, and French.[79]

St. Charles Borromeo had a school from the outset. Lay teachers staffed it for its first twenty-three years, and enrollment hovered between 100 and 130. Father Christian Denissen, pastor throughout those years, spent much of his energy in a futile fight with Bishop Foley over title to an east-side acreage known as the "Church Farm." Denissen maintained that the valuable parcel belonged to St. Charles by terms of a bequest and that the parish needed the money to build a school, church, and rectory. Ecclesiastical authority and its limits were once again at issue. Neither side emerged a clear winner. Rome did not uphold Bishop Foley's unlimited prerogative to dispose of the property, but Father Denissen and St. Charles parishioners learned that they must share any proceeds with other parishes.[80] All the while, the school limped along with three lay teachers in an inadequate old building.

When Father Denissen died in 1912, the new pastor decided to start a parish "rebirth" with the school and immediately brought seven IHM sisters to help. Children had to be turned away on the first day for lack of room. Parishioners were willing to raise money, and within two years a new school replaced the "ancient" structure that the sisters had wryly christened "the ark" when they first arrived. Enrollment took a quick leap. By 1913–14, St. Charles school had nearly 450 pupils, a number that continued to climb until by 1922 the priest and sisters agreed the parish warranted a high school.[81] It was, said the proud pastor, the result of "increasing membership of the parish and the mounting prestige of the school."[82]

The school represented the diversity in the parish, and the school curriculum mirrored the sisters' usual plan, which emphasized the development of skills in English, literature and writing, the sciences, and mathematics. Here as everywhere they taught, the sisters insisted on classes that were manageable in size. There were fourteen teachers in 1925, eleven sisters and three laypersons.[83] The IHM congregation had Belgian sisters from their founding, their curriculum remained based on the model originally brought from Belgium, and their longtime spiritual director, Father Joos, was Belgian. By the time they came to St. Charles Borromeo, however, it was their reputation for excellence as educators that most interested the pastor and parents.

Detroit's Belgians never provided the same target for nativists as other immigrant groups. They filtered in more slowly and won respect for their various enterprises and willingness to work. Their neat homes impressed their neighbors, and even their avid interest in such sports as pigeon racing, bowling, and bicycle racing charmed outsiders. The small but solid Belgian middle class of truck farmers and businessmen helped establish the Belgians' reputation by the time that poorer, less skilled Belgians arrived to work in auto plants. Moreover, the "white" Belgians escaped turn-of-the-century racial stereotyping that focused on "swarthy" Southern and Eastern Europeans.

Soon after 1907, when the upswing in Belgian immigration began, Belgian factory workers won widespread sympathy along with the rest of their countrymen as their neutral homeland became a corridor once European powers went to war in 1914. Local concern centered on the Belgian laborers and auto workers who had come ahead to find employment, work hard, and save money to provide passage for their families. Now, wives and children still back home were in the midst of a war that was not of their making. Within a year, Father Syoen had sailed across the Atlantic with the intent of gathering as many of these wives and children as he could. The entire city rejoiced when he returned with 108.[84] After the war, emigration erupted and hundreds of Belgians were bound directly for the place they familiarly called "the City."

A new Belgian National parish, St. John Berchmans, started with Sunday masses in a little machine shop in the summer of 1923 until a frame church went up the next year on Mack and Chalmers. The Polish Sisters of St. Joseph from Stevens Point opened a one-room school for all eight grades in the building that doubled as a school during the week and the church on Sunday. Makeshift swingboards attached to the back of the pews served as desks. While the students studied, a canvas cloth separated the sanctuary from the body of the church. If a funeral mass was scheduled, classes were canceled, students helped take the canvas down, and then they assisted at the mass.[85]

In the mid-1920s St. John Berchmans enrolled 369 children, Our Lady of Sorrows 477, and St. Charles Borromeo 648, of whom at least a third were from Belgian families in the parish.[86] Although they clustered in those three parishes, Belgian names frequently appeared on parochial school class lists and graduation bulletins across the city. Belgian families were most heavily concentrated in the Seventeenth and other east-side wards, but Belgian families were always in all of the city's wards.[87]

Scattered as much as the Italians and even more than the Hungarians, it appears that Belgians were willing to send their children to a nearby Catholic school, especially one attended by other Northwestern Europeans and second- or third-generation American Catholics. Perhaps they more complaisantly attended German, Irish, or territorial parishes because they found a satisfactory welcome. Belgian children were physically indistinguishable from others from Northwestern Europe, and Belgian adults did not arouse suspicion or aversion. In addition, several parish pastors or their assistants shared their Belgian heritage, and many more were familiar with the country through the diocesan connection with the American College at Louvain, where selected seminarians studied after Bishop Lefevere helped establish it.

Even though the Detroit Belgian community was less than half the size of either the Hungarian or Italian communities, apparently more Belgian children attended parochial schools than children from either of those two groups. They studied under teachers, usually second- and third-generation Irish and German IHMs, Dominicans, or Polish sisters, who did not focus on the Belgian culture. When they learned a foreign language it was not Flemish. Nourished by an active community with an abundance of social clubs and sporting associations that included children as well as adults, parents may have had less concern that their children would be cut off from Old World traditions. Belgian parents seemed willing to embrace parochial schools for their religious value and for an education that they, like so many other Catholics, deemed superior to the public schools.

Father Francis Van Antwerp, the grandson of immigrants from the Netherlands, was one of the most prominent priests in the diocese and for decades an active advocate of parochial education. Unflagging in his enthusiasm still in the late 1920s, he had helped establish the first diocesan school board with the Belgian Monsignor Joos in the 1880s. As a child, Father Van Antwerp was a pupil in one of the city's IHM schools, and he remained a loyal champion of that congregation, convinced that education was salvation on earth as in heaven. From his pulpit at Our Lady of the Rosary parish and everywhere he went throughout the city, the loved and respected "Father Van" carried the same message: Catholic schools were the only option for those who would keep the faith. Any type of Catholic education was better than none, but *good* Catholic schools were the highest imperative. Belgian Catholic parents experienced less difficulty than some when it came to acting on those priorities.[88]

THE EXPANDING POLISH COMMUNITY

The major development within parochial education after the 1890s was the rapid increase of Polish schools and their escalating enrollments. In the first quarter of the new century, Detroit's Polish Catholics were a driving force behind the ethnic parish and its institutions and associations. They had strength of numbers as an invaluable resource toward their chosen end. From the turn of the century an influx of Polish immigrants accompanied the growth of the auto industry, until, as the local press exclaimed, Detroit had the fourth-largest Polish population in the world—behind only Warsaw, Lodz, and Chicago.[89]

The new immigrants were substantially different from the German Polish who dominated in the nineteenth century. Fewer German Poles came to America after 1893 because conditions in the homeland had improved at the same time there was a depression in America. Growth in the twentieth-century Detroit Polish population resulted from the large number of Russian Poles who began immigrating to America toward the end of the nineteenth century and from the thousands of families who came from Austrian-held Galicia. Galicians were the last phase in that movement of people—often called the Polish emigration *za chlebem* [for bread]—which began during the 1870s and ended with World War I. Of them all, Galician Poles arrived as the most economically depressed and socially backward.[90] Like those who came before, however, the newcomers wanted more than bread.

Starting parishes and, almost always, a school alongside within the first year, Polish immigrants described their expectations in much the same terms as those who introduced the first Polish school at St. Albertus fifty years earlier. Parents at Our Lady Help of Christians, just one of twenty-three Polish grade schools in the mid-1920s, wanted whatever education their children would need to make their way in America but expected "more of their school than mere intellectual training." They demanded "spiritual development and character formation" and training "in the knowledge of the language of their forefathers."[91] Similarly, a small group of Poles who settled on the west side near the Clippert Brickyards were determined "to assure their children of a Catholic Education" and wanted "to preserve the traditions of their forefathers." They decided "to seek pastoral care in their own native language" and in 1917 opened St. Stephen Church and a school that could accommodate 1,500 youngsters.[92]

New parishes organized classes wherever priests and parents could find space—in private homes, church halls, and even in a converted bakery. Financially stretched and trying hastily to provide proper quarters, parish building conflicts sometimes wound up in court. St. Hyacinth parishioners were aroused to sue over their priest's land purchases, and one Polish priest sued the Polish contractor over collapsed concrete.[93] Sometimes parishes tussled with each other over turf. When St. Hyacinth organized, St. Stanislaus parishioners did not want another so close and would not open their doors when canvassers came around to ask about the feasibility of a new parish.[94] Each episode gained publicity, but more often Polish Catholics won praise for their remarkable accomplishments. Polish parishes and schools doubled almost every decade. Nine schools in 1913 enrolled 8,705, and by 1925 twenty-three schools had a combined enrollment of 22,867. That meant that 46 percent of all parochial students were in Polish schools.[95]

The local press had begun to run favorable articles in praise of the "discipline which [the] gentle women in the brown habits maintain." The sight of orderly and well-behaved recesses was "astonishing." The boys "in particular" furnished an "agreeable contrast" to their compatriots at public schools nearby. With their fathers working for "wages of $1.25 to $1.75 a day" and supporting a parochial school while paying taxes to support a public one, one reporter felt "safe in prophesying that these boys will become good mechanics and industrious, well-to-do citizens, and the girls happy wives and mothers."[96]

There was remarkable consistency in the education Polish children received from the 1880s through the 1920s. Almost half of all Polish gradeschoolers continued to have Felician teachers. A majority of the others studied with Sisters of St. Joseph, the women who left the School Sisters of St. Francis to establish their own Polish community and motherhouse in Stevens Point, Wisconsin, in 1901 (chapter 5). In addition to their earliest Detroit parish grade schools at Sweetest Heart and St. Francis of Assisi, they added St. Thomas the Apostle in 1916. By 1925 the three schools enrolled 4,537 children, but the sisters stretched their slim ranks still farther to take on St. Bartholomew and Ascension parishes in the following two years.[97]

Parents and priests deliberately invited one community of teachers in preference to another. Some thought the Felicians had a greater concern for preserving Polish language, literature, and culture. Other parishes rejected the Felicians for cultural or political reasons and invited the Sisters of St. Joseph or the Sisters of St. Francis instead. The St. Joseph sisters remained proud that although they "cherished their Polish heritage" they did not have the same preservation "zeal" as congregations, including the Felicians, whose founders profited from a Polish aristocratic background.[98]

Each major community was preoccupied with internal political disputes few outsiders knew about, and the women were exhausted by the demands of being "good religious" as well as capable professionals. Every St. Joseph sister learned, according to guidelines provided in their Constitution of 1912, that she must keep "eyes on God and her pupils," and "without neglecting her religious duties" she must "labor indefatigably in the cause of education." The "end in view" regarding education was to "guide the children on the way of salvation," to "teach the science that will be most useful to them," and to "train them so that they will not only be good Christians and law-abiding citizens themselves, but be able to inspire others with a love for all that is true, noble and good."[99] It was a set of goals that the best Protestant Progressives could not have bettered; meeting them would have given pause to John Dewey.

The Sisters of St. Joseph did not have their own normal school and were hard-pressed even to provide high school diplomas for the teachers who went off to manage classrooms.[100] Like Felicians, they studied on Saturday and during summers. Bright young women were sometimes chosen for special opportunities. In 1912 three Sisters of St. Joseph went to the IHM's academy in Monroe for "two solid years of high school: Latin, algebra, ancient history and the rest."[101] That represented a considerable expense—the St. Joseph Congregation paid the IHMs $2,543.40 for tuition and boarding. Before long, Mother Superior Mary Boleslaus decided the associations a sister might form if she went away to study presented too great a risk. The three young women left Monroe soon after she sent the community a letter expressing strong disapproval of "a spirit of worldliness."[102] They returned to the common pattern. One spent the next twenty-two years completing her high school courses and earning a B.A. degree, teaching all the while.[103] Only a few gained the opportunity for full-time study, even when the congregation's leaders decided to take advantage of the Sisters' College at Catholic University during the 1920s.[104]

Congregations were always preoccupied with the need to find funds to maintain and educate themselves. Money was saved and stretched by sharing work. Novices cleaned and cooked in the motherhouse, and teaching sisters mopped, polished, and cleaned the school toilets when the children went home. The Felicians' Sister Catherine, who had accompanied Father Dabrowski from Wisconsin to Detroit in the early 1880s, remained a tireless fund-raiser to her death in the 1930s. She wrote countless letters to the likes of Detroit's mayor and Frank Murphy, then governor-general of the Philippines. "I am an old retired, hard of hearing nun," she explained in her pleas. She appealed to old family friends and relatives for a check at Christmas to surprise "my good Mother Superior." During Lent she recommended that her relatives might fast "from good drinks and Club entertainment" or "from ice cream and shows" and then send her the money. Sometimes Sister Catherine appealed to strangers: "As I read in a paper about your daughter's engagement with Count Potocki and noticing the wealth you both posses . . . it came to my mind to write."[105] She kept a careful tally, jotting down on the rough draft of each letter the sum that came back in response.

Thrust into the unaccustomed role as businesswomen in charge of substantial budgets and huge financial obligations, it is little wonder that congregational leaders sometimes had trouble setting priorities. Their serious sense of purpose prompted an occasional eccentric decision, however. In the 1920s the Sisters of St. Joseph spent almost $3,000 for a "valuable" bird, egg, and butterfly collection obtained from the curator of the Milwaukee museum. When they proudly ensconced it in their Stevens Point motherhouse academy the local paper described the collection of eggs—hummingbird, swan, eagle, ostrich, and loon—as one of the most "complete collections of birds' eggs in the middle west."[106] It was renown they could ill-afford at the time, given the dozens of women in the congregation who could speak neither Polish nor English according to correct rules of grammar and who were teaching without a high school education.

Despite it all, Polish sisters were unrelenting in the effort to do their best to influence pupils they had for "only a short time."[107] Many Polish families had at least six children, each attending for a turn and then going to work. Children had to be put in classes on the basis of their abilities rather than age. Some could read and write Polish and English because their parents were educated in America. Others could read and speak only in Polish, but some spoke Polish yet could not read or write even though they were already in their early teens.[108] That meant the schools were overcrowded in the lower grades yet unable to develop solid programs beyond the fourth or fifth grade.

Until after 1910, when Pope Pius X issued a decree permitting children as young as seven to receive their first Holy Communion, children commonly made their first communion when they were in the fourth and fifth grade. Sometimes they were twelve or thirteen. With that sacrament accomplished, enrollments subsequently fell off. Until enforcement of compulsory education laws stiffened after World War I, communicants could slip out of the classroom to full- or part-time work. Sisters joined with priests to try to convince parents to sign up their older children for school rather than keeping girls home or sending boys to the factories. Many parents thought extended education for girls was unnecessary, however, because they could be instructed by their mothers just as their mothers had been instructed by their grandmothers in Poland. For males, parental resistance to continued education was complicated by the lack of industrial arts or trades programs in Catholic schools. Some families favored sending boys to public schools for such training, but there they "were faced with culture shock" because "nowhere was there the protective Polonian spirit." Targets of ridicule or beatings, too many of the boys who dared to enroll soon dropped out.[109] Dropping out of grade school was a pattern general to other working-class groups and other cities, however. In New York City in 1913, for example, only a third of those who entered grade one completed grade eight.[110]

Harried classroom teachers enlisted older children to help the younger; sometimes the tutoring experience encouraged girls to join the sisters' ranks. Many more Polish girls did decide to join religious congregations by the early twentieth century, perhaps because "taking the habit" was socially acceptable and inexpensive. It remained their most available avenue of upward mobility.[111]

More of these young recruits were familiar with America than the older generation of Polish sisters. The leading study of Catholic education reported that in 1909 and 1910, "Fully fifty per cent of the Sisters in Polish schools speak English and Polish with equal fluency, and about eighty per cent or so were born in America or have spent all but the years of their earliest infancy here."[112] The sisters' lack of familiarity with the Polish language began to have the potential for problems, however.

Most Polish parochial schools continued an "even distribution" between the use of Polish and English throughout the 1920s, long after anti-German sentiment forced that language into the status of an elective "foreign language" in German parish schools.[113] In order to maintain teachers who could instruct pupils in Polish, in 1922 the Felicians sent two women for graduate study at the Jagiellonian University in Cracow, and three others followed them across the 1920s. Once educated, the women took up the same mission that Father Dabrowski had assumed more than fifty years earlier. Through the 1930s and into the 1940s this small core worked to preserve the language by teaching college classes in Polish and providing materials in Polish. Working sometimes with Felicians from the Chicago or Buffalo provinces who had also studied in Poland, they collaborated on a Polish-language course for Felician high schools, translated Polish versions of the Baltimore Catechism, wrote units in Polish for the study of religion in each of the eight grades, wrote texts including a Polish grammar, and developed workbooks.[114] Priests continued to sermonize on the need for children to learn Polish in school, and Polish parochial schools continued to teach classes in the language until World War II, when Polish American boys found they could not be promoted or even go to confession because they spoke and wrote Polish better than English.[115]

As early as the 1890s some within the Polish community had begun to have doubts about their schools, and critics became more outspoken in the twentieth century. Socialists were particularly vehement about the need for educating Polish children to the level of others, as was the Polish Women's Alliance, which called for sending children to secondary schools, especially public schools because they were free.[116] Some secular newspapers repeatedly pointed out the failures of Polish attitudes about education. One typical article, "Do Not Ruin Our Children's Lives," contrasted the situation of Polish children and students of other nationalities: "It is not strange therefore that among thousands of street sweepers and factory laborers only a handful of non-Polish people could be found, the rest are Poles."[117] The Communists, who had a Workers' Home in Detroit, published a newspaper from 1920 that gave much attention to education, urging readers to sign up for evening school and send children to public school.[118] They wanted the clergy out of the lives of Polish immigrants.

More common were groups that went on the defensive, some of them seeking to preserve parochial schools through radical changes. The Federation of Lay Polish Catholics, organized in 1911, aimed to wrest control from the clergy and give laypersons the right to supervise parish administration and schools. Bishops reacted sharply to the group, viewing it as a greater threat than the Communists because its members were within the church. Parishioners were forbidden to read Federation papers, and in cities like Milwaukee and Chicago, where the organization was especially strong, priests sometimes refused to bury members of the Federation in Catholic cemeteries.[119]

The two largest Polish organizations, the Polish National Alliance (PNA) and the Polish Roman Catholic Union (PRCU), struggled over the need for and the meaning of education. The PNA, created in 1880, was the largest fraternal organization in America by the mid-1920s, with 220,000 members nationally. More middle class and secular than the PRCU, the PNA was also more concerned with Polish nationalism. It sought the recreation of Poland and wanted that new nation, when it came, to be defined by secular rather than church decisions.[120] The PNA did not advocate an end to parochial schooling but criticized the poorly trained priests and nuns who taught Polish children, demanded an improved level of instruction, and advocated state supervision as the lever to bring about improvement. At the Polish Immigrants' Congress in May 1910 a PNA leader who was also a well-regarded Polish historian made the point that neither American public schools nor Polish parochial schools served Polish children well enough. Public schools were too alien and "thus dangerous for the Polish spirit and for the external forms of Polish nationality." Parochial schools were too far removed from the authority of the nation.[121] It was, for the PNA, the reason to welcome state involvement in setting standards. With the development of external accreditation by the 1920s, theirs was the course Polish schools would accept (chapter 8). Still, by then, the more conservative educational aims, reflected by the PRCU, were so firmly in place that "state standards" could not dislodge the influential role Polish language and culture continually played in the parochial school curriculum.

The PRCU was initially organized in Detroit in 1873 by a local Polish priest. It developed as the organization clergymen preferred because it saw the immigrants' most important task to be the preservation of Polish culture and religion in America. Toward those ends, the PRCU emphasized that Poles should honor their traditions and obey their clergy.[122] The PRCU, in keeping with its convictions, was especially supportive of the Polish seminary. It provided scholarships, in contrast to the PNA, which did not fund theology candidates.[123]

Some middle-class Poles supported the mainstream clerical line associated with the PRCU, but it was the PNA that won heaviest support from the middle class. By 1906 in Detroit, the PNA had twenty-five affiliated groups, with a total membership of 1,500, and it continued to attract a larger local following than the PRCU.[124] Taken together, both groups amounted to a relatively small share of the Polish community, but their messages and influence filtered through newspapers, parish councils, informal discussions, and clerics' sermons.

Often in conflict during the 1890s, the organizations edged toward a more common agreement when middle-class leaders grappled with the huge and poorer twentieth-century Polish influx. The PNA and PRCU no longer struggled over whether immigrants must call themselves Polish Catholics or Catholic Poles, an issue that once seemed of uppermost importance.[125] They could and should be Polish and Catholic. How to reconcile that identity with being an American was more problematic. Ordinary Polish immigrants in Detroit were alert to PNA concerns about recreating Poland and agreed, often actively, with the need to rein in the power of clergy over matters of finance. Like the PRCU, however, they were primarily interested in the future of their children in America.

By the war years and into the 1920s Polish leaders and the rank and file felt their best intentions were under siege. Nativists were bearing down from one side while a generation changed by growing up in America whittled away on the other. Separate schools, their earliest line of defense, remained the favorite solution among the vast majority of Detroit Poles. Parish schools seemed the best means to both Polonize and Americanize the second and third generations. If children stayed within the parish, they would not associate with those who might make them embarrassed about their parents' foreign ways. At the same time they could learn what Americans needed to know for material success and responsible citizenship.

In Detroit, Clara Swieczkowska and the Polish Activities League she cofounded represented the local staunch upper-class position that favored and fostered a Polish and Catholic identity among the immigrants. Swieczkowska, born in 1892 to immigrant parents, grew up within sight of the St. Albertus steeple. She attended grade school in the parish, went on to Cass High School, and added special courses in Detroit's business college. Her father was associated with the *Rekord Codzienny* (Polish Daily Record), founded in 1913 to offset "the somewhat anticlerical stance" of the *Dziennik Polskii* (Polish Daily News), which had been in publication since 1904. After taking courses in journalism and sociology at the University of Michigan, in 1920 Clara Swieczkowska joined her father's effort and became editor of the religious, school, and society news. She devoted her columns and various other activities to the cause of a reunited Poland and to the preservation of Polish culture in America. In 1923 she co-founded the Polish Activities League, a group of women who separated themselves from the League of Catholic Women so they could concentrate on Detroit's Polish community. The Polish Activities League aimed to help immigrants adjust to their new lives without resorting to "ill-advised attempts" at "Americanization." Children of Polish heritage, they believed, needed Polish, Catholic educations.[126] In Detroit, these middle- and upper-class Polish women did not need to launch a crusade; instead, they nourished sentiments already prevailing among the Polish working class.

As of 1921, 65 percent of Detroit's Polish children were attending parochial schools, a proportion second only to Chicago.[127] Most of the others had spent at least a few years "with the sisters," preparing for their first Holy Communions. Polish children who resorted to public schools, like twenty boys and fourteen girls from St. Casimir's in 1910, were careful that it was "by permission of the Rt. Rev. Bishop."[128] With a new parish school opening almost every year, Polish children had less cause—or excuse—than most of the other new immigrants to resort to "outside" schools of any sort unless they went on to high school.

THE STILL-INHOSPITABLE PUBLIC SCHOOLS

The public school system continued to present special disincentives for the large Polish community. Although more grade schools had been provided in immigrant neighborhoods, Polish children would have benefited most from public intermediate schools because their parish programs at that level were either limited or nonexistent. Despite nativists' claims that the board of education's building program favored foreigners, the newest intermediate schools were not conveniently accessible to Polish youths, even had their parents decided to let them continue on. In 1921, in the four new and elaborate intermediate schools that were studded with swimming pools, gymnasiums, shops, art rooms, and music rooms, only 3.7 percent of the students were Polish.[129]

Other developments further discouraged Polish parents from considering public schools. Reforms introduced in the first decades of the century emphasized English language and literature with vigorous determination. Neither the Polish language nor culture had any credence in the curriculum. Moreover, once Detroit pioneered IQ testing in 1910 and subsequently began tracking students, immigrants were especially vulnerable, regardless of any ambitions or preferences they might have.

On another front, in a highly publicized political battle one group among the school reformers attacked Ralph and Anthony Treppa, members of an old, prosperous Polish Detroit family. The reformers were led by Laura Osborn, an outspoken temperance advocate who deemed bar-owner Ralph Treppa morally unfit to serve when he was named principal of an evening school in 1907. The saloonkeeper could not, she insisted, be a proper role model for students in the largely Polish night school. His brother, Anthony, was one of the few Poles elected to the school board, still ward-based at the time. Anthony Treppa, as head of the controversial textbook committee, became a target of the reformers in 1910–11. Osborn and her supporters blatantly distorted facts to accuse Treppa of wasting thousands of dollars in book purchases and alluded that he was part of a conspiracy involving liquor dealers.[130]

The reformers accomplished their real goals with the ouster of Superintendent Wales Martindale in 1912 and with the successful referendum in 1916 that restructured the forty-two-person board of education to an "efficient" body of seven elected at-large. Polish voters bought into campaign arguments that a small board would mean better education and supported the referendum, although not so overwhelmingly as voters in most other wards. With the election of the first new board their chances of exercising influence were clear. All seven members were listed on the social register and each was a prominent businessman or professional, with the exception of Laura Osborn, the reformer who had led the attack on the Treppa brothers.[131]

In the view of reformers who came to their task with an anti-foreign bias, Poles were just part of the whole problem. An Italian who taught night school was fired in 1908 because he worked days as a bookkeeper in a brewery.[132] The idea of using immigrants to teach immigrants lost ground as the population seeking night school education grew. With enrollment in Americanization classes leaping from three thousand in 1912 to twenty-seven thousand in 1922, the Detroit public school superintendent determined that it was necessary to have the best instructors, which meant "wide-awake, socially efficient American instructors."[133] The system stopped hiring immigrants as teachers for Americanization courses.

Ethnic leaders supported the night school program, but the demeaning level of instruction was not lost on the editor of the *Polish Daily Record*. In 1915 he wrote indignantly to the sponsoring Detroit Americanization Committee that one instructor might have drawn a picture of a cow rather than drop to all fours to mimic one. "The Polish people talked a great deal in their homes about the antics of the teachers," and in the editor's opinion that detracted from the "value of the lesson."[134] For the most part, the protracted campaign to bring about educational reform sustained derogatory images of Poles on one side and on the other reinforced Poles' distrust of the entire public school operation. They may have voted for the small board plan because they hoped for a better system, but Polish Detroiters continued to avoid the public schools throughout the next decade.

THE HAMTRAMCK EXPERIENCE

Polish perceptions of the unwelcome reception they might expect from Detroit public schools contrasted with the situation in nearby Hamtramck. A 2.09-square-mile enclave surrounded by Detroit, Hamtramck developed on the edge of Detroit's west-side Polish neighborhood. From a rural village with about five hundred in 1900 it mushroomed to a full-blown industrial city after the Dodge Brothers' auto plant located there in 1910. For decades it would rank as the largest Polish city in America. By 1920 two-thirds of the 48,615 Hamtramck residents were Polish-born, and most of the rest were of Polish extraction.[135] When it became a municipality in 1922, the first mayor was Polish and the board of education was composed exclusively of Poles.[136]

By the mid-1920s, 66 percent of all Hamtramck children attending school were in the public system, and public school students were predominantly Polish Catholics. A student nationality survey in 1925 found that 5,400 of 7,526 public school pupils were Polish, more than half of them not yet citizens.[137] Hamtramck public schools grew at an average rate of about 27 percent, compared to 6 percent for non-public schools in the early 1920s.[138] Still, parochial schools enrolled at least as many Polish Catholics as public schools. Three parishes, all built after 1909, handled the parochial students in classrooms more crowded than most any Polish parish school in Detroit. At St. Florian's, Hamtramck's largest parochial grade school in 1925, twenty-seven Felicians sisters and three lay teachers taught 2,217 pupils. The Felicians also taught at Our Lady Queen of Apostles, which enrolled 1,316, and the School Sisters of St. Francis conducted the school at St. Ladislaus, which had 1,540 students. In contrast to Hamtramck public school classrooms that had a student capacity of forty-five, the parochial schools commonly had more than seventy pupils in a classroom.[139]

Families in Hamtramck often made calculated use of both public and parochial schools. Catholic school enrollment was heaviest among children between the ages of seven and twelve, the years when they prepared for the sacraments of Communion and Confirmation. Because Hamtramck public schools provided convenient kindergartens, children often started in public school, shifted to parochial school for the grades that provided the most critical religious instructions, and then went back to public school, which had more complete upper-grade programs. Polish became a standard part of the junior high curriculum, and public schools enrolled 1,467 youths aged fourteen or fifteen in 1925, whereas non-public schools had only 217 in the same age group.[140] None of the Hamtramck parishes provided a high school throughout the 1920s, and parents who decided on secondary education sent children to the public school, other than the few who chose the new Polish Catholic high school at St. Josephat's or the Felician Academy, both some blocks from Hamtramck's border.

Although junior high and high schools were the fastest-growing sectors of Hamtramck's public school system during the 1920s, dropout rates escalated in this working-class Polish community once children reached sixteen; 58 percent of sixteen-year-olds and 85 percent of seventeen-year-olds were no longer in school.[141] Where Detroit had twenty-one children in the twelfth grade for every hundred in the fifth, Hamtramck at the same time had only three for every hundred.[142] Yet Hamtramck High enrolled 655 in 1925, substantially more students than were in all of Detroit's Polish Catholic high schools combined (chapter 7).[143]

Public school leaders took a careful, statistical look at their students and decided they should develop an industrial and vocational program. It was also necessary, the board of education believed, to make provision "for all other types of opportunity, in order that every child may be accorded the training which is best fitted to the development of his native ability."[144] To take advantage of training that would bring higher pay or a more fulfilling career would postpone a teenager's earnings, however. It was the working-class family's predicament.

Hamtramck helps shed light on decisions Polish immigrant families in the working class were making. They may have believed they had few choices when it came to cutting education short, given the expenses they must stretch to meet. About 85 percent of Hamtramck's household heads were factory workers, half of them unskilled.[145] Nonetheless, nearly 78 percent of the city's residents owned or were buying their their own homes by the mid-1920s.[146] They also made steady contributions to build and maintain their large churches, and then there were the sums they took to one of the many exchanges up and down the main streets, conscientiously turning dollars into money orders to send back home. To manage it all, wives took part-time housekeeping jobs while daughters and sons left school as soon as they could start to work. As far as one public school survey could determine, 65 percent of boys who left school in 1924–25 immediately entered the factories.[147] Even though Hamtramck Poles made more use of the public school system than their countrymen in Detroit, they decided they could not afford the extent of its opportunities.

The Polish middle class had little sympathy with the choices their poorer countrymen were making. Parents, they charged, selfishly exploited children. Some leaders and newspaper editors could sound as vitriolic as nativists when they ranted about Polish immigrants' failure or unwillingness to understand how important education was to success in America. They correctly assessed that thousands of Polish children were at a disadvantage. So, too, were other Catholic immigrant children if their parochial schools could not help counter the economic liabilities of growing up in poor, working-class families.

GRADE SCHOOLS FOR THE SECOND AND THIRD GENERATION

Parish schools may have become more significant than ever by the time of World War I, with the city now larger and social expectations more complex. The Catholic hierarchy had come to the firm conclusion that parish grade schools were invaluable and that ethnic parish schools remained acceptable. A new Code of Canon Law promulgated in 1918 made the obligation to attend parochial school explicit and also ensured immigrants' rights to continue establishing national parishes. But permission to create a juridical national parish—which had legal status and the right to priests of the same national origin as parishioners—was a decision resting with the Vatican rather than bishops after 1918.[148] At the same time it preserved ethnic parishes, the Code promoted the development of territorial parishes and thus earned regard as a masterful compromise; now bishops encouraged the descendants of immigrants to join territorial parishes rather than establish new ones based on nationality.[149] The Code of Canon Law, coupled with the economic gains made by the middle and lower-middle classes in Detroit, contributed significantly to both the ethnic and class-based territorial parish schools that proliferated after 1918.

Long-time differences among Catholic grade schools did not fade. The gap between strong and weak parish schools, if not wider than before, mattered more in the new twentieth-century city. Working-class immigrant parishes continued to vary in curriculum, class size, facilities, and quality of instruction. Meanwhile, as Detroit's economy changed, second- and third-generation immigrants of every nationality were promoted into the middle class and could provide schools with smaller classes, newer facilities, and better-trained teachers. Sometimes second- and third-generation Irish, German, Belgian, and Polish children began to meet in the same schools.

When the longer-established immigrants moved from their first ethnic parishes, their familiar sisters, whether in black, blue, or brown habits, went with them. And, again as earlier, fewer different religious communities taught Detroit children compared with places such as Chicago, which had fifty separate orders by the time of World War I. Between them, by 1925 the Felicians and IHMs taught almost half the city's Catholic students; the Sisters of St. Joseph and their parent community, the Sisters of St. Francis, instructed another quarter of the children.

The Dominicans began developing as a significant influence, however, once the unfriendly Bishop Foley died and Bishop Michael Gallagher replaced him. Foley had repeatedly encouraged the Adrian Dominicans to accept schools in the Chicago Archdiocese, able to shunt them off because of the significant increase in women who were joining all religious congregations. For Irish and German parishes, Foley continued to favor the IHMs, and, lacking Polish sisters, the Dominicans seemed no help on that front. The Hungarians' Holy Cross school remained the one assignment Bishop Foley permitted Dominicans to take in the city of Detroit until 1911, when he "reluctantly" gave in after the pastor of the Belgian parish, Our Lady of Sorrows, "harassed" him for a year.[150] The Dominicans developed a local network of supportive priests and parishioners from among their families and friends and began infiltrating the suburbs, starting with St. Mary's of Royal Oak, Michigan, in 1916. "Eyebrows were raised," but St. Mary's priest and congregation would have no other sisters, and eighty-three-year-old Bishop Foley "had begun to nod."[151] The Dominicans' long-time "alien footing in Detroit" finally ended three years later when Bishop Gallagher granted "spontaneous approval" for them to take over schools at St. Gabriel and St. Ambrose.[152] Not only was Gallagher familiar with their solid reputation in Grand Rapids and Chicago, but the growing community of second- and third-generation Catholic women also fit well with the needs developing quickly as second- and third-generation Detroit Catholics established new neighborhoods.

The Dominican provincial house in Adrian had its own certification program from 1896, and selected sisters had attended Catholic University's summer school for sisters. Once state requirements loomed, however, Dominicans rushed to summer school at Ypsilanti State Normal and Detroit Teachers' College, where fifty-six gained certification in 1921–22. In 1925 the Dominicans gained state approval to grant certification at their own St. Joseph's College in Adrian, incorporated just six years earlier.[153]

Many priests and parishioners viewed the Dominicans as more flexible, adaptable, and perhaps more malleable than certain other communities of teachers. They did not have the firmly fixed educational theory common to IHMs, and because their leaders were convinced assimilationists they did not have a commitment to either German or Polish culture and language. Still, like other congregations of women, Dominican superiors insisted on assigning and monitoring their own sister-teachers. When one priest asked that a sister be removed because she was inclined to be tomboyish, her long-time superior, Mother Camilla, replied, "Ah, yes, she is, Father, but she has a great heart. She is so lovable in the school and in the house that we could never take her away from the children and the sisters. Let us try to tone her down without changing her." When another priest wanted a "sour" sister transferred, Mother Camilla "shook her head" and persuaded him that the woman was a "prize lemon."[154] By 1925 the Dominicans staffed nine parish schools in the city.

The "long blue line" of IHMs meanwhile retained a dominant place and extended their reach (fig. 7). By 1925 the IHMs staffed fifteen of the city's sixty-three parochial schools and taught almost twelve thousand students, a quarter of the city's parochial pupils. They had more than double that number of students in other schools throughout the diocese. Concerned not to overextend their pool of teachers, they accepted schools selectively. As a result, IHM schools were able to keep class size within the same range as public schools without resorting to the half-days periodically necessary within the public system. At their largest school, Holy Redeemer, which enrolled 1,762 students in the grade school and the girls' high school in 1925, the sister superior assigned thirty-two sisters and hired nine additional lay teachers.[155]

IHM educational goals had changed little from the 1870s when they embraced Dupanloup's and the St. Andre System's philosophy. They remained convinced that Dupanloup was correct in writing that "we must have a profound respect for what the wisdom of the ages has sanctioned, what the very nature of things . . . demands and insists upon." Steeped in his legacy, they independently decided they should combine the wisdom of the ages "with what is demanded by the conditions of the present, the march

Figure 7. Regarded by other communities as a dominating "long blue line," a reference to the color of their habits, the IHM congregation's influence indeed stretched far. In this 1933 or 1935 photograph, the full extent of their ranks is not visible. Several dozen novices and postulants marched ahead of these professed sisters in a eucharistic procession on the grounds of their Monroe, Michigan, motherhouse. (Archives of the Sisters, Servants of the Immaculate Heart of Mary)

of time, the progress of the human mind, and the changed conditions of society."[156] Feeling justified, IHM "master teachers" revised the grade school course of study in 1910 to make English the "backbone of the curriculum" and then again in 1930 when they were intent on enriching core subjects and making use of "scientific research by the best educators of today."[157]

All IHM grade and high school teachers were certified before state law required it in 1925. By that point many had a bachelor's degree, and fifteen of the high school teachers held masters of arts degrees.[158] In the process of educating themselves at considerable expense, IHM leaders renegotiated salary arrangements. In addition to the music teacher's salary at each school, they gained a fourth of the music money earned from private lessons. By 1919 the bishop announced that he was increasing teacher salaries $200 to $250 a year for all sisters teaching in the diocese. Eight years later the minimum went up to $40 a month.[159]

Over the years, certain premier schools requested IHM teachers. The bishop asked them to direct the Cathedral parish schools, and when the Jesuits moved their university from downtown to a developing section in northwest Detroit in the mid-1920s the priests established Gesu parish for the adjacent middle-class Catholic neighborhood and invited IHMs to staff the school. By then the sisters were in the process of relocating their own women's college from Monroe to become Marygrove College on a campus they were building less than a mile away from the Jesuits' University of Detroit. Within three years Gesu was a model elementary school where carefully supervised Marygrove student teachers practiced on the city's upper-middle-class Catholic children. Many of their parents had once learned the same lessons from IHM sisters in parishes such as St. Joseph's, St. Vincent's, or Holy Trinity.

The IHMs opened other schools in new working-class neighborhoods developed by lower-middle-class, second-generation Catholics, and the sisters also maintained their original schools. Back in those old parishes, immigrant arrivals and children whose parents were left behind studied the same curriculum from the same books as the children at Gesu. The sisters continued to rotate every few years from one parish to another. At St. Vincent's, still one of the outstanding parochial schools in the city, sisters noted in their convent chronicle at the end of the 1925–26 school year that "the type of pupils was noticeably changed—as the environment did not attract" and "the older members of the parish began moving out to more restricted districts." Still, they were pleased. "There was very good attendance," and "we had very nice pupils."[160] Nearly all six hundred families were English-speaking "Americans."[161] There were fewer students—777 compared with 878 in 1917 and 950 in 1900—but the school had the same number of teachers, which meant that class size was smaller than before. St. Vincent's students studied literature and science, drilled on grammar, arrived early to do mental arithmetic between the first and second bells, said prayers, and heard about how to eat a banana properly. Here were children of the working class who learned the same lessons as children of the middle class at Gesu or Blessed Sacrament Cathedral School.

Several schools had become more class-based than ethnic in character, with a mixture of nationalities. That was especially true in such older parishes as St. Mary's, with its few black students and Hungarians, Syrians, Italians, and Irish. St. Charles Borromeo had a mixture of Germans, Belgians, and Polish.[162] A new parish could not count on being homogeneous, even if planners wanted it that way. St. Louis the King was built to the far north edge of the city when Bishop Gallagher received real estate from a Polish donor on the condition that a Polish Catholic Church be established on it. Felician sisters agreed to staff the school, but when it opened in 1924 Polish children were just part of a cosmopolitan group that included Italians, French, Irish, Germans, and other assorted Catholics from the area.[163]

Schools remained an important part of church politics. Reminiscent of the Kolasinski controversy, Bishop Gallagher asked Felician sisters to start a school at St. Stephen's on the west side of Detroit in 1918 and Our Lady Help of Christians on the north side in 1924. Both parishes were placed deliberately to offset progress of the schismatic independent Polish national-al churches, and both were intended to reclaim "misled" Polish parents or prevent others from straying.[164] Felicians also went to Resurrection parish in 1921 as soon as that independent church "reconciled" with the diocese.[165] In each case, the sisters' presence helped assure Poles that theirs was a par-ish in good standing. The schools encouraged parish membership and helped persuade new families to settle in the vicinity. St. Stephen's initially opened with six grades, four sisters, and 329 children; ten years later it offered all eight grades, had a staff of twelve sisters and two lay teachers, and enrolled 1,029 children.[166]

The number of pupils per classroom is a ready if superficial sign of the inequalities in parochial grade school education. An average of seventy-five to eighty-five students in each classroom was common in Polish schools. Meanwhile, the teacher-pupil ratio was dropping in the schools attended by Germans and Irish, immigrants or their descendants, and in those old central city parishes with a variety of nationalities. Territorial parishes in neighborhoods of lower density also had fewer children in each classroom. Indeed, a principal occasionally expressed some displeasure when new ad-jacent parishes siphoned off enrollment from her established school.

Children in poorer parishes were not uniformly disadvantaged. At a point in the mid-1920s, for example, when the original Irish parish of Most Holy Trinity had been substantially affected by out-migration and served a pre-ponderantly lower-middle- and working-class population, the grade school retained many staff members from its earlier era, had the same curriculum as before, and maintained a ratio of thirty-four students per teacher. A few miles to the west, however, the Polish school at St. Casimir's drew from a similar working-class population, but there Felician Sisters, some just out of high school, handled classrooms in which the average size was seventy-four and where four children were packed into seats originally intended for two.[167]

It is mostly in retrospect that such disparities assume significance. In the first quarter of the twentieth century, America meant widened opportuni-ties, and Detroit, with its substantial Catholic middle class, represented how high the children of immigrants might aim. Grade schools were prerequi-sites for secondary schools, which led in turn to college and the professions. But even the illiterate could earn factory wages that bought houses, built churches, and amazed relatives left behind in Europe. Not all parents were able or willing for their children to go on for more schooling. Not all children were equally prepared to continue, trapped as much by their grade schools as by their ethnic or class origins.

The advantages immigrant children gained by studying with teachers who shared their language or were willing to support their family's religious values are not readily calculated. Certainly, from early immigrant priests to currently imminent historians, many have made a favorable case. Their own parochial schools helped immigrants "minimize the contest" between generations, according to Oscar Handlin, as well as resist the "onslaught of the surrounding Protestant culture on their faith and traditions," according to John Higham.[168] Too many youngsters grew up without an "even" chance through a combination of circumstances—which included a flawed early education. Still, the various parochial grade schools offered immigrants' children a more certain haven than the public schools and experiences sufficiently appreciated that the graduates, once adults, sought the same for their children.

Detroit parish schools took on a herculean task that Detroit public schools had not chosen, dared, or imagined. Parochial schools managed it as well as they did out of dedication to purpose. Sylvia Tackowiak was just one of the Polish immigrant daughters who went on to high school, joined the convent, and became part of the teaching profession. It was a path she selected, perhaps by the age of ten, because of her parochial school experience.[169]

Parish grade schools, sixty-thee of them by the mid-1920s, were wooden and brick monuments to the impact parochial education had on Detroit's economy, politics, neighborhoods, and public schools. The impact parochial schools had on the city's children, for good and for ill, may perhaps be understood only through the very individual perceptions of Sylvia Tackowiak and all the others.

Surely these many schools were sometimes liberating and sometimes limiting, regardless of a child's ability, talent, or nationality. Grade school was an almost universal experience for Detroit children by the time of the Great Depression. Whatever a grade school education might mean to immigrants and their children, the advantages depended importantly on circumstances of chance. For all of the current statistically laden enthusiasms on behalf of education—to assess curricula, to do content analysis of texts, to factor in class size, to measure student "outcomes," and to legislate teacher "accountability"—perhaps we can learn from the past. It would be worthwhile to improve upon chance.

7   *Higher Ambitions: Secondary Schools*

... never say the public school is just as good and costs me less—this
is not true, because education without religion is no education.
—Father F. J. Van Antwerp, Our Lady of the Rosary pastor, in
A Catholic Manual of Instruction and Official Guide (1926)

PAROCHIAL grade schools sifted Catholic immigrants and their
children from Protestants, Jews, and other Catholics, to the approval of
parishioners and, as events of the 1920s would show, with the approbation
of most Detroiters. When the city's Catholics began to develop their separate secondary schools by the last quarter of the nineteenth century, it was
for many of the same reasons they built elementary schools. Intending to
prepare students for the world of broadened opportunity where they might
mingle equally with peers of any nationality or religion, Catholic high
schools often elaborated on established patterns.

Organized efforts to introduce separate Catholic secondary institutions
followed in the wake of public initiatives. The first tax-supported high school
opened in Detroit in 1858, just a few years after the divisive issue of tax funding for Catholic schools soured attitudes. The acknowledged "founding father" of the public high school was D. Bethune Duffield, who, with his Presbyterian minister father, had led denunciations of Bishop Lefevere, parochial
schools, and Catholics during the school question controversy. Duffield's active role, pervasive Protestant influence at all levels, and the public school drift
toward secularism discouraged Catholics from embracing the advantages of
a public high school. But the enthusiasm of almost all residents was limited,
and enrollment lagged. Not until 1876 were all four secondary grades finally
under one roof.[1] Grade school, or a few years beyond, would be the limit of
education for many children well into the twentieth century. Youngsters in
Detroit proved even less likely to stay in school than were those in other large

Michigan communities such as Grand Rapids, Battle Creek, and Bay City once Detroit's unskilled job opportunities blossomed.

The educational distance began to widen gradually among America's children, however, separating those who could manage extended schooling from those who could not.[2] Nationally, it was becoming a matter of concern to some observers that isolated farm children, restricted to one-room rural schools, were falling behind the opportunities afforded urban children. By the late 1870s the University of Michigan and the state normal school at Ypsilanti were admitting high school graduates without examination. Meanwhile, diversification in Detroit's economy expanded the spectrum of jobs, with new advantages going to young men and women who had at least some secondary schooling. Catholics who were alert to the opportunities wanted their children to have these chances for fortune, but still they worried about safeguarding the faith.

By the mid-1870s when the Third Plenary Council issued its firm demand for a Catholic education for grade school children, parents, grade school teachers, priests, and church spokesmen were already beginning to be apprehensive about those trickling into the new public high schools. Secondary schools seemed to present special risks, they thought, for youngsters who were still impressionable but forming independent friendships and approaching a marriageable age. Elsewhere, the central Catholic high school gained a "great impetus" and became a "clear and high ideal" when Thomas E. Cahill, a wealthy Philadelphia resident, left money in his will in 1879 to build and operate a boys' Catholic high school.[3] A comparable girls' high school developed a few years later.[4] Benefactors came forward in other cities, and central, sex-segregated boys' and girls' Catholic high schools became the norm. In Detroit, however, parents, priests, and sisters preferred to build on familiar experiences.

Jesuit priests opened the doors to the city's first Catholic preparatory school for boys in 1877, just a few blocks from the brand new public high school opened the year before, and the Christian Brothers soon started a commercial program for boys even before the public school had one in place. Those institutions were not options, however, for studious immigrants' daughters whose interest in becoming teachers made high school almost mandatory. The Irish at Most Holy Trinity became the first parish to offer a high school for their girls, graduating a class of young women from an abbreviated program in 1881. Several other parishes scrambled to do the same or better, thwarting the bishops' preferences for a central Catholic high school.

The development of private Catholic academies and high schools on the base of ethnic parish grade schools required teachers able and willing to provide secondary courses and students sufficiently prepared to advance. That meant children of the Irish and Germans came to have the advantage first. It also meant that because parochial high schools were almost uniformly taught by sisters, they were initially available only to girls. Not until the early twentieth century, when the bishop tacitly permitted sisters to teach older boys, did sons from poorer families have access to a Catholic secondary education more affordable than that provided in the Jesuit and Christian Brothers' schools.

The Catholic institutions were tiny by comparison with the city's public high schools. More like small-town public high schools, the education students received varied in quality from outstanding to marginal, depending on the teachers and curricula. Parish schools lacked the range of courses, physical facilities, and the extracurricular opportunities a central school might have afforded. Because of their small student bodies, however, teachers were able to provide classes more like tutorials, which, at their best, matched the education of expensive elite prep schools. The many ethnic parish high schools also meant that many Catholic youths, even those of the same nationality, grew up with little occasion to mingle with countrymen living on the other side of town.

Each Detroit Catholic high school came to have its own niche and atmosphere. Parish chauvinists liked to describe why their schools were "the best," even among other Irish schools or other German schools. They would tick off distinctions that might have seemed insignificant to outsiders and, in fact, often were. Nonetheless, parents might deliberately select one neighborhood over another because of its parish school. A cadre of priests developed diocesan visibility as leaders because of the schools they helped guide. Students, in the process, earned reputations or made contacts based upon the schools from which they graduated.

THE JESUIT HIGH SCHOOL

Certain schools were so distinctive as to command recognition beyond the Catholic community. Chief among them was the Jesuit's Detroit College. Detroit College occupied a privileged place from the time Bishop Borgess initiated it to provide Catholic education for boys, especially the sons of the middle class and the wealthy who were enrolling in the public high school in growing numbers. Some Catholics had hoped to bring the Jesuits to Detroit for years. In the 1840s the elite order had rejected a request from

Bishop Rese, accepting instead an invitation from Cincinnati's bishop. That city was then nearly five times larger than Detroit and was also closer to the Jesuit headquarters in St. Louis.

Within a few years after he arrived, Borgess approached the Jesuits on behalf of the diocese. He had studied with the Jesuits at St. Xavier's College, and the years he spent as chancellor of the Cincinnati diocese helped give him contacts with Jesuit leaders. He knew, as well, that the bishop of Cincinnati helped persuade Jesuit fathers to establish St. Xavier's College by turning over a church to them. Borgess had tried unsuccessfully to make that kind of arrangement with the Basilian fathers before approaching the Jesuits. But although he had offered the German parish church, St. Mary's, to the Basilians, he offered the much finer cathedral parish of SS. Peter and Paul to the Jesuits. His generosity served several purposes.

SS. Peter and Paul, of all the parishes, had the greatest gap between parishioners. Territorial rather than ethnic since the time it was established by Bishop Lefevere, it had remained a fashionable church of the wealthier Catholics in the central part of the city. It also attracted a contingent of poorer and transient families who took up residence in cheap housing tucked among businesses and industries. The situation created problems for the parish school. Vocal upper-class parents had been displeased in the 1860s when the IHMs replaced the Christian Brothers as their sons' teachers, and a few withdrew them in favor of boarding schools out of state. Those same parents often chose to send daughters to the Madames' Sacred Heart Academy. A number complained openly that they did not want to send their children to SS. Peter and Paul's school because of the poorer children who were there. By winning the Jesuits and providing them with that church, the bishop would give wealthy parishioners an elite school for their sons conveniently close to home and prestigious Jesuit priests as their church pastors. Other Catholic parents throughout the city whose sons were bright and motivated would have the opportunity to provide an enviable Catholic education if they could afford it.

In April 1877 Bishop Borgess and the Missouri Jesuit provincial entered into an agreement that gave Detroit its Jesuit "College or School." The Jesuits received six lots, the church, a pastoral residence, school buildings, and "parochial charge" of the parish. Should they later decide it was "necessary or advisable to change the location" of their school, they could move it to another part of the city and build a church and organize a parish nearby.[5] It was an option the fathers would exercise in the mid-1920s.

The Jesuit school started out with the gifts of valuable land and buildings in place, significant financial advantages. The IHMs, Felicians, and other communities of women had to raise donations and work for the money to build their own institutions. Parishes had to pay the diocese interest when they received building loans—3 percent compounded annually from 1905 to 1920, when interest went up to 6 percent because "the Diocesan funds are being invested at the rate of 6 percent."[6] The Jesuits also went into debt, however, in borrowing almost $30,000 to purchase and remodel a large three-story brick home opposite their residence for the new school venture. The priests did not take a teaching salary. Running the school on "sort of a family basis" instead, they pooled various sources of money, including collections from SS. Peter and Paul, the salary for two priests at that church (which totaled $1,000), and stipends for helping minister to neighboring parishes.[7]

The Jesuits spent money frugally but still managed to afford more than most parish schools. Before the first academic year opened, the fathers ordered fifty double desks at $3.75 apiece, an unattainable luxury for crowded Polish schools. Books to start a library came from Jesuit houses in St. Louis, Chicago, and Cincinnati. Tuition of $40 a year and a book bill that added up to $9.37 for the older boys also helped set the school apart from the outset.[8]

Detroit College, in Jesuit tradition, was conceived as a seven-year program that would lead to the bachelor's degree (fig. 8). The course of instruc-

Figure 8. This massive main building of the University of Detroit, new on the Jefferson Avenue campus in 1889, symbolized the equally solid place Jesuit-trained students were carving out in the city. (Emil Lorch Collection, Michigan Historical Collections, Bentley Historical Library, University of Michigan)

tion envisioned a three-year academic department corresponding to the second, third, and fourth years of high school, followed by the four-year collegiate department. The academic department became known as University of Detroit High School in 1911, when the university was chartered. Initially, Detroit College had to offer a class of "rudiments" for boys not sufficiently advanced to get into the high school program. Other boys, judged able, were placed into the second or even third year of the high school program when they entered. As with parish high schools, advanced levels were added year by year; the collegiate department began offering classes in 1881.

The high school program was the most immediately interesting to Detroiters. It received favorable coverage not only the diocesan *Western Home Journal* but also in the *Evening News, Free Press,* and the German *Die Stimme der Wahrheit.* The Jesuit "image" warranted attention, too. The *News* made haste to explain the Jesuits and their purpose in Detroit, aiming to reassure the "average American" who "must have experienced a small thrill of horror" upon learning "this dreaded order had actually established a branch in Detroit."[9] The *Western Home Journal* described the Jesuits as ardent in their support of political liberty and having the respect of the American heroes George Washington, Ben Franklin, and Andrew Jackson.[10] That newspaper and its successor, the *Michigan Catholic,* hammered on the role the Jesuits' school played in support of democracy. The image and reputation of the school developed most, however, from its demanding curriculum, from the esprit de corps it cultivated among its loyal students, and from the popular college athletic teams that won visibility for the whole Jesuit enterprise.

Before the school opened, the fathers distributed the plan of studies intended eventually to include "the doctrines and evidences of the Catholic Religion, Logic, Metaphysics, Ethics, Astronomy, Natural Philosophy, Chemistry, Bookkeeping, Arithmetic, the Latin, Greek, English, French and German languages."[11] The school year ran from the first Monday of September to the last Wednesday of June, and the school day—longer than in public high schools—extended from 8:30 A.M. mass through 4 P.M. Parents were urged to insist that their sons study at home for two to three hours every evening.

Fostering competition and rivalry were favorite motivating techniques. Students took monthly tests, and the priests handed out monthly bulletins indicating "conduct, application, progress and attendance." At the end of each semester, for all the community to see, the diocesan newspaper listed the names and scores of boys who took and scored above seventy-five in the semiannual examinations.[12] Each June the school's catalog printed the standing of the boys in merit points. Parents whose sons were at the bottom, or perhaps just not near enough to the top, felt a share of the boys' shame. Publishing the ratings reinforced the lesson that this was a serious academy.

In 1877, the first year, the Jesuits admitted seventy-four boys. Four of them, from wealthy Catholic families, came back from Notre Dame's prep school and another had returned from St. Xavier in Cincinnati. For the remainder of the century the annual number of new admissions varied, usually between 80 and 105 in 1900. The private high school was beyond the means of many families. Not only was the $40 tuition prohibitive but books were also far more expensive than in parish schools, and the dress suits required for special events meant higher clothing costs. Some middle- or lower-class families afforded the Jesuit education by pooled earnings, help from relatives, by paying in monthly installments of $5, or by scholarships.[13] So many boys worked part-time and weekends to help meet their costs that after a few years the Jesuits had to give up their preference for a midweek break, which had meant that boys went to school on Saturday rather than Thursday. One alumnus thought the economic differences among students "worked for democracy." Boys whose fathers and mothers denied "themselves of real necessities to put their boy through" met with "a few lily-white youngsters who wore sweet little curls and [a] beautifully laundered . . . collar, whose adoring parents used to bring them to and from school in their vehicles." The "little darlings had their purple and fine linen soiled . . . and twists taken out of their curls during the rough 'recess' play of their poorer and perhaps envious fellows." It worked out, he thought, so that some of the rich boys "actually learned to fight, a valuable addition to other kinds of knowledge."[14]

Attending Detroit College required other assets than money, however. Boys needed an adequate grade school preparation and teachers or priests who would push them on. The first year, one or two students came from each of the German and Irish grade schools; St. Mary's sent seven and Most Holy Trinity sent six. The pattern held for decades, and the school remained dominated by German and Irish families. Year after year a disproportionate number of boys were from Trinity grade school—sixty-three in the first ten years of the school's existence. In most years before World War I, Trinity grade school graduates made up at least 10 percent of each new class.[15] Bonds of cooperation between parish teachers and priests and the men at Jesuit High could help a boy gain access or ease his way; beside the name of one Trinity boy went the notation, "Nervous, tender treatment." Here and there in the record book were instructions, penned in, to send "reports and bills to Fr. Savage." It seems likely that the long-time priest at Trinity occasionally helped pay a boy's way.[16]

Sisters tapped certain students who they thought had academic promise. One Corktown boy expected to go to work after finishing St. Aloysius grade school until one of the sisters summoned his mother to advise her, "This boy deserves a chance to go on." His mother, a widow, ran a boardinghouse to support her three children, but the sister's assessment "changed all of our plans," as the grateful boy later recalled it. He was placed in the Jesuit's high school as a junior, graduated with the highest average even though he was the youngest boy in the class, and went on to become a lawyer.[17] Such stories fill anniversary booklets. Missing are the memoirs of boys who did not attract a sister's attention, whose parents needed their wages immediately, or who failed along the way.

Boys with Polish surnames or from Polish grade schools were slow to arrive at the Jesuit high school even though the city had a number of large Polish parish grade schools by the early 1890s. Occasionally, someone made an encouraging gesture. In 1891 eight boys came from St. Casimir's, all on half-tuition.[18] But Polish schools did not begin to contribute students on a regular basis until nearly 1916. The reasons were as complex as the Polish community itself. Some Polish parents active in church politics were likely unwilling to send their sons to the "establishment" Jesuit school favored by the bishop and dominated by Irish and Germans. Polish parents also had their own Polish seminary where boys could study for a time before making a final commitment to the priesthood. And then, too, many were unprepared by their grade schools for a high school so demanding as the Jesuit regimen. One of the two boys who went from St. Hyacinth found it quite a change from classrooms where "almost everything was given in Polish."[19] Unfortunately, Polish parishes did not offer their own high school opportunities until after World War I—and sometimes not then. The real lure for Polish boys was not the public high schools but rather the factories, which were their neighborhood centers.

Each year the Jesuit high school did attract Catholic boys who had attended public grade or high schools, and a few Protestant parents also sent their children—the record book noted two Episcopalians in 1892. And in the early years of the school's existence there were always a few boys who came from rural Michigan, out of state, or from nearby Canada. Some lived with relatives while they went to school, and the Jesuits helped make boarding arrangements for others.

The boys cemented their separate experience at Detroit College by ceremonies repeated annually until they were traditions—like the faculty-student procession across school grounds and into church for the "Red Mass" of the Holy Spirit that marked the beginning of each school year. They reinforced their classroom relationships in literary and debating societies and with baseball and football teams; they built camaraderie through shared tales of what they had endured from priests who banned tobacco on the grounds, ripped off "slouch" hats, denounced "cheap theaters," or meted out a "jug"— which meant detention minutes after school. They gave themselves status by calling their teachers "Professor" or "'Fessor" rather than "Mister."[20]

Some parents objected that the school's classical education, which required Greek in addition to Latin, was not adequately preparing students for the broader society. Perhaps the Jesuit fathers regarded the objection as an indication of ignorance on the part of the otherwise admirable, "sturdy" immigrant "working people" who came from "cottages of Ireland" and "small farming towns of Germany." But for a time the Jesuits adapted. Within the first month of the 1880 school year they agreed to start a commercial class for "those boys" who were "unwilling to study the classics."[21] It was not just a local concession; the Jesuit high school in Chicago also offered a commercial track. The *Western Home Journal* made haste to tell Catholics they were wrong anyway in the "very widespread" impression about the Jesuits: The fathers' "partiality for literature and the sciences" did not prevent their attention to children who wanted to become competent and successful business men. They made "every provision for this influential portion of the community."[22]

Before the turn of the century, however, the Jesuits dropped the commercial course from their high school, and even earlier they had discontinued the class of "rudiments" for those not prepared for the high school program. At the beginning of the school year in 1899 "about twelve new students were rejected . . . because of too little arithmetic."[23] Protests, complaints, and arguments about the needs of students did not deter them from the conviction that a liberal education was "the only course that fully develops all the faculties, forms a correct taste, teaches the student how to use all his powers to the best advantage, and prepares him to excel in any pursuit, whether professional or commercial."[24] That kept the numbers smaller, but it also made the diploma decisively "college preparatory," one more definitive option within the framework of Catholic education. With 515 students in 1925, the school was at capacity and turning boys away.[25]

Those who were admitted and who graduated became part of a widening solid cadre of middle- and upper-class Catholics who understood and accepted the lesson of mutual interdependence their Jesuit fathers articulated. After one successful fund-raising drive, the rector's article in the student newspaper spoke to the way Catholic men must behave as consumers of goods and services. Students should remember, he said, that almost all the subscribers were "engaged either in professional or mercantile pursuits here in Detroit." They had helped the institution. Was it not "proper" that friends of the institution "should remember this when in need of professional services or when about to transact business?" After all, that would be a "practical way of showing that . . . gratitude . . . is not a mere sentiment, but a real recognition of valuable service rendered."[26] It was an obligation the privileged shouldered with clear awareness of its advantages to each other.

ST. JOSEPH'S COMMERCIAL COLLEGE

Despite giving the appearance of making decisions in accord with their intellectual training, the Jesuits' timing also suggests their pragmatic planning. A commercial course with a $20 yearly tuition had become available for Detroit Catholic boys when the Christian Brothers started a three-year program at St. Joseph's parish in 1889. The first class of twelve had graduated just a year before the Jesuits dropped their commercial option.

St. Joseph's Commercial College grew on top of the grade school in that near-east-side German parish that was also evolving into a commercial district. Then the largest parochial elementary school in the city, St. Joseph's had nearly 950 students and 12 teachers.[27] The Christian Brothers had been teaching the boys there while IHM sisters taught the girls; now the brothers supplemented their staff and encouraged promising boys to stay on for the new curriculum. The Commercial College was a proud accomplishment for St. Joseph's pastor and parishioners, who had also just erected a new church building with twin spires and statues imported from Germany. The commercial program was the first venture of its kind in the city, opening when commercial education was becoming a significant national trend.

St. Joseph's Commercial College was headed by a succession of Germans from the Christian Brothers community.[28] They made German a standard part of the curriculum, which emphasized Christian morality along with shorthand, bookkeeping, and typing within a framework of strict, almost military, discipline. It was a distinctly "Catholic" commercial school and as such different from the Detroit High School of Commerce, opened around the turn of the century with courses intended especially to prepare girls for office work.[29]

St. Joseph's program attracted many students from other parishes, boys who came from across the city on foot or by streetcar. The $20 tuition was an investment working-class families were willing to afford, hoping their sons could indeed then manage to become part of Detroit's white-collar world. Entrants came most often from families that had avoided the city's factory jobs. The fathers of one typical group included a timekeeper at a stove company, two contractors, a clerk at a hat store, a clerk at Ferry Seed, a fireman, a clerk at Western Union, a conductor, a metal worker, a chauffeur, and four salesmen—real estate, caskets, shoes, and hats.[30]

At the Commercial College, as at the Jesuit high school, the sons of Irish and German immigrants met and studied together. But in the 1920s there were still few boys from Polish, Italian, or Hungarian families, even though St. Joseph's parish itself included a thousand Italians, four hundred Hungarians, and three hundred Poles before World War I.[31] The Commercial College held its own even after the parish began to dwindle, but the student body was never as large as the Jesuit high school. There were 106 students in 1903, 115 in 1916, and 338 in 1925.[32] Despite the financial advantage larger enrollments would mean, however, the Christian Brothers maintained a stringent policy and dropped students whose academic work was poor. Between 1917 and 1922 a total of 138 students graduated but 86 left the program. A few "went to work," as terse notations in the record book would explain. Most, however, were "advised to withdraw" because of "spotty" grades or "horrible grades."[33] The brothers got out the word, one way and another, that parents and potential employers should feel confident that all students at "St. Joe's Commercial" were carefully monitored.

The graduates, usually between the ages of seventeen and nineteen, were positioned for the city's white-collar job market that exploded alongside the auto industry. St. Joseph's parish would later claim and celebrate the commercial school's place: "From it came some of Detroit's leading business and financial wizards."[34] More accurately, the school was one piece of a pattern that characterized the era when work in Detroit was transformed—and with it the opportunities of its residents. By 1920 the Germans and the Irish, immigrants and second-generation, had a high percentage of white-collar office workers, nearly 23 percent for German Americans and 28 percent for Irish Americans. Both ethnic groups were also well represented among the city's proprietors. By comparison, 81 percent of the immigrant and second-generation Poles and 77 percent of the Hungarians were factory workers.[35]

PARISH HIGH SCHOOLS: THE IHM PRECEDENT IN IRISH PARISHES

Between them, University of Detroit High and the Commercial College enrolled 437 boys in 1915—nearly as many as Philadelphia's Central Boys'

Catholic high school.[36] Meanwhile, the idea of providing a Catholic high school opportunity for Detroit's girls had developed alongside plans for educating boys "with the Jesuits" or at "St. Joe's." By the time secondary education became more obviously important, the parish high school had a headstart.

Locally, Irish parishes and their IHM sisters pioneered the idea of adding a secondary program for girls to parish grade schools. Patterning the curriculum on the one they developed for their flagship academy in Monroe, the IHMs first introduced a high school program for girls at the Irish "mother church," Most Holy Trinity, and then at the adjacent and newer Irish parish of St. Vincent's. Trinity began offering high school courses and graduated the first students from an abbreviated academy program in 1881. St. Vincent's, adding one year at a time, boasted the first full-fledged Detroit parish high school in 1893.[37] Not to be outdone, Trinity expanded its high school course to completion and also soon graduated students through a full curriculum. It was this type of "healthy rivalry" that stimulated other efforts across the city and led each group of parishioners to claim that their school was the "first" or the "best" in one accomplishment or another. Trinity and St. Vincent's became prototypes for the others and established the local "image" of parochial secondary education. Even the reluctant *Michigan Catholic* began to see the advantages. Women were "truly not mentally inferior" but had a "different organization of faculties." Schooling with religious direction might keep them from becoming "almost completely unsexed" or "vain and light minded, affected, and unobservant to their duties."[38] Parents, priests, and an encouraging Bishop Foley began to decide that if daughters could be protected from the worst dangers, why not give them the best advantages? By 1915 the IHMs conducted eight of the nine parish high schools operating in Detroit.

When Trinity and St. Vincent's parishes initiated female high schools, both had substantial grade school "feeder" populations. In 1887 Trinity had a total of 682 students, 313 of them girls; St. Vincent's had 912 students, of whom 456 were girls.[39] Trinity had the longer history and a reputation among the sisters themselves as the "outstanding" IHM parish grade school. Nonetheless, St. Vincent's (fig. 9) became the better-regarded high school within the Catholic and non-Catholic community, in part because its neighborhood developed a generation later, dwindled later, and maintained a strong high school after Trinity's closed at the end of the 1920s. These pioneering schools were, in fact, much alike. They were taught by many of the same individuals because of shifts back and forth from one year to the next. Students in both schools followed a course of study identical to the academy

Figure 9. St. Vincent's school, church, and rectory on Fourteenth Street between Dalzelle and Marentete, knit together the lives of parishioners, adults, and children. Mostly immigrant or second-generation Irish families, they took great pride in developing a school they regarded as superior to the older Irish neighborhood around Most Holy Trinity a few blocks to the east. (Archives of the Sisters, Servants of the Immaculate Heart of Mary)

in Monroe—generally duplicated by the other Detroit parishes that had added IHM high schools. And nearly all students came from Irish families, as did many of their teachers—sometimes from the parish itself.

From its start, St. Vincent's had a substantial middle class within the congregation. Compared with Trinity, which was its parent parish and a mile to the east, the immediate neighborhood around St. Vincent's had more large houses and more big lots. St. Vincent's parishioners were in a mix of occupations, however, not too different from the people who went to Trinity although more likely to be the young, upwardly mobile, second-generation Irish. Bits of wisdom offered in St. Vincent's Sunday bulletins spoke to families who still identified with the working class: "Vanderbilt can write a few words on a sheet of paper and make it worth 5 millions—that's capital. A man who works ten hours a day and shovels three or four of tons of earth for $1.50—that's labor."[40] They were families whose hopes for their children matched the ambitions their priest and nuns shared.

Both parishes benefited immeasurably from strong priests. Father James Savage at Trinity and Father James Gregory Doherty at St. Vincent's had long tenure and were trusted by the parishioners, important in the diocese, and committed to educating the young. The two men gained the status of "irremovable pastors" and remained side by side at the neighboring parishes for almost forty years, beginning in the late 1880s.[41] They were part of the small group of "priest-consultors" who helped bishops make policy decisions. Both also served for years on the diocesan school board. Doherty was a member from its introduction in 1887, and the *Michigan Catholic* regularly put considerable stock in his evaluations of parish schools. In the diocese Doherty was a leader among "strict constructionists," who favored requiring Catholic parents to send children to parochial schools. Young and vigorous in the years when the Third Plenary Council decrees on Catholic schools were new, Father Doherty prodded parishioners to press on with a high school for girls, persuading them to build and equip the two-story brick St. Vincent Academy that opened in 1893. Like the grade school, as a collective parish effort the high school was either free or charged only a small monthly sum. He was soon and constantly describing the whole St. Vincent enterprise as "the best school in the state."[42]

The young women in high school at St. Vincent's and Most Holy Trinity were challenged with a course of study almost as rigorous as the one for boys who studied with the Jesuits at University of Detroit High. St. Vincent's did not offer commercial classes until 1916, when "to meet the present demand for a Commercial course, the Rev. Pastor announced the opening of a class."[43] By that time IHM secondary schools were firmly set on a course of their own that merged the usual two types of Catholic girls' schools: the school that aimed at "culture and distinct womanly accomplishment" and the school that aimed "at teaching a girl how readily to earn her own living."[44] College, especially a normal training program, was becoming a realistic opportunity for the well-prepared high school graduate whose parents were willing and able to send her on.

The curriculum the sisters offered at St. Vincent's and Most Holy Trinity gave students the choice of four separate college preparatory courses by the end of the 1890s. The "classical course," with mathematics, history, physics, botany, four years of Latin, and two years of Greek, led to the A.B. diploma. The "Latin course" substituted two years of French or German for Greek. The "scientific course" required an additional year of U.S. history and chemistry while reducing language to a total of four years. The "English course" further reduced the language requirement, substituting English history and English literature in place of two years of language.[45] Records suggest that students often opted for the difficult Latin course or were steered into it, depending on the sisters' assessment of their potential. Between 1916 and 1925, thirty of fifty-one Holy Trinity graduates received the Latin or

Latin/scientific diploma. Notations in the St. Vincent's records indicate the same pattern; through the mid-1920s only a few graduated with the "easier" English diploma.[46]

Regardless of the intended program, the sisters emphasized science and mathematics, and each year students took literature, history, rhetoric, composition, Christian doctrine, and church history. They balanced those heavy academic loads with such "finishing school" touches as penmanship, drawing, singing, and constant lessons in proper manners from their *Good Form* manual with few updates from the previous era.[47]

Beyond any assets such as natural ability, studiousness, or parental support, those who proved capable of such a challenging high school curriculum had the great advantage of grade school teachers who knew precisely what material they must master in advance and made sure they learned it. Once a parish opened a high school, its priest and sister-principal were especially attentive to the grade school that would promote pupils upward. Father Doherty examined children in the parish grade school each month, in part to keep an eye on their teachers. He worked with any sister he considered deficient, and among themselves the community of women knew he would not hesitate to dismiss someone midyear if she could not improve. The priest infrequently had such problems, however, because he made a practice of identifying the best of the sisters when he sat on the board that conducted the annual diocesan teacher certification examinations. Each year he went in person to the motherhouse in Monroe to select the teachers he wanted. He was looking for those characterized, he said, by "Tact, Talent, and Push."[48]

The IHM sisters welcomed the zeal of priests like Savage and Doherty, whose ambitions meshed with their own. The congregation of women had been building their professional competence beyond normal school training for some time and by 1905 had sisters sufficiently educated to inaugurate St. Mary College, the first Catholic college for women in Michigan. Initially, it was a junior college course for women added on top of their Monroe academy, just as they had introduced high school programs at Holy Trinity and St. Vincent's. Within two years St. Mary College was offering a course of study leading to the B.A. degree with the option of an accompanying teacher's certificate.[49]

Intended for laywomen, the college was a chance for their high school graduates to continue studying with the sisters, but enrollment remained small for the first ten or fifteen years. The greatest initial significance of the college was its importance to the sisters' professionalization. The existence of the college strengthened educational opportunities within the mother-house, and the need for professors provided a good reason for the brightest sisters to advance beyond the bachelor's degree. The same year the college opened, IHM leaders began a twenty-five-year practice of sending one postulant a year to the University of Michigan for an undergraduate degree. They ventured this despite the university's reputation among Catholics as a dangerous center of free thought—a notion fed by frequent editorials in the *Michigan Catholic*. Deliberately, they sent postulants rather than professed sisters in order to evade the chancery's power to end the practice. They embarked on the resourceful plan at a time when prestigious Catholic colleges would not admit women. Once Catholic University opened its summer school for sisters in 1911 they sent five there, but meanwhile they persisted in the determination to educate a core at the University of Michigan. Educational ambitions of supportive, well-placed priests such as Doherty and Savage helped the community ignore any disapproval.

Community leaders tapped some sisters to go on for the master's of arts degree as soon as they completed the bachelor of arts.[50] The unilateral decision to advance the education of one sister over another left an occasional woman harboring a long-term grudge against her sister superior, left others feeling they had been assessed as "too dumb," and required some women to study fields that served community needs rather than personal interests. Nonetheless, in its totality the workable plan served the greater good. By the early twentieth century, the pool of IHM sisters prepared to teach high school classes was expanding with the demand for their services.

Judged against Detroit's public high schools, the first Catholic high schools remained small. With fewer than a hundred students, St. Vincent's graduated 334 students from 1893 through 1927; between twelve and twenty-five graduated each year in the late 1910s and early 1920s.[51] A few came from outlying parishes that did not yet have their own high schools; students rarely came from one of the other three ethnic parishes in the district—Bohemian, French, and German. Typically, students lived in the neighborhood and had attended grade school at St. Vincent's.

The fictional Mr. Dooley, Irish wag and pulse, observed parents' new preoccupation with identifying careers for their six-year-old sons: "'Tis a big question . . . an' wan that seems to be worryin' th' people more thin it used to" when "ivry boy was designed f'r th' priesthood" even though his parents knew "th' chances was in favor iv a brick yard." Proudly, they now spied talents and told each other, "'Tis th' fine lawyer he'll make. . . . He'll be a gr-reat journalist. . . . We must thrain him f'r a banker."[52] Out of similar determined devotion to "our boys," and perhaps to boost enrollment, the

IHMs began accepting males into their high schools soon after the turn of the century. Bishop Foley's benign neglect of policy helped; after the late 1890s he had ignored the collective decision of bishops in the Cincinnati province that stated that boys could remain with the sisters only until the age of fourteen.[53] There were not enough brothers and priests available to teach all the boys moving up.

By 1915, when IHMs staffed eight of the nine parish high schools in Detroit, all but two admitted boys, although the coeducational schools still attracted nearly four or five times more girls than boys.[54] Between 1908 and 1927 St. Vincent's high school graduated thirty-eight boys, significantly fewer than the number from the parish who went through the Jesuit's University of Detroit High School.[55] But parents, pastor, and sisters never encouraged boys to stay on in the parish. Unless some special circumstance made it necessary, it would be "better for them" to go to "The High."[56]

The postwar expansion of parishes coincided with increased emphasis on secondary education, and newer Irish parishes followed the lead of those more established. By 1922 there were thirteen IHM-staffed high schools in Detroit. Holy Redeemer, the predominantly Irish school at Dix and Junction, developed into one of the largest parochial school plants in the country. For a time, boys and girls studied separately at Redeemer. IHM sisters taught the grade school children and high school girls while the Brothers of Mary taught the high school boys—390 of them by the mid-1920s, when total parish school enrollment reached more than 2,100.[57]

Trinity's all-female high school remained small, hovering between thirty and forty. It drew even more heavily from within the parish than St. Vincent's, but its older neighborhood was changing and there was substantial turnover in the Trinity student body. Of those who were ninth-graders in 1915, only one was among the sixteen who graduated from Trinity four years later. In all, about 160 graduated from Trinity's high school between 1892 and 1925.[58] Probably as many Trinity boys graduated from the Jesuit high school in that period. Most years the number of boys from Trinity who entered "The High" was about the same as the number of girls in the parish high school. By World War I, Trinity regularly sent twelve to fifteen boys a year to University of Detroit High.[59]

Public school records are not broken down by religion, and parish reports do not stipulate the number of Catholic students in public high school. It appears, based on priests' annual reports, that the total number dropped over the years in parishes that had their own schools and sufficient capacity. In 1900 Father Doherty, angry that the church hierarchy did not take a harder line, complained that nearly a hundred children from St. Vincent's were in public school "because they are free to go to any school they please." By 1916 public schools claimed only fifteen from St. Vincent's, the children Father Doherty could not recapture because, to his disgust, their "parents are indifferent."[60] Around the same time, twenty or thirty children from Trinity were in public schools. In many cases that was the fault of "poor worthless Parents" or "mixed marriages," according to Father Savage. But, he also explained in his annual report to the bishop, "Some have permission." It is likely that the priest more willingly granted permission when poor families wanted to send their sons to public high school. Tuition reached $60 at the University of Detroit High School by the turn of the century when Father Savage was receiving and no doubt paying the bills for some boys from the parish who went there.

Irish families who sent children on to Catholic high schools represented a range of occupations. Among those who graduated from St. Vincent's and Trinity between 1893 and 1925 and whose families can be located in the city directories, a substantial proportion had fathers in white-collar or retail occupations. Of the fathers, 47 percent were either professionals, white-collar workers, or non-retail and retail proprietors. Another 26 percent of the fathers were craftsmen, skilled, or semiskilled workers; 15 percent were unskilled. The fathers of almost 13 percent of the graduates were deceased. Generally, these statistics reflected the distribution of Irish family heads within the city's economic structure.[61]

Parents who sent children through high school were aware of the opportunities an education could bring their daughters as well as their sons. A shortage of Detroit public school teachers added incentive. Nearly all girls from St. Vincent's parish who completed high school entered the work force for at least a few years and most became teachers, either as laywomen or nuns. In 1920 the yearbook reported that the parish had given eighty-five teachers to the public school, sixty-five of whom were teaching at the time in Detroit. About a hundred others had become nuns, turning to a religious vocation more often than boys; only thirty-two from the parish had become priests.[62]

Catholic girls generally proceeded through Detroit Normal Training School on the path to the public school teaching profession. Located on West Grand Boulevard and Grand River in Northwestern High School, it was especially convenient for west-side Irish girls and led to almost automatic hiring at the end of the two-year course. Along with St. Vincent's, there were about six or seven parishes that might have been well represented within the public school staff in 1920, and Catholic teachers were becoming more common in public schools. Still, at a time when the teaching staff numbered about two thousand they remained decidedly underrepresented compared to the proportion of Catholics in the city.

GERMAN PARISH HIGH SCHOOLS

German parishes were slower to add high schools than the Irish, and, affected by neighborhood changes, those they started first remained smaller. Grade schools in the old German parishes, especially those in the center of the city, were already shrinking by the time the high school movement gathered steam. By 1913, for example, St. Mary's, the original German parish, had 212 pupils in its grade school, and the nearby Sacred Heart parish school, also German, had 275. Between them, the two were down about seven hundred grade-schoolers compared to enrollment at the turn of the century. The School Sisters of Notre Dame, who taught in both schools, sent their most promising boys to the Jesuits or to St. Joseph's Commercial, conveniently located in the same lower-east-side section as the parishes.

At the German parishes of St. Joseph's and St. Boniface's, the IHM sisters introduced high school programs in the first decade of the twentieth century but grappled with enrollment difficulties. St. Joseph's graduated its first female high school student in 1904, and then only three more in the next nine years. A few girls earned diplomas for completing the two-year course of instrumental music or the commercial course added in 1903.[63] Meanwhile, the sisters advised some students "on account of existing circumstances at that time" to finish at St. Mary's Academy in Monroe, and at least one girl from St. Joseph's graduated from Holy Trinity.[64] St. Joseph's did not have a third full-time high school teacher until 1922 in preparation for accreditation. The parish continued instead to give more emphasis to its boys' Commercial College, adding a four-year high school course in 1921.[65] Still, the girls' enrollment began to climb in the 1920s until there were nearly 150 students in the high school; between 1904 and 1927 St. Joseph's graduated eighty-three girls.[66]

Parents who promoted a high school at St. Joseph's struggled always with change and with a decline in the number of parish families—from a high of a thousand in 1894 to five hundred by 1913.[67] Even though the numbers of Syrians, Italians, Poles, Hungarians, and other newcomers nearly equaled the German population in the parish by 1913, most girls who went through the high school were German. Many had lived in the parish their whole lives.[68] Across town on the west side, the German parish of St. Boniface graduated its first high school girls in 1910, but that IHM school remained small. When the city purchased parish buildings to make way for a new highway in 1925, St. Boniface's parishioners closed their high school and concentrated instead on the grade school.[69]

Even as early as the late 1860s, German families had begun establishing parishes at what were then the edges of the city, and the trend accelerated when businesses and new immigrants changed the central city. In those more distant, stable neighborhoods, German schools expanded. St. Anthony's, planted by Bishop Lefevere on what was then the far eastern side, and St. Elizabeth's to the north each enrolled more than a thousand grade school students in 1925. Most German parochial schools were taught by the School Sisters of Notre Dame from Milwaukee or the Sisters of Christian Charity from Wilkes-Barre, Pennsylvania. Both communities faced demands from other bishops who desperately needed German-speaking sisters, and both were concerned to maintain good grade school programs. Understandably, they were reluctant to stretch their resources to start high schools.[70]

Opportunities for children from German Catholic families expanded by the mid-1920s once the second and third generation moved into new middle-class parishes and acquired a greater interest in a Catholic high school education than in a German Catholic education. The growing role of the Dominican sisters in Detroit along with the expansion of IHM high schools helped meet their needs. So, too, did the two Catholic "central" high schools Bishop Gallagher insisted upon in the late 1920s. Located in the former Cathedral school on the near north side and not far east of Woodward, Girls' Central opened in 1927 and was staffed by IHM sisters. Boys' Central—soon commonly known as Catholic Central or "C.C."—opened a year later under direction of the Basilian Fathers.[71] The schools were easily accessible by streetcar and intended to serve parishes that could not sustain a high school, as the bishop hastened to assure priests who might view them as competition to their own existing high schools.

If they lived on Detroit's northeast side, German, Irish, and Polish boys had one more option when De La Salle Collegiate opened for class in 1926. The school was the idea of businessmen who were alumni from St. Joseph's. They saw the area around the central-city parish changing to a section crowded by black residents, businesses, and small factories. Loyally, they did not want the fate of their old teachers, the Christian Brothers, to be dependent upon that parish. Many De La Salle backers were early graduates of "St. Joe's Commercial" who recognized that boys had come to need a different type of high school preparation if they hoped to advance into the professional or business school programs many colleges including the University of

Detroit now offered. One member from St. Joe's class of 1892 donated property, organized a board of trustees, and helped raise money so the Christian Brothers could get a bank loan to start De La Salle. A few years later the trustees themselves sponsored a loan so the brothers were not indebted to local banks. The four-year prep school gained accreditation from the University of Michigan and the University of Detroit in 1929. By 1937, despite the depression, there would be 465 boys in attendance.[72]

POLISH PARISH HIGH SCHOOLS

Overwhelmed by their grade schools, Polish parishes had trouble providing high school education. Of itself, secondary education also intensified several of the very issues that polarized the Polish community, leader from leader and parent from parent. Certain critics inside and outside the church charged Polish Catholic clergy with intentionally perpetuating a narrow parochial education to prevent immigrants from learning to assert their rights or exercise independence. Polish socialists were convinced that Polish children were forced into the lowest-paying work when parents insisted upon a parochial education which, from city to city, failed to meet public school standards. Catholic intellectuals in both the Polish National Alliance and the Polish Roman Catholic Union championed parochial school reform early in the twentieth century in order to preserve their schools, fearful that parents would otherwise take recourse in public schools.[73]

In 1912 the Congress of Polish Priests met in Detroit. This first-time convention of American Polish priests approved a new parochial school curriculum designed by the Polish rector of St. Stanislaus Kostka College in Chicago. The plan would strengthen academic offerings and initiate courses such as biology, offered in public schools but not available in Polish parochial classrooms. Priests endorsed the curriculum, recognizing it as an ideal for which to aim although it could not be widely implemented because too few schools had even eight grades or the equipment needed to teach these subjects. More problematic, the available pool of sisters for Polish schools remained too small and the women were lacking in education themselves. Despite other serious obstacles, the rector who wrote the program insisted that parishes must be the bases for schools rather than the centralized system gaining popularity among groups such as the National Catholic Education Association.[74]

A handful of Polish Catholic secondary schools for boys operated in cities with large Polish communities. Even in Chicago, however, attendance remained small. Nationwide in 1914, Polish secondary schools enrolled just over five hundred students.[75] The only secondary programs available within Detroit's Polish Catholic institutional framework were at the SS. Cyril and Methodius Seminary and the Felician Academy.

The seminary's prep school was limited to boys who intended to become priests. In 1900 the entire enrollment was 156, but by 1909 the student population had doubled and was a mix of local boys and those who came from across the country. Polish grade schools served seminarians well. A boy from St. Hyacinth recalled that he "learned more Bible History in eighth grade at St. Hyacinth than in the seminary."[76]

Every year some young men decided against the priesthood, but Father Dabrowski expelled one particularly active group of twenty-eight students in 1903 when they submitted a list of grievances and went on strike. Their complaints suggest that conditions could produce disgust with, rather than enthusiasm for, education, even in a selective school setting where pupils and teachers were of the same nationality and purpose. The rebels were angry about the lack of respect for their dignity, poor sanitary conditions, inadequate food, and widespread theft.[77] Boys who did not proceed on to the seminary nevertheless obtained a secondary education they could not have received anywhere else within the framework of Polish Catholicism. Some went on to attend the University of Detroit, which had opened schools of engineering, law, and commerce by World War I.[78] Yet the number of high school- or college-educated Polish boys in Detroit remained too small to encourage or influence the rest.

The Felician Academy, until 1920, admitted only those girls who wanted to join the Felician community as nuns. Like boys at the seminary, some girls stayed only a few years and then, better prepared than when they arrived, left for public school or jobs. The academy offered only a two-year secondary course until the sisters added a third year in 1904. In 1910 the mother superior decided to send three young "aspirants" to St. Mary's Academy in Monroe to complete high school, but the superior general in Europe quickly ordered an end to that. Claiming it was too expensive, her real concern was that such an arrangement would contribute to weakening the "spirit of the congregation" in the girls at an early stage in their development as Felicians.[79] It was the much the same worry that caused the St. Joseph's mother superior to withdraw the three sisters who went to study at Monroe in 1912 (chapter 6).

With growing urgency Felician leaders in Detroit stretched their resources to add a fourth year in their academy, and by 1914 the sisters-in-training were able to complete high school within the motherhouse. Because the young women who taught in their parish schools came out of this academy, the expanding pool of high school graduates helped improve the grade schools. Nevertheless, the Felicians did not have women adequately prepared to provide the high school programs some Polish parents wanted. Parishes meanwhile hesitated to hire lay teachers, reluctant to take on such an expense and resistant to depart from their grade school habit of a sister-faculty.

In 1914 Detroit had eleven Polish parochial grade schools. Many with only a four- or five-year course of instruction were hard-pressed to advance beyond that accomplishment because of the rush of Polish immigrants into Detroit.[80] The Felicians' earliest school, St. Albertus, added the last two years and did not graduate eighth-graders until 1908.[81] It was a bittersweet triumph for the sisters, when, leaving them no time to catch their breath, St. Casimir's and other parishes they staffed immediately asked for upper grades, too.

By 1917 Felician leaders began to move a few sisters on to college, sending five young academy graduates off to Washington for full-time study at the sisters' teachers' college at Catholic University. When they completed their degree work a second group went for full-time study, and then others in succession. Some sisters began enrolling closer to home as part-time students in the Detroit Teachers College or St. John's University in Toledo. The Felicians continued, however, to avoid contact with the IHMs, whose St. Mary's College for women was available in close-by Monroe.

Like other congregations, the Felicians enhanced their convent academy so it could better serve their needs. Realistically, they set out to arrange affiliation with Catholic University, a form of school certification available to parochial schools throughout the country. That affiliation meant graduates from the Felician Academy could be admitted to many colleges, including Detroit Teachers, without college entrance examinations. To be eligible, a high school had to offer a four-year course of study, which had to include three units in English and three in another major area, two each in a language, religion, and mathematics, one each in natural sciences and social sciences, plus electives. To receive credit under this system, high school students had to pass examinations sent out and then graded by Catholic University faculty. Readying themselves and the students, the Felicians brought in two laywomen with degrees to help strengthen the high school curriculum; one had an M.A. from Columbia and the other an A.B. from the University of Michigan.[82] By the spring of 1919 academy seniors began taking the Catholic University examinations.

The Felicians made their academy available in 1920 to day students who were not in the convent, which made it the first four-year Polish Catholic high school in Detroit for girls (fig. 10). For a time, however, only a limited number of lay students were accepted because the sisters gave priority to girls who

Figure 10. The science laboratory in their academy (in 1929) was just one more place the Felician sisters expended scarce resources in order to make their schools more competitive. (Archives of the Felician Sisters, Presentation of the B.V.M. Province, Livonia, Michigan)

had made a commitment to join the Felician order. With more girls interested in that vocation than ever, many of the 198 students who graduated from the academy between 1924 and 1934 became Felician sisters and moved quickly into classroom teaching. The academy, in effect, became the high school for girls who attended St. Albertus grade school. The parish never "considered having a high school of its own," as the pastor explained in 1945, "because in a way, a greater part of this need has always been taken care of by the Felician Sisters Academy directly across the street from us."[83] Pastor and parishioners must have believed that girls were the "greater part" of the need.

Three Polish parishes in Detroit did introduce high school diploma programs throughout the 1920s, adding a year at a time. All three high schools, taught by Felicians, followed much the same course of studies the sisters used in their academy—the course prescribed by Catholic University and based on syllabi sent from the university's professors.

In 1915 St. Josaphat became the first Polish parish with a ninth grade and the Felicians' first venture into parochial secondary education. Some parents were agitating to give their children the advantage of high school, and the new pastor, Father Joseph Lempka, pushed the initiative. He perhaps had enough influence to persuade the Felicians to start the venture because he had been chaplain in the Felician motherhouse. The school also had financial support from Tomasz Zoltowski, a grocer and brewer who had originally donated the land to establish the St. Josaphat parish.[84] Father Lempka had shown no previous signs of the educational vision that marked his contemporaries Father Doherty at St. Vincent's or Father Savage at Trinity. As chaplain, he had been primarily concerned that the Felicians should not study too much lest they neglect their religious responsibilities. The sisters' own director of education regarded Father Lempka as a hindrance to their progress and tried to counter his influence with hers, urging, "The better teacher you are, the better a religious you can become. Education does not detract from spirituality but serves to enhance it."[85]

Just as Father Lempka failed to appreciate such this perspective, he undoubtedly underestimated the demands connected with operating a high school. Circumstances at St. Josaphat proved especially problematic because at the time the high school was getting underway Polish families began moving out of the parish. World War I and the auto boom opened service jobs that quickly brought black migrants to Detroit from the South. In 1911 Detroit's black population was 4,111; by 1920 it was 40,838 and growing by a thousand arrivals a week, according to the Detroit Urban League's estimate.[86] As the newcomers edged from the crowded near-east-side black section northward toward St. Josaphat's borders, Polish immigrants left for other neighborhoods. From a high of about 790 grade school students in 1922–23, parish enrollments plummeted to 460 by 1929.[87]

High school enrollment grew while the grade school declined, however. Even after families left St. Josaphat's their high-school-aged children came back. Students came also from other parishes without high schools—Sweetest Heart, St. Albertus, St. Hyacinth, Immaculate Conception, and even from west-side Polish parishes. The school added its tenth and eleventh grades in 1921, but attrition was high. Although the high school had seventy students in 1924, it was not until 1926 that four students became the first graduating class, "a small but energetic group determined to finish their high school education at St. Josaphat."[88] By the time the high school opened, several other parishes had been coeducational for more than a decade, and St. Josaphat followed their lead. Like the parish grade school, its high school represented an equal proportion of boys and girls, and the boys proved as likely to graduate as the girls. In 1929 the senior class included thirteen boys and seven girls.[89]

By 1927 St. Casimir and St. Stanislaus had become the second and third Felician grade schools in the city to add high schools. St. Casimir opened a ninth grade for twenty students in 1927, and eleven seniors graduated four years later.[90] St. Stanislaus was larger and offered a variety of classes to meet the needs of students interested in either an academic or commercial program, but its science and mathematics classes focused on boys because of the notion that they would "benefit" from them more than girls.[91]

Although small and without special facilities like gymnasiums, Polish parish high schools offered a range of extracurricular activities—clubs, social and athletic events, religious retreats, and dramatic and musical groups. Students helped produce a monthly school paper, joined the Catholic Students Mission Crusade, and became part of a growing cadre of high school alumni loyal to the parish high schools and "their" special sisters. Each year a few graduates from Felician high schools went on to local colleges or universities and then joined the ranks of Polish community leaders who urged more education upon the next generation.[92]

The poignant struggle to provide higher education for Polonia's children is nowhere more evident than among the "Polish Sisters of St. Joseph," as Detroiters called them. They separated from the School Sisters of St. Francis and replaced them in Detroit just when the city's Polish immigration began to explode. In 1925 the sisters' grade school at Sweetest Heart enrolled 1,495, St. Francis 1,668, and St. Thomas the Apostle 1,374 (chapter 6).[93] The same burgeoning demand for their services divided efforts of the Sisters of St. Joseph among small Wisconsin towns, large immigrant centers like Chicago and Cleveland, and distant Polish parishes in Texas and Connecticut. They had all they could do to handle their grade schools.

Despite their huge grade school "feeder" populations in Detroit parishes, the sisters could not manage to establish a permanent four-year high school program throughout the 1920s. They started a ninth-grade program at Sweetest Heart in 1923, discontinued it the next year when the principal went for full-time study at Catholic University, and then started it again in 1928. Their only other high school in Detroit, St. Thomas the Apostle, would not open until 1937.[94]

It was the Felician sisters who, like the IHMs, became a common denominator among the high school students they taught across the city. By 1933 alumni from the Felician Academy, St. Josaphat, St. Casimir, and St. Stanislaus jointly organized the Felician Alumni.[95] But Polish Catholic high school alumni were few. Neither were there many Poles among public school graduates. In this regard Detroit Polish Catholics fit into a pattern common among their countrymen. In Hamtramck—where seven of ten school children were Polish in 1925—only about 42 percent of the sixteen-year-olds and 15 percent of the seventeen-year-olds attended school.[96]

Leo J. Nowicki, one St. Hyacinth grade-schooler who escaped the factory line to become a graduate from the University of Michigan College of Engineering, lamented the lot of his peers. Only two of the twenty-five in his eighth-grade class went to college so far as he knew. Born in Poland, he could not speak enough English to tell the teacher in his public school kindergarten that someone had stolen his lunch. At St. Hyacinth he learned English along with Polish history and Polish culture and then he went to public high school. There, it was the principal, a Polish immigrant himself, who encouraged Nowicki to go on to the University of Michigan. Only two girls and three boys in his 1921 Northeastern High School class were from Polish homes. As a freshman college student, Nowicki went back to Detroit every weekend to work as a clerk in a Polish-owned clothing store. Once his classes interfered with the weekend job, he fired furnaces and washed dishes in fraternities. By 1947 he was a member of the Detroit common council, proud of his accomplishments but disappointed that "the rapidly expanding automobile industry" with its many unskilled jobs combined with the low economic status of average Polish families to trap so many other young men and women.[97]

When it came to the Polish parish high school there was a reversal of the grade school dilemma. At the grade school level teachers and classrooms could not be found fast enough to keep up with the need. So few Polish students enrolled in high school, however, that it was difficult to develop programs that might lure others. Still, by the time Polish high schools emerged, there were precedents to encourage their supporters' ambitions. Certain small parish high schools had, indeed, developed enviable academic reputations. It was a goal not beyond reach.

VIEWED FROM OUTSIDE AND IN: ALL OF A PIECE

By the time of World War I there was no doubting Catholics' determination to multiply their parish grade schools and promote high schools under church auspices. The second and third generation continued to reinforce rather than relinquish the institutional separatism preferred by their immigrant parents. By their insistent example, they helped promote the practice among new immigrants. There was no mistaking it from any vantage point—Catholic schools at every level were a substantial feature of the whole educational picture in Detroit (table 5).

As the web of Catholic schools became more complex, outsiders tended to view them "all of a piece," just variations in shading—like the sisters'

Table 5. Parish Schools in Detroit for Selected Years

	1887		1900		1913		1925	
	Schools	Students	Schools	Students	Schools	Students	Schools	Students
IHMs	6	3,539 (55.7%)	8	4,367 (37.1%)	11	7,845 (34.0%)	15	11,669 (24.01%)
Felicians	3	863 (13.6)	3	2,124 (18.0)	7	6,261 (27.5)	12	11,545 (23.5)
Srs. of Christian Charity	1	250 (3.9)	3[b]	1,404 (11.9)	5	2,853 (12.5)	4	3,380 (6.9)
School Srs., Notre Dame	2	1,125 (17.7)	3	1,373 (11.7)	4	1,843 (8.1)	4	2,331 (4.7)
Srs., Holy Name of Jesus and Mary	1	193 (3.0)	2	772 (6.6)	2	827 (3.6)	3	1,086 (2.2)
Madames of Sacred Heart	1	305 (4.8)	—	—	1	160 (0.7)	—	—
Srs. of St. Joseph	—	—	—	—	2	2,444 (10.7)	9	7,883 (26.0)
Srs. of St. Dominic	—	—	—	—	2	506 (2.2)	9	5,590 (11.4)
School Srs., St. Francis	—	—	3	1,494 (12.8)	1	49 (0.2)	4	4,505 (9.2)
Srs., "S.H.M."	—	—	—	—	—	—	1	403 (0.8)
Franciscan Brothers	1[a]	76 (1.2)	1[c]	—	—	—	1[c]	390 (0.8)
Christian Brothers	—	—	—	120 (1.0)	—	—	1[c]	182 (0.4)
Lay	—	—	1	120 (1.0)	—	—	2	217 (0.4)
	15	6,351	23	11,774	35	22,788	63	49,181

Source: Compiled from First Annual School Report MS. in Sister M. Rosalita [Kelly], *No Greater Service: The History of the Congregation of the Sisters, Servants of the Immaculate Heart of Mary, Monroe, Michigan, 1845–1945* (Detroit: Congregation of the Sisters, Servants of the Immaculate Heart of Mary, 1948); and *Hoffmann's Directory,* 1900, 1913, 1925; Account Books, Item 39, 1894–1916. Archives of the Archdiocese of Detroit. Figures are not always in agreement from source to source.

a. Shared with School Sisters of Notre Dame.

b. Plus one shared with the IHMs.

c. Shared with the IHMs.

different-colored long clothing. Catholics who paid attention understood the gulf that separated their schools, appreciated what the various schools accomplished, and recognized what was yet to be done. More commonly, Catholics congratulated themselves on their own particular parish institutions and cared little about the others. But by 1920 the heterogeneous Catholic community necessarily joined forces to defend its schools as a whole.

Michigan residents had endured too many unsettling developments too quickly for comfort: the exploding auto industry with its dizzying economic implications, the heavy immigration of Central and Southeastern Europeans, an expanding urban black population, an array of state and local political innovations, and a confusing venture to make the world safe for democracy. An urge to somehow ensure order prompted a variety of responses. The ever-pervasive faith in institutionalized education as the means to teach "right values" made these institutions a sure nerve center; parochial schools were a certain object among supporters and critics alike.

From 1918 a movement gathered steam among parochial school critics who wanted to require that all children attend public schools. In response, Catholics were forced to divert significant energy and large sums of money to the defense of their schools. To their gratification and even to their surprise, they found support from outsiders who approved some particular aspect of Catholic education and, accordingly, were willing to let the whole of it prevail. As political events of the 1920s would demonstrate, Catholic schools had scrambled to a place on the high ground.

8 The Measure of Success: Challenges to Parochial Education in the 1920s

> Why not let the Catholic schools go right on with their work of turning out well-educated children, children who become good men and women and who help to make this a better nation.
> —E. G. Pipp [a Presbyterian], *Pipp's Weekly* (1920)

PAROCHIAL education in Detroit carved out its distinctive place in a seventy-year period bracketed by the school question in the 1850s and the anti-parochial amendment in the 1920s. Between those two formative encounters in the political forum Catholic schools came not only to serve certain objectives the faithful had for them but also to acquire meaning for good and for ill within the broader community. At each point, parochial education was a lightning rod for community frustrations with democracy and the repository of a firm conviction that schooling would make the necessary difference in the lives of people and nation. In the 1850s the issue had centered around whether Catholics had a right to claim tax support for their schools. In the 1920s the issue took a very different turn: Did Catholics and other denominations have a right to maintain schools?

Even before World War I pressed loyal Americanism with new urgency, a groundswell developed for an amendment to the Michigan constitution that would require all children to attend public schools. Catholic schools were generally acknowledged, by friends and foes alike, as the real quarry, but the amendment that went before the voters in 1920 and 1924 threatened others' well-being. It equally targeted all parochial and private schools, raised questions over constitutionally guaranteed rights, and had important implications for public school finances. The net was wide enough to sweep other constituencies together with Catholics to wage this particular fight; support from allies, whether high-minded or self-serving, brought in needed votes. But Catholic schools emerged with more than victory at the polls. During the course of the campaign, prominent outsiders deliberately signaled that Catholic schools were respectable. Too, the general public became aware that parochial schools presented valuable financial advantages to public school districts such as Detroit. Accordingly, after the amendment was twice defeated, parochial schools became an acknowledged segment of mainstream education, and their students were safely entitled to study toward faith and fortune, unfettered except for public accreditation standards.

Throughout the early 1920s the controversy over parochial schools proved the most influential issue in Michigan politics. Murky contests for elective or appointive offices revolved around personalities. Such eccentric developments as Henry Ford's embattled race for the U.S. Senate in 1918 disrupted alliances for a time, and orthodox conservatives clashed with party moderates and independents. But the Republican Party was nonetheless so strong that it dominated the state with an ease it had not enjoyed since the late nineteenth century. Even in Detroit, Catholic ethnics helped the party win every seat in the Michigan house and senate in 1920 and 1924. In races where the school amendment became entangled in campaigns for office, those conflicts usually played out in the Republican Party primary and had little effect on altering voter strength between the two major parties.

Of considerable and enduring political importance, however, the school amendment issue caused thousands of citizens—many of whom were recent immigrants—to realize their personal stake in the workings of the political process and the power of collective action. Often those new to the polls were among the industrial working class who a decade later became unionized New Deal advocates. The school issue proved more energizing than the idealistic reforms designed to encourage voter participation; that was especially the case among amendment opponents because they, more than proponents, were newcomers to American politics. The amendment campaign relied upon opportunities recently provided by Michigan reformers, however: the right to the initiative, petition, and referendum added to the state's constitution in 1913; Detroit's smaller "reform" public school board dating from 1917; the new 1918 city charter, with a nonpartisan nine-person council elected at-large; and woman suffrage, which became possible in Michigan by 1919. In light of those little-tried innovations, each side was necessarily enterprising and justifiably apprehensive. Tools such as the petition and referendum, as intended, addressed citizens' concerns more surely than foot-dragging or balky state legislators.

LAUNCHING THE SCHOOL AMENDMENT EFFORT

Distrust of parochial schools first emerged as a political issue in March 1916, when seven Detroiters organized the Wayne County Civic Association with the purpose of introducing a bill before the state legislature that would require all elementary school children to attend public schools.[1] Defeated there, proponents decided to try the opportunity for citizens to initiate legislation. If enough registered voters (10 percent of the number who voted for governor in the immediate past preceding election) signed a sponsoring petition, a measure could go on the ballot for popular vote.[2] Ironically, some who now took advantage of the right to petition had opposed this and other reforms when the 1908 constitution was written; the right had been added as an amendment only after continued progressive pressure.[3] In December 1918 the Wayne County Civic Association filed petitions bearing forty-eight thousand signatures with the secretary of state.

Petitioners sought to put an amendment on the ballot which, if approved by voters, would add two new sections to Article XI on education in the constitution. Section 16 would stipulate that "all residents of the State of Michigan between the ages of five and sixteen years shall attend the public schools in their respective districts until they have been graduated from the eighth grade" (or as many years as provided in the district school if it did not extend through grade eight). According to section 17, the legislature would "enact all necessary legislation to render effective section 16."[4]

Sponsors of the amendment were "inspired not by love of our Public Schools but by their hatred of Catholics," snapped the editor of *The Iconoclast.*[5] It was uniformly labeled the "anti-parochial school amendment" by all opponents, including the three major Detroit newspapers. Amendment supporters, in moments of candor, accepted that label as descriptive of a worthy goal.

Challenges to many signatures temporarily derailed the amendment, but the attendant publicity helped give momentum to its enthusiasts. The legislature passed a new state law in 1919 that required all schools in Michigan to conduct classes, except for religious instruction, in English.[6] But that was not enough for militant patriots and fearful xenophobes. On February 19, 1920, Wayne County Civic Association president James A. Hamilton was back at the secretary of state's office with an initiative petition claiming signatures of 114,000 who favored placing the school amendment on the November ballot.[7]

Canadian-born Hamilton, a sometime longshoreman, miner, restaurant operator, and bricklayer, had become the most visible leader in the school amendment campaign. He was vice president of the Wayne County Civic Association in 1918 and its president by 1920.[8] Financial backers of the school amendment effort managed to remain anonymous. S. S. Kresge, whose dime-store fortune started in downtown Detroit, publicly disclaimed rumors that he was a contributor.[9] Even though pro-amendment forces were not so administratively organized and may not have spent as much as amendment opponents, their four-year effort was surely expensive. The source of pro-amendment funding became so troubling once the Ku Klux Klan grew in strength that in 1924 the legislature passed a law requiring financial disclosure by any group that initiated a petition.

A week after presenting the petition, Hamilton's supporters rallied in Lansing and endorsed his candidacy for governor on the Republican ticket in the August primary. The school amendment was his single issue. The Wayne County Civic Association retitled itself the Public School Defense League, reaching for a statewide constituency on behalf of cause and candidate. As a politician, Hamilton was ambitious rather than reasoned or visionary. He was mum about his background, but critics accused him of failed business enterprises and shrinking from service during the war.

Although a lightweight candidate, Hamilton had all the makings of a demagogue who had hit upon the right place and time for the issue he championed. The number of signers on the school amendment petition in 1920 made it the largest filed on any moral issue up to that time, including prohibition, which had succeeded in 1916 via the petition route.[10] Catholics, after hoping nearly two years earlier that the movement would fail "in the present attitude of the Michigan people towards it," now recognized that they must organize their defense in earnest.[11]

Each side employed first one political tool then another. Legal maneuvering to keep the amendment off the ballot met with initial success. Secretary of State Coleman C. Vaughan ruled on July 9 that the proposed amendment was unconstitutional and refused to submit it to the electorate. He had acted upon the opinion of Attorney General Alexander Groesbeck, who held that the state has the right to regulate and supervise private institutions of learning but would be in conflict with the Fourteenth Amendment if it were to suppress them.[12] Groesbeck was running for governor in the August primary among a broad field of nine candidates that included Hamilton, but only Hamilton's supporters charged that political self-interest motivated the attorney general's advisory opinion. No one recalled or mentioned that Groesbeck, an active Mason, grew up a Catholic until a brief seminary experience disillusioned him.[13]

As a next recourse the Public School Defense League turned to the state supreme court. On September 26 a majority ruled that an amendment could not be declared unconstitutional in advance of becoming part of the constitution. Furthermore, said the justices, the secretary of state could not exercise judicial powers and the court issued a writ of mandamus ordering the amendment to appear on the November ballot. Groesbeck, now the front-runner in the gubernatorial race as a result of the primary, remained "firmly convinced of the unconstitutionality of the proposed amendment." And, as he pointed out, although the supreme court disagreed with him by ruling the amendment must go before the voters, that decision did not mean the court viewed the amendment as constitutional.[14]

Defeated in the primary and out of the governor's race, Hamilton put all his resources into the amendment campaign. It had been apparent since the Wayne County Civic Association first set out to acquire signers for their petitions, however, that Hamilton's followers needed little leading. The growing number of Catholics alone provoked dangerous animosities and encouraged their diverse enemies to make common cause. The new immigrant churches and schools going up in working-class neighborhoods aroused special resentment among those white, Protestant, working-class Detroiters convinced that Catholics gave primary and unquestioning allegiance to the pope. Most who shared Hamilton's cause were at least third- or fourth-generation Americans, angry that they must face competition with foreigners. Their hostility increased during the postwar economic downturn that hurt the auto industry.

Meanwhile, in small-town and rural Michigan, except for scattered immigrant settlements, the population was overwhelmingly native-born and Protestant. Farmers burdened by mortgages were in an angry mood when the market for their produce fell off, not to recover until 1923. Local professionals and merchants also felt the pinch. Long mistrustful of an alien Detroit, those who lived outside the city jealously guarded their disproportionate influence in the state legislature and zealously approved laws such as prohibition to promote morality—especially needed, they thought, in cities and among Catholic immigrants. By 1920, however, Michigan had more urban than rural residents for the first time, and the 1908 constitution mandated reapportionment in 1923. Recent political reforms such as direct election of U.S. senators were ominous signs to the "old stock" in rural communities who recognized correctly that they stood to lose state legislative seats and might be outvoted in statewide contests.[15]

During World War I, patriotic demands for 100 percent Americanism spurred designs on parochial schools. The conclusion of the war and the inconclusive peace seemed evidence to some that traitorous foreign influences required continued vigilance at home and abroad. Press accounts gave considerable attention to the Michigan soldiers who constituted the bulk of the "Polar Bears"—the regiment which, amid much local controversy, remained stationed behind in Archangel, Russia, until the summer of 1919 as part of the government's futile and confusing design to help Britain and France oust the new communist regime. Worse, it seemed to alarmists, the Bolsheviks were likely lodged in Detroit's very midst. During the nationwide Red Scare of 1919, the Justice Department rounded up more than eight hundred possible "enemy aliens" in Detroit following a raid upon suspected socialist and communist dance houses, offices, and restaurants.[16] Although no one was convicted, some citizens were convinced of a local communist threat because Attorney General A. Mitchell Palmer had seen fit to order the raids.

THE CAMPAIGN OF 1920

Hamilton charged that parochial schools were hotbeds of Bolshevist ideology. Bolshevist doctrine, he claimed, was strikingly similar to Catholic dogma in its insistence upon unthinking obedience. That was just one reason he set forth in various editions of the *Michigan Public School Amendment,* a rambling paperback tract that grew more lengthy as the anti-parochial school movement gathered momentum. Many of his points emphasized familiar patriotic claims. Public schools were the "melting pot of America, and the very cradle of Democracy," whereas parochial schools were formed and were "being used only to perpetuate some foreign language, custom, or creed." Just as past generations ultimately realized that slavery and polygamy must be abolished, the time had come to abolish parochial schools. He listed practical reasons for requiring public school education, buttressed here and there by miscellaneous figures. According to Hamilton's calculations, Detroit "would be able to put every child in a public school without an additional school room," given the building plans already underway. And public schools had 35 percent more "air space per child," plus better-ventilated forced air.[17]

Customarily, Hamilton's side pandered to prevailing prejudices. One of his associates, Helen Jackson, posed as a former nun, replete with convent tales common among anti-Catholics in the nineteenth century. Parochial schools, Hamilton confidently asserted, "have furnished 65 percent of the criminals of the country, public schools 5 percent and foreigners and illiterates 30 percent." The pope, who controlled the parochial school curriculum, had been "in alliance" with the Central Powers during the war, as had his Italian, German, French, and Irish emissaries.[18] And pity the children. Their Catholic parents did not themselves have religious liberty because the church held the threat of hell over their heads.[19]

A compatriot of Hamilton, Reverend Eli J. Forsythe, in a pamphlet entitled *Michigan School Amendment: The Religious Side,* set forth perhaps the only other published rationale.[20] Forsythe, a Detroit minister and reputed psychic, gave occasional speeches that were much less temperate than his printed pamphlet. When he took to the lecture circuit, Forsythe thundered in lurid detail about the "wrong women" who were having babies, threatening, thereby, "to exterminate the American Protestant home." The American nation could be saved only if the state regulated birth rates and if the Bible returned to public schools.[21]

When the campaign to mandate public education got underway, Catholics had cause to worry. They composed only about 20 percent of the population statewide. Detroit was their stronghold, where perhaps as many as 40 percent were at least nominal Catholics.[22] Of Detroit's population, just under a million in 1920, more than 60 percent were either immigrants or the children of immigrants and most were Catholic.[23] But in Detroit, where their growing numbers gave them potential voting power, Catholics had long found it difficult to make common cause. They had not agreed in 1850 over the school question and had been divided over various local political contests, especially since the 1890s. Catholic churches collectively offered confessions in at least twelve foreign languages by 1920. Certain new groups such as the Syrians and Maltese were growing by the thousands every month, and several immigrant communities quarreled internally. The Polish National Church, for example, created dissension in the Polish community.[24] That meant that Catholic leaders had to reconcile and mobilize more nationalities than ever before in order to make their numbers count.

Even before the state supreme court handed down its ruling, Catholics formed the Educational Liberty League to direct a campaign against the amendment. Chaired by a prominent businessman, John A. Russell, the Liberty League had an executive committee of four other laymen, but Bishop Michael Gallagher was a key participant.[25] In July 1920 he bought the *Michigan Catholic,* part of a multipronged plan to strengthen the institutional church.[26] Now, the *Michigan Catholic* delivered the chancery's perspective and promoted the bishop's objectives. Unlike the need for a voice that had initiated the *Catholic Vindicator* in the 1850s, however, all three major newspapers in Detroit now sided with the Catholics. Still, the first issue under diocesan ownership was devoted to attacking James Hamilton and the Public School Defense League—an absurd mistitle, Catholics objected, because public schools were not under attack and needed no defense. Because Catholics in Michigan were parceled into three dioceses, each under separate archbishops, they did not effect a coordinated campaign, but Bishop Edward D. Kelly of Grand Rapids and Bishop Frederick Eis of Marquette roused their dioceses by organizing committees in every parish.

On August 20, Detroit Catholics met in their separate churches to hear spokesmen explain the Educational Liberty League's planned campaign. Closely resembling the tactics of a political machine, the strategy divided the parishes into districts that corresponded with Detroit's election districts. Districts were then subdivided into precincts, and a committee was appointed for each election precinct within the parish. Often there were several because of the wide geographical reach of ethnic parishes. Some such "precincts" as defined by one parish undoubtedly overlapped with other "parish precincts" when each drew, selectively, from the same multiethnic neighborhood. According to the plan, a precinct committee member would canvass an assigned area, alerting all voters to the amendment issue and urging them to show up at the polling place in November.[27] The strategy relied on saturation contact with every potential Catholic voter and emphasized the need to use canvassers who could speak the language of the person whose vote the league was hoping to influence.

Just recently eligible to vote, women became critical to the success or failure of the amendment campaign. Analysts were not agreed in 1920 about whether women would register, turn out, or vote with any independence in their first chance to choose a U.S. president. On the school issue, however, Catholics counted on women to be committed to the right position, calculated the number of their votes, and exhorted them to do their civic duty. Never mind that Cardinal Gibbons had held that woman suffrage would tend to increase "this searing social evil, divorce." It need not, as he warned, bring "moral looseness, discord, and dishonor in the sacred family circle."[28] Rather, according to the *Michigan Catholic,* women must "help make politics clean." More to the immediate point, "Here in Michigan our parochial schools are in jeopardy. In fact the Catholic schools of the country are in jeopardy."[29] Women voters could save them. When the last chance to register was only a week away, Bishop Gallagher sent a special reminder to convents. Sisters were to *"register now,* . . . pray earnestly for success," and offer "Holy Communions and aspirations."[30]

For years, Detroit's immigrant daughters had been attending school in high percentages and, as a group, staying in school longer than boys. Many were ready and willing to mobilize without much prodding. Religious communities, generally better educated than the laity and long charged to train youngsters to be responsible citizens, were no doubt pleased to do their part. Most IHMs had registered long before the bishop's letter came, and at least one candidate for judge of the probate court in Monroe solicited their votes. Up for reelection, he sent them sample ballots, said he hoped he had won their confidence by his administration of probate and juvenile courts, and assured them he was against the amendment by the "bolshevik author."[31]

Getting out the word and the vote took money. To the Catholic hierarchy such an unwelcome expense could not have come at a more inconvenient time. From the moment he arrived in 1918, Bishop Gallagher had envisioned a massive building program that included a residence, chancery building, cathedral, and other costly projects such as the schools, hospitals, and colleges that he urged upon parishes and religious congregations.[32] In the spring of 1920 the bishop launched a fund-raising drive to build a diocesan seminary that proceeded, now, alongside the drive to save parochial schools. Door-to-door solicitors plus pulpit appeals brought $9,000,000 in pledges for the seminary in the first year, one-third of it already paid by 1921.[33] Meanwhile, as the fall election approached, parishes began collecting for the "school defense fund" at every Sunday mass.

Contributions testified to an almost bottomless yet selective generosity. Most Holy Trinity, a working-class and comparatively small parish, turned over $1,644 to the fund—raised in just September and October. It was only one of the several "special collections" taken. In addition to pledges for the new seminary, Trinity parishioners dug into their wages to help the "Holy Father," the Indian and Negro collection, the Holy Land, Catholic University, and the "Polish Sufferers." During the two months preceding the election, their donations to the school fund nearly equaled the amount Holy Trinity parishioners gave toward heating their church throughout the entire year of 1920.[34] Many other Catholics made these same choices. Parish contributions to the defense fund were frequently more than their donations to all other special collections combined.[35] In November, Bishop Gallagher estimated that Catholics had spent $150,000 to defeat the amendment.[36]

No record shows how the Educational Defense League spent its money. The bishop and the league's steering committee likely did recognize that people who donated even small sums would take an interest in the ballot proposal. Fund-raising drives could help get out the vote, much as wartime Liberty Loan drives had whipped up support for American participation in the European conflict. The league clearly needed money, however, to print the bulletins, pamphlets, booklets, sample ballots, and mailings it issued by the gross. To make the case for a no vote on the amendment, the Educational Defense League also ran large newspaper advertisements with quotes from widely respected Michigan Protestant and Jewish leaders who defended parochial schools.

Literature of the league's own making spelled out the Catholic case for parochial schools. One pamphlet, *Thirty Reasons Why You Should Vote No,* countered Hamilton's list of reasons in favor of the amendment and summarized the most frequent arguments made by the Catholics throughout the 1920 and 1924 campaigns. The anti-school amendment was certain to increase taxes; it was also un-American and unconstitutional. From the Catholics' perspective the amendment represented the same Kaiser-like state domination they fought in the war against Germany, and further, by striking at religious training, it was "an aid" to the godless Bolsheviks. It was injurious to the state because "thousands will leave Michigan as our forefathers left Europe in search of religious freedom." Perhaps the most interesting point on the list of thirty, albeit infrequently used, was the claim that the amendment was "dangerous to the home" because it would bring "race suicide" just as it did in France following the "assault" on religion, "for without religion men and women are slow to assume the burden of families."[37]

While Catholics organized their defense, so, too, did others whose schools were equally in jeopardy. Missouri Synod Lutherans mounted a vigorous statewide campaign comparable to the Catholic effort. They were a separate, conservative wing among Lutherans, insistent on preserving their German culture through their own schools. Lutherans had nearly two hundred schools in the state, although some were in small rural churches where the pastor was the teacher.[38] All too familiar with wartime intolerance when German Americans had tried valiantly to demonstrate their patriotism, pastors and laity now spoke up. Their campaign slogan "Whose Is the Child?" demanded parental rights over education.[39]

The eight-member Lutheran Executive Campaign Committee set up headquarters at the Tuller Hotel, organized the state into fifty-eight districts, and requested that every congregation establish a group of minutemen or "fighting units" to visit individual Lutheran homes.[40] It was time, said one Detroit clergyman, to follow in the tradition of a legendary Revolutionary War pastor who cast off his cassock, went before his congregation wearing a Continental army uniform, and announced, "There is a time for preaching and praying and there is a time for fighting."[41] To equip them with ammunition the headquarters engaged "nearly an entire publishing establishment" to issue postcards, posters, handbills, pamphlets by the bundle, and fifty thousand "Whose Is the Child?" campaign buttons. Like Catholics, Lutherans considered women's votes to be vital for defeating the amendment. Women from Detroit churches formed the Lutheran Mothers' League of the State of Michigan to rouse "every woman and every mother to the wanton injustice and wrong . . . and to urge the necessity of drastic action at the ballot box for the sake of American ideals."[42]

"The school amendment is overshadowing the presidential election in many parts," a Lutheran pastor in Manistee reported by mid-October. "The Finns in Kaleva," representative of an important concentration in northern Michigan, "are on our side."[43] Lutheran organizers were preoccupied with enlisting their own voters, a second front of considerable concern to them. Some Lutherans objected to joining forces with Catholics, convinced all along that "we must down the Catholic church. It is our duty to liberate the Catholic child."[44]

Several Lutherans complained that most parochial schools belonged to the "very orthodox" Missouri Synod congregations that would not cooperate or even meet with other followers of Martin Luther. It was a point that Hamilton also enjoyed raising.[45] The executive secretary of the Lutheran Schools Committee replied to one critic with a typical reassurance: "I believe that I can understand your sentiments . . . since, being a Lutheran, I cannot be anything else than anti-Catholic." He offered a pragmatic rationale for working with Catholics, however: "Coercion and persecution" would not "break the political or spiritual activities" of the "Romish church." Rather, persecution would only make Catholics more political. It was "not only probable" but also "practically certain" that they would gain and wield the balance of power in the state legislature, because "certain legislative districts could return Catholic legislators, if they so desired." Still, he did not back away from his central conviction about the "inherent right . . . [the] inalienable and a natural right" of Catholic parents to educate children along religious lines, "provided of course, they also meet the requirements of the state."[46]

Dubious Lutherans may have been somewhat mollified, because other long-time warriors against the papacy were also allying with Catholics in this particular battle. Although Congregationalists, Methodists, and Presbyterians throughout the state were sometimes considered "doubtful" votes, Baptists were the only major group whose ministers either refrained from comment or sided with the Public School Defense League.[47] Detroit clergymen were especially active in denouncing the amendment. They joined to sign newspaper statements, and, from their pulpits, Presbyterian, Methodist, Episcopalian, and Congregational ministers identified agnostics and Bolsheviks as the "bad company" backing the school amendment. They were the common enemy of Catholics and Protestants alike.[48] Protestant clergymen emphasized a history more recent than the Reformation. Characteristically, one Grand Rapids pastor reminded his flock that it was in Michigan where "four men once sat down before a table, a Catholic priest, a Congregationalist, a Methodist and a Presbyterian and laid the foundations of the State University."[49]

The *Detroit Free Press* thought it worthy of the same bold type as their headline about recognition of Mexico: "JEWS, GENTILES ONE ON SCHOOLS." The subheading summed up the editor's pleasure: "Hebrews, Protestants, Stand Beneath Crucifix; Fight for American Ideals."[50] Dating from the 1860s, early in their development as a community, most Detroit Jewish families sent their children to public school and provided religious instruction after hours or on weekends—the same course of action Hamilton and the Public School Defense League now recommended to Catholics and Lutherans. But Temple Beth El's Rabbi Leo Franklin, the most prominent Jewish leader in the city, was quick to oppose this amendment "conceived in bigotry."[51] Across the state in Kalamazoo, Rabbi Philip P. Waterman emphasized, "I repeat that I favor the public school as opposed to the private or parochial schools, but I feel that this is not a matter where it is fair or wise to exercise coercion."[52]

There were yet other corners of support. The "absolutely non-sectarian" Private Schools Association headquartered in Lansing came to the defense of its member schools, many of them elite day and boarding schools.[53] Dutch Reformed pastors also rallied to the defense of their schools, although comparatively few in number. And Seventh-Day Adventists spoke out with reasons of their own. Field Secretary Rev. W. F. Martin warned that larger church groups would start a move for compulsory education in public schools in self-defense if church schools were closed.[54]

Whatever motives others might have for opposing the amendment, Catholics welcomed their company. In a move known to "shatter church rule," Bishop Gallagher opened the pulpit at Blessed Sacrament Cathedral for a "mass meeting" in which all the speakers were non-Catholic, including three clergymen—the pastor of the First Unitarian Church, the rector of St. Joseph's Episcopal Church, and the rabbi from Temple Beth El.[55]

Many civic and religious leaders shared a conviction that much more was at stake than the future of parochial and private school education or the principle of separation of church and state, which worked to the advantage of parochial schools in this instance. They frequently invoked the Fourteenth Amendment. Across the years, the Fourteenth Amendment and numerous Supreme Court cases had sharpened American opinion about constitutionally guaranteed rights. Attorney General Groesbeck was just one who maintained that "the right of the parent to exercise a reasonable control over the education of his off-spring . . . is one of the most sacred rights preserved for the individual under the federal Constitution." Frank Leland, a University of Michigan regent and lawyer, agreed with Groesbeck and said the school amendment "would not be constitutional even if it were passed."[56] One after another, politicians, civic leaders, and clergymen lined up behind that position.

Hamilton countered on behalf of the amendment's legality: "Inasmuch as our democracy has decided that all its children be educated and has provided facilities for that purpose," it was "plainly evident that it proposed to compel attendance only at its own institutions." Because it had been "admitted by all" that the state has the right to decree that all children must go to school, "the state cannot allow its children to attend any schools outside of its own institutions."[57] Men like Groesbeck dismissed such reasoning, and Hamilton's rhetoric helped swell the Lutheran chorus: "Whose Is the Child?"

While flag-waving warnings about the "foreign" and despotic proclivities of Catholic schools helped fuel the amendment drive, appeals to patriotism were routine among those who opposed it. Speaking before the Eighty-seventh Annual Diocese Convention, Episcopal Bishop Charles D. Williams described the move to ban parochial schools as part of what Americans had just fought against in war. "In the name of one hundred percent Americanism we seem to be Prussianizing America."[58] Similarly commonplace was the indictment of the amendment as un-American and un-Christian, a "cowardly attack" expected only in countries run by communists and socialists who forced children into state schools.[59]

Leaders repeatedly alluded to the delicate balance that maintained peace and order in polyglot Detroit. Catholic leaders deftly played up the concern, running advertisements that reprinted portions of speeches. Governor Albert E. Sleeper cautioned that the amendment would "engender bitterness and suspicion and distrust where now, mutual trust and good feeling to a large extent prevail." Groesbeck abhorred the "ill feeling and acrimonious discussion among the people" that the amendment tended to foment, and President Frank Kedzie of the Michigan Agricultural College believed it introduced "one more element tending to unrest."[60]

Although Detroit was an especially fragile, fragmented community, taxpayers were of one mind in their skepticism concerning government expense. Shrewd leaders did not neglect the financial implications associated with a shift of all parochial school children into public classrooms. Apart from those who paid taxes and also supported separate schools, until this campaign there had been little mention of the financial advantages parochial schools provided non-Catholic taxpayers and public schools. Now, reform elites, business leaders, and public school administrators pushed this fundamental factor into a place of high visibility. Finally, finances may have offered voters the single most compelling argument.

Jeffrey Mirel, in his history of Detroit's twentieth-century public schools, has observed that a broad consensus favored their expansion and improvement between 1907 and the Great Depression. The system would be sufficiently impressive in the 1920s to win accolades as "foremost in the ranks of cities" and even as "one of the finest in the world."[61] For several years, then, a transformation of Detroit's public schools had been underway. Detroiters had been generous about school funding, but it remained an expensive process. During the course of the school amendment campaign, men such as Board of Education president John Hall put financial facts of life into focus. Detroit had better public schools for the money because so many children were educated in parochial schools. There was an additional clinching argument not often mentioned before this campaign, perhaps to avoid arousing Catholics to angry demands: Michigan's Primary School Fund allocations for Catholic children went to public schools.

By state law every public school district received a per-capita payment from the Primary School Interest Fund for all children of school age in the district, regardless of whether those children attended public, private, or parochial school.[62] It was the major source of state funding, often amounting to nearly a quarter of the total school revenue.[63] In July preceding the academic year of 1920–21, the state allocated $10 per child from the fund plus an additional 64 cents from miscellaneous money. Detroit public schools received $1,446,436.61 from the fund but enrolled 139,010 children in grades K–12 that year.[64]

As budget-wise public leaders understood perfectly, each child educated in private or parochial school not only saved expense but also added actual dollars to the district's budget. Now, in the midst of the amendment debate, many residents were astonished to learn from the board president that Detroit netted between $30,000 and $40,000 based on the count of parochial school children without the cost of educating those children. As Hall explained to one audience after another, in systems like Detroit's, parochial school children were a boon to public school budgets.[65] If the amendment were to pass, public schools would have more children but no more funding unless districts approved tax increases.

Primary School Fund money went exclusively for teachers' salaries. Because salaries had gone up in 1920–21, and with per-pupil capital spending also at an all-time high that year, concerned leaders could not afford to be subtle. It was no time to require public school attendance.[66] Frightening figures poured forth. The amendment would undoubtedly hurt the local economy, warned Frederick C. Martindale, one of the Republican candidates for governor. Because it would cost Detroit taxpayers an additional $6,000,000 by his estimate, he expected people would avoid settling in Detroit because homeowners would have such a heavy tax burden.[67]

Each side had its own estimate of the number of children who would be added to public school rosters and budgets. Hamilton claimed that 47,707 children attended Lutheran, Seventh-Day Adventist, Greek Orthodox, Russian Orthodox, private, Lithuanian, and Roman Catholic schools in Detroit.[68] According to Lutheran statements, as of 1920 the 185 Lutheran day schools throughout Michigan had 10,354 pupils and 209 teachers, and nearly 103,000 children attended parochial or private schools statewide.[69] The Educational Liberty League reported 550 schools operated by various religious denominations, 2,500 teachers, and an enrollment of about 120,000 in 1920.[70] "To carry the school amendment into effect will cost $70,000 for new buildings," the Lutheran campaign claimed. Furthermore, it would require many additional teachers. The resulting expense would "most likely place out of existence the public institutions for the care of the feeble-minded, epileptics, deaf mutes and the blind."[71]

One clause of the proposed amendment required that children would have to attend their own district schools. Some interpreted that to mean blind and deaf children would no longer be able to attend special schools, and it also displeased parents whose children crossed district boundaries for better or closer schools. Beyond such concerns there were more financial implications. According to Board President Hall, the teachers' retirement fund would lose about $23,000 a year—approximately the amount it received in 1919 from tuition fees charged the nearly six hundred children whose homes were outside the Detroit district. If the amendment were to pass, he cautioned, there "will not be a cent of tuition fees to go into the retirement fund." The *Detroit Free Press* reported that "trustees pricked up their ears" upon hearing this and resolved "to lay the matter before the 4,100 teachers in the public schools in order that they might know what they are voting for when they go to the polls."[72]

Hamilton and the Public School Defense League came up with financial answers. Catholics and Lutherans would save "approximately $18 a year per child," the amount it cost parents to maintain their schools.[73] Furthermore, Catholics would have the chance to demonstrate patriotism. They could lend their school buildings to the state, and their teachers could continue to contribute their services. Although Hamilton did not try to reconcile these recommendations with his claims that parochial schools were overcrowded and their teachers inadequate, he implied that this was at least an acceptable short-term remedy. Former parochial teachers would be supervised and book choices taken out of the hands of the clergy.[74]

As Hamilton's opponents saw it, however, his willingness to commandeer private property and coerce labor were further examples of his "un-Americanism." This "virtual seizure" would surely send Catholics and Lutherans to the Supreme Court, according to one Detroit lawyer. And, should the Court uphold any such condemnation, "there'll be an uproar that will end in serious trouble." Moreover, he judged that more than three thousand teachers in parochial and private schools would refuse to work for boards of education if their schools were closed and "no law could make them accept positions as teachers."[75]

If there were any lingering doubt about numbers, Catholics paraded their evidence before the public in one final statement. On Sunday, October 31, 1920, just two days before the election, more than fifty thousand parochial school children from Detroit and outlying towns joined their elders and "well wishers" in a march through Detroit's streets to the baseball stadium at Navin Field. There, a crowd estimated at between eighty-five and a hundred thousand attended an outdoor mass to pray that their schools "might not be wiped out by the vote at the election Tuesday."[76]

Initiated by Bishop Gallagher, the event's organizers planned carefully, and the crowd was "picturesque in the extreme."[77] Nearly 1,500 sisters attended the mass "in obedience to the Rt. Rev. Bishop's orders."[78] They arrived in a procession of automobiles and, conspicuous in their black, blue, and brown habits, filed into a large section of reserved seats. It was the first such public appearance by a group of sisters in the nation's history. Some marched through the streets and into the stadium side by side with their pupils, no doubt keeping an eye on the flag each child carried. Concerned over every impression, the bishop had charged teachers to be sure all flags were "upright" and not "trailing in the dirt."[79] More flags were carried by ten thousand Catholics, nearly all of them in uniform, who had served in the nation's wars. There were also nursing sisters who had done duty in France, Catholic Boy Scouts in uniform, and representatives from every Catholic activity in the city.

Row after orderly row, the thousands marched onto the field following bands trumpeting "Onward, Christian Soldiers." Significantly, as the friendly press made clear, the tune had been written by an Episcopalian minister and used by Theodore Roosevelt when he held his "Armageddon convention" at Chicago in 1912. Patriotism and religion entwined all day. Well-rehearsed children sang out when it was time for the "Star Spangled Banner," "Holy

God We Praise Thy Name," and "Our Country and Our Schools Forever," a song written especially for the occasion.

Father Patrick R. Dunigan celebrated the mass. Not long back from the French front, he had served as chaplain for Michigan soldiers in dugouts, forests, and sometimes "under shell fire." Bishop Gallagher preached a conciliatory sermon, dwelling on the cooperation between Catholics, Lutherans, the Dutch Reformed, and the Seventh-Day Adventists. He praised the "spirit of justice" among public officials and the press who condemned the amendment and "deplored the spirit of bigotry that would set Catholics and Protestants at each other's throats."[80]

The *Detroit News* hailed the mammoth demonstration as a "petition in boots." Marchers were workers of "all kinds," all products of the parochial schools and "all of them citizens doing their work . . . contributing to the prosperity and happiness of Detroit and the State of Michigan." Readers were advised not to miss a key message of the Navin Field mass, however: "Detroiters who have never seen the great parochial schools of Detroit welcome their thousands of child students in the mornings and pour them forth after school closes" should understand "the task that would confront the community if it were suddenly called on to furnish parochial school children with public school accommodations."[81]

On the following Tuesday, Detroit polls recorded the largest vote in the city's history. Initiated into the political process out of self-interest, many voters registered who had not previously thought to participate. On October 17, the last day for registrations, people were already in line when booths opened at 8 A.M., and clerks had to work overtime that night. Districts inhabited largely by Lutherans and Catholics reported especially heavy registrations.[82] As many as 90 percent of the registered voters turned out, and they voted unusually early—half of them by noon—despite a morning-long downpour. According to observers, women "cast ballot for ballot with the men" in nearly all sections of the city. The large turnout, the city's newspapers agreed, came about not because of the general election or the race for the presidency but because of the interest in the proposed school amendment and "the determination of the opposition . . . to swamp it under an overwhelming vote."[83]

Four years earlier, 73,148 Detroiters had voted on a ballot proposal to restructure the Detroit school board significantly.[84] Nearly four times as many votes were cast in the city on the amendment, with approximately 90 percent of all registered voters going to the polls. In the diocese of Detroit, where two-thirds of the total state vote was cast, 63 percent opposed the amendment.[85] Statewide, the tally was 610,699 against to 353,818 for the proposition.[86] Catholics, although only about 20 percent of the state's voters, had achieved a monumental triumph thanks to the impressive support from a variety of corners.

But the election gave evidence that the Catholic vote, so heavily tied to the Democratic Party in the nineteenth century, was an independent bloc that might be mobilized by either party. Catholics contributed importantly to Groesbeck's election as governor, and every member of Michigan's 1921 legislature would be a Republican.[87] As the primary elections of 1918 and 1920 made apparent, Michigan's two major parties did not divide along lines of ideology, politicians did not array dependably along any single liberal-conservative spectrum, and neither religion nor ethnicity nor wealth offered a dependable predictor of political behavior. Voters pulled instead from a grab bag of candidates and issues, selecting according to their own best interests as best they could calculate them. The statewide Republican sweep in 1920, then, reflected the politics of self-interest more than any "politics of consensus."

THE CAMPAIGN OF 1924

Defeat at the polls did not mean that those who supported the school amendment acquiesced in the majority's will. The stakes, they believed, were too high. There seemed reason to carry on the cause. The first of the "emergency" national immigrant quotas in 1921 and 1924 alerted Americans that many members of Congress agreed that foreigners were dangerous, yet there was no accompanying change in the flow of immigrants throughout the 1920s. They continued to arrive in Michigan cities such as Detroit and Flint, coming either directly from Europe or, more often, from other cities. Many were Catholic; in 1920 alone Detroit had opened two new Polish parishes, two that were Lithuanian, and one each for the Maltese, Syrians, and Mexicans.[88] Friends and foes alike had every reason to imagine that more would come and that the new ethnic parishes would add new parochial schools.

Those who were disappointed over the defeat of the school amendment still found reasons to persevere because of favorable precedents. Residents in states from Maine to Nebraska to Oregon were moved to political action. Oregon voters, by 101,000 to 15,000, passed an initiative amendment in November 1922 that would, by 1926, require all children aged eight to sixteen to attend public schools.[89] The amendment was scheduled to be heard by the U.S. Supreme Court in 1924, and both supporters and opponents were predicting victory.

Local parochial school supporters continued to store up funds for another likely assault from pro-amendment forces even while wanting to think "the psychological moment for the enemy has passed," as the hopeful Lutheran Executive Secretary Baur wrote to a friend in January 1922. "The people are becoming more and more disillusioned as to the peculiar ideals that were propounded during and after the war." He also recognized that in the lingering postwar depression, "They have less money and therefore more reason to worry about their own affairs."[90] It was the worry about their own affairs, however, that helped sustain the search for scapegoats. By the spring of 1924 Hamilton had enough signatures to put the amendment back on the November ballot. It read much the same as in 1920, except the mandatory attendance age was raised from five to seven and it no longer required that students must attend their district school.[91]

The campaign was a replay of 1920. Only the organized involvement of the Ku Klux Klan set it apart, contributing to a more virulent anti-Catholicism than before. The first kleagle arrived in Detroit in the summer of 1921 to recruit members. After slow initial growth, a new and better organizer helped boost the Michigan Klan to seventy thousand by 1924, with nearly half the members in Detroit.[92] The mushrooming black urban population helped the organizers. In 1900 there had been only about sixteen thousand blacks in Michigan, by 1920 there were sixty thousand, and by 1930 there would be more than 169,000.

Imperial Wizard Hiram Wesley Evans, new to the post in 1923, wanted to move away from hate-mongering and emphasize "positive" concerns—education, temperance, the flag, Protestantism, morality, and charity. Under his leadership the Klan began to champion separation of church and state, meanwhile insisting that the Bible should be read in school every day.[93] In short, the Klan had taken over the position held by mainstream Protestants in the mid-nineteenth century. The school amendment was a ready-made issue, offering Klansmen a chance to line up alongside some "solid citizens" who otherwise disdained them and their tactics. The Klan took up the school amendment with unsophisticated and crude patriotic rhetoric. "We'll take every child in all America and put him in the public schools of America. . . . We will build a homogeneous people; we will grind out Americans just like meat out of a grinder." Thus proclaimed Imperial Wizard Evans in a celebration of American independence on July 4, 1924.[94]

Catholic, Lutheran, Seventh-Day Adventist, and Dutch Reformed churches and the Private Schools Association picked up where they left off in 1920, only now they had the advantage of hindsight. Catholic organizers decided against a massive Navin Field rally this time, apparently worried that it might profit opponents who liked to warn about encroaching Catholic hordes. They concentrated instead on getting out the Catholic vote. Bishop Gallagher activated the Catholic School Defense Campaign Committee, sometimes still known as the Educational Liberty League. Again it enlisted the priest and two laymen from each parish to ensure that all Catholic citizens would register and vote.[95] A preelection experiment during Sunday masses in one parish had showed that as many as 14 percent marked sample ballots incorrectly—this in a parish "not made up of foreign-born or uneducated people, but presumably intelligent voters." Packets of sample ballots quickly went off to every parish priest, along with the bishop's directive to use them after the gospel and after discussing the importance of voting "to save our schools."[96]

Catholics employed the ethnicity issue however they could make it work. Polish parish meetings denounced the Ku Klux Klan's position that teaching a foreign language was detrimental to the loyalty of students. And Polish community leaders warned that passage of the amendment would mean an end to instruction in Polish. An Italian priest, mindful of the city's eighteen thousand Italians, likened the amendment to the new immigrant quota law—one more slap in the face to the southern nations of Europe who fought side by side with Americans. Before certain audiences, however, Catholic spokespersons made the case for their schools as important agents of Americanization.[97]

Catholics took on exhaustive mail projects, enabled by sisters and their pupils who folded and addressed for hours. Letters went off to the 60,661 Michigan voters who signed the petition to put the amendment on the ballot in an effort to verify whether those people had actually signed, and, if so, whether they fully grasped the purpose of the amendment or thought, perhaps, that they were merely supporting compulsory attendance. Some admitted that they did not understand it initially and were willing to vote against it now; others claimed Hamilton's group used trickery or fraud.[98]

As before, there was contact between the Lutheran and Catholic campaign headquarters. The two denominations shared information and tended to supplement one another's work without carrying out joint projects. The Lutheran Committee sent questionnaires to candidates for elective office, querying them about their position on parochial schools, a precaution they had begun in the 1922 election. Cover letters apologized, "It is not customary for the Lutheran church, which has always stood for the principle of complete separation of Church and State, to inquire about the attitude of candidates on political questions." In this instance, "however," they had to make an exception. Based upon responses, they prepared a list of acceptable candidates for their voters and shared it with Catholic organizers.[99]

The Lutheran Schools Committee also took pains to counter pro-amendment literature that claimed the wartime draft had proved that there were high rates of illiteracy among Michigan inductees and that parochial schools were to blame. An inquiry to the War Department brought a major general's reply: "No complete statistics on illiteracy in the Army have been compiled," and "no attempt has been made . . . to classify by States such data." The School Committee thereupon issued its own data from U.S. Census facts showing only 3 percent of Michigan's population aged ten and over to be illiterate, whereas the national average was 6 percent.[100]

The campaign prompted more legislative tinkering with the right to petition when doubts emerged about the financial backers of the amendment. Hamilton refused to name his sources of support, taken by many to mean that he had Klan backing. With Governor Groesbeck's encouragement, the state legislature passed a bill in 1924 that required all who resorted to the initiative to give a sworn statement of sources of money, how it was expended, and a promise that no deception had been used in procuring votes.[101]

Support was even more broad-based in 1924 than in 1920. In a show of solidarity with Catholic compatriots and citing Catholics' wartime loyalty, the Wayne County Council of the American Legion urged veterans to vote against the amendment. Prominent Masons spoke up on behalf of parochial schools, even though Masonic lodges were active in the Oregon move to require that all children attend public schools. When fifty Catholics and fifty Masons in Utica, New York, forged an alliance by founding the Hamilton-Jefferson Association in October 1924, the city's newspapers showed considerable enthusiasm. Monroe Catholics and Masons quickly formed a chapter, and the Detroit Tourist Convention Bureau rushed off a telegram urging the association to hold its first national convention in Detroit.[102]

Meeting in the summer of 1924, the National Education Association's representative assembly upheld the "American public school as the great nursery of broad and tolerant citizenship" but passed a resolution that acknowledged also the "contributions made to education by private institutions." The NEA concluded that "citizens have the right to educate their children in either public or private schools, when the educational standards of both are approved by the State educational authorities."[103] The position went out to Detroit public school teachers in their fall bulletin.

Financial arguments again provided amendment opponents with their centerpiece. To handle the needed city services for its booming population and physical expansion, Detroit's bonded debt increased across the decade from $25.5 million in 1920 to $255.4 million in 1930. The per-capita tax jumped from $26.84 to $53.44 during the same period. Almost a quarter of every tax dollar went to public schools.[104] During the 1924 amendment campaign, ten Protestant clergymen, two rabbis, and a lengthy list of leading businessmen, all of whom described themselves as "non-Catholic," issued a joint statement in the city's newspapers. The group offered alarming facts. Passage of the amendment would "cause distress, strife and chaos" if the 125,000 additional parochial children had to attend the overcrowded public schools where thousands were already on half-days. It would also cost $70,000,000 for new schools plus $9,000,000 annually for maintenance, books, and teachers. Too, the group took the softer slant: The amendment was "an attack upon our general educational system which has worked happily for generations."[105] One signatory was attorney Divie Bethune Duffield, descendent of Reverend Duffield, who had fought so fiercely against Catholic schools in Detroit seventy years earlier.

In the September primary it was the Republican contest that mattered because, given the party's statewide domination, the Republican candidate would win November's general election. A group calling itself the Michigan Anti-Klan Committee distributed literature endorsing candidates, including Groesbeck for governor and James Couzens, under attack by the Klan because his wife was a Catholic, for senator. With the experience of primaries still new, the committee added a careful reminder, "It will do no good to vote . . . except a Republican ballot." The Klan prepared a handbill listing its ticket, and Imperial Wizard "Evans orders" said they should distribute the flyers by airplane.[106]

Groesbeck defeated Hamilton and Frederick Perry, a Lenawee County minister and field organizer for the Klan who also entered the seven-way Republican gubernatorial primary. But the results encouraged the pro-amendment side because Hamilton placed second and between them Hamilton and Perry received 208,469 votes to Groesbeck's 348,955.[107] The *Michigan Catholic* warned that the foe had become much stronger and began weekly reminders with such headlines as "DEFEAT THREATENS UNLESS CATHOLICS RALLY TO SCHOOLS."[108]

In the general election in November, attention focused on the amendment and the mayor's race in Detroit. The mayor's race became a three-way competition among Joseph Martin, John Smith, and Charles Bowles when Bowles, the third-place winner in the September primary, launched a write-in campaign with Klan backing. Bowles, who grew up in the small Michigan town of Yale, was educated as a lawyer at the University of Michigan and was a high-ranking Mason who held office in several lodges. Many residents, worried over increased governmental costs and rising crime of all sorts, approved his campaign emphasis on fiscal efficiency and "strict law enforcement."[109]

Under the new city charter of 1918, the mayor ran as a nonpartisan, but Martin, Smith, and Bowles were established Republicans. The two candidates whose names were on the official ballot had Catholic ties. Joseph Martin, a council member and acting mayor, had been educated in public schools. His religion somehow escaped the records, but he had graduated from the University of Detroit at a time when most students there were Catholic. An auditor and accountant, he was in private business after holding various city posts, some gained through the patronage of former mayor James Couzens.[110] Martin was the candidate favored by established business and civic leaders. During the campaign, Bishop Gallagher publicly denied rumors he was supporting Martin. He would not "express any choice" but "cared only" for defeat of the anti-parochial school amendment.[111]

Candidate John W. Smith grew up Catholic in a poor German Polish family on Detroit's east side. One of seven children and with a widowed mother, Smith never went beyond elementary school. In his youthful poverty and scrappy survival Smith was similar to Hamilton, who had been on his own from the age of twelve. Smith earned his living as a plumber and steamfitter until he gained a series of patronage jobs in the Republican Party through his early and powerful mentor John C. Lodge.[112] Smith capitalized on Ku Klux Klan support for Bowles, and his base developed among Catholic, Jewish, black, and recent immigrant voters who recognized the Klan as their enemy. Speaking around town in Catholic churches on the eve of the election, he linked the Klan's highly visible demonstrations on Bowles's behalf with their support for the school amendment.[113]

Voter registration proceeded apace with population growth, and election day in November brought the heaviest turnout in Detroit's history: 308,415 voted in the mayoral race. The final tally gave John Smith 116,807, Bowles 106,679, and Martin 84,929. Bowles's vote was well beyond the estimated thirty-two thousand Klan members in Detroit and carried the lower-middle-class sections, cutting into Martin's strength.[114]

Had it not been for a large number of ballots spoiled when voters misspelled his name, Bowles would have become mayor. His near-success stunned election-watchers around the country who made much of his Klan backing. He was almost "totally unknown," wrote the *Christian Century*, appalled by Klan strength in the nation's fourth-largest city.[115] In fact, however, his opponents also had unimpressive credentials and experience, were little known outside party circles before the campaign, and were caught up anyway with party infighting. Smith had alienated the Groesbeck faction as a result of his bid for power in Wayne County in 1920.[116]

Men such as James Couzens, Republicans of established substance and reputation, had moved on to larger political arenas, and Democrats were divided. Consequently, the party was weak. Others expressed their "civic concerns" on boards and stayed clear of elective office to tend their flourishing businesses. Recorder's Court Justice Frank Murphy, just then beginning a career that would lead him to the mayoralty, governor's office, and U.S. Supreme Court, wrote in 1924 that politics in Michigan displayed "an inordinate amount of lack of character," with office-seekers who appeared to be "little attached to principle or political conviction."[117]

The amendment that would have required all children to attend public schools went down to defeat almost 2 to 1—760,571 to 421,471. It was a bigger margin than four years before. Majorities in sixty-three of Michigan's eighty-three counties voted against it. Wayne County tallied 263,786 opposing and 100,690 favoring the amendment, while Marquette County, with its multiethnic mining families, recorded the most lopsided vote against the amendment—10,390 to 3,614.[118] Seemingly resolved by voters with regard to Michigan, the Supreme Court ultimately settled the issue in 1925. The Court had been deliberating over the Oregon law after a federal court found it unconstitutional in 1924. In *Pierce* v. *the Society of Sisters,* the high court ruled that parents had the right to send children to nonpublic schools in lieu of public schools.[119]

Just as in the 1850s, Catholics came away from this political experience frightened by the number of their enemies, more aware of the protections offered through building coalitions, and better skilled in the use of the political process. As Smith's election to the position of mayor demonstrated, Catholic candidates could win; Frank Murphy was just beginning his career. Still, the political process did not embrace part-time, blue-collar politicians from recent immigrant neighborhoods. They stood little chance in at-large elections for the seven-member school board, had they been interested. And, in contrast to the old forty-two members, the new nine-member Detroit Common Council, elected at-large, discouraged would-be ward politicians. Working-class immigrants were profiting again from the auto economy that revived in 1923, and some among them were relieved and willing to let bigotry shift more of its focus upon Detroit's black community. Some were also willing to join neighborhood groups such as the Waterworks Association, which, in an effort to keep blacks out, sparked the celebrated Ossian Sweet case in 1925. Showing little interest in sustained cooperation beyond their class or kind, for the remainder of the 1920s Catholics generally turned back to tend families, homes, and parishes.

GRATEFULLY: STATE ACCREDITATION

Whatever their class or nationality, Catholics came away from the school amendment episode feeling more justified in their course than ever. This time, outsiders not only helped rescue parochial education but also heaped praise upon the products of their schools. Still, there was no misunderstanding it: Their allies often had self-interest at stake and their enemies were unrepentant. It was no time to let down the guard. Catholics were willing, sometimes eager, to further establish the measure of their success through state accreditation of their teachers and schools.

Pro-amendment forces contributed unwittingly to legitimatizing Michigan's parochial schools. Nearly all politicians, educators, Protestant ministers, and those ordinary citizens who bothered to write letters to newspapers supported the right of parochial schools to exist so long as those schools met the standards set for public schools. It was time to ensure this. In April 1921 the state legislature passed the Dacey bill, which provided for the "supervision of private, denominational and parochial schools," including the qualifications of teachers. A $12,500 appropriation would initially fund the supervision.[120] The act took effect in 1925.

It was not a measure put forth by those who had opposed parochial schools. Rather, the bill's sponsor was a twenty-six-year-old Republican, Vincent P. Dacey, a second-generation Irish Catholic educated in Detroit's parochial schools and a graduate of the University of Detroit.[121] His bill passed in the state senate by a vote of 28 to 4 and the house by 74 to 9.[122] Opposition came almost entirely from legislators who lived outside metropolitan Detroit. They, along with their constituents, favored the school amendment, wanted all children in public schools, and believed spending the state money it would take to supervise "sectarian" parochial schools violated the state constitution.[123]

Just like the school amendment, the Dacey bill swept in all private and denominational schools. But with its headline, "PAROCHIAL BILL PASSES SENATE" the *Detroit News* correctly assessed the bill's chief concern: parochial schools, specifically the numerous Catholic schools.[124] Despite a long-standing determination to stay free from state control, various Catholics recognized that this move was now in their schools' best interest. Even the National Catholic Welfare Conference, formed in 1919 to speak for the bishops, saw reason to approve when one state after another introduced accreditation.

Catholics might close ranks to defend their schools from outsiders, yet among themselves they were more realistic and far less confident about segments of parochial school education. The newest immigrants and their schools were especially vulnerable to criticism. Progressive educational theorists coupled with wartime patriotism were helping a young generation of Irish and German prelates push old Americanist arguments farther. They especially wanted to Americanize the Polish. Chicago's Bishop George William Mundelein had begun efforts to disband the Polish Seminary at Orchard Lake soon after he became bishop in 1916.[125] Bishop Gallagher's new diocesan seminary offered an alternative to the more assimilated Polish boys interested in the priesthood.

Some critics within Polish community itself thought the parish schools were too limited and limiting. Second-generation Polish Americans, anxious for their children to escape predestined factory slots, wanted schools that would give them an equal start with other children. The Polish National Alliance called for state supervision of schools early in the twentieth century, and certain Polish journalists in the United States had been attacking Polish schools at least as long. One writer, Helen Piotrowska, recommended that all children should be sent to public school after making their First Communion; at the least, Polish parochial schools in America should be centralized into one system.[126] Just as Polish immigrant leaders embraced Americanism via Polish civic and political clubs in the 1920s to stave off critics, school champions recognized that if their teachers and curricula measured up to statewide accrediting standards they could wave off doubters on that front.[127]

Meeting the standards in fact proved more invigorating than difficult. The new law stipulated the amount of time classroom teachers must give to those subjects the state required for an eighth-grade diploma; beyond that, schools could offer other subjects, including religion and foreign language. Michigan grade school teachers could teach for three years with a "limited certificate," which meant at least one year of college work. The next step, a grade school certificate, required another sixteen hours of college credit accomplished by any of several routes, including county normal schools that certified teachers for one- and two-teacher rural schools and the IHMs' St. Mary's in Monroe, approved to grant teacher certification in 1919. A teacher with four years of college qualified for a "life certificate."[128] But there was a loophole even here because anyone who had taught for ten years before August 18, 1921, was automatically entitled to a state certificate for teaching in private and parochial schools. Still, parochial school grade teachers were not so deficient, on the whole, as teachers in one-room rural district schools, a group often singled out by state legislators and educators who saw their weak preparation as reason for concern.

Measuring up to accrediting standards set for high schools posed more challenges, notably for congregations whose sisters were less educated and for parishes just trying to introduce secondary programs on top of their grade schools. The minimum qualification for a high school teacher was two years of college or normal training, but half of all academic sections had to be taught by faculty with degrees. Demands edged up; after January 1, 1933, all academic subjects, grades nine to twelve, were to be taught by teachers who had completed at least four years in an approved institution. Again there was some leeway. Because the standard was not retroactive within a given high school, so long as teachers did not move they could continue to teach without a four-year degree.[129]

Even though teachers had some time to conform to minimum state requirements, the state's normal schools reported a large number of summer school applications from parochial school teachers before the bill ever took effect. The Lutheran Schools Committee also sent letters to their colleges such as Concordia in Milwaukee to alert officials that students wanting to teach in Michigan by 1925 would face new requirements.[130] The state superintendent of public instruction anticipated that half of all parochial school teachers would qualify two years ahead of schedule.[131]

Some congregations had a head start in meeting the standards. For more than twenty years, the IHMs had dispatched selected groups of sisters to study at Catholic University, Notre Dame, and the University of Michigan. As soon as the Dacey bill was passed in 1921, congregation administrators hurried others off to the Michigan State Normal College in Ypsilanti or the Detroit Teachers College. When the Dacey Law became effective in September 1925, every IHM grade and high school teacher held at least the minimum qualifications required for her assignment. By that time, 56 grade school teachers and 114 high school teachers had a bachelor's degree and 15 high school teachers had a master of arts degree.[132]

To determine whether a school merited accreditation, inspectors from the University of Michigan would visit it, armed with their twelve central standards and a formidable checklist of questions. A four-year high school must have at least a three-person faculty—that could include the superintendent, "provided he teaches the major portion of his time." The number of pupils per teacher "should not be excessive," generally "one teacher for every twenty pupils." Teachers should not have more than six recitations per day; five would be better. The superintendent or principal was to give evidence that teachers increasingly used "improved" and "progressive" methods. The curriculum was to be adapted to needs of the community. Moreover, there was to be evidence of a "serious effort" to improve study habits of pupils, to attend to pupils' health through appropriate exercise programs, and to provide extracurricular activities. Library and laboratory rooms were not only to be suitable, but there was also to be evidence that pupils used these materials. Students should be prepared by their program of studies to meet the entrance requirements of the University of Michigan. Accreditors would also be examining records of freshmen who went on to the university as a means of determining the "efficiency of instruction and the general intellectual and moral tone" of the secondary schools that trained and recommended them to the university.[133]

These standards were much more rigorous and detailed than the form of "affiliation" schools had commonly entered into with Catholic University. Under that arrangement, a high school had to offer an approved four-year course with a total of fifteen units and follow a syllabus prepared by the university for each subject. Catholic University faculty wrote, mailed out, and then graded an annual examination for all students, and the university kept a record of students' grades and credits. The university also issued high school diplomas that enabled students to be admitted without further examinations to many colleges, including Detroit Teachers' College. A number of Catholic schools continued this affiliation even after University of Michigan and the attendant North Central Association approval was secure.[134]

Some Catholic high schools faculty were happy to demonstrate that they matched public school standards without difficulty. The IHMs had gained University of Michigan accreditation for their first school in 1915, when they requested it for their prized St. Vincent's in Detroit. To meet the university's requirements for their other schools, they needed to make only minor adjustments. At St. Joseph, for example, the IHMs hired "a secular" for the grade school "so Sr. Alfreda could go to the High School" as the third teacher there in preparation for a visit from the Ann Arbor examiner.[135]

Longer-established high schools had an edge. Examiners readily granted accreditation in the 1920s to the IHMs' Holy Trinity and Our Lady of Help high schools even though, in declining neighborhoods, they were already on the wane and were closed by 1930. The Jesuits' University of Detroit High School had been accredited through the University of Michigan for more than twenty-five years before the Dacey Law. In a statement typical of a string of evaluations that always brought the coveted three-year stamp of approval, University of Michigan professor A. S. Whitney pronounced the Jesuit teachers "all so excellent it is impossible to specify" when he visited in May 1900.[136]

Meeting the demands of accreditation prodded or empowered priests and sister-superiors to improve teachers and facilities in general. External standards proved especially significant in parishes that were just developing high schools. Outside evaluators "expected" lighting of the "approved type" and library books, but they also dipped down to examine the parish grade school closely. Because "the high school work depends so largely on the type of work done in the grades" they expected more of these parish grade schools than otherwise. At St. Stanislaus, sixteen of the thirty-eight elementary teachers had completed fewer than two years of training—sufficient to meet minimal requirements for a grade school. But in terms of preparing children to advance the deficiency counted as one more reason for the University Committee on Accredited Schools to delay the high school's accreditation when it finally had all four grades in place.[137]

Accreditors did not interfere with the right of schools to teach foreign languages, but they did keep watch on the proportionate place it held in the curriculum. Again, Polish schools were most likely to come in for criticism. "Teaching eight units of a foreign language out of a total of less than nineteen units of academic subjects" seemed excessive, one examiner chided St. Casimir's principal. He "would strongly suggest" two years of Latin and two years of either Polish or French "(preferably Polish)."[138]

Accreditors were careful also to observe how well pupils and teachers used English. "Obviously the matter of English is a real problem in your school," noted the examiner at St. Stanislaus, devoting two of his six major criticisms to this. "Situated as you are [in the midst of a Polish neighborhood] probably extra time and effort should be put upon oral English work."[139] The same examiner was harsher still in his assessment of St. Casimir's High School. Until the principal could offer "every assurance" that the school was doing everything possible about pervasive deficiencies in use of the English language, "one would hardly be justified in recommending accrediting for your school." Even the stark white walls and ceilings caught his disapproving attention. "As the opportunity presents itself," they would look better "decorated in light buff and cream."[140] The sisters apparently made certain improvements in short order, because within a few months St. Casimir's had provisional accreditation for one year. It would be eleven years, however, before St. Casimir's gained the coveted three-year accreditation and an A high school ranking.[141]

As a whole, Catholic high schools in Detroit satisfied the accreditors, often demonstrating greater strength in terms of curriculum and the number of accredited teachers than small-town schools of comparable enrollments.[142] Priests, sisters, and parents agreed in advance of school accreditation visits that embarrassing weaknesses were to be avoided if possible. If problems were found, they tried to attend to them as quickly as could be managed, whether it took paint or more library books or more summer classes for teachers. When approval came, it was announced from the pulpit on Sunday. Accreditation was an accomplishment for the whole parish to claim.

The Writing on the Wall

"May I suggest that you have this certificate framed and hung in a prominent place? It will give to any who are interested the information that your school is deserving of this high recognition."[143] It was just a form letter "To the Officials of an Accredited High School," but it was signed by M. L. Burton, president of the University of Michigan and chair of the University Committee on Diploma Schools. Little doubt that the certificate went on a prominent wall in a "suitable frame" and the form letter went into a labeled file, carefully saved.

And so it was that Detroit's parochial schools affirmed their place, to the satisfaction of enough majorities—voters, taxpayers, Catholic parents, accrediting committees, legislators, and the children, too. The majority of children educated at parochial schools from this generation would grow up to send one more generation along the familiar path. It was a chance to grow up to practice their faith and prosecute their fortune.

AFTERWORD

DETROITERS were unaware, when they resolved the question about educating their children in the 1920s, that the Great Depression was about to hit their city with effects more catastrophic than in most places. Enrollment in Catholic schools increased during and after the amendment debates, perhaps because of the considerable attention to them but primarily because of the rapidly growing Catholic population. On the last day of 1929 Pope Pius XI issued the encyclical *Divini Illius Magistri* (Christian Education of Youth). According to this, Catholics were bound in conscience to attend Catholic schools. Locally, parents who heard the message filtered through Sunday sermons could be pleased and reaffirmed in their course. The pope also claimed that Catholics' schools had the right to state support. On that point, even though Michigan Catholics might agree with the pontiff in principle they understood his words had little relationship to political or financial reality.

Detroit Catholics persevered as they had all along, quite familiar with stretching to afford their schools. The depression years meant just more of the same economies. The city's population began to level off, adding fewer than fifty thousand new residents between 1930 and 1940, but parochial enrollments continued to climb. Grade schools absorbed more from the enlarged pool of children born to young immigrants who had flooded the city throughout the auto boom. Hard times coupled with child labor legislation eliminated the chance of jobs for older youths, who now stayed in school longer. The high school population tripled in diocesan schools between the depression and the outbreak of World War II. Public school enrollments climbed, too. Reeling because state and local economic devastation came alongside the demands of newly unionized teachers, the public system would likely have been in chaos had the amendment passed in 1924 and moved all children into public classrooms.

Preoccupied top-level school leaders in both the parochial and public sectors attended most to administrative concerns. Bishop Gallagher appointed Monsignor Carroll Deady as school superintendent in 1934, a post he would hold until 1957. Under the determined Deady, Catholic schools finally came into one centralized system. This, like accreditation, had two sides. Regulations handed down from the central office improved weak schools but, so far as more assimilated Catholics and their teachers viewed it, the bureaucracy placed unnecessary limitations on their schools. Even so, long-standing patterns held firm; with religious congregations of women most in control of classrooms, the differences from one Catholic school to another persisted.

The Catholic central high schools, one opened for girls in 1927 and one for boys in 1928, grew on the base of parishes that lacked the ability to sustain their own secondary programs. They never supplanted the preferred habit of coeducational parish high schools, however. Catholics who moved to the city's newest neighborhoods or on to the suburbs after World War II copied the churches and schools of their youths. Often they took along their familiar sisters. The Felicians or Sisters of St. Joseph staffed parish schools established by third-generation Polish families in Warren, Sterling Heights, and Harper Woods. IHMs, School Sisters of Notre Dame, or Dominicans staffed schools in the new third-generation Irish and German parishes and were also the congregations most often invited to "assimilated," upper-class parishes in places such as Bloomfield Hills and Grosse Pointe.

Annexations had increased Detroit's sprawl to seventy-nine square miles by the end of the 1920s, and new suburbs began to stretch far beyond. Once the city became physically large, there was little occasion for its thousands of parochial school children to weave within the public fabric until they went to work. Moreover, for many Catholic women the work world would be an infrequent or brief experience unless they stayed single. Auto mobility, then, did not really change routines of the old, nineteenth-century "walking city." Rather, in a real sense, Catholic children who grew up within the city boundaries through the 1960s remained children of bounded neighborhoods centered around their parishes. They were the adults who, when asked "Where are you from?" replied, "St. Vincent's," or "St. Casimir's," or "Holy Redeemer." Only if asked while more than fifty miles away might they append, "in Detroit." By the 1970s they were puzzled, sometimes angered, if charged with "abandoning the city." After all, they countered, they never left "old Trinity," where they gathered on St. Patrick's Day and to which they sent "perpetual remembrances" for ancestors' souls in the form of generous contributions that went to help its current poor. Or, they never forgot Sweetest Heart, where they went to see children married, grandchildren baptized, and friends buried.

Could it have been otherwise? Historically, immigrants and the native-born expected schools to accomplish the magic such an enchanted and blessed nation surely might bestow. Their intention—the moral and material well-being of succeeding generations—was not misplaced. Although they embraced the American notion that success would likely come by dint of individual effort and personal worthiness, a different tradition prevailed when it came to organized education. Education was thought to have an obligation to foster the collective good. That, of course, was the rub.

When it came to schooling their children, it proved difficult for Detroiters to imagine soon enough how the collective good might emerge if they separated religious education from secular education. Those nativists who demanded a single public system neither respected nor would have tolerated what such an education might have accomplished at its best. Even the well-intentioned could not conjure up a single system that might address assorted heritages to everyone's satisfaction. Had they been able to envision such a plan, the expense would have frightened off taxpayers and politicians.

Successive generations of Detroiters could have trusted one another more all along the way from the 1830s. Had immigrants and the native-born recognized their common values rather than fearing their ethnic and religious differences, Detroiters, with their comparative wealth of resources, might have taken uncommon risks. As it happened, at least the democracy they prized enabled them the freedom to go their separate ways.

Notes

AAD	Archives of the Archdiocese of Detroit
AFSLM	Archives of the Felician Sisters of Livonia, Michigan
BHC	Burton Historical Collection, Detroit Public Library
DLSHS	De La Salle Collegiate High School
MHC	Michigan Historical Collections, Bentley Historical Library, University of Michigan
MHTGS	Most Holy Trinity Grade School
St. VJH	St. Vincent Junior High School
SSIHM	Archives of the Sisters, Servants of the Immaculate Heart of Mary
UDHSJA	University of Detroit High School and Jesuit Academy

Chapter 1: On Common Ground

1. Observation likely by Richard R. Elliott, speaking of his Irish immigrant father's vision, *Detroit Catholic Vindicator*, 30 April 1853, 4.

2. Sister M. Rosalita [Kelly], *No Greater Service: The History of the Congregation of the Sisters, Servants of the Immaculate Heart of Mary, Monroe, Michigan, 1845–1945* (Detroit: Congregation of the Sisters, Servants of the Immaculate Heart of Mary, 1948), 18–19; Sister M. Rosalita [Kelly], *Education in Detroit prior to 1850* (Lansing: Michigan Historical Commission, 1928), chap. 2; Floyd R. Dain, *Education in the Wilderness* (Lansing: Michigan Historical Commission, 1968), 16.

3. [Kelly], *Education*, 27.

4. Ibid., 41, 42.

5. For discussion of New York and the Free School Society, see Diane Ravitch, *The Great School Wars, New York City, 1805–1973: A History of the Public Schools as Battlefield of Social Change* (New York: Basic Books, 1974), chap. 1.

6. Dain, *Education in the Wilderness,* 80, citing letter from Richard, writing under a pseudonym in the *Detroit Gazette,* 1 Aug. 1817, 2.

7. Ronald P. Formisano, *The Birth of Mass Political Parties, Michigan, 1827–1861* (Princeton: Princeton University Press, 1971), 93, cites debates during the Michigan constitutional convention in 1835.

8. Paul M. Judson, OSA, "Sketch of the Life of Father Gabriel Richard, 1767–1832," *Records of the American Catholic Historical Society* 37 (Sept. 1925): 285–88.

9. [Kelly], *Education,* 135, citing *Michigan Territory: Laws,* 1:879.

10. John C. Springman, *The Growth of Public Education in Michigan* (Ypsilanti: Michigan State Normal College, 1952), 9–10, citing "The First Annual Report of the University of Michigania," from the manuscript record book of J. L. Whiting, MHC.

11. [Kelly], *Education,* 178, lists those among the group.

12. George Pare, *The Catholic Church in Detroit, 1701–1888* (1951, repr. Detroit: Wayne State University Press, 1983), 361, citing Letter to Didier Petit of the Society for the Propagation of the Faith, 22 Dec. 1825 (all subsequent citations are to this edition).

13. [Kelly], *Education,* 183, citing criticism in the *Northwestern Journal,* May 1830.

14. Dain, *Education in the Wilderness,* 101; [Kelly], *Education,* 201–2.

15. Timothy L. Smith, "Protestant Schooling and American Nationality, 1800–1850," *Journal of American History* 53 (March 1967): 685.

16. Dain, *Education in the Wilderness,* 145; see also chaps. 9 and 10 for a detailed discussion of school legislation.

17. [Kelly], *Education,* 198; Dain, *Education in the Wilderness,* 102.

18. Dain, *Education in the Wilderness,* 197.

19. Ibid., 30, citing Askin Papers.

20. [Kelly], *Education,* 50–56.

21. Elizabeth Williams was born in 1786 and died in 1843; she was the sister of the first mayor and niece of Joseph Campau. Elizabeth Lyons was born in 1786 and died sometime after the late 1830s; she was the daughter of an Indian trader and Elizabeth Chene, who was from an old French Detroit family. Angelique Campau was born in 1766 and died in 1838; she was related to the Campau family.

22. Julius P. MacCabe, *Directory of the City of Detroit* (Detroit: William Harsha, 1837), 30–31.

23. MacCabe, *Directory,* 31.

24. [Kelly], *Education,* 315; Eleanor Luedtke, *Caritas Christi: The Daughters of Charity of St. Vincent de Paul, 1844–1994, 150 Years of Service to Detroit* (Southfield, Mich.: Providence Hospital and Sarah Fisher Center, 1994), 9.

25. Silas Farmer, *History of Detroit and Wayne County and Early Michigan,* 2 vols., 3d ed. (1884, repr. Detroit: Gale Research, 1969), 1:735 (all subsequent citations are to this edition).

26. R. R. Elliott, "Rev. Thomas Cullen," *American Catholic Historical Researches* 13 (Oct. 1896): 177–78; Farmer, *History of Detroit,* 1:721.

27. [Kelly], *Education,* 315–16, citing *U.S. Catholic Directory* (1844), 49.

28. Ibid., 315.

29. Charles Oliver Hoyt and R. Clyde Ford, *John D. Pierce: Founder of the Michigan School System* (Ypsilanti: Sharf Tag, Label and Box Co., 1905), 105.

30. Ibid., 81; Dain, *Education in the Wilderness,* 206–7, quoting Ellwood P. Cubberly, *Public Education in the United States* (Boston: Houghton, Mifflin, 1919), 129–31, notes that other states had similar offices but had established them by statutes that could be revised or rescinded by legislators.

31. For a thorough discussion of debates during the Constitutional Convention of 1835, see Norman Drachler, "The Influence of Sectarianism, Non-Sectarianism, and Secularism upon the Public Schools of Detroit and the University of Michigan, 1837–1900," Ph.D. diss., University of Michigan, 1951, chap. 1.

32. Farmer, *History of Detroit,* 1:736.

33. William Locke Smith, *Education in Michigan* (Lansing: W. S. George, State Printers and Binders, 1881), 17.

34. Dain, *Education in the Wilderness,* 263.

35. Floyd R. Dain, "Public School Education in Detroit," *Michigan History Magazine* 45 (Dec. 1961): 358.

36. *Journal of the Senate of the State of Michigan, 1840* (Detroit: George Dawson, 1840).

37. Farmer, *History of Detroit,* 1:738–39.

38. "Report of the Superintendent of Public Instruction," *Journal of the Senate of the State of Michigan, 1837* (Detroit: John S. Bagg, 1837), document no. 7, 30.

39. [Kelly], *Education,* 326.

40. "Report of the Superintendent of Public Instruction," *Michigan Senate Journal, 1837,* document no. 7, 30–76.

41. Ibid., 32–33.

42. [Kelly], *Education,* 325.

43. Ibid., 327.

44. "Report of the Superintendent of Public Instruction," *Michigan Senate Journal, 1837,* document no. 7, 30.

45. [Kelly], *Education,* 330, writes that Cornelius O'Flynn, a Tralee-born Trinity parishioner and a member of the state legislature, urged that the request be passed into law, and she maintains O'Flynn was the only member of the Wayne County delegation to vote for this. Michigan legislative documents do not show him as a member during this period, however.

46. Ira Mayhew, *Popular Education for the Use of Parents and Teachers, and for Young Persons of Both Sexes* (New York: Harper and Brothers, 1850), 338. The proportion in Wayne County was better than that of the state as a whole. The states ahead of Michigan were Connecticut, New Hampshire, Massachusetts, Maine, and Vermont.

47. Dain, "Public School Education," 358.

48. *Documents: Journal of the House of Representatives of the State of Michigan at the Annual Session of 1843* (Detroit: Ellis and Briggs, 1843), document no. 10, 51.

49. Formisano, *Mass Political Parties,* 141–43.

50. Drachler, "Influence of Sectarianism," 33, 36.

51. Ibid., 33, 39.

52. D/Education, Board of, clipping from *Detroit Free Press,* Jan. 1859, BHC.

53. [Kelly], *Education,* 325, citing Pitcher's report.

54. Leslie Tentler, *Seasons of Grace: A History of the Archdiocese of Detroit* (Detroit: Wayne State University, 1990), 14–17, discusses the Rese years. Lefevere's title was as administrator of Detroit and coadjutor bishop with right of succession, because Rese retained the title of bishop until his death in Germany in 1871.

55. Reverend Dean O'Brien, "Memoir of the Late Hon. Richard Robert Elliott," *Michigan Pioneer and Historical Collections* 37 (1909–10): 653.

56. Letter to the French Missionary Society written in the early days of his episcopate and reprinted in "One Hundredth Anniversary," 6, booklet in SS. Peter and Paul parish file, AAD.

57. Pare, *Catholic Church,* 441–43.

58. Luedtke, *Caritas Christi,* 12.

59. Clarence M. Burton, *History of Wayne County and the City of Detroit, Michigan,* 5 vols. (Detroit: S. J. Clark, 1922), 1:783.

60. Tentler, *Seasons of Grace,* 86–87, citing Lefevere to Mrs. R. E. Hamilton, 28 Aug. 1854, Letterbooks, 2, AAD.

61. *Detroit Free Press,* 11 Feb. 1853, 2.

62. *Detroit Daily Advertiser,* 28 Feb. 1853, 2.

63. Tentler, *Seasons of Grace,* 21.

64. *Detroit Daily Advertiser,* 28 Feb. 1853, 2.

65. James Dale Johnston, *Johnston's Detroit Directory and Business Advertiser, 1853–54* (Detroit: Daily Tribune Publishing, 1853), xiv.

66. The Board of Education of the City of Detroit, *Histories of the Public Schools of Detroit* (Detroit: Mimeograph from Publications Department, 1967), 1:601–2.

67. Smith, *Education in Michigan,* 131.

68. Mayhew, *Popular Education,* 209.

69. Formisano, *Mass Political Parties,* 228, citing the *Catholic Vindicator.*

70. Charles R. Starring and James O. Knauss, *The Michigan Search for Educational Standards* (Lansing: Michigan Historical Commission, 1969), 57–58.

71. Mayhew, *Popular Education,* 209.

72. Ibid., 210–11.

73. Resolution passed by the House of Representatives, Feb. 27, 1849, and subsequently adopted by the Senate, cited in Mayhew, *Popular Education.*

74. Mayhew's *Popular Education* bears an 1850 publication date but apparently did not appear locally until at least 1852.

75. Richard R. Elliott, MSS, vol. 7 (of 27), describing his father's decision to send his children for schooling at Most Holy Trinity in the 1840s, BHC.

76. Hoyt, *John D. Pierce,* 151.

CHAPTER 2: THE SCHOOL QUESTION OF THE 1850S

1. *Documents: Senate and House of Representatives of the State of Michigan* (Lansing: Geo. W. Peck, 1853), document no. 5, in Jeremiah O'Callaghan's minority report, 5.

2. U.S. Bureau of the Census, *Compendium of the Seventh Census of the United States: 1850* (Washington: A. O. P. Nicholson, 1854), 192.

3. Johnston, *Detroit Directory, 1853–54,* xiv.

4. Occupational and property ownership figures are based upon data collected from the U.S. manuscript census rolls, as reported in my earlier study, *The Irish on the Urban Frontier: Nineteenth-Century Detroit* (New York: Arno Press, 1976). The data set is available from the Inter-University Consortium for Political Research (ICPR), the University of Michigan, Ann Arbor.

5. Excellent analysis is offered in John C. Schneider, *Detroit and the Problem of Order, 1830–1880* (Lincoln: University of Nebraska Press, 1980), 7–22.

6. Formisano, *Mass Political Parties,* 231–32.

7. *Detroit Free Press,* 15 Dec. 1852, 2.

8. *Detroit Daily Advertiser,* 10 Dec. 1852, 2; *Detroit Free Press,* 11 Dec. 1852, 2.

9. Leudtke, *Caritas Christi,* 15–19.

10. Formisano, *Mass Political Parties,* 230.

11. *Detroit Free Press,* 7 Jan. 1853, 3.

12. *Detroit Free Press,* 28 Dec. 1852; Formisano, *Mass Political Parties,* 222.

13. *Detroit Free Press,* 7 Jan. 1853, 3.

14. Luedtke, *Caritas Christi,* 19–20.

15. *Detroit Weekly Tribune,* 31 Oct. 1854, 4.

16. Luedtke, *Caritas Christi,* 20–21. This, she writes, reflects the growing number of German Protestants in the city.

17. *Detroit Free Press,* 14 Jan. 1853, 2. Pare, *Catholic Church,* 685–86, provides a sketch of Father Shawe.

18. Farmer, *History of Detroit,* 1:751.

19. *Documents: Senate and House of Representatives of Michigan, 1853,* document no. 3.

20. Ibid., document no. 20.

21. *Detroit Catholic Vindicator,* 4 June 1853, 4.

22. *Detroit Free Press,* 5 Jan. 1853; "Report of the Proceedings and Debates in the Convention to Revise the Constitution of the State of Michigan, 1850," xxvi–xxxi, in Drachler, "Influence of Sectarianism," 18.

23. *Documents: Senate and House of Representatives of Michigan, 1853,* document no. 5, in Jeremiah O'Callaghan's minority report.

24. See especially the *Detroit Free Press* and the *Detroit Daily Advertiser* in December 1852 and January 1853.

25. *Detroit Free Press,* 15 Dec. 1852, 2.

26. Carl Kaestle, *Evolution of an Urban School System* (Cambridge: Harvard University Press, 1973), 152.

27. *Documents: Senate and House of Representatives of Michigan, 1853,* document no. 6, report of the majority of the Committee on Education.

28. *Journal of the House of Representatives of Michigan, 1853,* 222.

29. Johnston, *Detroit Directory, 1853–54,* xiv.

30. Ravitch, *School Wars,* 67–68.

31. See Formisano, *Mass Political Parties,* 222–29; and David L. Angus, "Detroit's Great

School Wars: Religion and Politics in a Frontier City, 1842–1853," *Michigan Academician* 12 (Winter 1980): 261–80.

32. *Detroit Daily Advertiser,* 25 Feb. 1853, 2.

33. For the most thorough study of this realignment in MichIgan, see Formisano, *Mass Political Parties.*

34. *Detroit Free Press,* 2 Feb. 1853, 2.

35. Based on estimates using the average family size for Irish in 1850 of 4.8 (4.5 for Germans), the total number of adults must have been more than seven thousand. Although women could not vote, they signed petitions and frequently initiated them in the interest of causes such as temperance and the education of females.

36. *Detroit Daily Tribune,* 12 March 1853, 2.

37. A careful analysis of the 1853 vote, showing ward-by-ward correlations between ethnicity and voter behavior, is provided in Angus, "Detroit's Great School Wars."

38. *Detroit Daily Advertiser,* 9 March 1853, 2.

39. Tentler, *Seasons of Grace,* 18–19.

40. *Detroit Daily Advertiser,* 1 March 1853, 2.

41. *Detroit Daily Advertiser,* 9 March 1853, 2.

42. *Detroit Free Press,* 25 Feb. 1853, 2.

43. *Detroit Catholic Vindicator,* 7 May 1853.

44. *Detroit Catholic Vindicator,* 30 April 1853, 1.

45. *Detroit Weekly Tribune,* 9 Aug. 1853, 6.

46. *Detroit Evening Tribune,* 2 Aug. 1854, 2.

47. *Detroit Free Press,* 5 March 1853, 2.

48. *Detroit Free Press,* 7 March 1853, 2.

49. *Detroit Daily Advertiser,* 9 March 1853, 2.

50. *Detroit Free Press,* 1 March 1854, 2.

51. *Detroit Free Press,* 8 March 1854, 2.

52. *Detroit Daily Advertiser,* 4 March 1854, 2 (emphasis in the original).

53. Sister M. Evangeline Thomas, "Nativism in the Old Northwest, 1850–1860," Ph.D. diss., Catholic University of America, 1936, 119–20.

54. L. W. Granger, *Wide-Awake! Romanism: Its Aims and Tendencies* (Detroit: L. W. Granger, 1854), 63.

55. Formisano, *Mass Political Parties,* the authoritative study on the rise of the Republican Party in Michigan, says the case for an alliance with Know-Nothings is strong.

56. Paul Kleppner, *The Cross of Culture: A Social Analysis of Midwestern Politics, 1850–1900* (New York: Free Press, 1970), 66; *Detroit Catholic Vindicator,* manuscript comments following the 29 April 1854 issue, written in 1892 by the indexer (R. R. Elliott).

57. *Detroit Catholic Vindicator,* 4 Nov. 1854, 2.

58. *Detroit Catholic Vindicator,* 29 Oct. 1853, 2, and 4 Nov. 1854, 2.

59. *Detroit Catholic Vindicator,* 23 Dec. 1854, 2.

60. *Detroit Catholic Vidicator,* 3 Feb. 1855, 2.

61. *Detroit Free Press,* 1 March 1855, 2.

62. *Detroit Free Press,* 14 March 1855, 2.

63. *Detroit Daily Advertiser,* 19 Feb. 1853, 2.

64. Formisano, *Mass Political Parties,* 256–57. Formisano makes the persuasive case that the legislature was paying off political debts owed Know-Nothings.

65. *Detroit Catholic Vindicator,* 18 Oct. 1856, 2.

66. A Catholic Layman [R. R. Elliott], "The Roman Catholics in Detroit," *Michigan Pioneer and Historical Collections* 13 (1888): 444–50.

67. *Detroit Catholic Vindicator,* indexer's manuscript comments following the April 29, 1854 issue.

68. *Detroit Catholic Vindicator,* 13 Oct. 1855, 2.

69. Alfred G. Stritch, "Political Nativism in Cincinnati, 1830–1860," *Records of the American Catholic Historical Society* 48 (Sept. 1937): 262–63.

70. *Detroit Weekly Tribune,* 3 May 1853, 6.

71. Ibid.

72. *Detroit Catholic Vindicator,* 14 July 1855, 1.

73. Sidney Hook, *Education for Modern Man* (1945, repr. New York: Alfred A. Knopf, 1966), 159.

CHAPTER 3: CHARTING THE COURSE

1. *The Second Annual Report of the Michigan Bureau of Labor and Industrial Statistics* [BLIS] *(1885)* (Lansing: State Printer, 1 Feb. 1884), 62, citing 1884 statistics.

2. Olivier Zunz, *The Changing Face of Inequality: Urbanization, Industrial Development, and Immigrants in Detroit, 1880–1920* (Chicago: University of Chicago Press, 1982), 105; Tentler, *Seasons of Grace,* 31.

3. Vinyard, *The Irish on the Urban Frontier,* 399. This calculation is based on immigrant and second-generation male heads of families.

4. Stephan Thernstrom, "The Last of the Immigrants," unpublished paper delivered at the annual meeting of the Organization of American Historians, spring 1970.

5. See Zunz, *Changing Face of Inequality,* chap. 1, for description of ethnic roles within sectors of the economy in 1880; see also Vinyard, *The Irish on the Urban Frontier,* for data on occupations in 1850 and 1880.

6. Stanley Lebergott, *Manpower in Economic Growth* (New York: McGraw-Hill, 1964), 541; BLIS, *Annual Report of the Michigan Bureau of Labor and Industrial Statistics (1890)* (Lansing: State Printer, 1 Feb. 1889), 153.

7. Persistence calculations were derived by matching city directories and manuscript census rolls. For methodology, see Vinyard, *The Irish on the Urban Frontier,* 357–63.

8. Bela Hubbard, "Detroit Real Estate," in Clarence M. Burton Scrap Book no. 4, BHC.

9. "Fiftieth Anniversary Booklet," ca. 1905, Most Holy Trinity parish, file 6.20, AAD.

10. Lawrence A. Cremin, *Transformation of the School, Progressivism in American Education, 1876–1957* (New York: Knopf, 1961), 8.

11. Daniel Putnam, *The Development of Primary and Secondary Education in Michigan* (Ann Arbor: George Wahr, 1904), 112.

12. Putnam, *Primary and Secondary Education in Michigan,* 150.

13. Ibid., 100–101; Detroit Board of Education, *Detroit Public Schools* (Detroit: Board of Education, 1911), 8–9.

14. Wilma Wood Henrickson, "'Too Bright for the Schools?'—Assistant Superintendent Mathilde Coffin," in *Detroit Perspectives, Crossroads and Turning Points,* ed. Wilma Wood Henrickson (Detroit: Wayne State University Press, 1991), 235, citing *Detroit Evening News.*

15. Calculations are based on Burton, *History of Wayne County and Detroit,* vol. 1, who gives the 1850 school census as 6,965 and enrollment at 4,250, and also the BLIS, *Second Annual Report (1885),* 62, which shows a total school population of 34,938 between the ages of five and seventeen, with 15,271 attending public schools and 8,317 in schools "not public" in 1884.

16. According to Zunz, *Changing Face of Inequality,* 234, 40 percent of the boys over the age of twelve born to American-born parents were at work in 1900. Attendance figures for 1884 are based on BLIS, *Second Annual Report (1885),* 62.

17. Ibid., 62. By 1884, for example, of the children between the ages of five and seventeen, 44 percent were in public school and 24 percent were in schools "not public."

18. Letter, 16 Oct. 1889, box 2, Birney-McClear-Hankerd Papers, MHC. Correspondence among the daughters and mother in the Hankerd family during the 1880s and 1890s offers insight into the relationships between the students and the sisters, as well as this family's attitude about Catholic education.

19. Sisters, Servants of the Immaculate Heart of Mary, *Building Sisterhood: A Feminist History* (Syracuse: Syracuse University Press, 1997), 38–39.

20. [Kelly], *No Greater Service,* 120–30; Mary J. Oates, "'The Good Sisters': The Work and Position of Catholic Churchwomen in Boston, 1870–1940," in *Catholic Boston: Studies in Religion and Community, 1870–1970,* ed. Robert E. Sullivan and James M. O'Toole (Boston: Roman Catholic Archbishop of Boston), 177. Rome refused to approve any new orders after 1752, permitting only congregations which, by definition, did not have the privilege of self-governance; exemption from episcopal interference was extended only to male orders.

21. SSIHM, *Building Sisterhood,* 48–49.

22. [Kelly], *No Greater Service,* 126; SSIHM, *Building Sisterhood,* 50.

23. Tentler, *Seasons of Grace,* 18–21.

24. [Kelly], *No Greater Service,* 134, citing letter from Joos to Lefevere, 31 March 1859.

25. SSIHM, *Building Sisterhood,* 54.

26. This theme recurs in Sister Mary Philip Ryan, OP, *The Alien Corn: The Early Years of the Sisters of Saint Dominic, Adrian, Michigan* (St. Charles, Ill.: Jones Wood Press, 1967).

27. "Motherhouse Chronicles," vol. 1: "Records of the Institution of the Sisters, Servants of the Immaculate Heart of Mary," SSIHM.

28. Sister M. Rosalita [Kelly], ed., *Achievement of a Century: The Motherhouse and Missions, Congregation of the Sisters, Servants of the Immaculate Heart of Mary, Monroe, Michigan, 1845–1945* (Congregation of the Sisters, Servants of the Immaculate Heart of Mary, 1948), 47.

29. This practice continued for a number of years, apparently. The St. Joseph's "Convent Chronicles" for 1872 still indicate that "a German teacher was appointed for each class." SSIHM.

30. St. Joseph's parish, box 32, SSIHM.

31. [Kelly], *No Greater Service*, 295–96; [Kelly], ed., *Achievement of a Century*, 65–66.

32. Most Holy Trinity parish, file 6.20, AAD.

33. [Kelly], *No Greater Service*, 248.

34. "The Menology of the Sisters, Servants of the Immaculate Heart of Mary, Monroe, Michigan, 1856–1944," 1:82, SSIHM (bound typescript obituaries in two volumes). These menologies (obituaries), each written by a contemporary who knew the deceased best, are often glowing tributes, but nonetheless they reveal a pattern of assignments that were deliberately based on just such assessments of the sisters' personal strengths.

35. He wrote against the University of Michigan after the turn of the century, by then deciding that it was dangerous for Catholic students. But the IHMs did not hesitate to continue sending young sisters there to be educated, skirting diocesan disapproval all the while (chapter 7).

36. "Menology," 1:294, SSIHM.

37. Interviews with several retired sisters, IHM motherhouse, Monroe, Mich., Feb.–April 1986.

38. "Correspondence," in St. Andre System files, SSIHM.

39. Robert D. Cross, *The Emergence of Liberal Catholicism in America* (Cambridge: Harvard University Press, 1958), 9–12.

40. For a perceptive discussion of Rousseau's educational ideas, see Joan Roland Martin, *Reclaiming a Conversation, the Ideal of the Educated Woman* (New Haven: Yale University Press, 1985).

41. Cremin, *Transformation of the Schools*, 101–15; Ravitch, *School Wars*, 111.

42. Folder no. 3, St. Andre System box, SSIHM.

43. Folder no. 5, St. Andre System box, SSIHM.

44. St. Andre Method typescript, chap. 3, St. Andre System box, SSIHM.

45. Ibid.

46. Catharine Beecher, *A Treatise on Domestic Economy* (1841, repr. New York: Source Book Press, 1970), 9 (all subsequent citations are to this edition); see also Martin, *Reclaiming a Conversation*, 105.

47. Letter from Mamie Hankerd, 3 Nov. 1891, box 2, Birney-McClear-Hankerd Papers, MHC.

48. Birney-McClear-Hankerd Papers, box 2, MHC.

49. Beecher, *Treatise on Domestic Economy*, 32.

50. *Good Form*, a sixty-eight-page pamphlet, was published by St. Mary's College, Monroe, Mich.; a handwritten notation dates it "prior to 1920." SSIHM.

51. Beecher, *Treatise on Domestic Economy*, 122; *Good Form*, SSIHM.

52. *Western Home Journal*, 28 June 1873.

53. Lists of texts are at SSIHM and in Farmer, *History of Detroit*, 1:742.

54. [Kelly], *No Greater Service*, 375–96.

55. Beecher, *Treatise on Domestic Economy*, 34.

56. [Kelly], *No Greater Service,* 382, citing the dedication in the 1910 course of study for IHM grade schools that indicates they viewed this as continuing their work of the previous sixty years.

57. Letter, 16 Oct. 1889, Birney-McClear-Hankerd Papers, MHC.

58. [Kelly], *No Greater Service,* 327. Dupanloup's philosophy had been developed in his three-volume *De l'education.*

59. Folder no. 3, St. Andre System box, SSIHM.

60. [Kelly], *No Greater Service,* 350.

61. James W. Sanders, *The Education of an Urban Minority* (New York: Oxford University Press, 1977), 59–60.

62. The menologies and the sisters' correspondence often made use of such descriptive characterizations.

63. "Menology," 1:294, SSIHM.

64. [Kelly], *No Greater Service,* 306.

65. Interviews with Sister Frances Clare and Sister Amadeus, IHM motherhouse, Monroe, Mich., Feb. 1986.

66. Based on manuscript records detailing the sisters' annual assignments, SSIHM.

67. "Menology," 1:288–99, SSIHM.

68. Ibid., 1:220–21.

69. Ibid., 1:196.

70. Ibid., 1:34.

71. Ibid., 1:150–52. The IHMs managed this type of arrangement without separating their congregation into two "choirs" as was common among European-based sisterhoods in which the "second choir" of housekeepers remained permanently subordinated.

72. [Kelly], ed., *Achievement of a Century,* 67–69.

73. Luedtke, *Caritas Christi,* 14 (emphasis in the original).

74. Ibid., 14.

75. Oates, "The Good Sisters," 191.

76. "Account Book for 1887–1900," Most Holy Trinity parish files, AAD.

77. "Account Book for 1886–87," Most Holy Trinity parish files, AAD.

78. "Account Book, 1887–1900," 184, Most Holy Trinity parish files, AAD.

79. "Account Books for 1886–87 and 1887–1900," Most Holy Trinity parish files, AAD.

80. Suzanne Fleming, "She Who Remained: Mother Mary Joseph Walker and the 'Refounding' of the IHM Congregation," in SSIHM, *Building Sisterhood: A Feminist History* (Syracuse: Syracuse University Press, 1997), contains superb letters detailing efforts to stretch money and save during the 1860s.

81. *Western Home Journal,* 28 June 1873.

82. Most Holy Trinity parish, file 6.19, AAD.

83. St. Joseph's parish, box 32, SSIHM.

84. [Sister Dympna], a School Sister of Notre Dame, *Mother Caroline and the School Sisters of Notre Dame in North America, 1892–1928,* 2 vols. (St. Louis: Woodward and Tiernan, 1928), 1:26.

85. [Dympna], *Mother Caroline and the School Sisters,* 1:53.

86. Ibid., 1:41–42.

87. Tentler, *Seasons of Grace,* 41.

88. [Dympna], *Mother Caroline and the School Sisters,* 1:35.

89. Ibid., 1:49–50.

90. Ibid., 1:292.

91. Ibid., 2:279–80.

92. Ibid., 1:293–95.

93. Ibid., 1:297.

94. This apparently was basic to their curriculum from the 1850s and still the case when Mother Caroline died in 1892.

95. [Dympna], *Mother Caroline and the School Sisters,* 1:296–98.

96. Ibid., 1:291.

97. [Kelly], *No Greater Service,* includes a table handwritten by the author (bound in select volumes of this book) detailing the school board's report. Hereafter cited as [Kelly], *No Greater Service,* First Annual School Report MS.

98. St. Mary's parish, file 30.13, AAD.

99. "The Hundredth Anniversary of the Arrival in Detroit of the First Organized Immigration from Germany" (small, paperbound booklet based on letters, interviews, and articles from the *Detroit News* and the *Detroit Abend Post,* covering the years between 1830 and 1930), MHC; [Kelly], *No Greater Service,* First Annual School Report MS.

100. Putnam, *Primary and Secondary Education in Michigan,* 220–21, citing a speech by Prof. Joseph Estabrook at the annual meeting of Michigan educators in 1869.

101. Donald L. Kinzer, *An Episode in Anti-Catholicism: The American Protective Association* (Seattle: University of Washington Press, 1964), 7. As Kinzer notes, this speech was reprinted in the *Catholic World* and won much attention in the diocesan newspapers.

102. Pastoral Letter, Fourth Provincial Council of Cincinnati, 21, 19 March 1882, SSIHM.

103. Sanders, *Education of an Urban Minority,* 23.

104. James W. Sanders, "Catholics and the School Question in Boston: The Cardinal O'Connell Years," in *Catholic Boston: Studies in Religion and Community, 1870–1970,* ed. Robert E. Sullivan and James M. O'Toole (Boston: Roman Catholic Archbishop of Boston, 1985), 160.

105. Oates, "The Good Sisters," 173.

106. Jay P. Dolan, *The Immigrant Church: New York's Irish and German Catholics, 1815–1865* (1975, repr. Notre Dame: University of Notre Dame Press, 1983), 105 (all subsequent references are to this edition).

107. Request, 26 June 1876, to the bishop from trustees who wanted to sell part of their property to help build a school; Ste. Anne's parish, file 14.10, box 14, AAD.

108. *Western Home Journal,* 25 Dec. 1875.

109. *Michigan Catholic,* 24 Jan. 1884.

110. "Oversize Miscellaneous" Account Book, School/Financial Data, 1881, AAD.

111. Pare, *Catholic Church,* 556; Sister M. Arthemise Dalton, OP, "The History and Development of the Catholic Secondary School System in the Archdiocese of Detroit, 1701–1961," Ed.D. diss., Wayne State University, 1962, 60.

112. Pare, *Catholic Church,* 556. BLIS, *Second Annual Report (1885),* 65, recorded 13,815 in public schools and 5,827 in Catholic schools. The Detroit school board reported 21,434 students in 1886, and the Catholic Diocesan School Board reported 6,351 in 1887.

113. Francis Cassidy, "Catholic Education in the Third Plenary," *Catholic Historical Review* 34 (Oct. 1948): 259–60.

CHAPTER 4: PROMOTING THE CAUSE

1. James Hennesey, SJ, *American Catholics: A History of the Roman Catholic Community in the United States* (1981, repr. New York: Oxford University Press, 1983), 109, 160–61 (all subsequent references are to the 1983 edition).

2. *Western Home Journal,* 22 Feb. 1873, editorial (emphasis in the original).

3. Reverend F. J. Zwierlein, "Bishop McQuaid of Rochester," *Catholic Historical Review* 5 (Jan. 1920): 317–18; Neil G. McCluskey, SJ, ed., *Catholic Education in America: A Documentary History* (New York: Teachers College, Columbia University, 1964), 87.

4. *Michigan Catholic,* 10 Feb. 1883, 1.

5. Jay P. Dolan, *The American Catholic Experience: A History from Colonial Times to the Present* (Garden City: Doubleday, 1985), 271; Josephine Marie Peplinski, SSJ–TOSF, *A Fitting Response: The History of the Sisters of St. Joseph of the Third Order of St. Francis,* 2 vols. (South Bend: The Sisters of St. Joseph of the Third Order of St. Francis, 1982, 1992), 1:72; Thomas T. McAvoy, "Public Schools *vs.* Catholic Schools and James McMaster," *Review of Politics* 28 (1966): 20.

6. Robert D. Cross, *The Emergence of Liberal Catholicism in America* (Cambridge: Harvard University Press, 1958), 140; Dolan, *The American Catholic Experience,* 271, quoting Norlene M. Kunkel, CSFN, "Bishop Bernard J. McQuaid and Catholic Education," Ph.D. diss., Notre Dame University, 1974, 200.

7. McAvoy, "Public Schools *vs.* Catholic Schools," 27–28.

8. McCluskey, *Catholic Education,* 72.

9. Tentler, *Seasons of Grace,* 189–90.

10. McCluskey, *Catholic Education,* 72.

11. *Michigan Catholic,* 18 Sept. 1884, 1.

12. McCluskey, *Catholic Education,* 90–91, citing Third Plenary decrees.

13. Ibid., 90.

14. Ibid., 92.

15. McCluskey, *Catholic Education,* 92.

16. Dolan, *The American Catholic Experience,* 272, quoting Bernard J. Meiring, *Educational Aspects of the Legislation of the Councils of Baltimore, 1829–1884* (New York: Arno Press, 1978), 94, 97.

17. Tentler, *Seasons of Grace,* 26; [Kelly], *No Greater Service,* 360–61.

18. Cassidy, "Catholic Education in the Third Plenary," 302; Tentler, *Seasons of Grace,* 233.

19. Letter, 4 Aug. 1883, Assumption Grotto parish, file 2.13, AAD.

20. Cassidy, "Catholic Education in the Third Plenary," 295, citing council decrees; McAvoy, "Public Schools *vs.* Catholic Schools," 37; Dolan, *The Immigrant Church,* 272.

21. *Michigan Catholic,* 25 Dec. 1884.

22. Ibid., reprinting Pastoral Letter of the Archbishops and Bishops to the Clergy and Laity; the same discussion is in Cassidy, "Catholic Education in the Third Plenary," 295, citing council decrees.

23. Dolan, *The American Catholic Experience,* 272.

24. Hennesy, *American Catholics,* 181.

25. Cross, *Liberal Catholicism,* 36–37.

26. Andrew M. Greeley, *The Catholic Experience: An Interpretation of the History of American Catholicism* (Garden City: Doubleday, 1967), 161.

27. Timothy A. Byrnes, *Catholic Bishops in American Politics* (Princeton: Princeton University Press, 1991), 20.

28. Reverend Earl Boyea, "John Samuel Foley, Third Bishop of Detroit: His Ecclesiastical Conflicts in the Diocese of Detroit, 1888–1900," M.A. thesis, Wayne State University, 1984, 8–9.

29. Sanders, "Catholics and the School Question," 26, referring to Archbishop William Henry O'Connell.

30. Dolan, *The American Catholic Experience,* 274–75.

31. Cross, *Liberal Catholicism,* 132–35.

32. This group was particularly incensed because Germans were just then opposing Wisconsin's Bennet Law and the Edwards Law in Illinois, which would provide for compulsory education and the teaching of basic skills along with American history, all in English.

33. Boyea, "John Samuel Foley," 35. Foley gained his position as bishop of Detroit through the support of Archbishop Gibbons.

34. [Kelly], *No Greater Service,* 360–70.

35. Ibid., 368; Tentler, *Seasons of Grace,* 92–93.

36. Putnam, *Primary and Secondary Education in Michigan,* 153–63.

37. [Kelly], *No Greater Service,* 370.

38. Lawrence D. Orton, *Polish Detroit and the Kolasinski Affair* (Detroit: Wayne State University Press, 1981), 12–16.

39. Thaddeus C. Radzialowski, "The View from a Polish Ghetto," *Ethnicity* 1 (1974): 127.

40. John J. Bukowczyk, *And My Children Did Not Know Me* (Bloomington: Indiana University Press, 1986), includes a perceptive discussion of the Resurrectionists.

41. Orton, *Polish Detroit and the Kolasinski Affair,* 17–18, discusses problems with this parish name. Initially, it was to be St. Adalbert (Sw. Wojciech), a saint revered by Prussian and Kashubian Poles. But it was recorded by the press and Borgess as Albert or Albertus, an entirely different saint. That more common name, St. Albertus, will be used in all subsequent references.

42. Sister Mary Remigia Napolska, "The Polish Immigrant in Detroit to 1914," *Annals of the Polish R.C. Union Archives and Museum* 10 (1945–46): 89.

43. Zunz, *Changing Face of Inequality,* 172–75; Napolska, "Polish Immigrant in Detroit," 34–35.

44. Zunz makes this point strongly, calling Polish accomplishments in Detroit a tour de force.

45. Orton, *Polish Detroit and the Kolasinski Affair,* 31–32.

46. Zunz, *Changing Face of Inequality,* 189.

47. Orton, *Polish Detroit and the Kolasinski Affair,* 33.

48. Borgess opened the short-lived St. Francis Seminary in Monroe in 1886 to serve as a preparatory seminary and secondary school; at the time, Detroit was still sending boys out of state to study for the priesthood, heavily funded by the diocese. See Tentler, *Seasons of Grace,* 50–51.

49. See Bukowczyk, *And My Children Did Not Know Me,* for a thorough discussion of this tension.

50. Boyea, "John Samuel Foley," citing letter from parishioners to Borgess, 6 Feb. 1883, St. Albertus parish files, AAD.

51. Peplinski, *A Fitting Response,* 1:37.

52. The best analysis of this issue is found in Leslie Tentler, "Who Is the Church? Conflict in a Polish Immigrant Parish in Late-Nineteenth-Century Detroit," *Comparative Studies in Society and History* 25 (April 1983): 241–76; thorough discussions are also provided in Orton, *Polish Detroit and the Kolasinski Affair;* Napolska, "Polish Immigrant in Detroit"; and in Eduard Adam Skendzel, *The Kolasinski Story* (Grand Rapids: Littleshield Press, 1979).

53. Orton, *Polish Detroit and the Kolasinski Affair,* 43, citing *Detroit Free Press,* 2 Dec. 1885, 5; *Detroit Free Press,* 28 Dec. 1885, 4.

54. Skendzel, *The Kolasinski Story,* 7; Sister Mary Janice Ziolkowski, CSSF, *The Felician Sisters of Livonia, Michigan* (Detroit: Harlo Press, 1984), 129–31.

55. Skendzel, *The Kolasinski Story,* 8, citing Waclaw Kruszka, *Historya Polska w Ameryce.*

56. *Michigan Catholic,* 10 Dec. 1885, 4.

57. Tentler, "Who's Is the Church?" discusses this idea to an extent.

58. See Orton, *Polish Detroit and the Kolasinski Affair,* 148–52, for an excellent account of the battle over church finances.

59. Melvin G. Holli, *Reform in Detroit: Hazen S. Pingree and Urban Politics* (New York: Oxford University Press, 1969), 64–67.

60. Holli, *Reform in Detroit,* 67.

61. Tentler, *Seasons of Grace,* 267; Kenneth T. Jackson, *The Ku Klux Klan in the City, 1915–1930* (New York: Oxford University Press, 1967), 128; John Higham, *Strangers in the Land* (1955, repr. Forge Village, Mass.: Atheneum Press, 1963), 80 (all subsequent citations are to this edition).

62. Donald L. Kinzer, "The Political Uses of Anti-Catholicism in Michigan and Wisconsin, 1890–1894," *Michigan History Magazine* 39 (1955): 312.

63. Drachler, "Influence of Sectarianism," 109.

64. Ibid., 117, citing *Detroit Journal,* 4 Oct. 1892.

65. Ibid.

66. Arthur B. Moehlman, *Public Education in Detroit* (Bloomington, Ill.: Public School Publishing, 1925), chaps. 10–12.

67. Moehlman, *Public Education in Detroit,* 133, 145.

68. Ibid., 13, 145.

69. Ibid., 148, citing *Report of the Board of Education,* 1896–97.

70. Ibid., 135.

71. Tentler, *Seasons of Grace,* 269.

72. *Detroit Evening News,* 11 April 1892, 1. Tentler, *Seasons of Grace,* 234–36, includes a detailed and perceptive account of Atkinson's place during this period.

73. Drachler, "Influence of Sectarianism," chap. 9; Moehlman, *Public Education in Detroit;* Tentler, *Seasons of Grace,* 271–72.

74. Higham, *Strangers in the Land,* 86.

75. Holli, *Reform in Detroit,* provides the authoritative account of the Pingree years.

76. Moehlman, *Public Education in Detroit,* 146–47.

77. These problems that preoccupied the bishops are thoroughly covered in Tentler, *Seasons of Grace.*

CHAPTER 5: POLISH PARISH SCHOOLS

1. Farmer, *History of Detroit,* 1:722–24.

2. Calculated from Account Books, Item 39, 1894–1916, AAD.

3. Jozef Miaso, *The History of the Education of Polish Immigrants in the United States,* trans. Ludwik Krzyzanowski (1970, repr. New York: Kosciuszko Foundation and Polish Scientific Publishers, 1977), 113–14; Orton, *Polish Detroit and the Kolasinski Affair,* 32.

4. Sister Mary Tullia Domain, CSSF, "Mother Mary Angela Truszkowska, Foundress of the Felician Sisters," *Polish American Studies* 10 (July–Dec. 1953): 82.

5. Thaddeus C. Radzialowski, "Reflections on the History of the Felicians in America," *Polish American Studies* 32 (Spring 1975): 27.

6. Michael Krolewski, *The Prayer of St. Hyacinth Parish, Detroit, Michigan (Poletown),* trans. Wojciech Wojtysiak (Northville, N.J.: Costombook, 1984).

7. Felician documents and histories refer to the priest as Father Honorat rather than as Father Kozminski, and that name will be used throughout. Characterization is by Radzialowski, "Reflections on the History of the Felicians," 23.

8. Ziolkowski, *The Felician Sisters,* 56–57, 118, 181–83.

9. Domain, "Mother Mary Angela," 83–85; Sister Mary Jeremiah Studniewska, "The Educational Work of the Felician Sisters of the Province of Detroit, 1847–1948," M.A. thesis, Catholic University, 1949, 35.

10. Ziolkowski, *The Felician Sisters,* 90, quoting Mother Monica, Polonia, Wis., to Mother Magdalen, Cracow, 1 Nov. 1879.

11. *Western Home Journal,* 9 Oct. 1880, 5.

12. Orton, *Polish Detroit and the Kolasinski Affair,* 33–34, 66–68.

13. Ziolkowski, *The Felician Sisters,* 103.

14. Based on "Names of the Pupils in the Seminary of the Felician Sisters Detroit, Michigan," MS, AFSLM.

15. Radzialowski, "Reflections on the History of the Felicians," 21–22.

16. Sister Cajetan to Father Honorat, winter 1884, quoted in Ziolkowski, *The Felician Sisters,* 107.

17. Sister M. Catherine [Pyterek], Memoirs MS, AFSLM.

18. Sister Mary Tullia Domain, typescript MS, AFSLM. This curriculum reflects the time as about 1900; see Sister Mary Jeremiah Studniewska, *The Educational Work of the Felician Sisters of the Province of Detroit in the United States, 1874–1948* (Livonia, Mich.: The Felician Sisters, O.S.F., 1962), 127–31.

19. Ziolkowski, *The Felician Sisters,* 121.

20. Zunz, *Changing Face of Inequality,* 234, 253.

21. "Names of Pupils in Seminary of the Felician Sisters of Detroit, Michigan," MS, AFSLM.

22. Tentler, *Seasons of Grace,* 231.

23. Zunz, *Changing Face of Inequality,* 233.

24. Ziolkowski, *The Felician Sisters,* 51–52.

25. Father Dabrowski to Mother Magdalen, 9 Jan. 1884, quoted in Ziolkowski, *The Felician Sisters,* 104.

26. Father Dabrowski to Mother Magdalen, n.d. (before Aug. 1883), quoted in Ziolkowski, *The Felician Sisters,* 104.

27. Ziolkowski, *The Felician Sisters,* 117.

28. Ibid. Ziolkowski describes Mother Monica as refusing to send out unprepared teachers but contradicts her own analysis by repeated, consistent examples of the superior's actions to the contrary.

29. Bukowczyk, *And My Children Did Not Know Me,* 43.

30. Ziolkowski, *The Felician Sisters,* 129–31.

31. *Detroit News,* 1 Dec. 1885, 4.

32. Orton, *Polish Detroit and the Kolasinski Affair,* 84, 96.

33. *Detroit News,* 6 Dec. 1885, 4.

34. *Detroit News,* 12 April 1886, 4.

35. *Detroit News,* 12 April 1886, 4. Tentler, "Who Is the Church?" analyzes the composition of supporters.

36. Orton, *Polish Detroit and the Kolasinski Affair,* 65.

37. Tentler, "Who Is the Church?" 260.

38. Orton, *Polish Detroit and the Kolasinski Affair,* 81, 83.

39. Ibid., 87–94.

40. Farmer, *History of Detroit,* 1:745–53.

41. Moehlman, *Public Education in Detroit,* 123.

42. *First Annual Report of the Diocesan School Board of the Diocese of Detroit, Michigan* (Detroit: Detroit Publishing Co., 1888), 16, 17, cited in Ziolkowski, *The Felician Sisters,* 125. [Kelly], *No Greater Service,* includes a table handwritten by the author (bound in select volumes of this book) detailing the school board's report.

43. Folder 1, box 4, Bishop Foley Papers, AAD.

44. [Kelly], *No Greater Service,* First Annual School Report MS.

45. Folder 1, box 4, report, 29 Aug. 1889, Bishop Foley Papers, AAD.

46. St. Casimir's parish, file 18.3, AAD.

47. Eduard Adam Skendzel, *The Detroit St. Josaphat's Story, 1889–1989* (Grand Rapids: Littleshield Press, 1989), 407–9.

48. Account Books, Item 39, 1894–1916, AAD.

49. Domain, "Mother Mary Angela," 87.

50. Studniewska, *Educational Work of the Felician Sisters,* 48–49.

51. Ziolkowski, *The Felician Sisters,* 183.

52. See Boyea, "Bishop John Foley," and James H. Moynihan, *Life of Archbishop John Ireland* (New York: Harper and Brothers, 1953).

53. *Pamietnik Ztotego Jubileuszu, Parafil Najstodszego Serca Marii Panny, 1890–1940* (Sweetest Heart Golden Jubilee Book), MHC.

54. Calculated from Account Books, Item 39, 1894–1916, AAD.

55. Peplinski, *A Fitting Response,* 1:95.

56. Ibid., 2:245, as articulated in 1912 by Sister Boleslaus when she was mother superior of the Sisters of St. Joseph in their constitution of that year.

57. Ibid., 2:234, 202–3, 39.

58. *Pamietnik Ztotego Jubileuszu,* 19.

59. Peplinski, *A Fitting Response,* 1:94, has two sets of figures for this period, placing the number of Polish sisters who were teaching at either seventy or eighty-three (87–94).

60. Ibid., 1:106.

61. Ibid., 1:107.

62. Ibid., 1:111, 86–87.

63. Ibid., 1:145–46.

64. *Pamietnik Ztotego Jubileuszu,* 27; Peplinski, *A Fitting Response,* 1:164.

65. Ibid., 1:168.

66. Ibid., 1:146–47.

67. Ibid., 1:204, citing Sister Thecla's memoirs describing the May 1902 incident.

68. Ibid., 1:169.

69. Ibid., 1:171.

70. Ibid., 2:245.

71. Sister Cajetan to Father Honorat, 1892–93, cited in Ziolkowski, *The Felician Sisters,* 106.

72. Father Honorat to Sister M. Catherine Pyterek, n.d., cited in Ziolkowski, *The Felician Sisters,* 152.

73. Ibid., 151–52.

74. Sister M. Catherine [Pyterek], Memoirs MS, AFSLM.

75. Studniewska, *Educational Work of the Felician Sisters,* 75, citing annals of St. Joseph School and Convent, Jackson, Mich.

76. Ziolkowski, *The Felician Sisters,* 182.

77. Reminiscences of Rochelle Dornatt, a grade school student during the 1950s, as told to me about 1974.

78. Ziolkowski, *The Felician Sisters,* 147. In 1900, life expectancy for women in the United States was 48.3 years. Childbirth and the complications associated with it were the primary killers.

79. Peplinski, *A Fitting Response,* 2:56–57.

80. Ziolkowski, *The Felician Sisters,* 110.

81. Ibid., 181, citing circular of Mother M. Cajetan, 17 Feb. 1902.

82. Based on various financial reports in parish files at AAD.

83. St. Albertus parish, file 12.9, AAD.

84. BLIS, *Annual Report of the Michigan Bureau of Labor and Industrial Statistics (1884)* (Lansing: State Printer, 1 Feb. 1885), 98, 130–31.

85. Miscellaneous clippings, AFSLM.

86. Ziolkowski, *The Felician Sisters,* 160–61.

87. Ibid., 106, citing Mother Monica to Reverend Vincent Barzynski, Resurrection parish, Chicago, 20 Aug. 1880.

88. St. Casimir's and St. Josaphat parish files, AAD.

89. St. Albertus parish, file 12.14, AAD.

90. Ziolkowski, *The Felician Sisters,* 160.

91. Miaso, *Education of Polish Immigrants,* 49–50.

92. Holli, *Reform in Detroit,* 66–67.

93. Ibid., 64.

94. Account Books, Item 39, 1894–1916, AAD.

Chapter 6: Parish Grade Schools Multiply

1. U.S. Bureau of the Census, *Fourteenth Census of the United States, 1920,* vol. 2: *Population* (Washington: Government Printing Office, 1922), 1103.

2. Ibid., 2:52. The total population was 993,678, of which 289,297 were foreign-born and 348,771 were of foreign-born or mixed parentage. The black population was 40,838, only 4.1 percent of the total but up sharply from 1910, when 1.2 percent (5,741) of the city's residents were black.

3. Sister M. Arthemise Dalton, OP, "The History and Development of the Catholic Secondary School System in the Archdiocese of Detroit, 1701–1961," Ed.D. diss., Wayne State University, 1962, 74–75.

4. Figures do not always agree or match, but the proportions hold. Calculations here are based on Catholic directory figures, on Jeffrey Mirel, *The Rise and Fall of an Urban School System, Detroit, 1907–81* (Ann Arbor: University of Michigan Press, 1993), table 1, and on Hamtramck Public Schools, *Housing the Children,* research series no. 1 (Hamtramck, Mich.: Board of Education, 1926), 102.

5. Erdmann Doane Beynon, "Occupational Adjustments of Hungarian Immigrants in an American Urban Community," Ph.D. diss., University of Michigan, 1933, reprinted and exerpted in *Geographical Review* 27 (April 1937): 11. The description of the bar is based on Beynon's interview with the saloon-keeper's widow.

6. U.S. Bureau of the Census, *Fourteenth Census of the United States, 1920,* vol. 2: *Population,* 936. This figure includes those born in Hungary, the 3,453 born in other foreign countries to Hungarian-born fathers, and the second generation born in America of Hungarian parentage.

7. Zunz, *Changing Face of Inequality,* 391, 357.

8. Beynon, "Occupational Adjustments of Hungarian Immigrants," 12.

9. Malvina Hauk Abonyi and James A. Anderson, *Hungarians of Detroit,* Peopling of Michigan series (Detroit: Wayne State University Press, 1977), 13–19; Beynon, "Occupational Adjustments of Hungarian Immigrants," 228.

10. Andrew Untener, "The Old Grad Remembers When," in Holy Cross School thirty-year homecoming booklet (1906–36), Holy Cross parish, file 4.13, AAD.

11. Zunz, *Changing Face of Inequality,* 389.

12. Untener, "Old Grad Remembers."

13. Beynon, "Occupational Adjustments of Hungarian Immigrants," 759.

14. Ibid., 756.

15. Abonyi and Anderson, *Hungarians of Detroit,* 26.

16. Beynon, "Occupational Adjustments of Hungarian Immigrants," 758.

17. James A. Burns, *The Growth and Development of the Catholic School System in the United States* (New York: Benziger Brothers, 1912), 336.

18. Beynon, "Occupational Adjustments of Hungarian Immigrants," 430–31.

19. Holy Cross School thirty-year homecoming booklet (1906–36), Holy Cross parish, file 4.13, AAD.

20. Holy Cross parish, file 4.7, AAD.

21. Beynon, "Occupational Adjustments of Hungarian Immigrants."

22. Ryan, *Alien Corn,* 130.

23. Ibid., 243.

24. Beynon, "Occupational Adjustments of Hungarian Immigrants," 760–61.

25. Untener, "Old Grad Remembers." Untener, in 1910, became the first graduate of Holy Cross grade school.

26. Ibid.

27. Holy Cross parish, file 4.9, AAD.

28. The Holy Cross School's thirty-year homecoming booklet lists graduates. Holy Cross parish, file 4.13, AAD.

29. Untener, "Old Grad Remembers."

30. *Emelekalbum, a detroiti, Michigan, Szent Kereszt Romai Katholikus Magyar Hitkozseg, Huszonot Eves Jubileumara* (Jubilate, 1906–31, Silver Jubilee of the Holy Cross Roman Catholic Church, Detroit, Michigan); and *Holy Cross Church, Detroit, Michigan, 1925–1971* (another jubilee book, ca. 1975), MHC.

31. Holy Cross parish, file 4.9, AAD.

32. Desiderius Nagy to Mother M. Augustine, OSD, mother general of St. Joseph's Convent, Adrian, Mich., 18 July 1930, Holy Cross parish, file 4.13, AAD.

33. Holy Cross parish, file 14.3, AAD.

34. Sister M. Camilla to Bishop Michael Gallagher, undated letter [spring 1930?], Holy Cross parish, file 4.13, AAD.

35. "Emelekalbum, a detroiti, Michigan," 24.

36. Beynon, "Occupational Adjustments of Hungarian Immigrants," 768; *Detroit Times*, 17 Aug. 1931.

37. Holy Cross parish, file 4.13, AAD.

38. Reverend John C. Vismara, DD, "Coming of the Italians to Detroit," *Michigan History Magazine* 2 (Jan. 1918): 120.

39. U.S. Bureau of the Census, *Fourteenth Census of the United States, 1920*, vol. 2: *Population*, 936. The Italian immigrant figure includes 320 born in some country other than Italy to Italian-born fathers.

40. "Sunday Magazine," *Detroit Free Press*, 12 April 1964.

41. Zunz, *Changing Face of Inequality*, 338, 393.

42. Gilbert Anderson, "A Study in Italian Residence, Succession in Detroit, Michigan," unpublished paper, 1934–35, apparently written by a student and on deposit at the Buhr Library, University of Michigan.

43. George P. Graff, *The People of Michigan* (Lansing: Michigan Department of Education, 1974), 101.

44. Archives of the Polish Women for Progress, *The Polish Activities League, 1923–1973* (Detroit, 1973), MHC.

45. Vittorio Re, *Michigan's Italian Community: A Historical Perspective*, International and Ethnic Studies series (Detroit: Wayne State University, 1981), 40–42.

46. Undated agreement between Bishop Foley and the Italian societies of St. Joseph, Madonna delle Grazie, St. Peter, St. Vincent de Paul, and Holy Cross parish, file 5.3, AAD.

47. Holy Family parish, file 5.1, AAD.

48. Re, *Michigan's Italian Community*, 44.

49. Pastor to Bishop Michael Gallagher, 11 Oct. 1922, Holy Family parish, file 5.3, AAD.

50. Father John C[?] to Bishop Michael Gallagher, 21 Dec. 1923, Holy Family parish, file 5.3, AAD.

51. A School Sister of Notre Dame [Sister Dympna], *Mother Caroline and the School Sisters of Notre Dame in North America*, 2 vols. (St. Louis: Woodward and Tiernan, 1928), 2:114.

52. [Dympna], *Mother Caroline*, 2:197.

53. *The Official Catholic Directory*, 1917 and 1925. The directory, a serial, is known variously as *Sadliers' Catholic Directory, Almanac and Ordo, Hoffmann's Catholic Directory*, and *Almanac and Clergy List*. Hereafter cited as *Catholic Directory*.

54. *Detroit News*, 23 May 1973, 15-E.

55. See as an example of typical articles on education, *La Tribuna Italiana*, 11 Sept. 1909 and 25 Sept. 1909.

56. Vittorio Re, *History of the First Italian Presbyterian Church of Detroit*, Occasional Papers in Ethnic Studies series (Detroit: Wayne State University Ethnic Studies Division, 1979), 12–15.

57. Re, *History of the First Italian Presbyterian Church*, 36.

58. Ibid., 14.

59. Minerva Maiullo, *A Tapestry of Memories* (New York: A. S. Barnes, 1972).

60. Sanders, *Education of an Urban Minority,* 69.

61. Dolan, *The American Catholic Experience,* 280.

62. Mirel, *Rise and Fall of an Urban School System,* 62. At the intermediate level, 3.7 percent of the public school population was Polish and 3.1 percent was Italian.

63. [Dympna], *Mother Caroline and the School Sisters,* 2:251.

64. Dolan, *The American Catholic Experience,* 280; Hennesey, *American Catholics,* 174, quoting Chicago's Archbishop James Quigley.

65. Hennesey, *American Catholics,* 173.

66. St. Joseph's parish, file 27.3, and St. Mary's parish, file 30.13, AAD.

67. *Detroit Free Press,* 24 Jan. 1994, 6A.

68. Robert Conot, *American Odyssey* (New York: William Morrow, 1974), 265.

69. Russell Magnini, "History of the Michigan Italians," in *Ethnic Michigan,* ed. Arthur Helweg (East Lansing: Michigan State University Press, in press).

70. Maiullo, *A Tapestry of Memories.*

71. U.S. Bureau of the Census, *Fourteenth Census of the United States, 1920,* vol. 2: *Population,* 936; U.S. Bureau of the Census, *Fifteenth Census of the United States, 1930,* vol. 2: *Population* (Washington: Government Printing Office, 1933), 248.

72. Zunz, *Changing Face of Inequality,* 217.

73. George P. Graff, *The People of Michigan* (Lansing: Michigan Department of Education, 1974), 95.

74. Philemon D. Sabbe and Leon Buyse, *Belgians in America* (The Hague: Lannoo, 1960), 212.

75. *Detroit Free Press,* 1 May 1911.

76. Ryan, *Alien Corn,* 265.

77. Our Lady of Sorrows parish, file 9.10, AAD.

78. Sabbe and Buyse, *Belgians in America,* 75.

79. Tentler, *Seasons of Grace,* 110–11.

80. The most intelligible discussion of the tangled church farm matter is provided by Tentler, *Seasons of Grace.*

81. [Kelly], *No Greater Service,* 530.

82. St. Charles Borromeo parish, file 19.7, AAD.

83. Ibid.; *Catholic Directory,* 1900, 1913, 1925; Account Books, Item 39, 1894–1916, AAD.

84. Sabbe and Buyse, *Belgians in America,* 76–77.

85. Ibid., 88–90.

86. *Catholic Directory,* 1925.

87. U.S. Bureau of the Census, *Thirteenth Census of the United States, 1910 Abstract* (Washington, D.C.: Government Printing Office, 1910), 623.

88. Our Lady of the Rosary parish files, countless articles in the *Michigan Catholic,* and anecdotal accounts in the IHM archives all reinforce the influential role Father Van Antwerp played.

89. Clipping from *Detroit News*, 9 May 1926, St. Hyacinth parish, file 23.23, AAD.

90. Buckowczyk, *And My Children Did Not Know Me*, 11.

91. Studniewska, *Educational Work of the Felician Sisters*, 109, citing the history described in the 1933 parish annual.

92. *St. Stephen Church, 1917–1977, Golden Jubilee Book*, MHC.

93. Clipping from *Detroit News*, 9 May 1926, St. Hyacinth parish, file 23.23, AAD.

94. Krolewski, *The Prayer of St. Hyacinth Parish*, 173.

95. Calculated from *Catholic Directory* annual lists.

96. *Detroit Free Press*, 22 June 1902.

97. Calculated from *Catholic Directory*, 1925; Peplinski, *A Fitting Response*, 2:511–13.

98. Ibid., 2:255.

99. Ibid., 2:245.

100. Ibid., 2:207–9.

101. Ibid., 2:248–49.

102. Ibid., 2:243.

103. The investment in education was at risk also because of the high mortality rate among sisters, a result especially of tuberculosis. Two of the three who went to Monroe soon died. Ibid., 2:249, 258.

104. Ibid., 2:205.

105. Handwritten drafts of letters, Sister M. Catherine [Pyterek], Memoirs MS, AFSLM.

106. Peplinski, *A Fitting Response*, 2:211.

107. Ibid., 2:245.

108. Krolewski, *The Prayer of St. Hyacinth Parish*, 291.

109. Ibid., 291–92.

110. Stephen Brumberg, "Tales Out of School," *Issues in Education* 2 (Fall 1984): 93.

111. Radzialowski, "Reflections on the History of the Felicians," 22.

112. Burns, *Catholic School System in the United States*, 317, citing "Confessions of a Polish Priest," *Catholic Standard and Times*, 12 Feb. 1910.

113. Ziolkowski, *The Felician Sisters*, 272.

114. Ibid., 272–73.

115. Radzialowski, "Reflections on the History of the Felicians," 27.

116. Miaso, *Education of Polish Immigrants*, 142.

117. Ibid., 142, citing "Nie niszez czieciom zycia" (Do Not Ruin Our Children's Lives), *Praca*, no. 1 (1919).

118. Miaso, *Education of Polish Immigrants*, 252.

119. Ibid., 159.

120. Bukowczyk, *And My Children Did Not Know Me*, 37.

121. Miaso, *Education of Polish Immigrants*, 150–51.

122. Bukowczyk, *And My Children Did Not Know Me*, 37.

123. Miaso, *Education of Polish Immigrants*, 205.

124. Orton, *Polish Detroit and the Kolasinski Affair*, 193.

125. Bukowczyk, *And My Children Did Not Know Me*, 46–47.

126. The Polish Women for Progress, *The Polish Activities League.*

127. Calculated from *Catholic Directory;* Bukowczyk, *And My Children Did Not Know Me,* 72.

128. St. Casimir's parish, file 18.5, AAD.

129. Mirel, *Rise and Fall of an Urban School System,* 62–63.

130. Ibid., 1, 12, 13.

131. Ibid., 28.

132. Ibid., 10.

133. Ibid., 18–19.

134. Zunz, *Changing Face of Inequality,* 316, citing Minutes, Committee on Education, 16 Dec. 1915, Americanization Committee of Detroit Papers, Arthur J. Tuttle Papers, MHC.

135. Hamtramck Public Schools, *Housing the Children,* research series no. 1 (Hamtramck: Board of Education, 1926), 14; Zunz, *Changing Face of Inequality,* 354.

136. Miaso, *Education of Polish Immigrants,* 247.

137. Hamtramck Public Schools, *Housing the Children,* 88.

138. Ibid., 23, 90.

139. Calculated from *Catholic Directory,* 1925.

140. Hamtramck Public Schools, *Housing the Children,* table 29, 102; Miaso, *Education of Polish Immigrants,* 247.

141. Hamtramck Public Schools, *Housing the Children,* table 29, 102.

142. Ibid., 28.

143. Figures are calculated from Hamtramck Public Schools, *Housing the Children,* table 9, 90. Figures are not available to show how many Polish students were in Detroit public high schools.

144. Ibid., 35.

145. Zunz, *Changing Face of Inequality,* 354.

146. Hamtramck Public Schools, *Housing the Children,* 12.

147. Ibid., 35.

148. National parishes within the American Catholic Church are of two types, nonjuridical and juridical. The former are territorial parishes in which most members happen to belong to one nationality group. They have indefinite and extralegal status and if the population of the neighborhood changes they are no longer assured of priests of the same national origin. See Thomas Monzell, "The Catholic Church and the Americanization of the Polish Immigrant," *Polish American Studies* 26 (Jan.–June 1969): 6–7.

149. Monzell, "The Catholic Church and Americanization," 607; McAvoy, "Public Schools *vs.* Catholic Schools," 28, 46.

150. Ryan, *Alien Corn,* 265.

151. Ibid., 285–86.

152. Ibid., 312.

153. Ibid., 293–95.

154. Ibid., 317.

155. *Catholic Directory,* 1925.

156. [Kelly], *No Greater Service*, 386, citing Dupanloup, *De la haute education intellectuelle.*

157. Ibid., 387.

158. Ibid., 565.

159. Ibid., 567; Dalton, "History and Development of the Catholic School System," 81–83.

160. St. Vincent's parish convent, "Chronicles of 1925–26," SSIHM.

161. This description of family composition as of 1921 is found in St. Vincent's parish, file labeled "Miscellaneous," item no. 24, AAD.

162. St. Charles Borromeo parish, file 19.7, AAD.

163. Studienewsa, *Educational Work of the Felician Sisters*, 106–8.

164. Ibid., 94–95, 109; Ziolkowski, *The Felician Sisters*, 271.

165. Ziolkowski, *The Felician Sisters*, 271–72.

166. Studniewska, *Educational Work of the Felician Sisters*, 94–95.

167. Calculations from *Catholic Directory*, 1925; also St. Casimir's files at AAD and materials located at St. Casimir's school and rectory.

168. Oscar Handlin, *The Uprooted* (New York: Grosset and Dunlap, 1951), 244; John Higham, *Send These to Me* (New York: Atheneum, 1975), 21.

169. Peplinski, *A Fitting Response*, 2:171.

CHAPTER 7: HIGHER AMBITIONS

1. Farmer, *History of Detroit*, 1:749; Putnam, *Primary and Secondary Education in Michigan*, 90, citing the superintendent of public education in 1872 who complained about lack of public support and opposition, even from "men of character and standing."

2. An 1884 school census showed 10,597 youths aged fifteen through eighteen. Of this population, 1,556 were in public school and another 927 were attending schools "not public." About a quarter of these teen-aged children were probably finishing the elementary grades. BLIS, *Second Annual Report (1885)*, 61–62; Detroit Board of Education, *Detroit Public Schools*, 66; Farmer, *History of Detroit*, 1:749–50.

3. Burns, *Catholic School System in the United States*, 363. Philadelphia's "Roman Catholic High School" finally opened in the early 1890s and by 1915 enrolled a majority of the city's boys who attended Catholic high school.

4. Hennesy, *American Catholics*, 187; Reverend James A. Burns, "The Condition of Catholic Secondary Education in the United States," *National Catholic Association Bulletin* 12 (Nov. 1915): 404, 364; Dolan, *The American Catholic Experience*, 292.

5. Herman J. Muller, SJ, *The University of Detroit, 1877–1977: A Centennial History* (Detroit: University of Detroit, 1976), 4–5, citing copies of letter of agreement in the ADD and the archives of the University of Detroit.

6. Blessed Sacrament parish, file 1.3C, AAD.

7. Muller, *University of Detroit*, 26–27, citing Father Dowling's letter to the *Michigan Catholic*, 22 Jan. 1891. Figures are different in Father P. Douglas Keller, S.J., et al.,

The Second Hundred Years: The University of Detroit High School and a Chronicle of the First Hundred Years, 1877–1977 (Detroit: University of Detroit High School, 1977), 4, which gives $21,500 as the amount spent, citing an original diary from the university's archives.

8. Muller, *University of Detroit*, 4–5.

9. Ibid., 6, citing *Detroit Evening News*, 8 June 1877.

10. *Western Home Journal*, 4 Aug. 1877.

11. Muller, *University of Detroit*, 20–21.

12. See, for example, *Michigan Catholic*, 14 Feb. 1884, 5.

13. Keller et al., *Second Hundred Years*, 21.

14. Muller, *University of Detroit*, 32, citing John A. Russell, "Days at Old Detroit College," *Varsity News Magazine*, midwinter, 1924–25.

15. Tabulated from Detroit College Record Books, 1877–1918, UDHSJA.

16. Detroit College Record Book, 1889, 1917–18, UDHSJA.

17. Keller et al., *Second Hundred Years*, 19.

18. Detroit College Record Book, 1891, UDHSJA.

19. Krolewski, *The Prayer of St. Hyacinth Parish*, 312–13.

20. Muller, *University of Detroit*, 20.

21. Ibid., 25, assesses the complaints in this manner in his study; regarding the change, he cites "First Monday in September," Memoranda 2, 1880–87, University of Detroit Archives.

22. Muller, *University of Detroit*, 26, citing *Western Home Journal*, 3 Sept. 1881.

23. Keller et al., *Second Hundred Years*, 21.

24. Muller, *University of Detroit*, 61, citing "Detroit College Catalogue, 1898–1899," 13.

25. *Catholic Directory*, 1925, 355; Keller et al., *Second Hundred Years*, 21, 30.

26. John Charles Manning Papers, box 1, MHC.

27. [Kelly], *No Greater Service*, First Annual School Report MS.

28. Br. Angelus Gabriel, FSC, *The Christian Brothers in the United States, 1848–1948: A Century of Catholic Education* (New York: D. X. McMullen, 1948), 356–57.

29. Detroit Public Schools, *Education in Detroit, 1916*, publication of the National Education Association, Feb. 21–26, 1916, 45. This public school had two- , three- , and four-year courses by 1916.

30. De La Salle High School student records, classes of 1917 and 1918, in principal's office at De La Salle Collegiate High School, Warren, Mich. (DLSHS), and *Detroit City Directory*, 1918.

31. "Parish/School Report, Fiscal 1913," St. Joseph's parish, file 27.3, AAD.

32. The 1916 figure is from Detroit Public Schools, *Education in Detroit, 1916*, 178; the 1925 figure is from *Catholic Directory*, 1925, 358. Enrollment peaked in the 1940s, with 495 students coming from sixty parishes. See Br. Angelus Gabriel, *Christian Brothers*, 357, 358.

33. Commercial School Record Book, DLSHS.

34. St. Joseph's parish, file 17.9, AAD.

35. Zunz, *Changing Face of Inequality,* 340–42; based on heads of households.

36. Burns, "The Condition of Catholic Secondary Education," 404, 416.

37. St. Vincent's parish convent, "Chronicles of 1925–26," SSIHM.

38. *Michigan Catholic,* 19 June 1884, 2.

39. [Kelly], *No Greater Service,* First Annual School Report MS. Trinity's enrollment figure includes some who were in the high school.

40. 1895 monthly calendar for St. Vincent's parish, SSIHM.

41. Father Doherty was at St. Vincent's from 1886 through 1926 when he died; Father Savage died in 1925.

42. Thus he annually referred to St. Vincent's when he filled out reports for the bishop. St. Vincent's parish, file 38.2, AAD.

43. St. Vincent's parish convent, "Chronicles of 1925–26," SSIHM.

44. Burns, "Condition of Catholic Secondary Education," 379.

45. [Kelly], *No Greater Service,* 393–95.

46. Calculated from archival records located in the principal's office, Most Holy Trinity Grade School, and in the principal's office at St. Vincent's Junior High School.

47. [Kelly], *No Greater Service,* 80–81.

48. St. Vincent's parish, file 38.2, AAD; [Kelly], *No Greater Service,* 460.

49. [Kelly], *No Greater Service,* 573–75.

50. "Motherhouse Chronicles," vol. 2, SSIHM; Tentler, *Seasons of Grace,* 231–32; [Kelly], *No Greater Service,* 496.

51. Calculated from St. Vincent's Record Book, St. VJH.

52. Finley Peter Dunne, *Mr. Dooley at His Best,* ed. Elmer Ellis (1949, repr. New York: Archon Books, 1969), 215.

53. Tentler, *Seasons of Grace,* 95.

54. Burns, "Condition of Catholic Secondary Education," 416. Burns's listing shows only seven parish schools, failing to include the German parishes of St. Joseph's and St. Boniface's.

55. Record Books, St. VJH.

56. Interviews with Sister Frances Clare and Sister Amadeus, IHM motherhouse, Monroe, Mich., Feb. 1986; both were graduates of St. Vincent's in the early 1920s.

57. *Catholic Directory,* 1925.

58. Record Book, MHTGS.

59. Record Book, UDHSJA.

60. Reports of 1900, 1905, 1916, in St. Vincent's parish, file 38.6, AAD.

61. Data are based on the archival lists of graduates from St. Vincent's from 1893 to 1925 and from Trinity during the same period, but with 1913 and 1914 missing for that school. Occupations were identified through the annual Detroit city directories. Occupational categories are those used by Zunz in the 1920 segment of *Changing Face of Inequality.* A total of 127 were possible to trace.

62. St. Vincent's Annual Feast Calendar, 1920, 5, St. VJH.

63. "Convent Chronicles, 1927," in St. Joseph's parish, file 27.9, SSIHM.

64. Ibid.

65. "Historical Data of Parishes," miscellaneous item no. 14, 1921, AAD.

66. "Convent Chronicles, 1927," in St. Joseph's parish, file 27.9, SSIHM.

67. "Historical Data of Parishes," miscellaneous item no. 14, 1921, AAD.

68. Based on baptism records matched with graduates, AAD.

69. [Kelly], *No Greater Service*, 457.

70. According to various typescript spiral notebooks prepared by the congregation as guides for classroom teachers and generously provided to me by their archivist, Sister Mary Thecla Malawey, SCC. It was the policy of the Sisters of Christian Charity to teach only grade schools—leading one outstate Michigan pastor to change to the IHMs in 1904. [Kelly], *No Greater Service*, 537; [Kelly], ed., *Achievement of a Century*, 92.

71. Father George Pare MSS, box 7.6, AAD.

72. Br. Angelus Gabriel, *Christian Brothers*, 358–60.

73. Miaso, *Education of Polish Immigrants*, 151.

74. Ibid., 165–66; Burns, "Condition of Catholic Secondary Education," 377–440.

75. Miaso, *Education of Polish Immigrants*, 194.

76. Krolewski, *The Prayer of St. Hyacinth Parish*, 312–13.

77. Miaso, *Education of Polish Immigrants*, 178.

78. Muller, *University of Detroit*, chaps. 5 and 6.

79. Ziolkowski, *The Felician Sisters*, 207–8.

80. Napolska, "Polish Immigrant in Detroit," 89.

81. Ziolkowski, *The Felician Sisters*, 205.

82. Sister M. Tullia Domain MS, 10, AFSLM; Ziolkowski, *The Felician Sisters*, 281–319.

83. Studniewska, *Educational Work of the Felician Sisters*, 132–33; Sister M. Tuilla Domain MS, 14, AFSLM.

84. Zunz, *Changing Face of Inequality*, 189.

85. Ziolkowski, *The Felician Sisters*, 204, quoting from her interview with Sister M. Adelaide Wysygorska, 30 Aug. 1980.

86. Zunz, *Changing Face of Inequality*, 288, citing Forrester B. Washington, "The Negro in Detroit," chap. 5, pt. A of "The Historical Background of the Negro in Detroit from 1800 to 1920" section, BHC.

87. Skendzel, *The Detroit St. Josaphat's Story*, 407–9.

88. Ibid., 402, 407–9.

89. Enrollment Report, Oct. 1929, in St. Josaphat's parish file, AFSLM.

90. Studniewska, *Educational Work of the Felician Sisters*, 143.

91. Records of the Office of the Principal, in St. Stanislaus parish file, AFSLM.

92. Enrollment Report, Oct. 1929, in St. Josaphat's parish file, AFSLM.

93. Peplinski, *A Fitting Response*, 2:511–13; *Catholic Directory*, 1925.

94. Peplinski, *A Fitting Response*, 2:207, 519.

95. Sister M. Tullia Domain MS, 14–15, AFSLM.

96. Hamtramck Public Schools, *Housing the Children*, 102. There was no Catholic parish high school within Hamtramck at the time; only eleven of the sixteen- and seventeen-year-olds in school attended "non-public" school, likely in the Detroit Catholic schools.

97. Leo J. Nowicki, "Profile of an American by Choice," typescript autobiography, 1975, MHC.

CHAPTER 8: THE MEASURE OF SUCCESS

1. Thomas E. Brown, "Patriotism or Religion," *Michigan History* 64 (July–Aug. 1980): 36.

2. Between 1908, when the constitution was adopted, and the early 1920s, by either legislative action or initiative, thirty-four amendments were proposed and more than half passed. "Preserve the Constitution of Michigan from Piecemeal Amendment," 1924, in "1920 Pamphlets" file, Anti-Parochial School Amendment Collection, SSIHM.

3. Willis F. Dunbar and George S. May, *Michigan: A History of the Wolverine State* (Grand Rapids: William B. Eerdmans, 1980), 518; F. Clever Bald, *Michigan in Four Centuries* (1954, repr. New York: Harper, 1961), 338.

4. Sample copy of the ballot in "Published Miscellanea" file, box 1, Lutheran Church–Missouri Synod, Michigan District, Lutheran Schools Committee Collection, MHC.

5. C. A. Windle, *Truth and Light on the Proposed Michigan School Amendment,* 8, in "Published Miscellanea, 1920" file, box 1, Lutheran Church–Missouri Synod, Lutheran Schools Committee Collection, MHC.

6. Tentler, *Seasons of Grace,* 449, citing *Michigan Catholic,* 6 March 1919, 4, and 17 April 1919, 4.

7. Brown, "Patriotism or Religion," 37.

8. Frank B. Woodford, *Alex J. Groesbeck: Portrait of a Public Man* (Detroit: Wayne State University Press, 1962), 111, describes the members of the "Committee for the Defense of Public Schools" as "teachers and public school administrators, supported by such professional hatemongers as the Ku Klux Klan." He offers no source for this, however, and the Klan was not yet involved with the amendment issue in 1920. Some teachers did speak up in defense of the amendment—in keeping with the long-standing NEA position about the advantages of public schools—but there is no evidence that that was the constituency of the group. Indeed, the amendment would not have served their self-interest, as the following discussion shows.

9. *Detroit News* clipping, ca. 1920, in "1920" file, box 1, Lutheran Church–Missouri Synod, Lutheran Schools Committee Collection, MHC.

10. Jules E. Guillaumin, "Catholics and the Proposed School Amendment in the Diocese of Detroit," 6, typescript, no. 918, Pare Collection, AAD.

11. *Michigan Catholic,* 8 Aug. 1918, 4. According to Tentler, *Seasons of Grace,* 445, the limited Catholic response to the 1918 petition was apparently due to the lack of a permanent bishop.

12. Pamphlet reprinting Groesbeck's statement in his advisory letter to Vaughn, in Anti-Parochial School Amendment Collection, SSIHM. Vaughan had contacted Groesbeck upon the request of the Reverend L. A. Sinn, a Lutheran pastor from Saginaw who was active in the campaign to defeat the amendment.

13. Woodford, *Alex J. Groesbeck,* 66–67.

14. *Detroit Free Press,* 3 Oct. 1920, 7.

15. Woodford, *Alex J. Groesbeck,* 234, notes that Wayne County gained seven more legislators by 1925 at the expense of districts throughout the state.

16. Senate Judiciary Committee, Hearings on Charges of Illegal Practices of Department of Justice, 66th Cong., 1 March 1921, U.S. Congressional Hearings, 41st–73d Congress, 1869–1934, 169:709–23, cited in Henrickson, *Detroit Perspectives,* 304–14.

17. James Hamilton, *The Michigan Public School Amendment* (Detroit: Public School Defense League, n.d. [ca. 1922]), 132 pp., Anti-Parochial School Amendment Collection, SSIHM. Another version of 129 pages with some slightly different information also circulated and is in the MHC.

18. Hamilton, *The Michigan Public School Amendment.*

19. Talk by Hamilton in a clipping from *Detroit Free Press,* 27 Oct. 1924, in "Catholic Activities" file, box 1, Lutheran Church–Missouri Synod, Michigan District, Lutheran Schools Committee Collection, MHC.

20. Eli J. Forsythe, *Michigan School Amendment: The Religious Side,* in "Published Miscellanea" file, box 1, Lutheran Church–Missouri Synod, Michigan District, Lutheran Schools Committee Collection, MHC.

21. "Published Miscellanea" file, box 1, Lutheran Church–Missouri Synod, Michigan District, Lutheran Schools Committee Collection, MHC, contains a copy of his pamphlet. In light of his speeches, authorship of the pamphlet seems questionable, given its careful attention to academic scholars and its reasoned tone. See also, in the same collection, the clipping from the *Michigan Catholic,* 19 June 1924, in "Forsythe" file.

22. Tentler, *Seasons of Grace,* 446, 298.

23. Melvin G. Holli and Peter d'A. Jones, *Biographical Dictionary of American Mayors, 1820–1980* (Westport, Conn.: Greenwood Press, 1981), 439, citing *Statistical Abstract of the United States, 1929* (Washington, D.C.: Government Printing Office, 1929), 46–49, and U.S. Bureau of the Census, *Fourteenth Census of the United States, 1920.*

24. "Official Report, Diocese of Detroit, 1920," 33, Anti-Parochial School Amendment Collection, SSIHM. The *Detroit Free Press,* 23 Oct. 1920, 1, reported that Malta had sent five thousand immigrants to Detroit since January 1, and the priest estimated that as many more would likely come in the next ten months.

25. The others were Patrick J. M. Hally, Ernest A. O'Brien, Malcom J. McLeod, and Charles A. Blaney. Guillaumin, "Catholics and the Proposed School Amendment," 7.

26. Tentler, *Seasons of Grace,* 312.

27. Guillaumin, "Catholics and the Proposed School Amendment," 7–8.

28. Karolena M. Fox, "History of the Equal Suffrage Movement in Michigan," *Michigan History* 2 (Jan. 1918): 104.

29. *Michigan Catholic,* 13 Feb. 1919, 4.

30. Letter from Bishop Gallagher, 9 Oct. 1920, noting that October 16 was the last chance to register, in "Correspondence" file, Anti-Parochial School Amendment Collection, SSIHM.

31. Letter from the Judge of Probate Court, 19 Oct. 1920, in "Correspondence" file, Anti-Parochial School Amendment Collection, SSIHM.

32. Tentler, *Seasons of Grace,* 309–11.

33. Ibid., 305.

34. "Account Book for 1914–17," Most Holy Trinity parish files, AAD. The fuel collection netted $1,746.47 toward a total fuel, light, and water expense of $2,334.25.

35. "Correspondence, from 'Official Report of the Diocese, 1920,'" 24–25, Anti-Parochial School Amendment Collection, SSIHM.

36. He estimated that between $300,000 and $500,000 was spent by all groups to defeat the amendment. Catholics spent $150,000, and Lutherans at least $70,000. *Detroit Times,* 3 Nov. 1920; Guillaumin, "Catholics and the Proposed School Amendment," 19.

37. *Thirty Reasons Why You Should Vote No,* in "Pamphlets" file, Anti-Parochial School Amendment Collection, SSIHM. This file holds many examples of the Educational Liberty League materials.

38. *Detroit Free Press,* 22 Oct. 1920, 2. Reports gave varying figures throughout the campaign.

39. Timothy Pies, "Historical and Contemporary Analyses of the Financing of Lutheran and Catholic Education in Michigan's Saginaw Valley," Ph.D. diss., University of Michigan, 1983, 82–83. The slogan was taken from a tract written by a professor at Concordia Seminary in St. Louis and was used in Oregon and similar campaigns.

40. Pies, "Historical and Contemporary Analyses," 83; "Minutes of the State Convention," 13 July 1920, in "Published Miscellanea" file, box 1, Lutheran Church–Missouri Synod, Michigan District, Lutheran Schools Committee Collection, MHC.

41. *Detroit Free Press,* 18 Oct. 1920, 7.

42. *Detroit Free Press,* 21 Oct. 1920, 2.

43. J. H. Todt to Henry Frincke, campaign manager, 13 Oct. 1920, in "Todt, J. H." file, box 1, Lutheran Church–Missouri Synod, Michigan District, Lutheran Schools Committee Collection, MHC.

44. "1920" file, and Letter from J. H. Todt, Feb. 1922, in "Todt, J. H." file, both in box 1, Lutheran Church–Missouri Synod, Michigan District, Lutheran Schools Committee Collection, MHC.

45. Windle, *Truth and Light,* 9. Windle was the editor of *The Iconoclast;* this small pamphlet is in both the SSIHM and MHC archives.

46. John C. Baur, executive secretary, to Dr. C. W. Brayman of Cedar Springs, 17 March 1922, in "File B," box 1, Lutheran Church–Missouri Synod, Michigan District, Lutheran Schools Committee Collection, MHC.

47. For a tally of the "Doubtful Forces" in certain counties, see "District Information" file, Lutheran Church–Missouri Synod, Michigan District, Lutheran Schools Committee Collection, MHC.

48. Reverend R. A. Brady, pastor of Central Methodist Church of Pontiac, quoted in *Detroit Free Press,* 25 Oct. 1920, 1.

49. Sermon by Congregationalist minister from *Grand Rapids Press* clipping, 18 Oct. 1920, in "1920" file, box 1, Lutheran Church–Missouri Synod, Michigan District, Lutheran Schools Committee Collection, MHC.

50. *Detroit Free Press,* 30 Oct. 1920, 3.

51. [Kelly], *No Greater Service,* 554.

52. *Detroit Free Press,* 26 Oct. 1920, 1.

53. "Pamphlets" file, Anti-Parochial School Amendment Collection, SSIHM.

54. Pies, "Historical and Contemporary Analyses," 90.

55. *Detroit Free Press,* 25 Oct. 1920, 1.

56. Groesbeck and Leland in Educational Liberty League advertisement, *Detroit Free Press,* 21 Oct. 1920, 10.

57. *Detroit Free Press,* 17 Oct. 1920, 20.

58. Pies, "Historical and Contemporary Analyses," 90, citing *Detroit News,* 19 May 1920.

59. *Detroit Free Press,* 21 Oct. 1920, 10, and 30 Oct. 1920, 3.

60. *Detroit Free Press,* 21 Oct. 1920, 10. This large advertisement, published and paid for by the Educational Liberty League, quoted several prominent men.

61. Mirel, *Rise and Fall of an Urban School System,* 43.

62. *Eighty-fourth Annual Report of the Superintendent of Public Instruction* (Lansing: Wynkoop, Hallenbeck, Crawford, 1922), 11–20, describes the history of the fund, dating from the Northwest Ordinance and made operational by constitutional provisions in 1837 and 1850.

63. Detroit Public Schools, *Education in Detroit, 1916,* 16, shows primary school money for 1914–15. A clipping from the *Detroit Free Press,* 27 Oct. 1924, showing that the primary school fund amounted to $14 per child in 1924, is in "Catholic Activities" file, box 1, Lutheran Church–Missouri Synod, Michigan District, Lutheran Schools Committee Collection, MHC.

64. *Eighty-fourth Annual Report of the Superintendent of Public Instruction,* 66–67, 62. The per-capita cost for instruction in Detroit public schools that year was $63.33.

65. "Anti-Parochial School Amendment," in "1920" file, 7, Anti-Parochial School Amendment Collection, SSIHM.

66. For budget figures, see Mirel, *Rise and Fall of an Urban School System,* 58 and 402.

67. Clipping from *Detroit News,* 20 June 1920, in "Published Miscellanea" file, Lutheran Church–Missouri Synod, Michigan District, Lutheran Schools Committee Collection, MHC.

68. Hamilton, *The Michigan Public School Amendment,* 129.

69. *Detroit Free Press,* 18 Oct. 1920, 7.

70. The "Correspondence" file, Anti-Parochial School Amendment Collection, SSIHM, shows the 1920 figure in a four-page statement by the Educational Liberty League. In 1924 Catholics estimated that 125,000 children in Michigan were attending Episcopalian, Adventist, Catholic, Lutheran, and Dutch Reformed Schools according to "The Truth about the School Amendment," 4, in Anti-Parochial School Amendment Collection, SSIHM.

71. *Detroit Free Press,* 23 Oct. 1920, 10.

72. *Detroit Free Press,* 2 Oct. 1920, 1. The *Eighty-fourth Annual Report of the Superintendent of Public Instruction,* 63, shows 594 nonresident pupils in 1919–20.

73. Windle, *Truth and Light,* 10.

74. Hamilton, *The Michigan Public School Amendment.*

75. *Detroit Free Press,* 20 Oct. 1920, 4.

76. *Detroit News,* 1 Nov. 1920, 1.

77. *Detroit Free Press,* 24 Oct., 1920, 27, and 29 Oct. 1920, 22. The parade and mass were under the auspices of the Detroit Diocesan Union Holy Name Society, but the event was planned at the request of Bishop Gallagher;

78. "Convent Chronicles, 1927" in St. Joseph's parish, file 27.9, SSIHM.

79. W. P. Bradley, general chair of the Navin parade, to Reverend Dear Sister, in "Correspondence" file, Anti-Parochial School Amendment Collection, SSIHM.

80. *Detroit News,* 1 Nov. 1920, 2.

81. *Detroit News,* 31 Oct. 1920, 1.

82. *Detroit News,* 17 Oct. 1920, 1.

83. *Detroit Free Press,* 4 Nov. 1920, 1.

84. Mirel, *Rise and Fall of an Urban School System,* 25.

85. According to the *Detroit Free Press,* 4 Nov. 1920, 1, 3, Wayne County went against the amendment by a vote of 179,186 to 94,542. The diocesan figure is from the "Official Report of the Diocese, 1920," 31, in "Correspondence" file, Anti-Parochial School Amendment Collection, SSIHM.

86. *Free Schools Bulletin* (Feb.–March 1924): 1, in "Press Articles" file, Anti-Parochial School Amendment Collection, SSIHM.

87. *Detroit Free Press,* 4 Nov. 1920, 1. Brown, "Patriotism or Religion," 38–39, shows a strong positive correlation between the percentage of Catholics in each county with the vote for Groesbeck.

88. "Official Report of the Diocese, 1920," in "Correspondence" file, Anti-Parochial School Amendment Collection, SSIHM.

89. *Free Schools Bulletin* (Jan. 1924): 4, in "Press Articles" file, Anti-Parochial School Amendment Collection, SSIHM.

90. John C. Baur to Prof. W. H. T. Dau, 25 Jan. 1922, in "File G," box 1, Lutheran Church–Missouri Synod, Michigan District, Lutheran Schools Committee Collection, MHC.

91. *Civic Searchlight Newsletter,* June 1924, in "Published Miscellanea" file, box 1, Lutheran Church–Missouri Synod, Michigan District, Lutheran Schools Committee Collection, MHC.

92. Kenneth T. Jackson, *The Ku Klux Klan in the City, 1915–1930* (New York: Oxford University Press, 1967), 129.

93. "The Public School Problem" (twenty-four-page statement outlining "fully" the the Ku Klux Klan policies toward public schools), in "Published Miscellanea" file, box 1, Lutheran Church–Missouri Synod, Michigan District, Lutheran Schools Committee Collection, MHC.

94. A typed statement by Evans is in "Published Miscellanea" file, box 1, Lutheran Church–Missouri Synod, Michigan District, Lutheran Schools Committee Collection, MHC.

95. *Michigan Catholic,* 24 July 1924, 1.

96. Bishop Gallagher to Rev. dear Father, 15 Oct. 1924, and sent to all parishes, in "Correspondence file," Anti-Parochial School Amendment Collection, SSIHM.

97. Clippings from *Detroit Free Press,* 12 Sept. 1924, and *Detroit News,* 14 Oct. 1924, in "Catholic Activities, 1924" file, box 1, Lutheran Church–Missouri Synod, Michigan District, Lutheran Schools Committee Collection, MHC.

98. Clipping from *Detroit Times,* 29 Oct. 1924, in "Catholic Activities, 1924" file, box 1, Lutheran Church–Missouri Synod, Michigan District, Lutheran Schools Committee Collection, MHC.

99. "File B," box 1, Lutheran Church–Missouri Synod, Michigan District, Lutheran Schools Committee Collection, MHC.

100. "Miscellanea" file, box 1, Lutheran Church–Missouri Synod, Michigan District, Lutheran Schools Committee Collection, MHC.

101. Clipping from unidentified newspaper, 23 May [1924?], in "Press Articles" file, Anti-Parochial School Amendment Collection, SSIHM.

102. "Hamilton-Jefferson Society" file, box 1, Lutheran Church–Missouri Synod, Michigan District, Lutheran Schools Committee Collection, MHC.

103. *Detroit Educational Bulletin* 8 (Sept. 1924): 24, in "Published Miscellanea" file, box 1, Lutheran Church–Missouri Synod, Michigan District, Lutheran Schools Committee Collection, MHC.

104. Sidney Fine, *Frank Murphy: The Detroit Years* (Ann Arbor: University of Michigan Press, 1975), 97, citing Sidney Glazer, *Detroit* (New York: Bookman Associates, 1965), 91, 94–97, 108–9; Detroit Bureau of Governmental Research, *Statistics,* 3, 4, 7, 14; "The Cost of Government of the City of Detroit, 1922–1923," *Public Business* (no. 71): 4; "The Cost of Government City of Detroit, 1925–1926," *Public Business* 3 (no. 17): 268.

105. Clipping from *Michigan Catholic,* 9 Oct. 1924, in "Catholic Activities" file, and clipping from *Detroit Free Press,* 5 Oct. 1924, in "Citizens Committee, 1924" file, both in box 1, Lutheran Church–Missouri Synod, Michigan District, Lutheran Schools Committee Collection, MHC.

106. "Published Miscellanea" file, box 1, Lutheran Church–Missouri Synod, Michigan District, Lutheran Schools Committee Collection, MHC.

107. Woodford, *Alex J. Groesbeck,* 224–27.

108. *Michigan Catholic,* 23 Oct. 1924, 1.

109. Jackson, *Ku Klux Klan in the City,* 133. The problem of crime in the 1920s is discussed in Fine, *Frank Murphy,* chap. 5.

110. Holli, *American Mayors,* 246–47; David Allan Levine, *Internal Combustion: The Races in Detroit, 1915–1926* (Westport, Conn.: Greenwood Press, 1976), 136–39.

111. *Detroit News,* 30 Oct. 1924.

112. Holli, *American Mayors,* 334. There is some dispute about Smith's ethnic background; some sources describe him as Polish.

113. Jackson, *Ku Klux Klan in the City,* 135.

114. Ibid., 128–33.

115. Ibid., 133.

116. Woodford, *Alex J. Groesbeck,* 119.

117. Fine, *Frank Murphy,* 187, citing Frank Murphy Papers and Hester Everad Papers, MHC.

118. "Ballots, Petitions, etc." file, box 1, Lutheran Church–Missouri Synod, Michigan District, Lutheran Schools Committee Collection, MHC.

119. The Supreme Court took up the case after a federal court found the Oregon law unconstitutional in 1924.

120. State of Michigan, *Journal of the House of Representatives of the State of Michigan, 1921* (Lansing: Wynkoop-Hallenbeck, 1921), 2:1046.

121. *Michigan Official Directory and Legislative Manual, 1921 and 1922* (n.p., n.d.), 692.

122. *Detroit News,* 29 April 1921, 10.

123. State of Michigan, *Journal of the House of Representatives of the State of Michigan, 1921,* 2:1046–47; *Michigan Official Directory and Legislative Manual, 1921 and 1922,* 690–708.

124. *Detroit News,* 29 April 1921, 10.

125. Miaso, *Education of Polish Immigrants,* 227–28.

126. Ibid., 152.

127. Bukowczyk, *And My Children Did Not Know Me,* 67.

128. John C. Springman, *The Growth of Public Education in Michigan* (Ypsilanti: Michigan State Normal College, 1952), 204.

129. Miscellaneous correspondence between the University of Michigan Committee on Accreditation and sister-principals, St. Josaphat and St. Stanislaus files, AFSLM.

130. "File B," box 1, Lutheran Church–Missouri Synod, Michigan District, Lutheran Schools Committee Collection, MHC.

131. Clipping from undesignated paper, June [1923?], in "Press Articles" file, Anti-Parochial School Amendment Collection, SSIHM.

132. [Kelly], *No Greater Service,* 564–65.

133. "Papers 1875–1933," box 1278/4855 in Bureau of School Services Collection, University of Michigan, MHC. Several accrediting reports and associated materials are in AFSLM. See, for example, "Accrediting Report Form," Oct. 1920, and "Interpretation of Standards for the Accrediting of High Schools by the University of Michigan," written by George E. Corrothers, director of university inspection of high schools, and Wray H. Congdon, inspector, both in St. Josaphat's parish file.

134. Sister Mary Tullia Domain, "The Seminary of the Felician Sisters," typescript MS, Nov. 1961, AFSLM. Studniewska, "Educational Work of the Felician Sisters," 135, notes that the Felician Academy remained affiliated with Catholic University from 1921 until 1927.

135. "Convent Chronicles, 1922" in St. Joseph's Parish file, SSIHM.

136. University of Michigan, Bureau of School Services, Papers, 1875–1933, in "Record" [1897–1907], 430, MHC.

137. Letters from University of Michigan examiner Wray H. Congdon, 6 Feb., 19 Feb. 1932, St. Stanislaus parish file, AFSLM.

138. Wray H. Congdon to Sister Mary Emmanuel, principal, 13 Jan. 1931, St. Casimir's parish file, AFSLM.

139. Wray H. Congdon to Sister Mary Vitolda, principal, 6 Feb. 1932, St. Stanislaus parish file, AFSLM.

140. Wray H. Congdon to Sister Mary Emmanuel, principal, 13 Jan. 1931, St. Casimir's parish file, AFSLM.

141. Studniewska, "Educational Work of the Felician Sisters," 143.

142. Papers in "Accredited Schools, Miscellaneous Materials, 1914–1929" file, University of Michigan University, Bureau of School Services, MHC.

143. "To the Officials of an Accredited High School," signed by M. L. Burton, president of the University of Michigan and chair of the University Committee of the University Committee on Diploma Schools, 5 Dec. 1921, Sister Mary Tullia Domain manuscript materials, AFSLM.

Index

Academy of the Ladies (Madames) of the Sacred Heart, 11, 194

Academy of Visitation Nuns, 80

Accreditation, 178, 209, 211, 244–49

African Americans: discrimination against, 167, 243; in Holy Family parish neighborhood, 163; population in early twentieth century, 215, 238, 272n2; schools for, 19, 62, 167, 188; as sister-teachers, 57–58, 60

African Episcopal Church, public school in, 24

Alexia, Sister (mother superior of School Sisters of St. Francis), 130, 143

Alfons, Sister M., 133

Amadeus, Sister (IHM, graduate of St. Vincent's), 280n56

American College at Louvain, 64, 172

American Home Missionary Society, 14

Americanist views, 104–5, 109, 245; on plenary council rulings, 93–96, 267n32

Americanization classes, 181–82

American Legion, Wayne County Council of, 240

American Protective Association (APA), 105, 106, 108

American Temperance Society, 14

Anti-Catholicism, 105–9; in Detroit public school politics before 1850, 24; in Europe, 89, 90; and school question, 38, 39. *See also* Anti-parochial school amendment

Anti-liquor laws, 32, 33, 44

Anti-parochial school amendment, 220–43; background of proponents of, 222–23, 282n8; and campaign of 1920, 225–37; and campaign of 1924, 237–43; Catholic response to petitions, 223, 282n11; constitutionality of, 223–24, 231–32, 243, 288n119; financial concerns and, 232–35, 240–41; funding for effort to defeat, 228, 237, 284n36; launching of effort to pass, 222–25; non-Catholic response to, 229–31, 232, 234, 235, 236, 238, 239–40, 241, 282n12, 284nn36, 39; parade in opposition to, 235–36, 286n77; and political reforms, 224, 283n15; positive consequences of effort to pass, 220–21, 244; provisions of amendment, 220, 222, 234; votes on, 236–37, 243, 286n85

Anti-Slavery Society, Michigan, 14

APA (American Protective Association), 105, 106, 108

Ascension school, 174

Assimilation, Americanist views on, 93, 94, 245

Atkinson, John, 108

Auto industry, 147, 243; Belgian workers in,

Society incentives, 166; before 1900, 71, 78–83; percentage of Catholic school children taught by in 1890s, 83; standards for admission to congregation, 80–81; textbooks used in schools taught by, 82; after World War II, 252
—at specific schools: Sacred Heart, 62, 79–80, 83; San Francesco, 163; St. Mary's, 23, 52, 79, 83
School Sisters of St. Francis, 112, 129–32, 174; background, 130; deaths from illness, 138; educational philosophy of, 131; fund raising by, 139, 140; housekeeping assignments, 133; living conditions, 137, 138; new candidates, 130–31; percent of Catholic students taught by, 185; Polish sisters, 130–31, 132–34, 271n59; religious life, 131; sanatoriums, 133, 140; and Sisters of St. Joseph, 131, 132–34, 140; teacher preparation, 130, 131–32, 140
—at specific schools: St. Francis of Assisi, 112, 129, 131, 132; St. Ladislaus, 183; Sweetest Heart of Mary, 112, 129–30, 131, 132, 137–38
School Sisters of St. Joseph. *See* Sisters of St. Joseph
Scotten, Daniel, 62
Secondary schools: Classical Academy (University of Michigania), 7–8, 10; curriculum for Felician teacher preparation, 120, 121, 128, 270n18; De La Salle Collegiate, 210–11; Detroit College, 192, 193–200, 195*fig.*, 207, 209, 247, 278–79n7; St. Joseph's Commercial College, 192, 200–201, 209, 279n32. *See also* High schools
Sectarian animosity, sources of, 19–27
Secular teachers. *See* Lay teachers
Segregation, of economic classes in Catholic schools, 151, 188; 1860s–1900, 85, 86, 109–10, 150–51; and school question, 45–46; during territorial era, 13
—: gender, in Father Gabriel Richard's Catholic school plan, 7
—: of new immigrants, 143; Catholic schools as way to segregate new immigrants from public schools, 110; in Italian community, 167
—: of Protestants from Catholics in Eighth Ward public school, 26, 42–43
Separation of church and state: constitution (Michigan) on, 16; in public schools before 1850, 16, 19–20

Seraphica, Sister (School Sisters of Notre Dame), 80
Seventh-Day Adventists, 231, 234, 238, 285n70
Shawe, Reverend Michael Edgar, 33, 34, 36, 40
Sicilians, 160–61, 166. *See also* Holy Family church and parish; Holy Family school
Sinn, Reverend L. A. (Lutheran minister), 282n12
Sisters of Charity, 161
Sisters of Christian Charity, 71, 210, 281n70
Sisters' College, at Catholic University, 175
Sisters of St. Dorothy, 164
Sisters of St. Joseph (School Sisters of St. Joseph, Polish Sisters of St. Joseph), 132–36, 174–75; and conflict in Polish community, 135; deaths from illness, 138, 276n103; educational philosophy of, 131, 174–75; establishment of, 131, 132–34, 140; financial decisions of, 176; and high schools, 216; new candidates, 135–36; percent of Catholic students taught by, 185; religious life, 174; teacher preparation for, 135–36, 175, 176, 276n103; after World War II, 252
—at specific schools: Ascension, 174; St. Bartholomew's, 174; St. Francis of Assisi, 134, 174, 216; St. John Berchmans, 171; St. Thomas the Apostle, 174, 216; Sweetest Heart of Mary, 135, 174, 216
Sisters of the Holy Family of Nazareth, 116
Sisters, Servants of the Immaculate Heart of Mary (IHMs): accreditation of schools, 246, 247; Americanist versus pluralist views on, 94; and anti-parochial school amendment, 228; basis for assignments of, 71–73, 263n34; and Bishop Lefevere, 59–60, 61, 62; certification of, 97, 187, 205, 246; curricula used by, 66–70, 71, 170, 187, 188; at Detroit schools before 1900, 61–78; in early twentieth century, 185, 186–88, 187*fig.*; educational philosophy of, 63–71, 111–12, 186–87, 264n56; before 1850, 22; 1850–1900, 45, 51, 57–78, 200; ethnic diversity of, 58, 63, 71, 264n71; and ethnicity of students/schools, 63, 71–72; Father Francis Van Antwerp's opinion on, 172; founding of order, 57–58; at French Catholic schools, 62; at German schools, 61, 62–63, 71, 77*fig.*, 77–78, 200, 209, 247, 252; habits worn by, 58; housekeeping assignments, 73, 264n71; at Irish schools, 62, 63, 71, 72, 73, 186, 188, 207,

252; living conditions, 76; orphanage operated by, 60; percent of Catholic students taught by, 185; at rural parish schools, 63; salaries, 74–75, 187; and school board inspections, 97; and St. Mary College, 205–6; at St. Mary's Academy (Monroe, Mich.), 57–60, 67, 70; teacher preparation, 63, 64–65, 70–71, 72, 187, 205, 246, 263n35; textbooks used in schools taught by, 68, 69, 188, 263n50; university education for, 206; after World War II, 252
—at high schools, 67; boys as students, 207; certification, 187, 205, 246; German high schools, 209, 210; Most Holy Redeemer, 186, 207; Most Holy Trinity, 202–3, 204–5, 247; before 1900, 67; after 1900, 186, 187, 202, 281n70; number of schools, 207, 280n54; St. Boniface's, 209; St. Joseph's, 209; St. Vincent's, 202–3, 204–5, 247; teacher preparation, 206, 246
—at specific grade schools: Blessed Sacrament, 188; Gesu, 188; Most Holy Redeemer, 62, 186, 207; Most Holy Trinity, 62, 72, 73; Our Lady of Help, 62, 247; St. Boniface's, 62; St. Charles Borromeo's, 170; St. Joseph's, 61, 72, 77fig., 200, 209, 247; St. Vincent's, 62, 72, 188
Sister-teachers: and anti-parochial school amendment, 227–28, 235, 239; Catholic school graduates as, 177, 190, 214, 280n56; differences between congregations summarized, 111–12; in early twentieth century, 185–88; 1850–1900, 45, 51–52, 56–71, 110; and ethnicity of schools and students, 58, 63, 71–72, 264n71; identification of potential high school students by, 198; salaries, 73, 74–75, 117, 139, 140, 141, 154, 187. *See also* Certification of teachers; *specific congregations*
—specific congregations: Daughters of Charity, 22, 32, 73–74; Daughters of Divine Charity, 157; Sisters of Charity, 161; Sisters of Christian Charity, 71, 210, 281n70; Sisters of St. Dorothy, 164. *See also* Dominican Sisters; Felician Sisters; School Sisters of Notre Dame; School Sisters of St. Francis; Sisters of St. Joseph; Sisters, Servants of the Immaculate Heart of Mary
—at specific schools: Ascension, 174; Blessed Sacrament, 188; Gesu, 188; Holy Cross,

154–55, 157, 185; Holy Family, 162; Most Holy Redeemer, 62, 186, 207; Most Holy Trinity grade school, 62, 72, 73–74; Most Holy Trinity high school, 202–3, 204–5, 247; Our Lady Help of Christians, 189; Our Lady of Help, 62, 247; Our Lady Queen of Apostles, 182–83; Our Lady of Sorrows, 169, 185; Resurrection, 189; Sacred Heart, 62, 79–80, 83; San Francesco, 161, 163; Santa Maria, 164; SS. Peter and Paul, 62, 194; St. Albertus, 112, 117, 139, 213; St. Ambrose, 185; St. Anne's, 62; St. Anthony's, 83; St. Augustine's School for Colored Children, 62; St. Bartholomew's, 174; St. Boniface's, 62; St. Casimir's, 112, 126, 127, 189, 213; St. Charles Borromeo's, 170; St. Florian's (Hamtramck, Mich.), 182; St. Francis of Assisi, 112, 129, 131, 132, 134, 174, 216; St. Gabriel's, 185; St. John Berchmans, 171; St. Josaphat's, 112, 126, 127, 141, 189; St. Joseph's, 61, 72, 77fig., 200, 209, 247; St. Ladislaus, 183; St. Louis the King, 188; St. Mary's, 23, 52, 79, 83; St. Stanislaus, 112, 127, 248; St. Stephen's, 189; St. Thomas the Apostle, 174, 216; St. Vincent's grade school, 62, 72, 188; St. Vincent's high school, 202–3, 204–5, 247; St. Wenceslaus, 126; Sweetest Heart of Mary, 112, 129–30, 131, 132, 135, 137–38, 174, 216
Sleeper, Governor Albert E., 232
Smith, John W., 241, 242, 243, 287n112
Southwestern High School, Hungarian students at, 158–59
Spalding, John Lester (bishop of Peoria), 93, 94
Spencer, Herbert, 87
SS. Cyril and Methodius Seminary, 120, 212; and attendance of Polish students at Detroit College, 198; Father Kolasinski's opinion on, 109; grade school at, 124; opening of, 100–101, 118
SS. Peter and Paul Cathedral and parish: Jesuits at, 194–95; opening of, 39, 40; Sicilian parishioners, 160–61
SS. Peter and Paul school, 62, 194. *See also* Detroit College
St. Albertus church and parish: closing of, 102; and conflict in Polish community, 101–3, 124–25; financing of, 101, 118, 140; naming of, 267n41; new church building, 100, 101–2, 118; opening of, 98; priests, 99–100; reopening of, 103

JoEllen McNergney Vinyard is a professor of history at Eastern Michigan University. She received her B.A. at Nebraska State College, Peru, her M.A. at the University of Kansas, and her Ph.D. from the University of Michigan. She is the author of *The Irish on the Urban Frontier* and *Michigan: The World around Us.*

Statue of Liberty–Ellis Island Centennial Series

The Immigrant World of Ybor City: Italians and Their Latin Neighbors in Tampa,
1885–1985 *Gary R. Mormino and George E. Pozzetta*
The Butte Irish: Class and Ethnicity in an American Mining Town, 1875–1925
David M. Emmons
The Making of an American Pluralism: Buffalo, New York, 1825–60 *David A. Gerber*
Germans in the New World: Essays in the History of Immigration
Frederick C. Luebke
A Century of European Migrations, 1830–1930 *Edited by Rudolph J. Vecoli and
Suzanne M. Sinke*
The Persistence of Ethnicity: Dutch Calvinist Pioneers in Amsterdam, Montana
Rob Kroes
Family, Church, and Market: A Mennonite Community in the Old and the New
Worlds, 1850–1930 *Royden K. Loewen*
Between Race and Ethnicity: Cape Verdean American Immigrants, 1860–1965
Marilyn Halter
Les Icariens: The Utopian Dream in Europe and America *Robert P. Sutton*
Labor and Community: Mexican Citrus Worker Villages in a Southern California
County, 1900–1950 *Gilbert G. González*
Contented among Strangers: Rural German-Speaking Women and Their Families in
the Nineteenth-Century Midwest *Linda Schelbitzki Pickle*
Dutch Farmer in the Missouri Valley: The Life and Letters of Ulbe Eringa,
1866–1950 *Brian W. Beltman*
Good-bye, Piccadilly: British War Brides in America *Jenel Virden*
For Faith and Fortune: The Education of Catholic Immigrants in Detroit, 1805–1925
JoEllen McNergney Vinyard